The big band sound comes to radio sponsored primarily by cigarettes

Armed Forces Radio Service broadcasts to servicemen during World War II

Milton Berle takes to the airwaves—1948

Kukla, Fran, and Ollie and creator Burr Tillstrom entertain children of all ages

Betty Furness advertises for Westinghouse—1952

Huntley and Brinkley bring the news—1957

President John F. Kennedy's funeral is broadcast worldwide—1963

Automated radio equipment changes programming procedures at some stations

"Sesame Street" is aired on public TV—1969

"Roots," a miniseries shown in 1977, had a record-breaking audience.

Portable equipment aids TV news gathering

Broadcasting helps celebrate the nation's bicentennial—1976

See/Hear

Critical Readers

Dan F. Baker   California State University, Long Beach

True Boardman   Westwood, California

Robert H. Farson   The Pennsylvania State University

James Fletcher   University of Georgia

Dana Hawkes   Palomar College

Boris D. Kaplan   Malibu, California

Joseph J. Keane   Pasadena City College

Deanna M. Robinson   University of Oregon

Jan Sprague   Waubonsee Community College

Howard L. Stevens   Suffolk County Community College

See/Hear
An Introduction to Broadcasting

Lynne S. Gross
Loyola Marymount University

web
Wm. C. Brown Company Publishers
Dubuque, Iowa

wcb

Wm. C. Brown
Chairman of the Board

Larry W. Brown
President, WCB Group

Book Team

Robert Nash	Executive Editor
Barb Grantham	Designer
Elizabeth Munger	Production Editor

Wm. C. Brown Company Publishers, College Division

Lawrence E. Cremer	President
Richard C. Crews	Publisher
Raymond C. Deveaux	Director of Sales and Marketing
David Wm. Smith	National Marketing Manager
David A. Corona	Director of Production Development and Design
Ruth Richard	Production Editorial Manager
Marilyn Phelps	Manager of Design

To April,
for her devoted overview.

Contents

List of Illustrations

Preface

Purpose
Broadcasting is one of the most potent forces of our world today. It influences society as a whole and it influences every one of us as an individual. Broadcasting is a very public, not private, business in the sense that the air through which radio and TV are broadcast "belongs" to everyone. No less does the broadcast product "belong" to everyone—through the click of a switch and the twist of a dial. Every one of us, as an individual *and* as a representative of society, has a right to become involved in broadcasting fare and has an obligation to understand why we need to interact with what is now called the electronic media. Some knowledge of the background and structure of the industry is an essential basis for this understanding. One goal of this book is to provide just that kind of specific knowledge.

Audience
The book is designed to give an overview of broadcasting for people interested in entering the field as a career and also for people interested primarily in gaining a better understanding of the assets and liabilities of instant communication. The book emphasizes factual information, but it also introduces and discusses many controversial aspects of broadcasting to stimulate readers to form their own opinions about goals for the present and future of broadcasting.

Organization of Book
The first four chapters of the book deal with history and technology to give the basic background necessary to understand the radio and television industries. The next three chapters discuss what is most familiar to most readers—programming. Chapters 8 through 11 cover the inner workings of the industry in terms of government regulation, self-regulation, advertising, and ratings. Public broadcasting and cable TV are handled in detail in chapters 12 and 13. Chapter 14, which deals with personnel, sketches the organization of broadcasting and should help students decide whether or not they wish to enter the field. Chapter 15 considers broadcasting in other countries. The final chapter, 16, is a crystal ball approach to the future of broadcasting.

The chapters do not need to be read in chronological sequence. However, some terms defined early in the book may be unfamiliar to people who read later chapters first. The glossary can help overcome this problem. It includes important technical terms which students may want to review from time to time. It also includes less important terms which students need not understand so precisely in order to follow the material presented but which they may want to add to their vocabulary. Words that are defined in the glossary are set off in bold face type the first time they occur within any particular chapter. Also included in the glossary are abbreviations that are used frequently in the broadcasting field. Even though the full name or term is spelled out in the text the first time it is used, memory might fail when the abbreviation appears alone later; it can be refreshed by a quick turn to the glossary.

As a further aid, a summary is provided at the end of each chapter, with important names and major terms and concepts printed in italics. Reading only the summaries cannot in any way substitute for reading the chapters, however. In fact, the summaries will probably be incomprehensible to someone who has not read the material. They are offered mainly as a quick review for students who wish to be assured that they remember significant points.

Over three hundred photographs, drawings, diagrams, and charts throughout the book are intended to be entertaining as well as informative. Some of the photos that have never been printed before testify to unsung but unique facets of broadcasting.

An Instructor's Resource Manual accompanies this textbook. It includes lists of sources for supplementary teaching materials; suggestions of lecture topics; resources for guest speakers; discussion and test questions; and additional background bibliography. Also included are two sample course outlines—one designed by Deanna Robinson for a ten-week one-quarter course, the other designed by me for an eighteen-week one-semester course.

This book represents the combined efforts of many people. The idea was first suggested to me by members of the Community College Telecommunications Association of California. Henry Leff, City College of San Francisco, devised the title. Dana Hawkes, Palomar College, used chapter drafts in teaching. His students' many suggestions for improvements were greatly appreciated. I am especially grateful to True Boardman, radio and TV writer-director, Boris D. Kaplan, former director of nighttime programs, CBS, and Joe Keane, former program director of KHJ-TV, for the time and judgment they gave to a critical reading of this book. I want to express my appreciation also to Dan Baker for his drawings and to Ray Burton, John Gregory, Tom Koehring, Don McCall, Gay Russel, Don Scouller, Doree Steinmann, and many of my students, first at Long Beach City College and then at Loyola-Marymount University. They read individual chapters, initial drafts, and outlines. Suggestions, factual informa-

Special Features

Supplementary Materials

Acknowledgments

tion, and photographs were supplied by many of my fellow governors of the Academy of Television Arts and Sciences as well as others in the broadcasting industry. I would also like to thank Elizabeth Munger for her excellent editing, Linda Lockhorn for long hours of typing, Barb Grantham for the attractive book design, and my husband and three sons for their tolerance and understanding while I was working on the text.

Lynne S. Gross

Preface

See/Hear

1 In the Beginning
A History of Radio

It is inconceivable that we should allow so great a possibility for public service as broadcasting to be drowned in advertising chatter.

Herbert Hoover, when he was
Secretary of Commerce

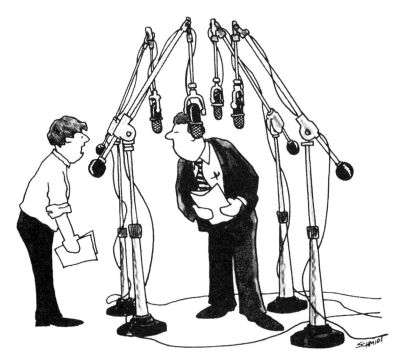

Cartoon copyrighted by *Broadcasting* magazine

"Don't forget to announce that this is our first quadraphonic broadcast."

The beginnings of radio are, in a sense, veiled in mystery and dispute. The early inventors lived in various countries and, in some instances, devised virtually the same inventions. Ironically, this was due in part to the fact that there was no communication system available for people to learn what others were inventing. This led to innumerable rivalries, claims, counter-claims, and patent suits.

The earliest inventions crucial to the field weren't even intended to be utilized for radio broadcasting. When **radio waves** were first discovered, there was consternation about the fact that they were so public. Many experimenters were involved in devising methods to make the airwaves private so that messages could be sent confidentially. Only a few visionaries foresaw the use of radio broadcasting as we know it today.

Early Inventions

Many people believe that radio originated in 1873 when James Clerk Maxwell, a physics professor at Cambridge University, England, published his theory of **electromagnetism.** His *Treatise on Electricity and Magnetism* predicted the existence of radio waves and how they should behave based on his observations of how **light waves** behave.[1]

Experiments to prove Maxwell's theory were undertaken by the German physics professor Heinrich Hertz during the 1880s. Hertz actually generated at one end of his laboratory and transmitted to the other end the radio energy which Maxwell had theorized. He thus proved that variations in electrical current could be projected into space as radio waves similar to light waves. In 1888 he published a paper, ''Electro-magnetic Waves and their Reflections,'' which served as a basis for the theory of modern radio transmission. Originally radio waves were called ''Hertzian waves,'' and today Hertz's name is used as a **frequency** measurement meaning **cycles per second.**[2]

Figure 1.1
James Clerk Maxwell
Smithsonian Institution
Photo No. 56859

Figure 1.2
Heinrich Hertz
Smithsonian Institution
Photo No. 66606

Figure 1.1

Figure 1.2

A battle was waged in the 1890s between General Electric (GE) and Westinghouse to have their patents adopted for nationwide electrical use. GE favored direct current (DC) and Westinghouse favored alternating current (AC). In 1896 Westinghouse won and AC became the national standard. Long-distance radio wave radiation is dependent on AC generation, so it was fortunate for radio that this was the adopted standard.

Guglielmo Marconi, often referred to as the "Father of Radio," expanded upon radio principles. Marconi was the son of a wealthy Italian father and an Irish mother. From an early age he was scientifically inclined and fortunately had the leisure and wealth to pursue his interests. Shortly after he heard of Hertz's ideas, he began working fanatically in his workshop, finally reaching a point where he could actually ring a bell with radio waves.

He then incorporated the Morse key into his system with the goal of transmitting Morse Code by radio waves. Until this time, the transmission of Morse Code had required the laying or stringing of wires from one reception point to another. To set his radio waves in motion, Marconi used Hertz's method, which was to generate a spark that leaped across a gap. To receive the signal, he placed metal filings in a glass tube. When the radio wave contacted the metal filings, they cohered to each other, and the glass tube then had to be tapped to loosen the filings to receive the next impulse. Marconi's first crude but effective system thus consisted of a Morse key, a spark, a coherer, and a tapper.

Having tested his invention outside his workshop by successfully transmitting throughout his estate and beyond, Marconi wrote to the Italian government attempting to interest them in his project. They replied in the negative. His determined Irish mother decided he should take his invention to England. There he received an 1897 patent and the financial backing to set up the Marconi Wireless Telegraph Company, Ltd. Under the auspices

**Figure 1.3
Guglielmo Marconi,
shown here with
wireless apparatus
about 1902.**
Smithsonian Institution
Photo No. 52202

Chapter 1

of this company Marconi continued to improve on **wireless** and began to supply equipment to ships. In 1899 he formed a subsidiary company in the United States, the Marconi Wireless Company of America. The famous transmission of the letter "s" across the Atlantic from Britain to New-foundland occurred in 1901 and was, of course, a great breakthrough for what eventually became radio.[3]

Although Marconi maintained a dominant international position in wireless communication, many other people were experimenting and securing patents in Russia, Germany, France, and the United States. Until this time the primary use of wireless had been as a means of Morse Code communication by ships at sea. Now some people were becoming intrigued with the idea of voice transmission.

A significant step in that direction was the work done by John Fleming of Britain in 1904. He developed the **vacuum tube** which led the way to voice transmission. It was later developed further by others, particularly Reginald Aubrey Fessenden and Lee De Forest.[4]

Fessenden, a Canadian-born professor who worked at the University of Pittsburgh, proposed that radio waves not be sent out in bursts—which accommodated the dots and dashes of Morse Code—but rather as a continuous wave on which voice could be superimposed. He succeeded in obtaining financial backing from two Pittsburgh financiers, and on Christmas Eve of 1906 he broadcast to ships at sea his own violin solo, a few verses from the Book of Luke in the Bible, and a phonograph recording of Handel's "Largo."[5]

Lee De Forest is known primarily for the invention of the **audion,** an improvement on John Fleming's vacuum tube. It contained three **electrodes** instead of two and was capable of amplifying sound to a much greater degree than previously. This tube was the most crucial key to voice transmission.

Figure 1.4
Lee De Forest, shown here with wireless apparatus about 1920.
Smithsonian Institution Photo No. 52216

De Forest, like Marconi, was fascinated with electronics at an early age and, like Marconi, secured financial backing to form his own company. However, De Forest experienced management-financial problems which frequently rendered him penniless and led him eventually to sell his patent rights to the Marconi Company and to American Telephone and Telegraph (AT&T).

De Forest was farsighted in his views of the way radio waves could be utilized, and he strongly advocated voice transmission for entertainment purposes. In 1910 he broadcast the singing of Enrico Caruso from the New York Metropolitan Opera House. Several years later he started a radio station of sorts in the Columbia Gramaphone Building, playing Columbia records in hopes of increasing their sales. He was also hopeful of increasing the sale of wireless sets so that more of his audion tubes would be sold.[6]

Early Control

During these early stages radio grew virtually without control. Initially the government became involved only to the extent of requiring certain types of ships to carry radios for safety purposes. Government concern became even greater after the word of the sinking of the *Titanic* was transmitted by the ship's wireless and received in New York by young David Sarnoff, who later became president of RCA. This transmission resulted in the saving of many lives.

In 1912 Congress passed an act that required everyone who transmitted on radio waves to obtain a license from the secretary of commerce. The secretary could not refuse a license but could assign particular **wavelengths** to particular transmitters. Thus ship transmissions were kept separate from amateur transmissions, which were, in turn, separate from government transmissions. All this was done without any thought of broadcasting as we know it today.

World War I

At the beginning of World War I the government took over all radio operation. Ship-to-shore stations were operated by the Navy, and many **ham** radio operators were sent overseas to operate radio equipment. Perhaps even more important, patent disputes were set aside for the good of the country. Marconi's company, still the leader in wireless, had aroused the concern of American Telephone and Telegraph by suggesting the possibility of entering the wireless phone business. AT&T, in an effort to maintain its supremacy in the telephone business, had acquired some wireless patents, primarily those of Lee De Forest. The stalemate that grew out of the refusal of the Marconi Company, AT&T, and several smaller companies to allow each other to interchange patents had virtually stifled the technical growth of radio communications.

With the onset of the war these disputes were set aside so that the government could develop the **transmitters** and **receivers** needed. World War I was also responsible for ushering into the radio field two other large companies, General Electric and Westinghouse. Both were concerned with electrical energy and were established manufacturers of light bulbs. Since both light bulbs and radio tubes require a vacuum, GE and Westinghouse assumed responsibilities for manufacturing tubes. GE had also been involved in the development of Ernst F. W. Alexanderson's invention of the **alternator** to improve long-distance wireless. During the war this alternator was perfected.

After the war the patent problem returned and as a result GE began negotiating with the Marconi Company to sell the rights to its Alexanderson alternator. The Navy, which had controlled radio during the war, feared that this sale would enable Marconi, a primarily British company, to achieve a monopoly on radio communication, so the Navy intervened and convinced GE president Owen Young to renege on the Marconi deal. This left GE sitting with an expensive patent it could not profit from because it did not control other patents necessary for its utilization. But the patent placed GE in an excellent negotiating position because of its value for long-distance transmission.

The Founding of RCA

What ensued was a series of discussions among American Marconi, AT&T, GE, and Westinghouse culminating in the formation of Radio Corporation of America (RCA). American Marconi, realizing that it would not receive Navy contracts as long as it was associated with British Marconi, transferred its assets to RCA. Individual stockholders received RCA shares for Marconi shares, and GE purchased the shares of American Marconi held by British Marconi. AT&T, GE, and Westinghouse also bought blocks of RCA stock and agreed to make patents available to each other. In the original agreement, GE and Westinghouse had exclusive rights to manufacture receiving sets; RCA had exclusive rights to sell them; and AT&T had sole rights to make, lease, and sell broadcast transmitters. Again, this was not undertaken with entertainment broadcasting in mind but with emphasis on ship-to-shore transmission.[7]

Among the employees of RCA who came from American Marconi was David Sarnoff, a Russian immigrant who had supported his family from a very young age, first as a newspaper boy and then as a Morse Code operator. At age fifteen he had become an employee of Marconi and as such, when he was twenty-one, received the tragic distress messages from the *Titanic*.[8]

Figure 1.5
David Sarnoff working at his radio station position atop the Wanamaker store in New York. It was here he heard the *Titanic*'s distress call, causing him to stay at his post 72 hours to report the disaster.
Photo courtesy of RCA

In the Beginning　　7

Further laws were passed which required radio equipment on ships, and these helped American Marconi's business to boom and Sarnoff's career to escalate. In 1915, at age 24, he wrote a memo to Marconi management suggesting entertainment radio. It read in part as follows:

I have in mind a plan of development which would make radio a "household utility" in the same sense as the piano or phonograph. The idea is to bring music into the home by wireless. . . . The problem of transmitting music has already been solved in principle and therefore all the receivers attuned to the transmitting wavelength should be capable of receiving such music. The receiver can be designed in the form of a simple "Radio Music Box" and arranged for several different wavelengths, which should be changeable with the throwing of a single switch or pressing of a single button.

The "Radio Music Box" can be supplied with amplifying tubes and a loudspeaker telephone, all of which can be neatly mounted in one box. The box can be placed on a table in the parlor or living room, the switch set accordingly and the music received. . . .

The same principle can be extended to numerous other fields as, for example, receiving lectures at home which can be made perfectly audible; also, events of national importance can be simultaneously announced and received. Baseball scores can be transmitted in the air by the use of one set installed at the Polo Grounds. The same would be true of other cities. This proposition would be especially interesting to farmers and others in outlying districts removed from cities. By purchase of a "Radio Music Box," they could enjoy concerts, lectures, music recitals, etc., which may be going on in the nearest city within their radius. . . .

It is not possible to estimate the total amount of business obtainable with this plan until it has been developed and actually tried out; but there are about 15,000,000 families in the United States alone, and if only one million or 7% of the total families thought well of the idea, it would, at the figure mentioned, ($75 per outfit) mean a gross business of about $75,000,000 which would yield considerable revenue.

Aside from the profit derived from this proposition the possibilities for advertising for the company are tremendous, for its name would ultimately be brought into the household, and wireless would receive national and universal attention.[9]

This idea was filed away as a harebrained notion, and Sarnoff had to wait for more propitious timing.

Early Radio Stations

Meanwhile, with restrictions lifted, many of the amateur radio enthusiasts began to experiment again. One of these was Professor Earle M. Terry of the University of Wisconsin, who broadcast weather reports and occasional music to farm areas near Madison.[10]

The publisher of the *Detroit News,* William E. Scripps, fostered interest in radio by using his newspaper to advertise his radio broadcasts, which in turn advertised his newspaper. In 1920 the Harding-Cox presidential returns were broadcast by having an office boy rush from the newspaper editorial office to the conference room where the radio "studio" was in

Figure 1.6
The *Detroit News* radio station first known as 8MK and then as WWJ. This picture from 1920 shows the method by which music was broadcast from a phonograph. Much of the transmitting equipment was developed by Lee De Forest.
Photo courtesy of the Automotive History Collection, Detroit Public Library

operation. It was estimated that in the neighborhood of 500 amateurs heard these results.[11]

In Pittsburgh Frank Conrad, a physicist and an employee of Westinghouse, resumed his amateur activities in his garage, programming music and talk during his spare time. A local department store began selling wireless reception sets and placed an ad for the sets in a local newspaper, mentioning that these sets could receive Conrad's concerts. One of Conrad's superiors at Westinghouse saw the ad and envisioned a market. Up until this time both radio transmission and reception had been for the technical-minded who could assemble their own sets, but it was obvious that sets could be preassembled for everyone who wished to listen to what was being transmitted.

Conrad was asked to build a stronger transmitter at the Westinghouse plant capable of broadcasting on a regular schedule so that people purchasing receivers would be assured listening fare. Thus Westinghouse in 1920 became the first company to apply to the Department of Commerce for a special type of **license** to begin a broadcasting service. It was given the call letters KDKA and authorized to use a frequency away from amateur interference. KDKA launched its programming schedule with the Harding-Cox election returns interspersed with music and then continued with regular broadcasting hours. Public reaction could be measured by the length of the lines at department stores where radio receivers were sold.[12]

KDKA's success spurred others to enter broadcasting. Foremost among these was David Sarnoff, who could now dust off his old memo and receive more acceptance for his idea. He convinced RCA management to invest $2,000 to cover the Jack Dempsey-Georges Carpentier fight on July 2, 1921, and a temporary transmitter was set up in New Jersey for the fight. Fortunately Dempsey knocked Carpentier out in the fourth round, for shortly after that the overheated transmitter became a molten mass. This fight, however, helped to popularize radio, and both radio stations and sets multiplied rapidly.

By 1923 radio licenses had been issued to over 600 stations, and receiving sets were in nearly one million homes.[13] The stations had low power, usually 10 to 15 watts, and were owned and operated primarily by those who wanted to sell sets—Westinghouse, GE, RCA, retail department stores, radio repair shops, newspapers wanting to publicize themselves, and college physics departments. One licensing aspect which would lead to later problems was that all stations were on the same frequency—360 meters. Stations in the same reception area worked out voluntary arrangements whereby they could share the frequency by broadcasting at different times of the day.

Early Programming

Programming was no problem in the early days. People were mainly interested in the novelty of picking up any signal on their battery-operated **crystal** headphone receivers. Programs consisted primarily of phonograph records, call letters, and performances by endless free talent who wandered in the door eager to display their virtuosity on this new medium.

One early station, WJZ, operated from a shack on the roof of a Westinghouse building in Newark, New Jersey. It was accessible only by an

Figure 1.8
The tent atop a
Westinghouse building
in East Pittsburgh
which served as KDKA's
first studio. It was the
cause of some of early
radio's unusual
moments—such as the
whistle of a passing
freight train heard
nightly at 8:30, and a
tenor's aria abruptly
concluded by an insect
that flew into his
mouth.
Photo courtesy of KDKA,
Pittsburgh

iron ladder and hatchway and programmed mainly time signals, weather, and selections on the Edison phonograph. On one occasion a woman was invited up to read a story, but after climbing the ladder and being pushed through the hatchway, she fainted.[14]

A woman who was a strong, speech-making advocate of birth control asked to be allowed on radio. The people at the station were nervous about what she might say, but when she assured them she only wanted to recite some nursery rhymes, they allowed her into the studio. She then broadcast, "There was an old woman who lived in a shoe/She had so many children because she didn't know what to do." She was not invited back.[15]

A young man in New Jersey wanted to let his mother know how he sounded over the air, so he dropped in at WOR, which had just opened a studio near the music department of a store. The singer they were expecting hadn't arrived yet, so this young man was put on the air before he even had time to notify his mother. He sang to piano accompaniment for over an hour, with a messenger rushing sheet music from the music counter to the studio.[16]

A man in Chicago wanted to discuss Americanism over a Chicago station and even submitted a script ahead of time. When he appeared at the station, it was with a group of bodyguards who covered the station premises to make sure that no buttons were pushed to take him off the air. It turned out that he was a potentate of the Ku Klux Klan and, digressing from the script, he extolled the virtues of white supremacy.[17]

The primary programming of the era was what was dubbed "potted palm music"—the kind played at teatime by hotel orchestras. Sometimes it was sung and sometimes it was played by a pianist or small instrumental group. Sopranos outnumbered all other "potted palm" performers.

Drama was also attempted even though engineers at first insisted that men and women needed to use separate microphones placed some distance from each other. Performers found it difficult to play love scenes this way. Finally it was "discovered" that men and women could share a mike.

From time to time radio excelled in the public affairs area. Political conventions and Presidential speeches were broadcast as well as the funeral service for Woodrow Wilson. The six-year-old son of Ernst F. W. Alexanderson, the developer of the alternator, was kidnapped, and it was a radio report of the child's description that was responsible for his recovery.

The Rise of Advertising

As the novelty of radio wore off, performers were less eager to appear and some means of financing programming had to be found. Many different ideas were proposed, including donations from citizens, levying taxes on radio sets, and requiring manufacturers and distributors to pay for operating stations. The reality of commercials came about largely by accident.

AT&T was involved mainly in the telephone business and was, if anything, unwilling to see radio grow because the demand for wired services might be diminished. Therefore, one of its entries into broadcasting was closely akin to phone philosophy. It established station WEAF in New York as what it termed a **"toll" station.** AT&T stated that it would provide no programming but that anyone who wished to broadcast a message could pay a "toll" to AT&T and then air the message publicly in much the same way as private messages were communicated by dropping money in pay telephones. In fact, the original studio was about the size of a phone booth. The idea did not take hold. People willing to pay to broadcast messages to the world did not materialize.

AT&T realized that before people were going to pay to be heard, they wanted to be sure that someone out there was listening. As a result, the nonprogramming idea was abandoned, and WEAF began broadcasting entertainment material, drawing mainly on amateur talent found among the employees. Still there were no long lines of people wishing to pay to have messages broadcast.

Finally, August 22, 1922 WEAF aired its first income-producing program—a ten-minute message from the Queensboro Corporation, a Long Island real estate company, which paid $50 for the time. The commercial was just a simple courtesy announcement because AT&T ruled out direct advertising as poor taste and an invasion of privacy. Many people of the era said advertising on radio would never sell products, and, in fact, every dollar of income which WEAF obtained was a painful struggle.

What eventually made the station succeed was the fact that AT&T was able to convince the Department of Commerce that WEAF should have a different frequency. The argument was that other broadcasters were using their stations for their own purposes while WEAF was for everyone and therefore should have special standing and not be made to broadcast on 360 meters like everyone else. As a result, WEAF and a few other stations were assigned to the 400 meter wavelength. This meant less interference and more broadcast time. The phone booth was abandoned, a new studio was erected, and showmanship took hold.[18]

The Formation of Networks

Because AT&T was still predominantly in the phone business, it began using phone lines for remote broadcasts. It aired descriptions of football games from Chicago and Harvard which came over long distance lines. It also established "toll" stations in other cities and interconnected them by phone lines—in effect, establishing a network.

During this time AT&T did not allow other radio stations to use phone lines and also claimed sole right to sell radio "toll" time. At first, other stations were not bothered because they were not considering selling ads. In fact, there was an anti-advertising sentiment in the early 1920s. Herbert Hoover, then secretary of commerce, stated that it was inconceivable that a service with so much potential for news, entertainment, and education should be drowned in advertising chatter.

However, as the AT&T toll network emerged and began to prosper, other stations became discontent with their second-class status. The fires of this flame were further fanned by patent disputes, by AT&T's apparent attempt to enter the receiver-manufacturing business, and by a Federal Trade Commission inquiry which accused AT&T, RCA, GE, and Westinghouse of creating a monopoly in the radio business.

A series of "behind-closed-doors" hearings was held by the major radio companies. The result of these complicated negotiations was the formation in 1926 of the National Broadcasting Company (NBC)—owned by RCA, GE, and Westinghouse—which was to handle broadcasting activities for the radio group. AT&T agreed to withdraw from the programming area and from the radio group in exchange for a long-term contract assuring that NBC would lease AT&T wires. That agreement was to bring the phone company millions of dollars per year. NBC also purchased WEAF from AT&T for $1 million, thus embracing the concepts of both networking and "toll" broadcasting.

In November of 1926 the NBC Red Network, which consisted of WEAF and a twenty-two-station national hook-up, was launched in a spectacular debut that aired the New York Symphony Orchestra from New York, Mary Garden singing "Annie Laurie" from Chicago, Will Rogers mimicking President Coolidge from Kansas City, and dance bands from various cities throughout the nation. A year later NBC's Blue Network was organized, made up of different stations across the country. Both networks added stations rapidly.

At first advertising on both networks was brief and low-key. Many advertisers simply associated their names with the programs—"Eveready Hour," "Ipana Troubadours," "Maxwell House Hour."

In 1932 GE and Westinghouse withdrew from RCA, largely because of a U.S. attorney general's order that the group should be dispersed and partly because David Sarnoff, now president of RCA, felt his company should be an entity by itself. Again a series of closed-door meetings resulted in a divorce settlement. RCA retained the radio manufacturing business, but GE and Westinghouse could now compete. RCA became the sole owner of NBC, and GE and Westinghouse received RCA debentures and some of the RCA real estate. In retrospect, it appears that RCA walked off with the lion's share of value. But all this happened during the depression, and GE and Westinghouse were not overly eager to hold on to what they thought might be an expensive broadcasting liability. NBC, in spite of the depression, moved to new headquarters in mid-Manhattan, dubbed Radio City.[19]

The beginnings of what eventually became the Columbia Broadcasting System occurred in 1927. Arthur Judson, disgruntled because Sarnoff had not accepted his offer to supply talent for the NBC network, established, with several associates, the United Independent Broadcasters. The original intent of the company was to supply talent to stations not in the network.

However, in the search for capital, the company joined with the Columbia Phonograph Company to form the Columbia Phonograph Broadcasting System. Judson's group was to supply talent and programs, and the Columbia group was to sell the programming to sponsors. Unfortunately sponsors were not eager to oblige, and the project failed, with Columbia Phonograph Record Company pulling out.

Several investors tried to keep the project afloat and changed the name to Columbia Broadcasting System. Finally the family of William S. Paley supplied needed capital, Paley became president, and the CBS network began to develop. It progressed steadily with Paley at the helm. He developed a workable network-affiliate relationship and during the '30s managed to lure much of the top radio talent from NBC to CBS.

Figure 1.10
William S. Paley
Photo courtesy of CBS

The forerunner of the American Broadcasting Corporation was formed in 1934 but in its early years did not achieve prominence. In 1942 the Federal Communications Commission enforced the **duopoly** rule, which prohibited a single company from owning and operating more than one national radio network. Thus forced to divest itself of its Blue Network, the National Broadcasting Company formed a separate company to operate it. In 1943 a group headed by Edward J. Noble bought the new corporation, then still called the Blue Network. It became the ABC radio network in June of 1945. In 1953 ABC merged with United Paramount Theaters in order to better its financial footing.[20]

A fourth radio network, Mutual, was formed in 1934 when four stations—WGN in Chicago, WLW in Cincinnati, WXYZ in Detroit, and WOR in New York—decided to work jointly to obtain advertising. This gradually was built into a network, but a network that never entered television. It experienced hard times when TV emerged and for a while was under Minnesota Mining and Manufacturing Company. It is now owned by Amway Corporation and has a healthy number of affiliates.[21]

A fifth network, the Liberty Broadcasting System, was organized in 1946 and at one time served about three hundred stations. However, this network did not survive the rapid expansion of television, and it suspended operations in 1951.[22]

Chaos and Government Action

The problem of overcrowding of the broadcast frequency continued to grow during the 1920s. Secretary of commerce Herbert Hoover was besieged with requests that the broadcast frequencies be expanded and that stations be allowed to leave the 360-meter quagmire, the frequency band on which all of them were broadcasting. He made various attempts to improve the situation by altering frequencies, powers, and broadcast times but was unable to deal with the problem in any systematic manner because he could not convince Congress to give him the power to do so.

By 1925 the situation had so deteriorated that the only remedy would have been to reassign frequencies being used for other purposes. However, under the existing law, the secretary of commerce was powerless to act in this regard. To add to the trouble, in 1926 a court ruling said that the secretary of commerce had no power to restrict any of the stations in any manner. Hoover threw up his hands and told radio station operators to regulate themselves as best they could.[23]

In 1926-27 there were some 200 new stations, most of them using any frequency or power they wished and changing at whim. The airwaves were complete chaos.

To help remedy this situation, Congress passed the Radio Act of 1927. The act proclaimed that radio waves belonged to the people and could be used by individuals only if they had a license and were broadcasting in the public "interest, convenience, and necessity."

All previous licenses were revoked and applicants were allowed sixty days to apply for new licenses from the newly created Federal Radio Commission (FRC). The commission gave temporary licenses while it worked out the jigsaw puzzle of which frequencies should be used for what purposes. In the end, it granted 620 licenses in what is now the **AM** band. The FRC also designated the power at which each station could broadcast. Ten stations were authorized to operate at 50,000 watts; seventeen were to use between 10,000 and 50,000 watts; most were between 100 and 10,000 watts; but over 150 were left in the quicksand of less than 100 watts.[24] As technical improvements became available—such as the **directional antenna** system—additional stations could be licensed.

Several years after the Radio Act, Congress passed the Communications Act of 1934, which created the Federal Communications Commission (FCC) and made permanent most of the provisions of the 1927 act. This act still governs broadcasting today. It sets forth such details as the composition of the FCC, the FCC's jurisdiction, the significance of call letters, the procedures for licensing, the causes for license revocation, and the treatment of political candidates. It also cautions against fraudulent statements and obscenities.

Figure 1.11

Figure 1.12

Figure 1.11
A carbon microphone,
the best quality
available during the
formative years of radio.
Photo courtesy of KFI,
Los Angeles

Figure 1.12
An early station setup
that includes a carbon
mike, a multitubed
audio board, and
Westinghouse receivers.
Photo courtesy of KFI,
Los Angeles

Figure 1.13
Home radio receiver
with speaker, about
1924.
Photo courtesy of RCA

Figure 1.14
A battery-operated radio
receiver from about
1923.
Photo courtesy of RCA

Figure 1.15
Early backpack equip-
ment for remote broad-
casting.
Photo courtesy of KFI,
Los Angeles

Figure 1.16
A mobile van which
NBC sported to cover
the New York scene in
the 1930s.
Photo courtesy of NBC

Figure 1.13

Figure 1.14

Figure 1.15

Figure 1.16

The "Golden Era" of Radio

With the chaotic frequency situation under control, radio was now ready to enter the era of truly significant programming development—a heyday which lasted some twenty years. Improvements in radio equipment helped. Earphones had already been replaced by loudspeakers so that the whole family could listen. The early **carbon mikes** were replaced by **ribbon mikes,** which had greater fidelity, and single-dial tuning replaced the three-dial system required on earlier receivers. For portability and use in automobiles, battery sets were introduced. However, the first portables were cumbersome due to the size of early dry batteries.

Radio became the primary entertainment medium during the depression. In 1930, 12 million homes were equipped with radio receivers, but by 1940 this number had jumped to 30 million. During the same period, advertising revenue rose from $40 million to $155 million. In 1930 NBC-Red, NBC-Blue, and CBS combined offered approximately 60 hours of

Figure 1.17
Amos 'n' Andy as they appeared when broadcasting from Studio B in NBC's Hollywood Radio City. Freeman Fisher Gosden is on the left side of the table with Madaline Lee, Charles Correll is at the right, and sitting in the left foreground is the "Here th' are" man, announcer Bill Hay.
Photo courtesy of KFI, Los Angeles

Figure 1.18
Jack Benny and his wife and co-star, Mary Livingston, in 1933. The "Jack Benny Show," sponsored for many years by Jello and Lucky Strike, featured such sure-fire laugh provokers as an ancient Maxwell automobile that coughed and sputtered, Benny's perennial age of 39 years, a constant feud with Fred Allen, and Benny's horrible violin playing.
Photo courtesy of NBC

sponsored programs a week. By 1940 the four networks (Mutual had been added) carried 156 hours.[25]

The first program to generate nationwide enthusiasm was "Amos 'n' Andy." It was created by Freeman Fisher Gosden and Charles J. Correll, who met while working for a company that staged local **vaudeville**-type shows throughout the country. Gosden and Correll, who were white, worked up a blackface act for the company and later tried this on WGN radio in Chicago as "Sam 'n' Henry." When WGN did not renew their contract, they took the show to WMAQ in Chicago and changed the name to "Amos 'n' Andy" since WGN owned the title "Sam 'n' Henry."

Correll and Gosden wrote all the material themselves and played most of the characters by changing the pitch, volume, and tone of their voices. Gosden always played Amos, a simple hard-working fellow, and Correll played Andy, a clever, conniving, somewhat lazy individual who usually

Figure 1.19

Figure 1.20

Figure 1.19
Ed Wynn, also known as "the perfect fool." He received this label originally because he performed in the first Broadway stage show broadcast on radio, titled "The Perfect Fool." Later Wynn starred in "The Fire Chief," a program sponsored by Texaco, and at one time he tried to form another radio network.
Photo courtesy of NBC

Figure 1.21

Figure 1.20
Lum and Abner, played by Chester Lauck (left) and Norris Goff. This comedy took place in the Jot 'Em Down grocery store in the supposedly fictional town of Pine Ridge, Arkansas. In 1936 the town of Waters, Arkansas changed its name to Pine Ridge in honor of Lum and Abner.
Photo courtesy of KFI, Los Angeles

Figure 1.21
George Burns and Gracie Allen. Many of the jokes of this program were plays on words based on Gracie's supposed empty-headedness. At one point Gracie started searching for her "lost brother" by suddenly appearing on other shows to inquire about him.
Photo courtesy of NBC

took credit for Amos's ideas. According to the scripts, Amos and Andy had come from Atlanta to Chicago to seek their fortune, but all they had amassed was a broken-down automobile which constituted the Fresh-Air Taxicab Company of America. Much of the humor of the show revolved around a fraternity-type organization called the Mystic Knights of the Sea headed by a character called Kingfish, who was played by Gosden.

WMAQ allowed Correll and Gosden to **syndicate** the show on other stations. Its success caught the attention of the NBC Blue Network, which hired the two in 1929 at $100,000 a year. Their program from 7:00 to 7:15 p.m. Eastern time became such a nationwide hit that it affected dinner hours, plant closing times, and even, on one notable occasion, the speaking schedule of the president of the United States.[26]

Many other comedians followed in the wake of the success of Correll and Gosden—Jack Benny, Eddie Cantor, Lum and Abner, Ed Wynn, Fred Allen, George Burns and Gracie Allen, Jimmy Durante, Edgar Bergen and Charlie McCarthy, Bob Hope, Fibber McGee and Molly, Arthur Godfrey, the Goldbergs, the Aldrich Family.

Music, especially classical music, was also frequently heard. There were broadcasts of the New York Philharmonic concerts and performances from the Metropolitan Opera House. As a special pet project of David Sarnoff, NBC established its own orchestra led by Arturo Toscanini. Sarnoff was also largely responsible for Walter Damrosch's "Music Appreciation Hour" aimed at young people. For lighter music, "Your Hit Parade" was introduced in 1935, and little-known singers such as Kate Smith and Bing Crosby took to the air. As the "big bands" developed, they too went out over the airwaves.

One program innovation was the audience participation show. Among many amateur hours, perhaps the most famous was the one hosted by Major Bowes. Quiz shows such as "Professor Quiz" and stunt shows such as "Truth or Consequences," hosted by Ralph Edwards, were attracting large and faithful audiences.

Many programs were developed for children, including "Let's Pretend," "The Lone Ranger," "Uncle Don's Quiz Kids," and "Little Orphan Annie." Art Linkletter gained fame for his interviews with children.

During the day there were continuing dramas such as "Stella Dallas," "One Man's Family," "Lorenzo Jones and His Wife Belle," "Ma Perkins," "Myrt and Marge," "Our Gal Sunday," "Backstage Wife," and "The Romance of Helen Trent." These came to be called "soap operas" because soap manufacturers were frequent sponsors. The segments always ended with an unresolved situation in order to entice the listener to tune in tomorrow. Most did. The scripts for a major portion of the soap operas came from a husband-wife team, Frank and Ann Hummert. They defined the basic idea for each series and wrote synopses of programs, then farmed the actual script-writing to a bevy of writers around the country, some of whom never even met the Hummerts.

Figure 1.22
Charlie McCarthy and ventriloquist Edgar Bergen (*right*) with W. C. Fields (*left*) and Dorothy Lamour. Charlie had a running feud with W. C. and a love affair with just about all the '30s and '40s beauties and even the '50s movie idol Marilyn Monroe.
Photo courtesy of NBC

Figure 1.23
Marian and Jim Jordan as Fibber McGee and Molly. One of the institutions of this program was the hall closet which, when opened, always unloaded its contents with ceremonial crashes. The commercials were integrated directly into the program when the announcer dropped by the McGee home and extoled the virtues of Johnson's Wax.
Photo Courtesy of NBC

Figure 1.24
Katherine Naiht, House Jamison, Ann Lincoln, and Ezra Stone of "The Aldrich Family." This program's familiar opening was "Henry, Henry Aldrich," to which Ezra Stone replied, "Coming, Mother." The program was based on the Broadway play "What a Life." It played as skits on the Rudy Vallee and Kate Smith shows before becoming its own show.
Photo courtesy of NBC

Figure 1.25
Arturo Toscanini and
the NBC orchestra.
Toscanini was coaxed
out of retirement in Italy
by David Sarnoff, head
of NBC and classical
music lover. A special
studio, 8H, was built for
the orchestra and was
referred to as the
world's only floating
studio because of its
unique construction.
Photo courtesy of NBC

Figure 1.26
Bing Crosby in 1949.
For a period of time the
crooner sang and ex-
tolled Minute Maid on
radio station WCAE in
Pittsburgh.
Photo courtesy of The
Coca-Cola Company

Figure 1.27

Figure 1.28

Figure 1.27
Tommy Dorsey's Band.
When cigarette com-
panies backed many of
the swing bands,
Raleigh-Kool sponsored
the Dorsey musicians.
Since the radio pro-
grams were performed
before live audiences,
the huge cigarette
packs did make an im-
pact.
Photo courtesy of KFI,
Los Angeles

Figure 1.28
Rudy Vallee *(right)* with
Charles Butterworth
(left), Helen Vinson, and
Fred Perry. Some of the
many stars who got
their start on this vari-
ety format show were
Bob Burns, Bob Hope,
Eddie Cantor, Alice
Faye, Milton Berle, and
Ezra Stone.
Photo courtesy of KFI,
Los Angeles

Figure 1.29
Dave Garroway (*right*) in
Pittsburgh. This future
host of the "Today"
show was a KDKA an-
nouncer from 1938 to
1940.
Photo courtesy of KFI,
Los Angeles

Figure 1.30
Major Edward Bowes of
"The Original Amateur
Hour." Some of the win-
ners from this amateur
competition formed a
touring Major Bowes
company which pro-
vided talent employ-
ment during the depres-
sion.
Photo courtesy of KFI,
Los Angeles

For drama, the networks first tried to rebroadcast the sound of Broadway plays, but they discovered that this was akin to sitting in a theater
blindfolded. As a result, the networks hired writers such as Norman
Corwin, True Boardman, Arch Oboler, Maxwell Anderson, and Stephen
Vincent Benet to script original dramas for radio. These dramas usually
employed many sound effects. The names of some of the series were "Lux
Radio Theater," "First Nighter," "Silver Theater," "Collier's Hour,"
"True Detective Mysteries," "Gangbusters," "The Shadow," and "Sher-
lock Holmes." In 1938 Orson Welles produced "War of the Worlds," a
fantasy about a Martian invasion in New Jersey, and an estimated 1.2
million people succumbed to hysteria. They panicked in the streets, fled to
the country, and seized arms to prepare to fight—despite the fact that the

"Mercury Theater" program included interruptions to inform the listener that this was only a drama. Some people felt that radio had become overly realistic.[27]

It was mainly the depression that brought about the growth of commercials. During the '20s, advertisements were brief, tasteful, and did not mention price. However, as radio stations and all the facets of the American economy began digging for money at any price, the commercial standards dissolved. Some advertisers felt commercials should irritate, and broadcasters, anxious for the buck, acquiesced. The commercials became long, loud, dramatic, hard-driving, and cutthroat.

Most of the radio programs were produced, not by the networks, but by advertising agencies. They found they could combine advertising effectiveness with human misery. Thus a large number of personal help programs developed. Listeners would send letters to radio human relations "experts" detailing their traumas, crimes, and transgressions and ask for help. Often this help had commercial tie-ins. Box tops had to accompany the letter to qualify it for an answer; or suggested help might involve the sponsor's drug product; or the contentment to be derived from puffing on the sponsor's brand of cigarette might be recommended. By 1932 more air time was spent on commercials than on news, education, lectures, and religion together. The commercials did succeed in bringing profits to NBC, CBS, and some individual radio stations. They also brought profits to the advertising agencies that were intimately involved in most details of programming, including selecting program ideas, overseeing scripts, selling and producing advertisements for the shows, and placing the programs on the network schedule.[28]

There were also many events which could be termed stunt broadcasts, such as broadcasts from heights, depths, widely separated points, gliders, and underwater locations. A two-way conversation took place between an aerial balloonist off the Atlantic coast and an airplane off the Pacific coast. A four-way conversation involved participants in Chicago, New York, Washington, and a balloon. One music program featured a singer in New York accompanied by an orchestra in Buenos Aires. A piano concert was performed from a blimp in the mid-Atlantic.

These stunt broadcasts paved the way for the broadcast of legitimate public events from distant points. In 1931 nineteen separate locations around the world participated in a program dedicated to Marconi. Radio carried descriptions of Admiral Byrd's 1933-35 Antarctic expedition and the 1934 burning of the ship *Morro Castle* off the New Jersey coast. People were able to hear the farewell address of King Edward VIII when he abdicated the British throne, the coronation of George VI, and the trial of the Lindbergh baby kidnapper.[29]

Radio also figured in politics of the day. President Franklin Delano Roosevelt effectively used radio for his "fireside chats" to try to reassure the nation during the depression. Louisiana's firebrand Governor Huey Long was often heard on the airwaves, and Father Charles E. Coughlin, a Detroit priest, tried to build a political movement through radio.

**Figure 1.31
A wartime plug for
NBC's programs.**
(Figure on next two pages.)
Photo courtesy of KFI,
Los Angeles

THE INCOMPARABLE AMOS 'N' ANDY, returning to air via NBC Friday Oct. 8.

THE INCORRIGIBLE BABY SNOOKS and Frank Morgan on Maxwell House show Thursday, 8:30 p. m.

THE INVENTIVE ARKANSAS TRAVELER, Bob Burns, back on air Thursday night.

THE INGENIOUS JACK BENNY, airing with all the gang at 4 p. m., Sunday.

THE INFALLIBLE H. V. KALTENBORN, commentator, heard four afternoons weekly.

NBC PROUDLY Presents:

RAMP, TRAMP, TRAMP. It's NBC's parade of stars marching along to open the fall and winter season of happy listening.

For dialers, the biggest news of all is the return of Amos 'n' Andy. The two old favorites introduce a brand new show on Friday, October 8 complete with guest stars, music and the kind of laughter which made Freeman Gosden and Charles Correll famous.

TRAMP, TRAMP, TRAMP.

"The Great Gildersleeve" started the parade by huffing and puffing his way back to his fans late in August. This is Hal Peary's third season on the air with his own program, and from the way the polls were going when he went off in June, it looks like his biggest.

TRAMP, TRAMP, TRAMP.

Fanny Brice, with more antics of

Page Four

26   Chapter 1

A Star-Bedazzled Parade Of Fast-Stepping Radio Entertainers, on March To Storm Your Listening

THE IMPERTINENT CHARLIE McCARTHY and Bergen for Chase & Sanborn, Sunday, 5 p. m.

her inimitable Baby Snooks, and Frank Morgan, with a new batch of tall stories, followed "Gildersleeve" to NBC microphones on the first Thursday in September.

TRAMP, TRAMP, TRAMP.

Edgar Bergen and Charlie McCarthy marched back from Newfoundland, where they entertained the troops stationed there. This season they are presenting Victor Moore and William Gaxton, in addition to Ray Noble's orchestra and the songs of Dale Evans.

TRAMP, TRAMP, TRAMP.

That bad little boy, Red Skelton, was next in line, and with him were the popular members of his cast—Harriet Hilliard and Ozzie Nelson and his band.

TRAMP, TRAMP, TRAMP.

An account of Bob Hope's travels while away from his radio show for the summer sounds like a review of the war headlines—England, Bizerte, Tunis, Algiers, Sicily. Back on the air with him for the new season comes another grand trouper, Frances Langford, who also went into the battle areas with Bob. And, of course, Jerry Colonna and Vera Vague will be on hand.

TRAMP, TRAMP, TRAMP.

And so they come. Those two top comedians, Jim and Marian Jordan, who have more delightful sessions with "Fibber McGee and Molly," ready for their listeners.

Eddie Cantor with another season of Wednesday night laughfests.

Jack Benny, another of radio's globe-trotters, only recently returned from the European and North African battlefronts.

And, of course, there are all the favorites who have been on NBC this summer and who will continue to make radio listening America's Number One pastime—"One Man's Family;" Bing Crosby; the Standard Symphony Hour; H. V. Kaltenborn and the other commentators who bring the world into our homes; Kay Kyser's "College of Musical Knowledge;" Ginny Simms; the Joan Davis-Jack Haley show; and the Sunday morning Westinghouse program.

Happy listening? Yes, indeed!

THE INGRATIATING FATHER AND MOTHER BARBOUR on "One Man's Family," Sunday, 5:30 p. m.

THE INIMITABLE FIBBER McGEE AND MOLLY, back with their friends Tuesday, 6 p. m.

THE INEXHAUSTIBLE LAUGH CREATOR, Bob Hope, back in his regular Tuesday spot, 7 p. m.

THE IRREPRESSIBLE LITTLE KID, as played by Red Skelton, Tuesday, 7:30 p. m.

The Press-Radio War

News was destined to become one of radio's strongest services, but not without a struggle. At first announcers merely read newspaper headlines over the air. The eminently successful CBS weekly series "The March of Time," was a combination of drama and news. Actors impersonating such figures as Mussolini, Franklin Roosevelt, Eleanor Roosevelt, and Huey Long acted out news in a manner which straddled the fence between fact and fiction.

In 1932 the Associated Press gave presidential election bulletins to the networks, and programs were interrupted with news flashes. Newspapers objected on the grounds that news on radio would diminish the sale of papers. From 1933 to 1935 a "press-radio war" ensued with the press insisting that news bulletins be limited to thirty words and that radio could not report "hot off the wire" news. Some papers boycotted radio by refusing to carry program schedules.

For a time, radio stations were unable to obtain news from the three **wire services**—Associated Press (AP), United Press (UP), and International News Service (INS)—but the press's hold on news gradually broke down. This was due in part to a court decision giving radio stations the right to read from already published news and in part to the fact that radio stations were permitted to have "commentators." These commentators often became thinly disguised news reporters.

Also, NBC and CBS began their own news-gathering activities. In the case of NBC, one man—Abe Schechter—gathered news simply by making telephone calls. Sometimes he scooped newspaper reporters because just about anyone would answer a call from NBC. In addition, Schechter could reward news sources with tickets to Rudy Vallee's show, which were highly prized. Most of the material Schechter collected was broadcast by NBC's prime newscaster, Lowell Thomas, but an item or two usually wound up on

Figure 1.32

Figure 1.32
The NBC radio mobile unit making contact with an airplane. This 1929 experimentation led to future possibilities for news coverage.
Photo courtesy of NBC

Figure 1.33
President Franklin Delano Roosevelt delivering a "fireside chat."
Photo courtesy of NBC

Figure 1.33

Walter Winchell's Sunday night gossip program. CBS set up a larger news force that included **stringers**—reporters paid only for material actually used. That network's top news commentator was H. V. Kaltenborn, who later became famous for his premature and incorrect announcement on the air that Thomas Dewey had defeated Harry Truman for the Presidency.

As world tensions grew, there was an increased awareness of news on the part of the public. Advertisers became interested in sponsoring news radio programs because of the growing potential listener market. At one point, UP and INS agreed to make their news available to advertisers who would then broadcast it over radio, but they would not make it available to radio stations directly. This arrangement led to a total breakdown of broadcast news blackouts, and radio began to develop as an important news disseminator. Americans heard actual sounds of the Spanish Civil War, of Germany's march into Austria, and they heard the voices of Hitler, Chamberlain, and Mussolini.[30]

World War II

The government did not take over broadcasting during World War II as it had during World War I. However, it did solicit the cooperation of radio for morale and public service announcements, bond purchase appeals, conservation campaigns, and civil defense instructions. Among the most famous of these solicitations were Kate Smith's marathon broadcasts for war bonds. Her appeals sold over $100,000,000 worth of bonds. Many of the plays and soap operas produced during the period dealt with the war effort, and some even tried to deal with the segregation problem, which was coming to a head because of segregation in the Armed Forces. Several soap operas presented Negroes (the preferred term at that time) in esteemed professional roles.

Figure 1.34

Figure 1.35

Figure 1.35
H. V. Kaltenborn, the dean of radio commentators. He received his greatest recognition during the 1938 Munich crisis, when he didn't leave the CBS studios for eighteen days and went on the air 85 times to analyze news from Europe.
Photo courtesy of KFI, Los Angeles

Figure 1.34
Walter Winchell with the signal key he used to accent his rapid-fire speaking style. He always worked with his hat on in the studio and always began his programs, "Good evening Mr. and Mrs. North and South America and all the ships at sea. Let's go to press."
Photo courtesy of NBC

The Army and Navy set up the Armed Forces Radio Service to entertain servicemen overseas by producing special programs and recording network programs for replay on troop-operated stations around the world. Propaganda broadcasting was begun over shortwave. Foreign countries did likewise. The Japanese programmed dulcet-voiced girls broadcasting appeals intended to demoralize American soldiers. "Tokyo Rose" was the cover name the Americans applied to them all.

The news function greatly increased with up-to-date material being broadcast at least every hour. Some of the best-known voices heard from overseas were H. V. Kaltenborn, William L. Shirer, Eric Sevareid, Howard K. Smith, Charles Collingwood, Richard C. Hottelet, Larry Lesueur, and, probably most important of all, Edward R. Murrow with his "This is London" broadcasts.

David Sarnoff, president of NBC, joined the Signal Corps and supervised the communication coverage for D day—June 6, 1944, the opening of the Allied invasion of France. William Paley, president of CBS, became a colonel dealing in psychological warfare. Special events such as President Roosevelt's war message to Congress, the signing of the surrender papers, and the events of D day were heard over radio. [31]

One result of the war was the perfection of audio tape recorders by means of which events could be recorded and played back whenever desired. Prior to the war, NBC and CBS had policies forbidding the use of recorded material for anything other than sound effects, and even most of those were executed live. This policy was abetted by the musicians' union, which insisted that all broadcast music utilize musicians rather than phonograph records. The Mutual Broadcasting Company permitted some use of recorded speech but was considered second-rate for doing so. As a result, the live programs usually had to be performed twice—once for the East and Midwest, and once again three hours later for the West Coast.

Figure 1.36
Correspondent Edward R. Murrow at his typewriter in wartime London.
Photo from United Press International

Figure 1.37
David Sarnoff, promoted to brigadier general during World War II.
Photo courtesy of RCA

Figure 1.38
William S. Paley serving as colonel in the U.S. Army during World War II.
Photo courtesy of CBS

Figure 1.36

Figure 1.37

Figure 1.38

The recording technique then used was usually phonograph **discs,** for the only magnetic recording known in America prior to World War II was **wire recording.** In order to edit or splice, a knot had to be tied in the wire and then fused with heat, making it a cumbersome and essentially unusable technique. During the war American troops entering German radio stations found them operating without any people. The broadcasting was handled by a machine that used plastic tape of higher fidelity than Americans had ever heard from wire. This plastic tape could be cut with scissors and spliced with adhesive. The recorders were confiscated, sent to America, improved, and eventually revolutionized programming procedures.[32]

Radio stations enjoyed great economic prosperity during the war. There were about 950 stations on the air when the war began. No more were licensed during the war, so those 950 received all the advertisements. A newsprint shortage reduced ad space in newspapers, and some of that advertising money was channeled into broadcasting. Institutional advertising became common because of high wartime taxes; companies preferred to pay for advertising rather than turn money over to the government. And with few consumer products to sell because industry was geared for the war effort, companies were happy to sponsor prestige programs such as symphony orchestra concerts. Thus radio station revenue increased from $155 million in 1940 to $310 million in 1945.[33]

After the war, radio networks appeared for a time to return to prewar programming—comedy, drama, soap operas, children's programs, news, public service. But a new phenomenon was beginning to appear upon the scene—the disc jockey. Several conditions precipitated this emergence.

The Changing Format

1) The FCC altered a ruling about identification of recorded material. Previously it had been necessary to identify all recordings as they were broadcast. Such frequent announcing would have stigmatized a d.j. show. But in the 1940s the FCC ruled that such announcements could be made only each half hour.

2) Several record programs broadcast in the middle of the night or as fillers during special event coverage had achieved interest and success and had produced benefits for advertisers.

3) A court decision of 1940 ruled that if broadcasters purchased a record, they could then play it without further financial obligation. This ended the practice of stamping records "not licensed for radio broadcast" and added legal stature to disc jockey programs.

4) In the mid '40s the musician's union, which had voted to halt recording, was appeased with a musicians' welfare fund to which record companies would contribute. This opened the door to mass record production.

5) Television began to siphon entertainment talent from radio, leaving it more and more dependent on the disc jockey.

6) Radios became more portable at the same time as Americans were becoming more mobile. The public appreciated the disc jockey shows, which could be enjoyed while listeners were engaged in other activities.

7) Station management appreciated the lower overhead, fewer headaches, and higher profits associated with disc jockey programming. A d.j. did not need a writer, a bevy of actors, a sound effects man, an audience, or even a studio. All that was needed were records, and these were readily available from companies who would eagerly court disc jockeys in the hopes that they would plug certain tunes, thus assuring sales of the records. This "courtship" tarnished the disc jockeys' image slightly in the late '50s when it was discovered that a number of disc jockeys had been engaged in "**payola**"—the practice of accepting money or gifts in exchange for favoring certain records.[34]

Postwar radio was, above all, prosperous. Advertisers were standing in line, and the main problem was finding a way to squeeze in the commercials. To the networks, especially NBC, this was a boon because it provided the necessary capital to support the then unprofitable television development. In order to invest even more in the new baby, nonsponsored public affairs radio programs dropped by the wayside, as did some expensive entertainment. Radio fed the mouth that bit it.

On the local level this prosperity created a demand for new radio station licenses as both entrepreneurs and large companies scrambled to cash in on the boom. The 950 wartime stations expanded in a rabbitlike fashion to well over 2,000 by 1950.[35] But the bubble soon burst as advertisers deserted radio to try the medium that featured both sound and sight. This left radio networks as hollow shells. The 2,000 local stations found that the advertising dollars remaining in radio did not stretch to keep them all in the black. In 1961 almost 40 percent of radio stations lost money.[36]

The period of the TV takeover tried the souls of radio men. Some attempted to hang on to yesteryear and maintain traditional programming, but this was grasping at a straw in the wind. Many swam with the tide and joined TV. Others succumbed to economic pressures and left the business. Still others groped for solutions to the problem and eventually settled for disc jockey domination. After a long, hard pull, the d.j.s won the favor of the public—and, hence, the advertisers—and once again radio assumed economic and social status.

Frequency Modulation—FM

FM was actually developed in the early 1930s by Edwin H. Armstrong. David Sarnoff mentioned to him that someone should invent a black box to eliminate **static.** Armstrong invented, not a black box, but a whole new system—frequency modulation. He wanted RCA to back its development and promotion, but Sarnoff had committed RCA funds to television and was not interested in underwriting an entirely new radio structure despite its obviously superior clarity and fidelity.

Armstrong continued his interest in FM, built an experimental 50,000-watt FM station in New Jersey, and solicited the support and enthusiasm of GE for his project. In the late '30s and early '40s an FM bandwagon was rolling, and some 150 applications for FM stations were submitted to the FCC. As a result, the FCC removed channel 1 from the TV band and awarded the **spectrum** space to FM. It also ruled that TV sound should be frequency-modulated. Armstrong's triumphant boom seemed just around the corner, but the war intervened and commercial FM had to wait. However, FM went to war installed on virtually every American tank and jeep.

After the war the FCC reviewed spectrum space and decided to move FM to another part of the broadcast spectrum. This move was violently protested by Armstrong and other FM proponents, for it rendered all prewar FM sets worthless and saddled the FM business with heavy conversion costs.

Armstrong was further infuriated by the fact that although FM sound was to be used for TV, RCA had never paid him royalties for the sets it manufactured. In 1948 he brought suit against RCA. Increasingly harassed and ill as the suit proceeded for over a year, he one day leaped from the window of his thirteenth-floor apartment to his death.[37]

FM continued to develop slowly. With television on the horizon, there was little interest in a new radio system. Many of the major AM stations acquired FM licenses as insurance in case FM replaced AM, as its proponents were predicting. They simply duplicated their AM programming on FM, which naturally did not increase the public's incentive to purchase FM sets.

However, as general interest in high fidelity music grew, FM's interference-free signal became a greater asset. In 1961 the FCC authorized **stereophonic** sound transmission for FM, which led to increased awareness of the medium by hi-fi fans. A further aid was a 1965 FCC ruling which stated that in cities of over 100,000 population AM and FM stations with the same ownership had to have separate programming at least 50 percent of the time. This ruling was extended in 1977 to limit stations in cities over 100,000 to 25 percent duplication and stations in cities of 25,000 to 100,000 to 50 percent duplication.[38]

Figure 1.39
Edwin H. Armstrong
Smithsonian Institution
Photo No. 43614

Radio Today

Radio today is station-dominated. The networks have disappeared as entertainment sources and have become primarily news services. Stations, whether network-affiliated or not, produce most of their own programming. This is mainly music announced by disc jockeys, although some stations feature all-news or all-talk **formats.** The most listened-to radio formats are usually popular songs. However, there are stations to appeal to every musical taste imaginable.

Radios have found a special niche in the automobile, where they are listened to by Americans on the go. Portable radios also accompany people to the beach, to mountain resorts, to the classroom, to parties. They make and break recording artists and make and break the current events of the hour.

Economically, radio stations are holding their own. The dollar has not deserted radio and, in fact, advertising revenues have soared to well above the postwar figures. But costs have risen, as have the number of stations, so the advertising butter must be spread thinly.

It has been a long, significant journey from Guglielmo Marconi to Wolfman Jack, with the labors and voices of thousands making important contributions along the way.

Summary Radio has developed from its early nonbroadcasting-oriented status through its heyday of entertainment and informational programming to its present emphasis on news and music.

Early inventions by *Maxwell, Hertz, Marconi, Fleming, Fessenden,* and *De Forest* were not used primarily for broadcasting as we think of it today but rather for communication. The government's first involvement was to require that ships carry radios for safety; it then took over radio during World War I. After the war RCA was established mainly so *patents* could be shared and radio could develop. *Sarnoff, Terry, Scripps,* and *Conrad* all contributed to the broadcast orientation of radio during the 1920s, when programming consisted mainly of records and performances by free talent. Advertising began when AT&T established a "*toll*" station, but it did not really take hold until the depression years. NBC's Blue and Red networks were established in 1926 followed by CBS, ABC, and Mutual. By the late 1920s the airwaves were chaotic, so a freeze was imposed in 1927 which led to the establishment of the *FCC* and the passing of the *1934 Communications Act. Amos 'n' Andy* began a programming era of comedies, dramas, music, children's programs, and soap operas which lasted for over a decade. News came to radio more slowly because of the *press-radio war.* During World War II radio cooperated with the war effort and broadcast news from the scene. After the war radio continued to grow until TV began siphoning its programming. A difficult adjustment period followed with radio settling into a *disc jockey*-dominated format that has been aided by the high fidelity possibilities of *FM.*

2 A Sound Look
Technical Aspects of Radio

Radio is TV with privacy.

Don McNeill, host of the
long-running radio show "The Breakfast Club"

"Something seems to be wrong with the cart machine."

Through the wonder of **radio waves,** a voice spoken in a small soundproof room or music played on a turntable or tape recorder can reach millions of ears. This is accomplished by converting the sound of the voice or music into electrical impulses and then sending these impulses through the air to radio sets located in homes, cars, pockets, or wherever their owners wish to place them. This sound conversion involves a great deal of equipment, generally beginning with microphones and ending with radio receivers.[1]

Microphones can be characterized by their pickup patterns and also by their internal construction. They can be designed so they pick up sound in varying ways. The four most common types of microphone are: **unidirectional,** which picks up sound mainly from one side; **bidirectional,** which picks up sound mainly from two sides; **cardioid,** which picks up sound in a heart-shaped pattern; and **omnidirectional,** which picks up sound from all directions.

Microphones

Each directional aspect has its own special uses. When only one person's voice is to be heard, such as that of a newscaster or sportscaster, a unidirectional mike is the best choice. It will pick up the person sitting in front of it and will minimize crowd or other distracting noises in the background. Bidirectional mikes had their heyday during the era of radio drama, for they enabled actors to face each other to deliver their lines. Cardioid mikes are very satisfactory for two people seated next to each other and thus are frequently used on TV talk shows. Omnidirectional mikes pick up overall crowd noises well and are often used for plays with large casts.

With respect to internal construction, there are three types of microphones used frequently in radio: the **dynamic** (or pressure) mike, the **ribbon** (or velocity) mike, and the **condensor** (or **capacitor**) mike. A dynamic mike consists of a **diaphragm,** a permanent magnet, and **coils** wrapped around the magnet. The diaphragm is positioned within the field of the magnet and responds to the pressure of sound. The sound waves of talking or other noise cause movements of the diaphragm and result in a disturbance of the **magnetic field,** which induces a small electrical current in the coils. This current then flows out the wire of the microphone as electrical impulses representing sound. Dynamic mikes are small, fairly inexpensive, sturdy, responsive to a wide range of frequencies, and less sensitive to wind than other studio mikes.

Ribbon mikes are constructed by attaching a metallic ribbon near magnets. This ribbon responds to the velocity, or speed, of the sound waves rather than the pressure and causes disturbances which result in electrical current. Ribbon mikes are usually bulkier, more fragile, and more sensitive to wind than dynamic mikes.

The condensor, or capacitor, type of studio mike uses an electronic component, the capacitor, to respond to sound. It requires power to operate, so capacitor mikes must have batteries attached to them. Capacitor mikes were therefore both cumbersome and expensive until recent technological advances improved this limitation. Capacitor mikes are now widely used and prized for their high fidelity.[2]

Figure 2.1
Microphone pickup patterns.

Figure 2.2
An omnidirectional dynamic microphone.
Photo courtesy of Electro-Voice, Inc., Buchanan, Michigan, U.S.A.

Figure 2.3
A unidirectional ribbon microphone.
Photo courtesy of Shure Brothers, Inc.

Figure 2.4
A cardioid condensor microphone.
Photo courtesy of Electro-Voice, Inc., Buchanan, Michigan, U.S.A

Figure 2.5
A bidirectional ribbon microphone.
Photo courtesy of Shure Brothers, Inc.

Omnidirectional

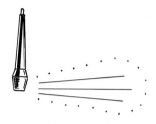

Unidirectional

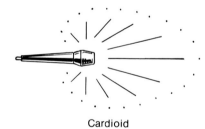

Cardioid

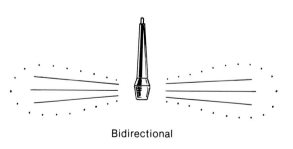

Bidirectional

Figure 2.1

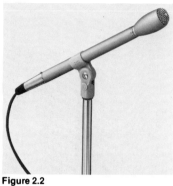

Figure 2.2

Figure 2.3

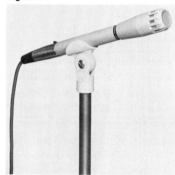

Figure 2.4

Figure 2.5

Figure 2.6
A broadcast quality
record turntable.
Photo courtesy of QRK
Electronic Products

Turntables

In an audio production facility, a turntable has two functions: (1) to spin a record at the proper speed, and (2) to convert the variations in the grooves of the record to electrical energy with the pickup arm.

A broadcast quality turntable consists of a heavy metal plate covered by a rubber or felt top. It will normally have a power switch to control the motor, a **gear shift** to select speeds, and an **equalizer** or filter to compensate for scratchy records. Next to the revolving table will be a pickup arm that houses the **cartridge** and **stylus** which actually pick up the signal from the record. The cartridge receives the minute vibrations from the stylus and converts them into variations in voltage, acting similarly to the magnet and coil in a microphone. These variations are then sent through wire to the control board. The stylus is a very small, highly compliant strip of metal, the end of which is made of hard material, usually diamond.

Since turntables are used by radio stations primarily for playing musical selections, a control room will usually have two turntables so that a disc jockey can **cue** one record while another is airing. Sometimes turntables will be used for **disc** commercials, but most stations choose audio tape for advertisements. Some stations are even pretaping their music, thus rendering their on-air turntables obsolete.[3]

Tape Recorders

Tape recorders are devices which rearrange the iron particles on magnetic tape so that sound impulses can be stored on the tape and played back at a later date. This rearranging of particles is undertaken by stationary **heads.** Quality recorders usually have three heads—one to erase, one to record, and one to play. The erase head is always positioned so that old material is erased an instant before new material is recorded. When the machine is in

Figure 2.7
Tape recorder head
arrangment.

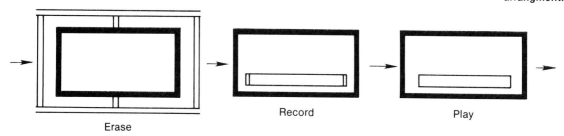

Erase

Record

Play

Figure 2.8

Figure 2.9

**Figure 2.8
A reel-to-reel recorder.**
Photo courtesy of Teac
Corporation of America

**Figure 2.9
A cartridge recorder.**
Photo Courtesy of Spot-
master

**Figure 2.10
A cassette recorder.**
Photo courtesy of Teac
Corporation of America

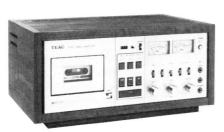

Figure 2.10

play, the erase and record heads are disengaged. Cheaper recorders have only two heads—one for erase and another for both play and record.

The three basic types of tape recorders are reel-to-reel, **cassette,** and **cartridge.** On a reel-to-reel recorder all the tape is initially on one reel and must be threaded past the heads to the take-up reel. This kind of machine lends itself to editing because the tape is readily accessible.

A cassette machine uses cassette tape, which is two reels already threaded inside a plastic container. The cassette is inserted so that the tape passes against the heads. Because of the small size, it is often used for taping material at locations away from the studio.

A cartridge machine is similar to a cassette machine in that the tape is slipped into a machine with no threading necessary, but the cartridge is constructed differently in that it is a container with a loop of tape. The tape is wound onto the center spool with the end next to the spool slightly raised. When the tape is cut from the master reel it can be spliced to the raised end, thus making a continuous loop. The cartridge, like the cassette, is inserted in the machine in such a way that the tape passes against the heads. Commercials are usually recorded on cartridges, for they are brief and can profit from a cartridge recorder's **cue tone** which automatically starts and stops the machine.

Most tape recorders can record at different speeds, the most common of which are 7 1/2 IPS (inches per second) and 3 3/4 IPS. This means either 7 1/2 or 3 3/4 inches of tape passes the head per second. The more tape that goes past the head, the better can be the recording quality because more frequency responses can be placed on the tape. For this reason, there are recorders that tape at 15 IPS in order to achieve high quality reproduction of musical sounds.[4]

Control Boards

The control board or console is the primary consolidating piece of equipment in any audio production facility. It has three primary functions: (1) to enable the operator to select any one or combination of the various **inputs** (microphones, turntables, tape players, etc.); (2) to amplify the sound; and (3) to enable the operator to route the inputs to a number of **outputs (monitor, transmitter,** tape recorder, etc.).

The various inputs come to the board through wires after they have been converted from sound to electrical impulses. For example, the signal from a microphone enters the board at a connection for microphone input. This mike signal consists of a very small voltage which the board directs through a **preamplifier** so that it is increased enough to be sent to the **potentiometer,** or pot. Here the resistance to the sound is varied, thus increasing and decreasing the volume. At the output of the pot there is a **key.** When the key is in the "off" position, the signal is stopped at this point; when the key is in the "on" position, the signal is sent to the program **amplifier,** the final amplification stage before being distributed. The signal is here amplified enough so that it can be sent through the line out to a tape recorder or transmitter.

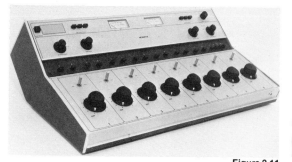

Figure 2.11

Figure 2.12

Figure 2.11
A fairly simple audio input-output board.
Photo courtesy of McMartin Industries, Inc.

Figure 2.12
A more complex board with slider controls for volume.
Photo courtesy of Cetec Broadcast Group

Figure 2.13
A twelve-input, four-output board which can be used for complex productions.
Photo courtesy of Opamp Labs, Inc.

Figure 2.13

At the "line out" position, the signal is also sent to the volume unit indicator (**VU meter**), a metering device which enables the operator to determine the level of sound going out the line. Here too, sound is sent to a monitor amplifier and then to a speaker which enables the operator to hear the signal.

The audio control board as discussed so far has only one input, a microphone. Since the purpose of the board is to mix sound, most boards have several inputs so that several mikes, turntables, and tape recorders can be on at once. By using the various controls, one song can be faded into another or a disc jockey can talk over a record as it is ending by turning down the turntable pot and turning up his mike pot. The individual sources are connected to each other after the key and before the program amplifier.[5]

Studios and Control Rooms

Gone are the days of velvet-draped studios with complicated sound effects gimmickry. In their place are all-in-one studio/control-room complexes, often no larger than a department store display window. They house the control board, the mikes, the turntables, the tape recorders, the record and tape library, and, somewhere tucked in the middle, the disc jockey-engineer-salesperson-station manager-janitor.

Figure 2.14
Diagram of a simple
audio control board.

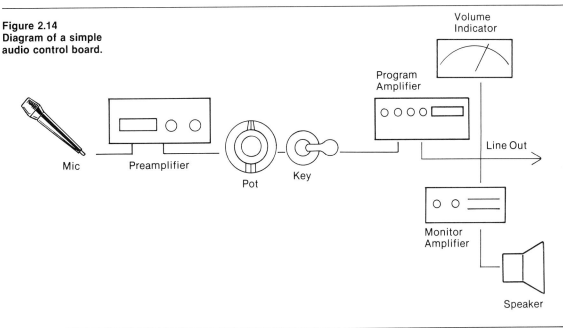

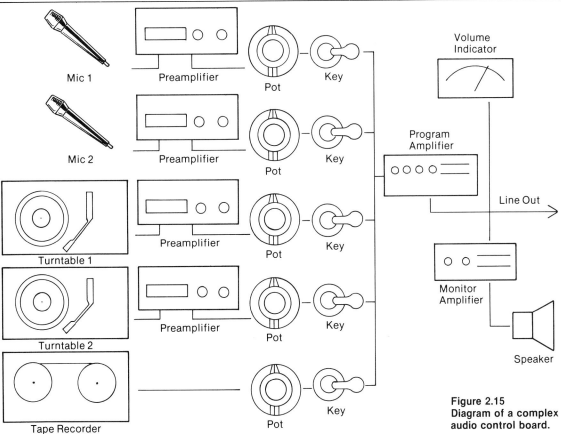

Figure 2.15
Diagram of a complex
audio control board.

Figure 2.16

Figure 2.17

Not all stations are this way, of course, but many small stations do operate primarily from one soundproof room, with perhaps a small outer reception area.

In larger stations the disc jockey and microphone are in one room called a studio, and the engineer, turntables, tape recorders, and board are in an adjoining room called a control room. Usually there is a soundproof window between the engineer who is spinning the records and the disc jockey who is announcing so they can communicate by hand signals. They can also communicate verbally through a talkback system when mikes are not being used on the air. A studio setup that large can usually also afford the luxury of genuine offices for the sales staff and the executives as well as a newsroom and record library.

Many stations contain several studio complexes so that tapes for later airing can be produced in one while another is on the air or being set up for on-air. There are even a few large studios with adjoining control rooms which produce talk shows or live musical groups.

Some radio stations have custom-built facilities, but many simply rent office space and soundproof as necessary.

Most small stations that originate all their programming in one to two studio complexes send the signals directly to the transmitter by phone line. However, where operation is more complicated, involving remote broadcasts or **network feeds,** a master control room is utilized. This control room will contain power supplies, monitors to hear the various sounds, **jack panels** to route the sounds in many different ways, and numerous other buttons, switches, and signal lights.

If the station is a network **affiliate,** it will receive programs originated in a network studio and then sent north, south, east, or west, often over thousands of miles of specially leased telephone lines. **Booster** amplifying equipment is located along these lines to keep the volume at a proper level. When the stations receive the network programs at their master control centers, they relay them to their transmitters.[6]

Figure 2.18
Automated radio equipment. The music is on the reels and the commercials and other announcements are on the carts.
Photo courtesy of Harris Corporation

Some stations have very little in the way of either studios or control rooms because they use equipment that allows them to broadcast on an automated basis. These stations operate mainly with multiple tape decks, some of which contain reel-to-reel music and some of which contain cartridge commercials. **Sub-audio** tones which cannot be heard over the air signal one tape recorder to stop playing music and another to start playing a commercial, or vice versa. Station-break taped announcements can also be inserted by use of specialized clock mechanisms. In this way a station can program for a whole day without having either a disc jockey or an engineer; the sound is sent directly from the tape deck to the transmitter.[7]

Automated Equipment

From the studio control room or master control room or automated tape deck, the sound, which is still in the form of variations of electrical energy, goes to the transmitter and then to the **antenna.** At the transmitter, it is **modulated,** which means this electrical energy is superimposed onto the **carrier wave** which represents that particular radio station's **frequency.** The electrical energy of the sound cannot go through the air itself because it is not of a high enough frequency. It must be carried on a wave which is of much higher frequency.

The transmitter generates this carrier wave and places the sound wave on it. This modulation can occur as either amplitude modulation (**AM**) or frequency modulation (**FM**). In amplitude modulation, the amplitude, or height, of the carrier wave is varied to fit the characteristics of the sound. In frequency modulation, the frequency of the carrier wave is changed. Diagrams of AM and FM waves are shown on pages 46 and 47.

FM is **static**-free, while AM is subject to static because this interference noise occurs at the top and bottom of the wave cycle. Since FM is dependent on varying the frequency of the wave, the top and bottom can be eliminated without distorting the signal. AM, however, is dependent upon height, so these static regions must remain with the AM.

Transmitters

Figure 2.19
Diagram of AM wave

Consider this to be an electrical wave representing the original sound.

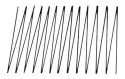

Consider this to be the carrier wave of a particular radio station. Notice it is of much higher frequency than the electrical wave.

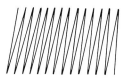

This would be the modulated carrier wave taking the sound signal. Note that the sound signal makes an image of itself and that the amplitude, or height, of the carrier wave is changed—hence, amplitude modulation.

Figure 2.20
Diagram of FM wave

Consider this to be the electrical wave representing the original sound wave.

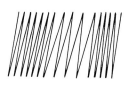

Consider this to be the carrier wave.

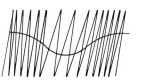

This would be the modulated carrier wave. The frequency is increased where the sound wave is highest (positive) and the frequency is decreased where the sound wave is lowest (negative). The amplitude does not change.

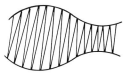

Perhaps this can be better seen by superimposing the sound wave over the carrier wave.

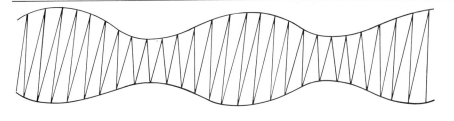

Figure 2.21
Comparison of AM and
FM waves.

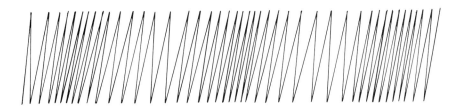

AM signals can travel great distances, sometimes around the world, while FM signals are **line-of-sight** and often cannot be heard if a building or hill comes between the transmitter and the radio attempting to receive the station. This phenomenon has nothing to do with the form of modulation, however, but rather is a function of the placement of the stations on the frequency band.

There is an entire **spectrum** of frequencies which encompasses much more than radio station carrier waves. At the low end is audible sound, which generally ranges from 15 cycles per second for low bass noises to 20,000 cycles per second for high treble noises. Most people do not have ears capable of hearing the entire range, so effective audible sound is actually a smaller portion of the spectrum. At frequencies higher than sound the continuum becomes radio waves, which can be neither heard nor seen but which are capable of carrying sound. Above radio waves are **infrared rays,** and then light waves, with each color occupying a different frequency range. After visible light come **ultraviolet rays, X rays, gamma rays,** and **cosmic rays.**

Within the radio wave portion of the frequency spectrum are many operations other than radio station broadcasting. The spectrum is also used for such functions as ship-to-shore radio, police calls, citizen band radio, "**ham**" operation, military communications, and, of course, television. In order to keep these groups from interfering with each other, various frequencies have been set aside for different purposes.

Two areas are set aside for radio station broadcasting. The FCC has assigned AM the range between 535 and 1605 **kilohertz** and FM the range between 88 and 108 **megahertz. Hertz** means **cycles per second,** kilo means thousand, while mega means million. Hence AM station carrier waves will be generated between 535,000 cycles per second and 1,605,000 cycles per

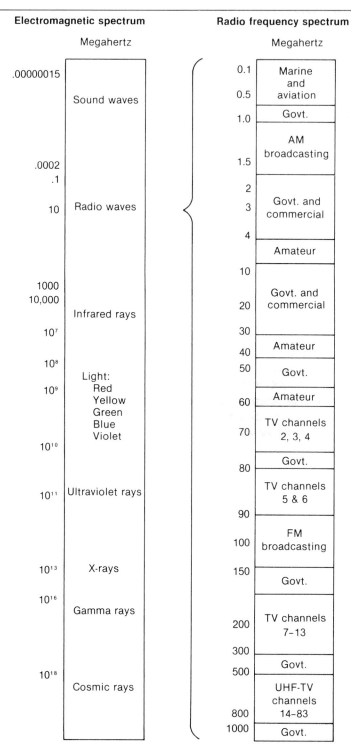

**Figure 2.22
Electromagnetic spec-
trum.**

In order to show all important elements, these charts are not drawn to scale.

second while FM station carrier waves do likewise between 88,000,000 cycles per second and 108,000,000 cycles per second.

As the radio wave portion of the spectrum progresses from its lowest to its highest end, its characteristics change so that the radio waves close to the **light waves** behave somewhat like light. That is why FM station output is likely to be lost behind buildings and hills. Light waves do not travel through buildings; hence FM that is near light on the spectrum tends toward being similarly obliterated.

AM, at the lower end of the spectrum, is not so affected, but these lower frequencies are affected by a nighttime atmospheric condition known as the Kennelly-Heaviside layer which, when hit by radio waves, bounces the wave back to earth. In this way waves can be bounced great distances— e.g., New York to London. FM is not affected by this layer—because of its position on the spectrum, not, again, because of its frequency modulation. Theoretically, if FM waves were transmitted on the normal AM frequency of 535 kilohertz, they could bounce, because the skipbounce is determined by the carrier frequency rather than the manner of modulation.

Individual AM and FM stations are not free to generate carrier waves at any point within the frequency ranges assigned to them, respectively. If they did so, there would be massive interference among stations. Instead, each station's particular carrier wave frequency is assigned. Although each station is given a specific frequency, such as 550 kilohertz, the frequency covers ten kilohertz if the station is AM and 200 kilohertz if it is FM. For example, an AM station at 550 kilohertz actually operates from 545 to 555 so that it can modulate the necessary information. Because FM stations have a broader **bandwidth,** they can produce higher fidelity and contain more information than can an AM station. This makes FM more adaptable to **stereo** and **quadraphonic** broadcasting and to the **multiplexing** of other services, such as background music for doctors' offices.[8]

**Figure 2.23
The heart of a transmitter, called an exciter.**
Photo courtesy of Harris Corporation

Antennas

After the radio waves have been modulated either AM or FM onto the proper frequency carrier wave at the transmitter, they are radiated into the air through the radio station antenna at the assigned frequency and power.

The FCC has established a complicated chart of frequency and power allocations to allow a maximum number of stations around the country to broadcast interference-free. Between 535 and 1605 kilohertz there is room for 107 stations of 10 kilohertz each, but there are actually over 4,200 AM stations nationwide. This is possible because many stations throughout the country broadcast from their antennas on the same frequency but in a controlled way that takes into consideration geographic location and power. The allocation chart divides AM stations into three categories—local, regional, and clear. Local channels operate with power not in excess of 2,500 watts during the day and usually less at night when the Kennelly-Heaviside layer is in effect. Obviously, it is possible for a local channel in San Francisco to share a frequency with many other stations in places such as Portland, New Orleans, Albuquerque, Chattanooga, and Miami. Regional stations cannot exceed 5,000 watts, and usually serve rural areas. Again, a regional station in Virginia can share a frequency with many areas, such as Nebraska, Maine, and Arizona. Clear-channel stations can operate up to 50,000 watts and often have signals that extend over several states. Originally, clear-channel meant that only one station in the country operated on that frequency. As the pressure for new stations increased, the FCC gradually allowed more stations to operate on the clear channels but did try to keep these channels free from interference by **directional antenna** systems and other means.

FM stations are divided into class A, class B, and class C stations. Class A stations may use power up to 3,000 watts and generally serve a very limited area. Class B stations serve a larger area and can use power from 5,000 to 50,000 watts. Class C stations, the most powerful, can use over 50,000 watts.[9]

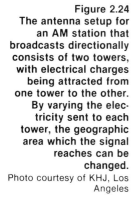

Figure 2.24
The antenna setup for an AM station that broadcasts directionally consists of two towers, with electrical charges being attracted from one tower to the other. By varying the electricity sent to each tower, the geographic area which the signal reaches can be changed.
Photo courtesy of KHJ, Los Angeles

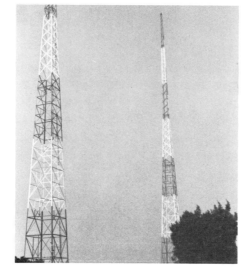

Chapter 2

The waves sent out from the radio station antenna are always in the air but can't be heard unless a radio receiver is turned on. The purpose of the receiver is to pick up and amplify radio waves, separate the intelligence from the carrier wave, and reproduce this intelligence in the form of sound.

The first stage of a radio receiver is the antenna which picks up the sound being sent out by the radio station antenna. From here the sound goes to the **radio frequency** amplifier, which has two purposes: one is to amplify the signal (carrier wave plus intelligence), and the other is frequency selection. This is accomplished by a device within the amplifier called a **tuner,** which makes it possible to tune in the signal to one particular radio station to the exclusion of other stations. If the tuner were not used, all stations broadcasting in the area of the receiver would be heard simultaneously.

Only the station tuned in gets to the end of the radio frequency amplifier. From here it goes to the **detector,** where the carrier wave is separated from the intelligence it is carrying. This detector then discards the carrier wave, which has already done its job, and feeds the intelligence in the form of electrical impulses to the following stage, the **audio frequency** amplifier. Here the impulses are strengthened and sent to the speaker, where the electrical energy is converted back into sound waves and the sound can be heard.

Thus has the message traveled full circle—from mike and turntable through an audio board, transmitter, and antenna to the speaker of a radio receiver.[10]

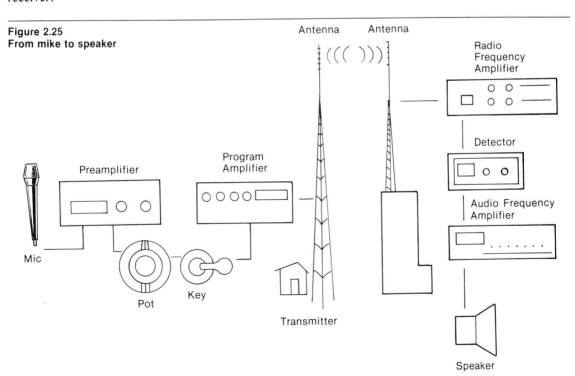

Figure 2.25
From mike to speaker

Antenna   Antenna

Radio Frequency Amplifier

Detector

Audio Frequency Amplifier

Preamplifier

Program Amplifier

Mic

Pot

Key

Transmitter

Speaker

Summary   Radio consists basically of transforming sound into *electrical impulses,* sending those electrical impulses through the air, and then transforming them back into sound. In order to accomplish this, radio stations employ *microphones, turntables, tape recorders, control boards, studios* and *control rooms, automated equipment, transmitters, antennas,* and *receivers.*

Microphones are characterized by their pickup patterns (*unidirectional, bidirectional, cardioid, omnidirectional*) and internal construction (*dynamic, ribbon, condensor*). A turntable employs a *power switch, gear shift, equalizer, cartridge,* and *stylus* to spin a record and convert variations in record grooves to electrical energy. Tape recorders rearrange *iron particles* on magnetic tape in order to store sound and are *reel-to-reel, cassette,* or *cartridge* in form. A control board selects *inputs, amplifies* them, and sends them to various *outputs.* In small stations, studios and control rooms are one and the same, while in larger stations talent and microphones will occupy the studio while an engineer, turntables, tape recorders, and an audio board are situated in the control room. Some stations operate with automated multiple tape decks. The transmitter superimposes *sound waves* in the form of electrical energy onto a *carrier wave* by either *AM* or *FM.* The antenna sends the *modulated waves* through the air. Radio receivers pick up and amplify radio waves, separate the information from the carrier wave, and reproduce the information as sound.

3 Telvolution
The Evolution of Television

> *Until a few years ago, every American assumed he possessed an equal and God-given expertise on three things—politics, religion, and weather. Now a fourth has been added—television.*
>
> Eric Sevareid, longtime
> broadcast newsman and commentator

"I'll bet Sarnoff is making a speech on TV tonight!"

To some people it may sound presumptuous to suggest that anything as young as television even has a history. To other people it may seem as though there were no history before television. Some say television is still in its infancy and others argue that it is past its prime. It has been dominantly in our midst only since 1952, but the years have been a blur of technological change and programming turnover.[1]

Early
Experiments

The first experiments with television employed a **mechanical scanning** process dependent on a wheel originally invented by the German Paul Nipkow in 1884. This wheel contained tiny holes positioned spirally. Behind the wheel was placed a small picture. As the wheel turned, each hole scanned one line of the picture.

Even though this device could scan only very small pictures, attempts were made to promote it commercially. C. F. Jenkins, an American, developed a workable system and formed a company in 1930 to exploit the idea. John Baird of Britain obtained a television license in 1926 and convinced the British Broadcasting Corporation to begin experimental broadcasting with a mechanical system.

At GE's plant in Schenectady, New York, Ernst F. W. Alexanderson began experimental programming in the 1920s by using a revolving scanning wheel and an image that was 3″ × 4″. One of his "programs," a science fiction thriller of a missile attack on New York, scanned an aerial photograph of New York which moved closer and closer and then disappeared to the sound of an explosion.[2]

While mechanical scanning was being promoted, others were developing **electronic scanning,** the system that has been adopted. One was Allen B. Dumont, who developed the **oscilloscope,** or **cathode ray tube,** a basic tool of electronic research that is similar to the TV receiver tube. Dumont was able to capitalize on this invention when the TV receiver market took hold in the 1940s.[3]

Another early electronic inventor was Philo T. Farnsworth, who in 1922 astounded his Idaho high school teacher with diagrams for an electronic TV system. He convinced a backer to provide him with equipment and in 1927 transmitted still pictures and bits of film. He applied for a patent and found himself battling the giant of electronic TV development, RCA. In 1930 Farnsworth, at age 24, won his patent and later received royalties from RCA.[4]

The RCA development was headed by Vladimir Zworykin, a Russian immigrant and onetime Westinghouse employee who had patented an electronic pickup tube called the **iconoscope.** In 1930, GE, RCA, and Westinghouse merged TV research programs at RCA's lab in Camden, New Jersey and incorporated Zworykin, Alexanderson, and other engineers into a team to develop television further.

This group systematically attacked and solved problems such as increased lines of scanning, definition, brightness, image size, and frequency of scanning. They started with a system that scanned sixty lines using a model of Felix the Cat as the "star" and then gradually improved this scanning to 441 lines.

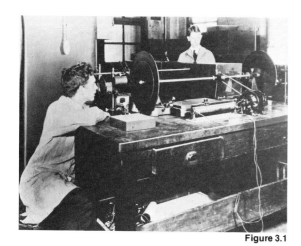

Figure 3.1

Figure 3.2

Figure 3.1
Early mechanical scanning equipment. Through a peephole J. R. Hefele observes the image recreated through the rotating disc. The scanning disc at the other end of the shaft intervenes between an illuminated transparency and the photoelectric cell. This cell is in the box which is visible just beyond the driving shaft.
Photo courtesy of A.T.&T. Co. Photo Center

Figure 3.2
The television receiving screen used during the first intercity TV broadcast on April 7, 1927. Dr. Herbert E. Ives, former director of electro-optical research at Bell Telephone Laboratories, stands beside this screen, which consisted of fifty neon-filled tubes, each divided into small segments, creating a pattern of light and dark areas to form a picture. Dr. Ives is holding a photoelectric cell from the transmitter. Early scanning equipment is seen at the left.
Photo courtesy of A.T.&T. Co. Photo Center

Figure 3.3

Figure 3.3
Felix the cat as he appeared on experimental 60-line black and white TV sets in the late 1920s. This picture was transmitted from New York City all the way to Kansas.
Photo courtesy of RCA

Figure 3.4
Ernst F.W. Alexanderson
Smithsonian Institution
Photo No. 51199

Figure 3.5
Allen DuMont (*right*) giving a personalized tour of the DuMont Laboratories to Lee De Forest.
Smithsonian Institution
Photo No. 73-11097

Figure 3.4

Figure 3.5

Figure 3.6   Figure 3.7

Figure 3.6
Philo T. Farnsworth in
his laboratory about
1934.
Smithsonian Institution
Photo No. 69082

Figure 3.7
Vladimir K. Zworykin
holding an early model
of the iconoscope TV
tube.
Photo courtesy of RCA

In 1932 experimental broadcasts were transmitted from the Empire State Building and three years later, in the midst of the depression, David Sarnoff, now president of RCA, announced that the company would invest millions in the further development of television. Experimental broadcasts continued with programs emanating from a converted radio studio, 3H, in Radio City. Actors wore green makeup and purple lipstick and simmered under the intensive lights.[5]

Sarnoff decided to have television displayed at the 1939 New York World's Fair. President Roosevelt appeared on camera and was seen on sets with 5″ and 7″ tubes.[6]

The "Coming Out" Party

In 1939 RCA's program schedule usually included one program a day from 3H, one from a mobile unit traveling the streets of New York, and several assorted films.

The studio productions included plays, bits of operas, singers, comedians, puppets, and household tips. The mobile unit consisted of two huge buses, one jammed with equipment to be set up in the field and one containing the transmitter that broadcast back to the Empire State Building. It covered such events as baseball games, wrestling, ice skating, airport interviews with dignitaries, fashion shows, and the premiere of *Gone With the Wind*. The films were usually cartoons, travelogues, or government documentaries.

Other companies established experimental stations and broadcast in New York. Sets, mostly manufactured by RCA and Dumont, increased tube size to 12″ and sold for $200 to $600. CBS began experimentation with color television utilizing a mechanical color wheel of red, blue, and green that transferred color to the images. This color system was not compatible with the RCA promoted system. In other words, the sets being manufactured could not receive either color or black and white pictures from the CBS mechanical system.

In 1940 a group led mainly by RCA personnel tried to convince the FCC to allow operation of the 441-line system. However, the FCC was not

Figure 3.8   Figure 3.9

certain that this system had adequate technical quality so established an industrywide committee of engineers, the National Television System Committee (NTSC) to recommend standards. This committee rejected the 441-line system and recommended the 525-line system, which the United States presently uses. CBS approached the committee with the idea of color television, but the committee did not think its system was of sufficient quality.

In May of 1941 the FCC authorized the full operation of 525-line black and white television. Originally there were to be thirteen very high frequency (**VHF**) channels, but channel 1 was eliminated to allow spectrum space for FM radio. Twenty-three stations went on the air, 10,000 sets were sold, and commercials were sought. The first commercial was bought by Bulova for $900 and consisted of a shot of a Bulova clock with an announcer intoning the time. All of this was called to a halt, however, in 1942 because of World War II.

During the war only six stations remained on the air, and most sets became inoperable because spare parts were not being manufactured. The NBC studio was used to broadcast air raid warden training programs; volunteers traveled to their local police station to watch this instruction. So, in a very limited way, television went to war.[7]

The Emergence of Television

TV activities did not resume immediately after the war, due in part to a shortage of materials. Also, it was expensive to build and operate a TV station, the initial investment ranging from $75,000 to $1.5 million. And then the owners had to assume that they would operate at a loss until enough receivers were in the area to make the station attractive to advertisers.

To add to the risk, there were rumors that all television stations might be moved to the ultra high frequency band (**UHF**), which had been explored during the war. CBS once again raised the question of color, stating that its color system was so well developed that TV station allocations should not be made until the color question was resolved. RCA represented a contrary position on the color issue and promised black and white sets on the market by mid-1946 with a color-compatible system to follow soon. In the fall of

1946 RCA did demonstrate a color system that was compatible, albeit unstable and unreliable.

In 1947 the FCC declared that CBS's color system would be a hardship on set owners because they would have to buy new sets. It therefore stated that television should continue as black and white and in the VHF range it had been using, channels 2 to 13.

The next year, 1948, television emerged as a mass medium. Stations, sets, and audience all grew over 4,000 percent within that one year. Advertisers became aware of the medium and networks began more systematic programming.[8]

The TV networks already existed before 1948 as offshoots of the radio networks. As early as 1945-46 television networks had been organized by NBC, CBS, and ABC. A fourth network, Dumont, was organized by Allen B. Dumont, who had developed the cathode ray tube and who owned a pioneer TV station in New York. However, most cities only had one or two TV stations, and NBC and CBS usually recruited them as **affiliates**, making it difficult for ABC and Dumont to compete. ABC survived because it merged in 1953 with United Paramount Theaters and thus gained an increase in operating funds. Dumont, however, went out of business in 1955.[9]

Television grew so uncontrollably in 1948 that in the fall of that year the FCC imposed a **freeze** on television station authorizations because stations were beginning to interfere with each other. Mindful of the days of radio chaos, the FCC wanted to nip the problem in the bud. Further reasons were that some of the characteristics of VHF had not been predicted, there weren't enough channels to meet the demand, and CBS once again raised the question of color. This freeze lasted until June 1, 1952. During this period there were 108 stations on the air and no more were authorized to begin operation.

What occurred between 1948 and 1952 could be termed an explosive lull. Many cities, including Austin, Denver, and Portland had no television stations. Others, including Pittsburgh, St. Louis, and Milwaukee, had only one. Twenty-four cities boasted between two and six stations. New York and Los Angeles were the only cities with seven. TV networking, then, could not be considered truly national. Nevertheless, sets, audience size, advertising, and programming continued to grow. By 1952 there were sets in 15 million homes. The largest ones had 20″ tubes and sold for about $350. TV advertising revenues reached $324 million. In TV cities, movie attendance, radio listening, sports event attendance, and restaurant dining were all down—especially on Tuesday night, which was Milton Berle night.

People with TV sets stayed home and often invited their friends over (or allowed their friends to invite themselves over) to watch this ex-vaudevillian's show, which included outrageous costumes, slapstick comedy, lavish productions, and a host of guest stars. "Uncle Miltie," on his "Texaco Star Theater," became a national phenomenon and the reason many people bought their first television set.[10]

The Freeze

Figure 3.10
Milton Berle in one of his outlandish costumes. His "Texaco Star Theater" was TV's first big hit.
Photo courtesy of NBC

During 1948-49, 30 percent of sponsored evening programs were sports—basketball, boxing, bowling, wrestling, roller skating. Among the wrestlers, both men and women, there was competition to outdo each other in costumes, hairdos, and mannerisms. The emphasis on sports was due, at least in part, to the fact that a large number of the first sets were in bars and taverns. During the 1949-50 season, sports comprised less than 5 percent of evening programming, and children's programming was tops, indicating that TV had moved to the home.

Other broadcasting fare of the freeze era included Sid Caesar and Imogene Coca in "Your Show of Shows," Ed Sullivan's "Toast of the Town," Groucho Marx's "You Bet Your Life," "Mama," "The Goldbergs," "Your Hit Parade," "Break the Bank," and "What's My Line?"

"Amos 'n' Andy" was brought to TV featuring black actors trained by Gosden and Correll. The program was condemned as an insult by the National Association for the Advancement of Colored People at its 1951 convention, much to the astonishment of the lily-white broadcasting fraternity.

For children there was Buffalo Bob and his puppet Howdy Doody, and for children of all ages, Burr Tillstrom's puppets starred with Fran Allison in "Kukla, Fran, and Ollie." From radio came such classics as "The Lone Ranger" and "Hopalong Cassidy." Talent shows abounded, led by Arthur Godfrey's "Talent Scouts" and Ted Mack's "The Original Amateur Hour." Faye Emerson hosted a 1950 talk show and found that what the public talked about most was the depth of her neckline.

Drama was begun with "NBC Theater," "Kraft Television Theater," "Philco Playhouse," and "Studio One." The first soap opera was "A Woman to Remember," which was forgotten after its first year, but others followed successfully in its wake. For example, "Love of Life," which began in 1951, was still strong more than a quarter-century later, with one of the original members still in the cast. "The Voice of Firestone" featured classical music, and Bishop Fulton J. Sheen preached religion on CBS in the same time slot as Berle on NBC.

In 1951 "I Love Lucy" began as a maverick of the TV world because it was filmed ahead of time while other shows were aired live. There was a stigma against film at the time, partly because it added to the cost of the show, and partly because the TV networks inherited the live tradition from radio and assumed that all shows should be produced live. But the film aspect was particularly useful and dramatic when Lucille Ball became pregnant, and hence the story line dealt with Lucy's pregnancy. The episode involving the birth of Lucy's baby was filmed ahead of time, and Lucille's real baby was born the same day the filmed episode aired—to an audience that comprised 68.8 percent of the American public.

TV newscasts of the '50s developed slowly. Networks found it easy to obtain news and voices, but pictures were another matter. At first they contracted with the companies who supplied the newsreels then shown in theaters. This didn't exactly fill television's bill because much of it was shot for in-depth stories, not news of the day. The networks also hired **stringers**

Figure 3.11

Figure 3.12

Figure 3.13

Figure 3.11
"Your Show of Shows," starring Imogene Coca (*left*) and Sid Caesar. The regular cast included Carl Reiner and Howard Morris. Some of the writers for the show were Mel Brooks, Woody Allen, and Neil Simon.
Photo courtesy of NBC

Figure 3.12
"You Bet Your Life," starring Groucho Marx (*left*) assisted by his announcer George Fenneman. The show had a quiz format but emphasized Grouch's witticisms. One feature was a stuffed duck which fell down from the ceiling if a contestant mentioned the "secret word." The contestant would then be entitled to an additional $100.
Photo courtesy of NBC

Figure 3.14

Figure 3.15

Figure 3.13
Marionette Howdy Doody and his real-life friend Buffalo Bob Smith. The show also featured Clarabell, the clown who never spoke, and an audience full of children. Each program began, "What time is it?" Followed by the audience's response, "It's Howdy Doody Time."
Photo courtesy of NBC

Figure 3.14
Kukla, Burr Tillstrom, Fran Allison, and Ollie. Burr operated and spoke for each one of the large cast of puppets while Fran conversed with them from in front of the puppet stage. The "Kukla, Fran, and Ollie" show was the first program to be televised coast to coast in color.
Photo courtesy of NBC

Figure 3.15
Lucille Ball, who will no doubt live forever in reruns. Early in her career there was hesitancy on the part of producers to allow such an attractive woman to turn herself into a comedienne.
Photo courtesy of Viacom Enterprises

in various cities to shoot film of events as they occurred, with the understanding that only the film used would be paid for. However, this could not begin to cover all the news. Networks set up their own film crews but limited budgets and bulky film equipment meant that camera operators could attend only planned events such as press conferences, coronations, political conventions, and ribbon-cutting grand openings. The fifteen-minute newscasts, by John Cameron Swayze on NBC and Douglas Edwards on CBS, tended to be reports on events which had been filmed earlier, limiting their timeliness.

Interview-type news shows were a further development with "Meet the Press," produced by Lawrence Spivak, beginning its long run of probing interviews with prominent people. "See It Now" was started in 1951 as a news documentary series featuring Edward R. Murrow and produced by Fred Friendly. A historical feature of their first program was showing for the first time both the Atlantic and Pacific Oceans live on TV. Most of their early information programs were a combination of filmed footage, some from the newsreel companies, and live commentary dealing with news issues.

The Kefauver crime hearings were also shown in 1951. At one point, witness Frank Costello objected to having his face televised, so the cameras focused on his hands as the audience tried to gain clues from his gestures.

The importance of TV to our political process was already becoming evident as the 1952 political nominating conventions were covered by the TV networks. NBC's coverage was sponsored by Westinghouse and brought fame to Betty Furness as she demonstrated refrigerators over and over on live commercials, including one never-to-be forgotten spot when the "easy-to-open" refrigerator door she had just described refused to open at all.[11]

Lifting the Freeze

In April of 1952 the FCC issued its "Sixth Report and Order," by which the freeze on new stations issued four years earlier was ended. It provided for 82 channels—12 VHF and 70 UHF. A table listed 2,053 allocations in 1,291 communities, 66 percent of which were in the UHF band. The stations were allocated in a pattern designed so that they would not interfere with each other. Ten percent of the allocations were set aside for educational television, but this number was later increased to 35 percent.

The creation of the 70 UHF channels was intended to accommodate the need and desire for more stations. The FCC, in placing both types of channels in cities, planned that they would be equal. In reality, they became first-class and second-class stations. UHF was technically not as effective as expected. Its weaker signal was supposed to be compensated for by higher towers, but this did not prove to work in practice.

People did not have sets which could receive UHF, so in order to tune in UHF stations, they needed to buy converters. Many were unwilling to do this, so UHF found itself in a vicious circle. In order for people to buy UHF converters, there had to be interesting programming material on UHF which they wanted to watch; in order to finance interesting program material, UHF stations had to prove to advertisers that they had an adequate audience. This situation was alleviated slightly by an amendment to the Communications Act which required all TV sets to be manufactured with both UHF and VHF reception capabilities after January 1963.

Because VHF stations were established first, they were the first to obtain network affiliations and hence capture the best programming. Consequently, UHF stations had to depend on **syndicated** material and local talent. A few have been successful with sports programming or special interest material such as Spanish language shows and religious programs.

As a result of these factors, a large proportion of UHF stations have generally been unprofitable. In recent years some have turned the profit corner, but the fate of UHF is still uncertain.

Overall, however, the lifting of the freeze led to an enormous rush to obtain stations, both UHF and VHF, even though some of the UHF ones later left the air. Within six months 600 applications had been received and 175 new stations had been authorized. By 1954, 377 stations had begun broadcasting, and TV could be considered truly national.[12]

To this fledgling industry came some of the country's best-known talent. They came from radio, from Broadway, and from film—all of which were experiencing downturns as television was burgeoning.

Blacklisting

Unfortunately, many of these people became caught in the **blacklisting** mania of the 1950s led by Senator Joseph R. McCarthy, a Republican from Wisconsin. A 215-page publication called *Red Channels: The Report of Communist Influence in Radio and Television* listed 151 people, many of whom were among the top names in show business, most of them writers, directors, and performers. Listed after their names were "citations" against them. Some of these charges were proved to be totally false, such as associating people with "leftist" organizations to which they had never belonged. Others were true but were "leftist" only by definitions of the perpetrators of *Red Channels*. These included such wrongdoings as belonging to an "End Jim Crow in Baseball Committee" and signing a cablegram of congratulations to the Moscow Art Theater on its 50th birthday.

Although many network and advertising executives did not believe these people were Communists or in any way unAmerican, they were unwilling to hire them, in part because of the controversy involved and in part because sponsors received phone calls that threatened to boycott their products if advertisements employed these people.

An affiliated organization, Aware, Inc., followed up *Red Channels* with a constantly increasing list of people described as "radical entertainers." A leading founder-supporter of Aware, Inc. was a supermarket executive who placed calls to advertisers warning that his supermarkets would not carry products advertised by actors on Aware's list or presented within programs written by leftist writers. He made threats to place signs near some products saying they were advertised by "Stalin's little creatures."

For the better part of a decade some well established writers were finding that all the scripts they wrote were "not quite right" and actors were told they were "not exactly the type for the part." Many of these people did not even know they were on one of the "lists" because these were circulated clandestinely among executives.

One of the many victims of the blacklist was the fine character actor Philip Loeb, who had for several years played the kindly father on the series "The Goldbergs." Due to sponsor pressure inspired by Aware, Inc., he was replaced and, despite his long-established reputation, found himself unemployable. Despairing, he committed suicide.

In time the blacklist situation eased. Ironically, broadcasting was influential in exposing the excesses of the Communist witch hunt, which had spread beyond the entertainment industry.

Edward R. Murrow and Fred Friendly presented as a "See It Now" program "The Case Against Milo Radulovich, A0569839." Radulovich had been asked to resign his Air Force commission because his sister and father had been anonymously accused of radical leanings. The program exposed some of the guilt-by-association tactics and was instrumental in helping Radulovich retain his commission. Later Murrow and Friendly prepared several programs on Senator Joe McCarthy, who had alarmed the country by saying that he had a list of hundreds of Communists in the State Department. The Murrow-Friendly telecasts helped reveal the falsity of that claim.

Later there was network coverage of the 1954 hearings of McCarthy's dispute with the Army. As the nation watched, McCarthy and his aides harassed and bullied witnesses. Public resentment built up against McCarthy, and the Senate voted 67 to 22 to condemn him.[13]

The Live Era

Programming of the '50s was predominantly live. "I Love Lucy" continued to be filmed, and several other programs jumped on the film band wagon as foreign countries began developing broadcasting systems. Americans could see a reuse of their products in other countries and hence a recouping of film costs. Reruns in the United States itself were as yet unthought of, although some programs were kinescoped so they could be shown at various times. These kinescopes were low quality, grainy film representations of the video picture. However, most of the popular series of the day originated in New York and were telecast as they were being shot.

This live aspect created problems for writers, actors, and technicians. Costume changes needed to be virtually nonexistent. The number of locales for a story was governed by the number of sets that could fit in the studio. Timing was sometimes an immense problem. In radio, scripts could be fairly accurately timed by the number of pages, but television programs contained much action, the time of which often fluctuated wildly in rehearsals. One writing solution was to plan a search scene near the end of the play. If the program was running long, the actor could find what he was looking for right away; if the program appeared to be moving too quickly, the actor could search the room for as long as necessary.[14]

Figure 3.16
A "Playhouse 90" show
entitled "The Country
Husband." Here Barbara
Hale (*left*) can't understand why Frank Love-
joy insists on personally
escorting Felicia Farr
home.
Photo courtesy of Colum-
bia Pictures Television

The programming of the early '50s is often looked back upon as the "Golden Age of Television." This is mainly because of the live dramas produced during this period on such programs as "Kraft Television Theater," "Studio One," "Robert Montgomery Presents," "Medallion Theater," "Playhouse 90," and the "U.S. Steel Hour." One of the most outstanding plays was Rod Serling's "Requiem for a Heavyweight," the psychological study of a broken-down fighter. Another was Paddy Chayefsky's "Marty," the heart-warming study of a short, stocky, small town butcher who develops a sensitive romantic relationship with a homely school teacher. Other highlights of the decade were Robert Alan Arthur's "A Man is Ten Feet Tall," Gore Vidal's "Visit to a Small Planet," Reginald Rose's "The Remarkable Incident at Carson Corners," and Milt Gelman's "Killer."[15]

All of these productions made abundant use of close-ups—the real emotion and action of the plays took place on actors' faces. Cameras were usually placed in the center of the studio with sets arranged in a circle on the periphery so the cameras could have easy access to each new scene.

Besides conventional drama, some innovative formats were tried, many of them the brainchild of Sylvester L. ("Pat") Weaver, the president of NBC from 1953 to 1955. One of these was the idea of the "**spectacular**," a show that was not part of the regular schedule but which was designed to expand the horizons of creativity. The most outstanding of the spectaculars was "Peter Pan," starring Mary Martin, which was viewed by some 165 million Americans.

Weaver was also involved in developing the "Today" and "Tonight" shows. "Today" started in Chicago as "Garroway at Large," an informal variety series. Its host, Dave Garroway, became host on the daily morning "Today" show and the format changed somewhat to include both news and variety. Another star of the show was J. Fred Muggs, a baby chimpanzee. The late nightly show "Tonight" originally starred Steve Allen, then picked up steam as Jack Paar became its controversial host.

Pat Weaver felt that programs should be network-controlled rather than advertising-agency-controlled. Most of the early TV and Golden Era radio program content had been controlled by the advertising agencies. Weaver developed a "**magazine concept**" whereby advertisers bought insertions in programs, and the program content was supervised and produced by the networks. This was used for "Today," "Tonight," and many of the spectaculars, somewhat to the chagrin of the advertisers.[16]

Other highlights of this early programming were "Victory at Sea," a documentary series recreating the naval battles of World War II; Elvis Presley performing on the Ed Sullivan show—from the waist up; the introduction of the crime-drama "Dragnet," which was the first show to bump Lucy from the top of the ratings; Liberace at the piano in his sequined attire; Jackie Gleason's comedy sketches, the most famous of which was "The Honeymooners"; "The Colgate Comedy Hour," with Donald O'Connor; and "Omnibus," a potpourri of cultural elements.[17]

Color TV Approval

The problems connected with color TV were not resolved until 1953. In 1950 the FCC finally accepted the CBS system of color even though it still had the drawback of being incompatible with existing black and white receivers. RCA immediately filed suit against its adoption, and companies other than CBS seemed unwilling to invest in manufacturing color sets under the CBS system. A state of confusion reigned in the industry as companies took sides in the conflict, causing general consternation to prevail.[18] Once again the National Television System Committee was called in to resolve the issue. It finally approved an alternate system similar to the one RCA had developed that was all electronic and compatible with the present black and white receivers. This method was adopted by the FCC in 1953, and even CBS supported it at the time.

However, for a long time RCA-NBC was the only company actively promoting color. NBC constructed new color facilities and began programming in color, but both CBS and ABC dragged their heels, and most local stations did not have the capital needed to convert to color equipment. Even more important, consumers were reluctant to purchase color TV sets because they were double the cost of black and white sets and the limited color programming did not merit this investment. The circularity was broken gradually. As more color sets were sold, the prices were lowered and programming in color increased, causing even more sets to be sold. Not until the late '60s were all networks and most stations producing color programs.

Films for TV

The days of live programming for other than news and special events began to disappear in the mid '50s for several reasons. One was the introduction of videotape in 1954. The expense of the equipment prevented it from taking hold quickly, but once its foot got in the door, it revolutionized TV production techniques. Programs could now be performed at convenient times for later airings. As the equipment became more sophisticated, stops could be made to allow for costume changes, scene changes, and the like. As the equipment became even more sophisticated, mistakes could be corrected through editing procedures. Scenes could even be taped out of sequence and assembled in order at a later time, in much the same manner as film. As the years progressed, just about all types of programming except the news was being pretaped.

However, the live era had begun to yield to film even before tape took hold. Film companies had been antagonistic toward TV, not even allowing TV sets to appear in movies. The 1953 merger of United Paramount Theaters and ABC cracked the film door, and ABC soon convinced several major film companies to begin producing film series for TV. Some of the early filmed TV series were "Cheyenne," "Colt 45," "Wyatt Earp," "Death Valley Days," "Rin Tin Tin," "Wagon Train," and "December Bride." As the foregoing list demonstrates, westerns predominated. By 1959 thirty-two western series were on prime-time TV. The one with the greatest longevity was "Gunsmoke," which revolved around Dodge City's Matt Dillon, Chester Goode, Doc, and Miss Kitty. Others of popular note were "Bonanza," "Maverick," "Have Gun, Will Travel," and "Tales of Wells Fargo."

Other types of programs took hold also, again mainly on film. The old crime-mystery formula surfaced on TV in such programs as "The Untouchables," "77 Sunset Strip," "Highway Patrol," "M Squad," "Perry Mason," and "I Led Three Lives." Fred Astaire presented a widely acclaimed 1958 special; Lawrence Welk began bubbly music in 1955; Dick Clark appealed to the teenagers with "American Bandstand"; and Leonard

Figure 3.19

Figure 3.20

Figure 3.21

Figure 3.19
Ward Bond starring as Major Adams in "Wagon Train." This series dealt with the trials and tribulations of settlers as they moved westward. After Bond's death in 1961, John McIntire took over the leading role.
Photo from MCA Publishing

Figure 3.20
A scene from the "Gunsmoke" episode "The Devil's Outpost." Guest star Robert Lansing portrays an outlaw attempting to free his brother from the custody of Marshall Matt Dillon. Warren Vanders (*right*) acts as a member of Yancy's gang.
Photo courtesy of Viacom Enterprises

Figure 3.21
"American Bandstand" hosted by Dick Clark (*center*). Dick was originally a Philadelphia disc jockey and became nationally prominent with his program of dancing teenagers.
Photo courtesy of Dick Clark Teleshows, Inc.

Bernstein conducted his first "Young People's Concerts" in 1958. For the younger kids there was such fare as "Captain Kangaroo," "The Mickey Mouse Club," "Lassie," "My Friend Flicka," and "Disneyland."

Among the public service programs, Fidel Castro appeared on "Meet the Press" and Nikita Khrushchev, amid much controversy, appeared on "Face the Nation" and then as the "star" of his tour of the United States. "See It Now" was phased to an occasional presentation, then dropped, and Edward R. Murrow's main program was "Person to Person," a series in which he interviewed political and social celebrities. Two young reporters, Chet Huntley and David Brinkley, teamed up for NBC's coverage of the 1956 political convention and found themselves a berth as nightly anchormen for the fifteen-minute network news.[19]

The TV boom continued in the late '50s—more TV sets, more viewers, more stations, more advertising dollars. But to this rising euphoria came a dark hour.

Figure 3.22
M.C. of "The $64,000
Question" was Hal
March (*right*). Gino
Prato, an Italian-born
New York shoemaker,
mops his brow while
listening to a four-part
question on opera.
Photo from United Press
International

Quiz programs on which contestants won minimal amounts of money or merchandise donated by companies had existed on both radio and television. However, in 1955 a new idea emerged in the form of "The $64,000 Question." Contestants were to be allowed to appear for a number of weeks against challengers to try to win huge cash prizes. Sales of the sponsor of "The $64,000 Question," Revlon, zoomed to such an extent that some of its products were sold out nationwide. The sales success and high audience ratings spawned many imitators— "The 64,000 Challenge," "Twenty-One," "Nothing But the Truth," "Treasure Hunt." Contestants locked in soundproof booths pondering and perspiring caught the fancy of the nation.

The Quiz Scandals

From time to time there were rumbles that some quiz programs had been fixed. Then in 1958 a contestant from the daytime quiz show "Dotto" claimed to have evidence that the show was rigged, and a contestant from "Twenty-One" described that program's irregularities. The networks and advertising agencies denied the charges, as did Charles Van Doren, the most famous of the "Twenty-One" winners. A grand jury and a House of Representatives subcommittee conducted hearings and found discrepancies in the testimony.

In the fall of 1959 Charles Van Doren appeared before the House subcommittee and read a long statement describing how he had been convinced in the name of entertainment to accept help with answers to questions in order to defeat a current champion who was unpopular with the public. Van Doren was also coached on methods of building suspense, and when he did win, he became a national hero and a leader of intellectual life. After several months on the program, during which he continued to be coached on questions, he asked to be released and finally was allowed to lose. His celebrity status followed him, and he initially lied, he said, so he would not betray the people who had invested faith and hope in him. Other witnesses from various programs followed Van Doren to testify to the means by which dull contestants were disposed of so that lively personalities could continue to win and hence hold audience attention.

In retrospect, it is apparent that the quiz scandals' negative effect on TV was short-lived. The medium was by then just too pervasive a force to be afflicted by such an incident. The networks set about rectifying the errors by canceling the quiz shows and reinstating a higher percentage of public service programs.

They also took charge of their programming to a much greater extent. The presidents of all three networks decreed that from here on most program content would be decided, controlled, and scheduled by networks, who would then negotiate time sales with advertisers. This was a further extension of Weaver's "magazine concept." Beginning in 1960, most program suppliers contracted with the networks rather than advertising agencies. This made life more profitable for the TV networks too, because they established profit participation plans with the suppliers.[20]

Reflections of Upheaval

Television journalism gathered force and prestige during the 1960s—the decade of civil rights revolts, the election of John F. Kennedy, space shots, satellite communications, assassinations, Vietnam, and student unrest.

The networks encouraged documentaries and increased their nightly news from fifteen minutes to a half-hour in 1963, thereby assigning increased importance to the news departments. Anchoring on camera for NBC were Huntley and Brinkley and for CBS was Walter Cronkite, the man to become known as the most believed American. Network news departments scored points over their print counterparts when President Kennedy agreed to having news conferences televised live. Although total news time and coverage increased, scheduling remained a problem. Rumbles from the newsroom could frequently be heard as its programs were placed at unpopular hours.

The quiz scandal had helped precipitate a rise in documentaries. To atone for their sins, networks increased their investigative fare. These documentaries were now easier to execute because technical advances allowed for the use of 16mm film rather than the bulky 35mm. Film and sound could now be synchronized without an umbilical cord between two pieces of equipment; and wireless microphones were becoming reliable, enabling participants to wander freely without having to stay within range of a mike cord.

As ongoing documentaries, ABC established "Close-Up," and the other networks offered "CBS Reports" and "NBC White Paper." One 1960 "Close-Up" program entitled "The Children Were Watching" dealt with the feelings of a six-year-old black child attending the first integrated school in New Orleans. NBC's first "White Paper" dealt unflatteringly with the U-2 affair. In November of 1960 "CBS Reports" aired "Harvest

Figure 3.23

Figure 3.24

Figure 3.25

Figure 3.23
A Huntley-Brinkley newscast. Chet Huntley broadcast from New York while David Brinkley, seen on the television screen, came from Washington, D.C.
Photo courtesy of NBC

Figure 3.24
A scene from an "NBC White Paper" entitled "The Decision to Drop the Bomb." Here Secretary of State James F. Byrnes (*left*) and President Harry S. Truman appear as they did on their way to the Potsdam Conference in 1945.
Photo courtesy of NBC

Figure 3.25
Filming preparations for "The Tunnel." NBC news correspondent Piers Anderton (*left*) reviews the building of this tunnel under the Berlin Wall with student Dominico Sesta (*center*) and cameraman Peter Dehmel. The 450-foot-long passage began in this basement of a West Berlin home.
Photo courtesy of NBC

of Shame" dealing with the plight of the migrant workers. It was narrated by Edward R. Murrow as one of his last CBS duties before leaving to become head of the United States Information Agency.

Other notable documentaries of the era included "Biography of a Bookie Joint," for which concealed cameras oversaw the operation of a Boston "key shop"; "The Real West," an authoritative report to counter the westerns that was narrated by Gary Cooper; a 1962 airing of "The Tunnel," for which NBC secured footage of an actual tunnel being constructed by young Berliners to bring refugees from East to West Berlin; "Cuba and Castro Today," a 1964 ABC program featuring Lisa Howard interviewing Fidel Castro in Cuba; "The Louvre," for which cameras were allowed inside the famous building for the first time; and "D-Day Plus 20," a reminiscence between Eisenhower and Cronkite filmed at Normandy beaches.

Many documentaries reported on the racial problem. "Sit-In" dealt with resistance to restaurant segregation; "Crisis: Behind a Presidential

Commitment" chronicled the events surrounding Governor George Wallace's attempted barring of the schoolhouse door to prevent blacks from attending the University of Alabama; "Black History: Lost, Strayed or Stolen" was narrated by Bill Cosby.

Civil rights actions were covered live—including the funeral of Medgar Evers, the black civil rights leader murdered in Mississippi; the march on Washington led by Martin Luther King; and the riots in the Watts section of Los Angeles. Television reacted to the civil rights movement in another way—it began hiring blacks. Radio too had been lily white, but not so visibly. Both media began hiring blacks in the '60s. Jackie Gleason's chorus included a black dancer. Ed Sullivan programmed black acts. Scriptwriters began including stories about blacks (which often were not aired in the South). Networks and stations hired black on-camera newsmen. A black family moved to Peyton Place. A black cowboy appeared on "The Outcasts." And Diahann Carroll as Julia became the first black heroine.[21]

Television has been credited, through the "Great Debates" between John F. Kennedy and Richard M. Nixon, with having a primary influence on the 1960 election results. Kennedy and Nixon converged for the first debate at the studios of WBBM, Chicago's CBS station. Kennedy, tanned from campaigning in California, refused the offer of makeup. Nixon, although he was recovering from a brief illness, did likewise. Some of Nixon's aides, concerned about how he looked on TV, applied Lazy-Shave, a product to cover five o'clock shadow. Some people believe that the fact that Kennedy appeared to "win" the first debate had little to do with what he said. People who heard the program on radio felt Nixon held his own, but those watching TV, especially the reaction shots of Kennedy and Nixon listening to each other, could see a confident, attentive Kennedy and a haggard, weary looking Nixon whose perspiration streaked the Lazy-Shave. Three more debates were held, and Nixon's makeup and demeanor were well handled, but the small margin of the Kennedy victory at the polls has often been attributed to the undecided vote swung to Kennedy during the first debate.[22]

Through the medium of television, Americans were able to witness the nation's race into space. In 1961 Alan Shepard was launched into outer space within the view of network television cameras. The next year John Glenn orbited the earth as viewers witnessed the blast-off and recovery. Subsequently televised pictures were sent from outer space and the moon, and television viewers witnessed Neil Armstrong's first step onto the moon.

Television profited in its own way from space exploration. In July of 1962 Telstar I, a communications satellite, was launched by AT&T and the National Aeronautics and Space Administration. This satellite carried, among other things, the first live television transmissions between Europe and the United States. Telstar I did not permit continuous transmission because its signal ceased when it dropped below the horizon on its elliptical orbit. This problem was solved in April, 1965 with the launching of the first **synchronous satellite**, Early Bird. A synchronous satellite travels in an orbit that is synchronized with the speed of the rotation of the earth, thus

Figure 3.26

Figure 3.27

appearing to hang motionless in space and allowing for continuous pickup and transmission of signals. Many other communication satellites have been launched since, linking the United States with such places as Hawaii, Japan, Africa, the Soviet Union, and South America.

In order to control satellite communication, Congress passed a 1962 bill establishing COMSAT, the Communications Satellite Corporation, which was set up as a private company with half the stock owned by the general public and half owned by communications companies. To handle international problems and policies involving satellite communications, an International Satellite Consortium (INTELSAT) was formed and joined by most of the countries friendly to the United States.[23]

Satellites have transmitted many noteworthy international events, such as Pope Paul's visit to the United States, splashdowns of U.S. space missions, track meets in Russia, Olympic games, international talk shows—and one particular United States' tragedy in 1963. From Friday, November 22, to Monday, November 25, 1963, there were times when 90 percent of the American people were watching television. As a New York critic wrote, "This was not viewing. This was total involvement." From shortly after the shots were fired at 12:30 Dallas time until President John F. Kennedy was laid to rest in Arlington Cemetery, television kept the vigil—Jacqueline Kennedy accompanying her husband's body from Parkland Hospital; reports of Lyndon Johnson taking the oath of office at 2:38 p.m.; the casket descending from Air Force One; Jacqueline Kennedy's blood-stained suit and stockings; the announcement of the capture of Lee Harvey Oswald as prime suspect; the arrival of dignitaries from the world over; weeping men and women; John John's salute; the transfer of the casket from the White House to the Capitol; the flashbacks to Kennedy during his presidential years; the first "live murder" ever seen on TV as Jack Ruby shot Lee Harvey Oswald; the procession to Arlington Cemetery; the eternal flame.

Many praised television for its controlled, almost flawless coverage. Some felt TV would have made it impossible for Lee Harvey Oswald to

Figure 3.26
One of the so-called "Great Debates." John F. Kennedy has his turn speaking while Richard Nixon and moderator Howard K. Smith look on. In the foreground are the newsmen who asked the questions.
Photo from United Press International

Figure 3.27
The Kennedy funeral. This off-monitor shot shows John-John saluting the flag covering his father's caisson.
Photo courtesy of Broadcasting magazine

receive a fair trial and that it was the presence of the media that enabled the Oswald shooting to take place.[24] In 1968 TV was to tell the news of two other untimely deaths—Martin Luther King, Jr. and Robert Kennedy.

For the first time in history, war came to the American dinner table. As the troop buildup began in Vietnam in the mid '60s, the networks established correspondents in Saigon. Filmed reports of battles appeared almost nightly on the evening news programs. The war resulted in an inner-circle battle at CBS. Fred Friendly, then president of CBS news, resigned when his network carried reruns of "I Love Lucy" rather than the Senate hearings on the escalation of war activities in Vietnam.[25] In 1968, amid rising controversy over the war, Walter Cronkite decided to travel to Vietnam to see for himself and returned feeling that the United States would have to accept a stalemate in that country.

Much of the controversy surrounding the war emanated from the country's campuses, where students were becoming increasingly dissident regarding various issues. This too was covered by the media, as was the 1968 Democratic convention in Chicago, where youths protested outside the convention halls against the steamrolling nomination of Hubert Humphrey. The media became embroiled in the controversy and were accused of inciting the riot conditions because they were covering them. The demonstrators seemed to be trying to attract media coverage. On the other hand, many people inside the convention hall learned of the protesting from seeing it on a TV monitor.[26]

The role of the media in the creation of news was debated frequently in the '60s and beyond as their image as a source of information increased.

A Vast Wasteland?   In 1961 Newton Minow, Kennedy's new appointee as chairman of the Federal Communications Commission, spoke before the annual convention of the National Association of Broadcasters. During the course of his speech, he stated the following to these broadcasting executives:

> I invite you to sit down in front of your television set when your station goes on the air and stay there without a book, magazine, newspaper, profit and loss sheet or rating book to distract you—and keep your eyes glued to that set until the station signs off. I can assure you that you will observe a vast wasteland.[27]

The term "vast wasteland" caught on as a metaphor for television programming. Needless to say, the executives were not happy with Minow's phrasemaking.

Television entertainment programming during the '60s was a case of "it's hard to keep the players straight." Few programs endured the decade, many vanishing quickly because they did not achieve substantial ratings. During the early '60s the dominant fare was violence. "The Untouchables," "Route 66," "Surfside 6," "The Roaring 20s," "A Man Called X," "Sea Hunt"—all featured murders, jailbreaks, robberies, thefts, kidnappings, torture, blackmail, sluggings, forced confessions, and dynamiting. Saturday morning children's programming was replete with violent cartoons.

Figure 3.28

Figure 3.29

Figure 3.30

Figure 3.31

A surge against violence, aided by Minow's challenge, brought forth a change to doctors' shows such as "Ben Casey" and "Dr. Kildare" and more comedies such as "The Dick Van Dyke Show," "Hazel," "Gilligan's Island," "Father of the Bride," "Gomer Pyle, USMC," "Mr. Ed," "Bewitched," "Batman," and the "Beverly Hillbillies." The last, a series about an Ozark family that struck oil and moved to Beverly Hills without changing their mountain character, headed the ratings but was heralded as the supreme example of the vast wasteland.

Spy shows such as "Mission: Impossible," "The Man from U.N.C.L.E.," "I Spy," and "Amos Burke" were plentiful for several years and brought with them a returning encroachment of violence. After the assassinations of Martin Luther King, Jr. and Robert Kennedy, a new wave of medical shows and comedies surfaced, augmented by a rash of variety shows—"Marcus Welby M.D.," "Medical Center," "Here's Lucy," "Laugh-In," "The Andy Williams Show," "Tom Jones," "The Smothers Brothers."

During the '60s, movies were better than ever—on TV. In 1961 "Saturday Night at the Movies" began a prime time movie trend that saw movies on all seven nights of the week by 1968. This rapidly depleted Hollywood's supply of films, so in 1969 ABC introduced a made-for-TV

Figure 3.32   Figure 3.33

Figure 3.32
"A Yank in Korea," one
of the movies to play
frequently on TV. Here
actors Lon MacCallister
(*left*) and Larry Stewart
discuss their plight.
Photo courtesy of Larry
Stewart

Figure 3.33
Robert Redford in his
first TV appearance.
This is a scene from an
episode of "Rescue 8"
entitled "Breakdown,"
aired in February of
1960. Redford was hired
by director Larry
Stewart to guest star
with leads Jim Davis
and Lang Jeffries and
from this launched a
well known career.
Photo courtesy of Larry
Stewart

movie series, "The Movie of the Week." These films had not been previously shown at theaters but were conceived for television viewing.

Talk shows with such hosts as Steve Allen, Dick Cavett, David Frost, Ernie Kovacs, and Merv Griffin became dominant in the '60s too. Johnny Carson took over "Tonight" from Jack Paar and proved equally controversial.

Specials of note included "Julie and Carol at Carnegie Hall," featuring the singing of Julie Andrews and Carol Burnett, Ed Sullivan's presentation of the Beatles, "My Name is Barbra" with Barbra Streisand, "Frank Sinatra: A Man and His Music," Vladimir Horowitz playing piano at Carnegie Hall, "Death of a Salesman," "The Magnificent Yankee," and Hallmark's presentation of "Macbeth."

Instant replay became an instant hit with sports fans, and the Super Bowl telecast of 1967 was preceded by much hoopla. As remote equipment made it easier to leave the studio, the quantity of sports broadcasting increased, and sports themselves changed to accommodate the new medium. Teams changed their playing times in order to avail themselves of larger audiences and added a few more playoffs to add to the excitement.[28]

The '60s were a period of great prosperity for television. Despite objections from TV's critics, the commercialism of the medium grew. When Herbert Hoover, who as secretary of commerce had decried advertising in the 1920s, died in 1964, NBC broadcast a tribute which was followed by a beer commercial, a political commercial, and a cigarette commercial.[29]

TV of the '70s

The cigarette commercials disappeared in 1972 as the result of a congressional bill passed barring the advertising of cigarettes on the broadcast media. This was motivated by the surgeon general's report linking cigarettes and cancer. Removing cigarette commercials from radio and TV, however, has not decreased smoking, with the result that there are constant pressures to reinstate the ads.[30]

Two other experiments of the '70s were **prime-time access** and the **family hour.** Prime-time access was promoted primarily by Westinghouse Broadcasting. It pointed out that the networks monopolized **prime time** by programming from 7:00 to 11:00 and suggested that some of this time should be programmed by the stations themselves in order to meet community needs as well as allow more room for syndicated programs. In 1971 this idea was adopted by the FCC, which ruled that networks would be allowed to program only three hours a night, leaving the other hour to the local stations. During this hour there were to be no old network programs or old movies; all programs had to be newly created. What resulted was station programming from 7:00 to 8:00 and network programming from 8:00 to 11:00. The rule was later altered to allow stations to program network news from 7:00 to 7:30 and to allow networks to program all four hours Sunday night. What was left, in reality, was 7:30 to 8:00 Monday through Saturday. Although prime-time access was established to allow stations to broadcast significant local programming, this is not what, in fact, happened. For the most part, the stations filled the time with the cheapest thing they could find—game shows and remakes of old formats.[31]

Family hour began in 1975 as an attempt to throttle sex and violence before 9:00 p.m., the time when children are usually in the audience. The family hour concept emanated from the code of the National Association of Broadcasters, an internal broadcasting organization, but there were those who believed it came about through subtle pressure by the FCC and hence represented an abhorrent attempt by the FCC to regulate program content. The family hour idea was widely opposed by writers, producers, and directors, who took the concept to court, where it was decided that the FCC had overstepped its powers and that the family hour restrictions should be removed from the NAB Code.[32]

The women's movement affected broadcasting in the '70s. Stations continued to hire and program blacks and Mexican-Americans but added female newscasters and stories about women in responsible positions.

Both public broadcasting and cable TV established places for themselves within the communications structure. Award of the 1970 "Emmy" to the "Andersonville Trial" as the best show of the year helped establish public television's place in the sun. Another prominent success was the children's program "Sesame Street."

Programming on commercial TV falls into two categories—news and public affairs on one hand, and entertainment on the other. However, there is some overlap as news programs attempt to achieve entertainment value by having news personalities banter with each other. The news has made news frequently, such as when it was accused of being biased with Eastern liberal establishment personnel. Highlights in the news and documentary area have been bicentennial specials, the coverage of President Nixon's trip to China, the Watergate hearings, and the documentary "The Selling of the Pentagon," which resulted in a congressional investigation.

Figure 3.34
The one-hour documentary special "Pollution is a Matter of Choice" explored the environmental questions throughout the country. Frank McGee (*insert*) was the on-camera reporter.
Photo courtesy of NBC

Figure 3.35
Mary Tyler Moore. After appearing on Dick Van Dyke's show for several years, Mary launched her own show, which went off CBS voluntarily after eight years.
Photo courtesy of MTM Enterprises

Figure 3.36
A bicentennial special. Producer-director Larry Stewart explains action to Richard Mulligan, as Thomas Jefferson, and Sorrell Booke, as John Adams, for the NBC 1976 program "Without Consent."
Photo courtesy of Larry Stewart

Figure 3.37
"The Bionic Woman," Lead Lindsay Wagner (*left*), director Larry Stewart (*center*), and Andrew Prine prepare for a scene of the episode "Rodeo," which aired in October of 1977.
Photo courtesy of Larry Stewart

Figure 3.38
Stars Peter Strauss (*left*), Susan Blakely, and Nick Nolte in "Rich Man, Poor Man." This miniseries based on Irwin Shaw's book started a proliferation of novels for TV.
Photo from MCA Publishing

Figure 3.39
A scene from "Roots," a David L. Wolper Production, depicting one of Alex Haley's ancestors who was sold into slavery in the New World.
Photo courtesy of The Wolper Organization, Inc.

Figure 3.35

Figure 3.36

Figure 3.37

Figure 3.38

Figure 3.39

Sports coverage has increased greatly during the '70s, including "Monday Night Football," nighttime world series games, and thorough Olympic coverage. In 1972 sportscasters transformed to newscasters as Arab terrorists captured and killed Israeli Olympic athletes.

Among comedy series, "All in the Family" struck a new chord by probing previously taboo topics of politics, ethnics, and sex. The program, with its bigoted resident of New York's borough of Queens, Archie Bunker, became a ratings leader. By the mid 1970s there were fewer movies on TV than at any time during the past decade, but some of the movies—including "That Certain Summer," which dealt with homosexuality—showed that censorship was becoming less restrictive. Spin-offs became popular. "The Mary Tyler Moore" show begat "Rhoda" and "Phyllis." From "The Six Million Dollar Man" came "The Bionic Woman," and "Happy Days" resulted in "Laverne and Shirley." The nighttime soap opera "Mary Hartman, Mary Hartman," refused by the networks, became a hit on independent stations. Novels dramatized for TV and shown on a series of different nights became a popular phenomenon, as proven by the success of programs derived from Irwin Shaw's *Rich Man, Poor Man* and Alex Haley's *Roots.*[33]

Television, born into a fast-paced society, has been forced into the role of an early bloomer. Within thirty years it has progressed from hot lights and green makeup to instantaneous worldwide communication.

Summary

Television has progressed rapidly in its short history, encompassing many changes in technology and programming.

Mechanical scanning experiments were begun in the late 1800s, and *electronic scanning* was developed somewhat later by *Dumont, Farnsworth, Zworykin,* and others. RCA displayed television at the 1939 World's Fair and several years later had a *525-line* black and white system approved by the FCC. World War II halted the development of TV, and after the war the *color question* and *UHF* possibilities further delayed it. In 1948 TV began growing so fast that a *freeze* was imposed until 1952. Programming during this period included "Texaco Star Theater," "I Love Lucy," sports, children's programs, dramas, and limited news and public affairs. The lifting of the freeze established both VHF and UHF stations. The 1950s saw *blacklisting,* live drama, and *"spectaculars."* CBS's color system was accepted and then rejected in favor of an RCA-backed system. In the late '50s live programming yielded to film and tape. Quiz scandals gave the industry a black eye. During the '60s broadcast journalism gained impetus reporting such events as civil rights uprisings, space shots, assassinations, war, and student unrest. Entertainment programs turned over rapidly during the decade. In the 1970s cigarette commercials disappeared, *prime-time access* and *family hour* appeared, and the women's movement, *public broadcasting,* and *cable TV* came to the fore.

4 How Pictures Fly Through the Air

Technical Aspects of TV

Television is a triumph of equipment over people.

Steve Allen, TV personality

Cartoon copyrighted by *Broadcasting* magazine

"Today's program, 'Accident Prevention in Home and Shop,' will not be seen due to technical difficulties."

The audio portion of television is basically FM radio. The sound is picked up from a microphone, turntable, or tape recorder, then mixed in an audio board and sent to the **transmitter** and out the **antenna** to be received by the home TV set. Sometimes before it is transmitted, it is stored, along with the picture, on videotape.

The video signal is usually picked up by several cameras and sent through a switcher where the picture to be aired is selected. This picture is then sent to a videotape recorder or directly to the transmitter and out the antenna in a manner similar to audio signals.[1]

Cameras

The picture begins in the television camera, which consists of a **viewfinder,** a **lens** system, and an electronic system. The viewfinder is simply a small TV monitor mounted on the camera to allow the camera operator to see the picture framed.

The lens system is similar to that of a photographic camera. With it, the camera operator selects and focuses the image and varies the light which strikes the tube of the television camera. Focusing is accomplished by adjusting a knob until the picture is sharp and clear. The focusing mechanism actually establishes a relationship that considers the distance between the lens and the object to be focused, but usually it is not necessary to calculate this because the eye can discern soft focus from sharp focus.

Light adjustment is accomplished by opening and closing an **iris** in the lens. If there is scant light in the room, the iris must be opened wide in order to take advantage of all available light; if there is profuse light, the iris can be partially closed. The degree to which the iris is opened or closed is measured in **f-stops.** The lower the f-stop, the wider open the iris is. Hence a

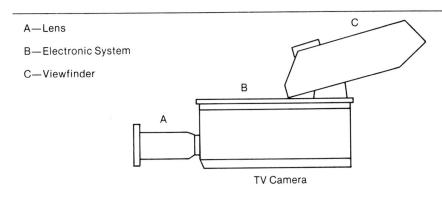

A—Lens

B—Electronic System

C—Viewfinder

TV Camera

**Figure 4.1
Parts of a television
camera.**

  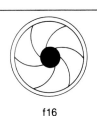

f1.9   f5.6   f16

**Figure 4.2
Lens openings corre-
sponding to different
f-stops.**

lens set at f/4.0 will be more open and let in more light than a lens adjusted to f/22. The more the iris is closed, the greater the **depth of field**—i.e., the range of distance from the camera within which all objects, close and far, will simultaneously be in sharp focus. If a room has only a little light and the iris is wide open with a low f-stop, then the depth of field will be shallow. The main technical reason lights are used in a TV studio is to enable the camera f-stop to be set high so the iris can be partially closed, thus allowing objects near the camera as well as farther away from it to be in focus. Lighting, of course, also improves contrast, establishes mood, and provides modeling so that a subject looks three-dimensional and separated from its background.

Prior to the 1960s most cameras had **fixed lenses** that could frame a picture at one specific point. For example, a fixed 25 mm lens mounted on a camera in the middle of a studio would show a wider shot than a 50 mm lens mounted on the same camera. These pictures could not change unless the camera was moved and the lens was refocused.

In the early days of television, four or five lenses were mounted on turning devices called a **turret.** This turret might be mounted with one 50 mm lens, one 75 mm lens, one 90 mm lens, and one 135 mm lens. When the camera's picture was not on the air, the camera operator could switch from one lens to another, thus obtaining a closer or longer shot for the next on-air picture.

Today most cameras have only one lens, a **zoom lens,** which can, on the air, move from a close-up to a long shot or stop at any point in between. Zooming can be accomplished by moving a ring mounted on the lens or can be handled more conveniently at the back of the camera by a push rod, crank, or handle.

Zoom lenses can be adjusted to vary focal length so that, without moving the camera position, more or less of the scene in front of the camera can fill the television screen. A zoom lens with a ratio of 4:1 can capture a wideshot that is four times as broad as its close-up. In other words, a 4:1 zoom might have a close-up that looks like that obtained with a 100 mm fixed lens and a long shot that looks like that obtained with a 25 mm fixed

**Figure 4.3
Simulation of picture as
taken with a 25 mm lens
(*right*) and with a 50 mm
lens (*left*).**

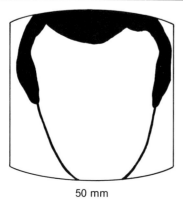

50 mm

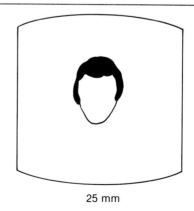

25 mm

Chapter 4

Figure 4.4
A 1952 camera with turret lenses.
Photo courtesy of RCA

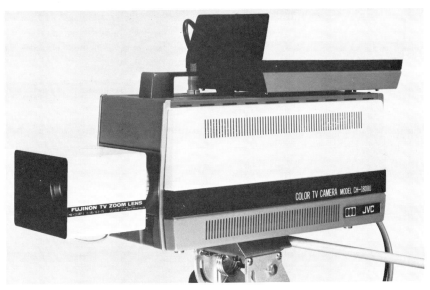

Figure 4.5
A television camera with a zoom lens.
Photo courtesy of JVC
Industries Company

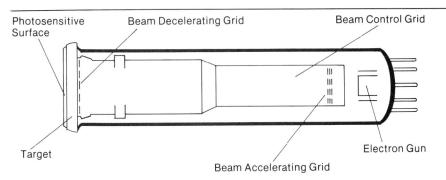

Photosensitive
Surface

Beam Decelerating Grid

Beam Control Grid

Figure 4.6
Television camera tube

Target

Beam Accelerating Grid

Electron Gun

How Pictures Fly Through the Air

lens. It could also frame any millimeter range between 25 and 100. A 10:1 lens might cover a range from 18 mm to 180 mm.[2]

The camera itself contains the electronic components that convert the image focused by the lens into electrical impulses. The main component is a tube which consists of an **electron gun,** a **target,** a **photosensitive surface,** and other auxiliary electronic elements. (See figure 4.6.)

The picture to be televised goes through the lens to the photosensitive layer of chemicals arranged in microscopic but individual dots. Each dot emits an electrical charge which varies in intensity depending on the amount of light hitting it. For example, the dots of the photosensitive layer reacting to a white shirt would give off a stronger electrical charge than the dots reacting to dark hair.

Electrical charges emitted from the back of this photosensitive plate hit a target and reproduce an electronic equivalent of the image. Each little speck of information on the target is then picked up individually so that it can be sent through a wire and later reassembled as a picture. The picking up of this information is accomplished through the use of an electron gun mounted at the back of the tube which generates a steady stream of electrons to **scan** the target in a very specific way. In the American system of television, the electron beam scans 525 horizontal lines, left to right, each 1/30th of a second. This means that every 1/30th of a second the camera manufactures one picture. It is not scanned as a whole picture, however. Within that 1/30th of a second the beam actually scans the target twice. On the first scan, it picks up information from every other line of the picture; then it returns to the top and picks up the remaining lines. In essence, it first scans the odd-numbered lines and then the even-numbered lines. The scanning of the odd-numbered lines takes 1/60th of a second and is referred to as one **field.** The scanning of the even-numbered lines also takes 1/60th of a second and is a second field. Both scans together require 1/30th of a second, referred to as one **frame.** Therefore, American television scans 525 lines at the rate of 30 frames per second or 60 fields per second. Since the human eye retains an after-image, it perceives all this as a constantly moving image. Other countries have different standards such as 636 or 840 lines, creating incompatibility. That means, for example, that an American TV set could not receive a program from a French transmitter.

Each frame contains about 200,000 separate elements, so the number of elements transmitted per second is approximately 6,000,000. Obviously they must be arranged in a systematic order, for if the electrons picked up random bits of information, the picture would be scrambled. In order to keep the electron beam hitting the target at exactly the right spot at the right time, a system of coils and grids is used to magnetically align the beam at the proper horizontal and vertical points and assure that it is traveling at the right speed. The gun, itself, never moves; its beam is simply adjusted by the magnetic elements.

If a camera is black and white, it has only one tube following this process, and the photosensitive surface, target, and beam react to the

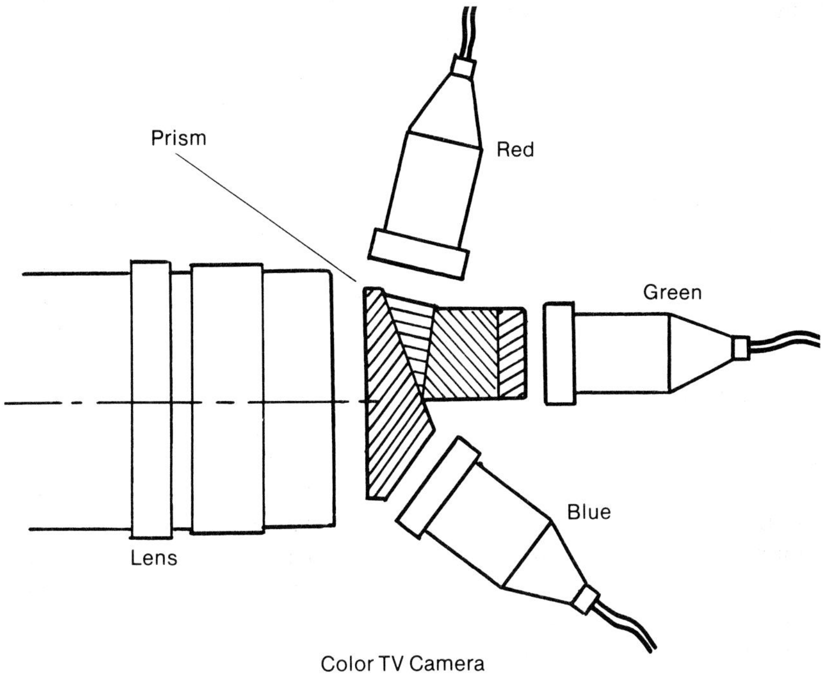

Figure 4.7
Color television camera
tubes.

Color TV Camera

varying shades of gray made by the scene being televised. If the camera is color, it usually has three tubes working simultaneously. As the image comes through the lens, it is multiplied into three by a **prism** with **filters** that send each of the primary colors—red, blue, and green—to a different tube. These tubes then respond to the intensity of the selected color.

Some color cameras have only one tube which picks up the various colors one after another. Other color cameras have four tubes, the extra one for luminescence, or essentially the black and white image. Some color cameras are complicated to set up initially and then to keep properly registered during production or over a period of time. They come with separate controls called camera control units, which are placed in the control room so that electronic adjustments can be made during production without interfering with camera movement in the studio.

There are several different types of television camera tubes, all of which operate in a similar manner. The original tube developed by Zworykin, the **iconoscope,** was relatively insensitive and required uncomfortably hot lighting. It was replaced after a few years' use by the **image orthicon** tube, which was large and expensive but sensitive enough to be the primary tube used by broadcasters for over twenty years.

Another tube, the **vidicon,** was also developed. It is cheaper and smaller than the image orthicon but not as sensitive to light or as capable of high resolution. Its main use has been in film projection and in closed-circuit television systems where top picture quality is not essential.

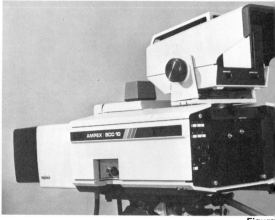

Figure 4.8

Figure

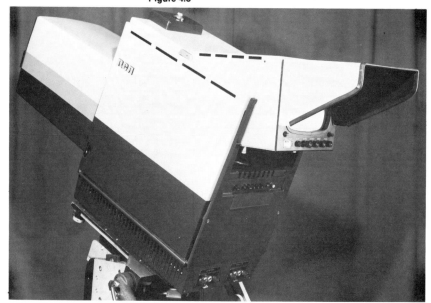

**Figure 4.8
Philips color camera,
Model LDK-25**
Photo courtesy of North
American Philips Corpora-
tion

**Figure 4.9
Ampex color camera,
Model BCC-10**
Photo courtesy of Ampex
Corporation

**Figure 4.10
RCA color camera,
Model TK-46**
Photo courtesy of RCA

**Figure 4.11
JVC color camera,
Model GC-4800U**
Photo courtesy of JVC
Industries Company

Figure 4.10

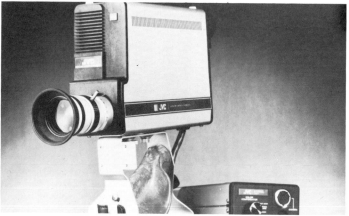

Figure 4.11

Figure 4.12

Figure 4.13

Figure 4.14

During the 1960s an improved version of the vidicon, the **plumbicon,** was introduced and is now the most utilized tube in broadcasting. Its highly sensitive compound of lead as the coating on the photosensitive surface makes the plumbicon as high a quality tube as the image orthicon with the added advantage of small size and lower cost.[3]

The camera unit (consisting of viewfinder, electronics, and lens) must be mounted on something so it can be moved about the studio. There are three basic types of mounting equipment: **tripod, pedestal,** and **crane.** A tripod is a three-legged stand. A pedestal is a large tube that allows the camera to move up and down by counterweight, hydraulic, or air pressure systems. A crane is a large machine which can raise the camera to a high level.[4]

Film Equipment

A great deal of what is programmed on television never is seen by a studio camera because it is produced on film. Obviously, movies which were first shown in theaters and are later run on TV are utilizing the film medium. But many of the visual elements of newscasts are on film, as are entire situation comedies, dramas, commercials, and documentaries.

The historical reason for this has been that film equipment is portable and easier to handle than television equipment, which is bulky and encumbered with long cables. This difference is disappearing and the lines between film and videotape becoming blurred as TV equipment becomes more portable. Videotaping has a distinct advantage in that the action taped can be viewed immediately while the film must be processed before it can be seen. Also, tape can be erased and used over while film stock cannot.

Film cameras associated with television work come in three sizes: 35 mm, 16 mm, and super 8 mm. These numbers refer to the width of the film each camera uses. The larger the frame, the better the picture quality. However, the larger the frame, the bulkier the camera needed to hold the film.

Since feature films must be shown on large movie screens, they are shot in 35 mm. When they come to the TV studio to be aired as old movies, they are either in the 35 mm format or have been transferred to 16 mm. For most of the filming executed for TV, 16 mm is adequate, and recently stations have begun converting to super 8 which seems to give enough quality while reducing bulk.

All film cameras have a lens, similar to a TV camera lens, which focuses and lets in light. Film is loaded on one reel and run to a take-up reel. In the process it passes behind the lens opening and records the picture on photosensitive chemicals which are used to store the latent images which the lens has focused. After the film is developed, it can be shown by use of a projector—35 mm, 16 mm, or super 8, depending on the size of the film. In the projector the film passes a light source which projects the picture through a lens.

If the film must be edited, this can be accomplished by physically cutting out the unwanted **frames** and taping or cementing the film back together. Editing equipment allows the film editor to see the film one frame at a time and then cut and splice it neatly.

All the foregoing has referred only to the picture part of the film. Many TV films, especially those for newscasts, are shot silent with narration added by the newscaster during the broadcast.

Often sound is needed during the filming, which adds another dimension to the filming equipment. Sometimes pictures and sound are recorded simultaneously on the same film—a method known as **single-system** sound recording. Other times the picture is recorded on the camera and sound is recorded on a tape recorder, the two being combined later through printing—a method known as **double-system** sound recording.

Single-system is easier to record but presents problems if the film is to be edited. Since it is physically impossible for a lens and the sound head to be at exactly the same place within the camera, the sound for a particular

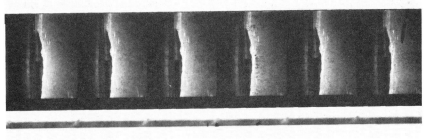

35 mm

16 mm

8 mm

Figure 4.15

Figure 4.15
Actual size of three sizes of film

Figure 4.16
A super 8 camera
Photo courtesy of Ehrenreich Photo-Optical Industries, Inc.

Figure 4.17
A 35 mm projector
Photo courtesy of Arriflex Company of America

Figure 4.16

Figure 4.17

**Figure 4.18
A Moviola film editor**
Photo courtesy of
Magnasync/Moviola Cor-
poration

frame precedes it by several inches. If the film is edited to suit the picture, some of the sound will be lost. With double-system sound, each can be edited separately and combined later along with other effects such as music, sound effects, and applause. Editing equipment needed for editing sound film is more expensive and complicated than that for picture only.[5]

Once a film has been shot, developed, and edited, it must be incorporated within the rest of the TV station equipment. Film is never projected directly in television; it is first converted to electronic material. This is done by projecting it through a **film chain,** which generally consists of a film projector, a slide projector, a set of mirrors, and a TV camera. Sometimes one film chain will incorporate several projectors, although only one can be shown at a time.

The film projector looks like any regular film projector, but it is specially designed to adapt film, which is usually shot at 24 frames per second, to TV, which operates at 30 frames per second. The projector compensates for the difference so a flutter will not appear on the TV screen.

The slide projector is used for 35 mm slides and usually can hold 36 slides in a dual drum. A dual lamp assembly allows slides to be changed

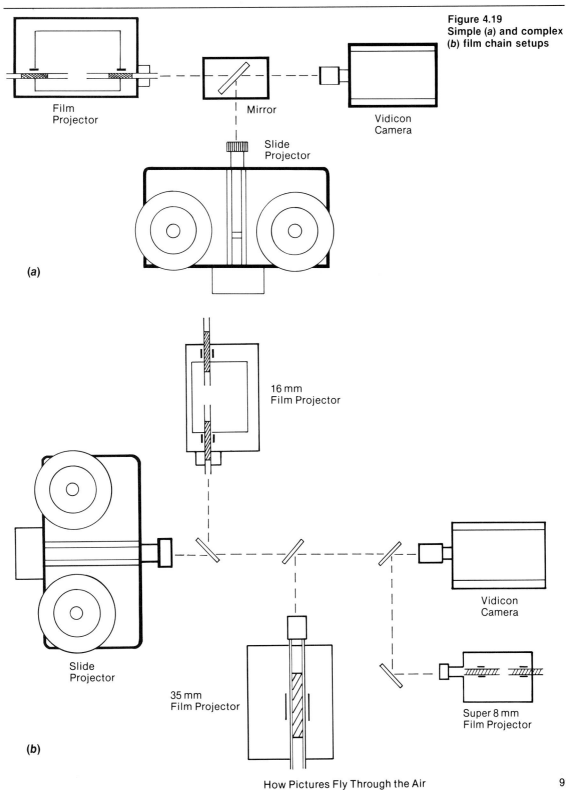

Figure 4.19
Simple (a) and complex
(b) film chain setups

Film
Projector

Mirror

Vidicon
Camera

Slide
Projector

(a)

16 mm
Film Projector

Slide
Projector

Vidicon
Camera

35 mm
Film Projector

Super 8 mm
Film Projector

(b)

How Pictures Fly Through the Air

rapidly without the blank screen phenomenon that occurs with most carousel projectors.

The mirrors are usually contained in a unit called a **multiplexer.** The purpose of the mirrors is to direct the various inputs of the film chain to the TV camera. This is accomplished by mechanically rotating or moving the mirrors so that they are in position to deflect the proper pictures.

The camera part of the film chain operates on the same principle as the studio TV camera. It scans the picture coming from the film or slide projector via the multiplexer and converts it to electrical impulses.[6]

Sync Generators

Most TV programs incorporate the inputs from several studio cameras and a film chain. If a program consists entirely of movies, then only the film chains will be used, but generally a number of video sources will be tied together. For example, a program might start with a series of slides from the film chain, then change to a long shot of the host on camera 1, followed by a close-up of a guest on camera 2.

Each camera input, operating by itself, is scanning top to bottom and left to right, one dot at a time. But there is no guarantee that they will all be scanning at the same point. In fact, they will probably be at entirely different points, as the diagrams in figure 4.21 show.

If the picture going out on the air is switched from one element to another, the picture will roll because it is not receiving the same information from all sources. In other words, the signal will become confused if it must search for a new scan point. In order to prevent this, a **sync generator** is employed in the system with the duty of sending information to all the cameras so that they all scan the same lines at the same time—i.e., they are in **sync.** A sync generator is a very undistinguished looking piece of equipment, usually literally a black box buried within the equipment and left untouched unless it develops a malfunction.[7]

Monitors

The pictures from the various cameras are displayed on **monitors** so that the director can see them and choose which picture he wants to go over the air. A monitor looks just like a TV set but, unlike a home TV set, it has special electronics so it can display a picture coming directly from a camera, and generally it has no tuner for selecting different channels.

A bank of monitors mounted near the director's chair are labeled according to their output: camera 1, camera 2, film chain 1, film chain 2, etc. Usually there will be two monitors which are larger than the others, one labeled "air" and one labeled "preview." The air monitor shows the director the picture chosen to be on-air at that moment while the preview monitor allows for setup of the next shot or some particularly difficult special effect.[8]

Switchers

A device called a **switcher,** consisting of buttons and levers, is used to place the proper picture on the air. For example, if the director wanted the picture on camera 1, the man operating the switcher would punch the button labeled "camera 1."

Figure 4.20
**A film chain in opera-
tion**
Photo courtesy of General
Telephone Company

Figure 4.21
Scanning

Figure 4.22
A bank of monitors
Photo courtesy of KHJ-TV,
Los Angeles

Figure 4.20

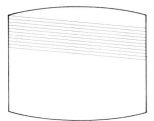
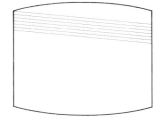
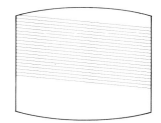

Studio	Studio	Film Chain
CAM 1	CAM 2	CAM 3

Figure 4.21

Figure 4.22

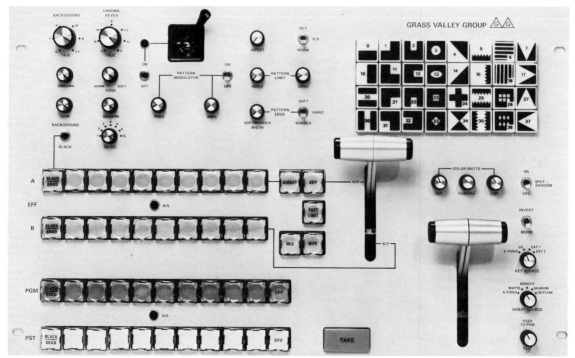

Figure 4.23

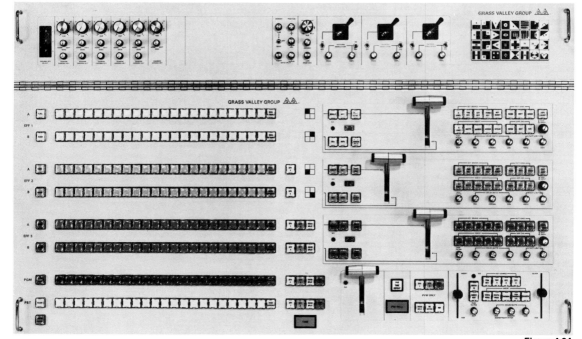

Figure 4.24

Figure 4.23
A fairly simple switcher
Photo courtesy of The
Grass Valley Group, Inc.

Figure 4.24
A complex switcher
Photo courtesy of The
Grass Valley Group, Inc.

There are several different ways the switcher can change from one picture to another. It can "**take**," which is a quick change from one picture to another, or it can "**dissolve**," which is a slow change where one picture gradually replaces another. If a **special effects generator** is incorporated in the switcher, it can wipe one picture across another, insert one picture in the corner of another, change pictures in starlike or wave motions, and execute many other unusual effects.

The complexity of the switcher depends on the number of inputs the studio system has and the number of different types of switching desired. Theoretically, a switcher could consist of two buttons if the only inputs available were two cameras and the only switching desired were "takes." A third button for "black" (nothing) might be added if it is desirable to have a blank screen before the program or at the end of it. If "dissolves" are desired, then three more buttons and a lever can be added to enable a slow transition from one picture to another or from a picture to black. As the number of inputs and number of special effects increase, so do the number of buttons—and the cost of the switcher.[9]

Studio and Control Room Design

The switcher, sync generator, audio board, and monitors are usually located in a control room, while the cameras are located in the studio. Usually the control room is situated near the studio but at a higher level so that cables from the camera and mike equipment can travel under the floor. In general, TV stations have at least two studios and control rooms so that one show can be setting up and rehearsing while another is taping.

Most broadcast studios are a minimum of 40 by 50 feet with ceiling heights of about 15 feet. This height is needed because lighting is used for TV operation and the lights must hang from a ceiling **grid.** Most studios have a curtain around the edge which can serve as a background, a floor that is smooth and extremely hard to permit smooth camera operation, and walls and ceilings that are acoustically treated to prevent outside noise interference. There should be no windows, since outside light would make controlled lighting impossible, and there should be a large soundproof door for bringing in scenery. Air conditioning is needed to compensate for the heat of the lights.

In addition, power outlets and outlets for cameras and microphones are needed so that sets can be placed at various spots in the studio with easy access for microphones, cameras, and power equipment. Most studios contain a loudspeaker system which enables the director to speak from the control room to the studio before or after taping. During taping, however, a loudspeaker system would be picked up by the microphones and interfere with the audio of the program content. It is necessary for the director in the control room to talk to the camera operators in the studio to give instructions during taping, so an **intercom** system connects all members of the crew. It consists of headphones and small microphones so that all can communicate with each other.

Because of its high noise level, the film chain is usually located in a separate room away from the studio and control room, often in the same area as the videotape recorders.[10]

**Figure 4.25
A studio setup at an
industrial company—
Hewlett-Packard.**
Photo courtesy of Hewlett-
Packard

**Figure 4.26
A studio setup at a
university—Loyola-
Marymount University.**
Photo courtesy of Loyola-
Marymount University

Figure 4.27
A control room at a community college— Cosumnes River College.
Photo courtesy of John Champagne

Figure 4.28
A control room of the NBC network.
Photo courtesy of NBC

Videotape Recorders

The television signal can be sent from the control room to the transmitter. However, it is more likely to be sent to the videotape recorder (VTR), where the impulses are placed on magnetic tape and stored to be played back at a later date. Unlike film, the "pictures" stored on videotape are not pictures the eye can see but rather are rearranged iron particles. In this way, videotaping is similar to audio taping, but there are some significant differences stemming mainly from the fact that much more needs to be recorded for a video signal than an audio signal—nearly 100 times more.

If video information were recorded by stationary heads as in audio tape recording, the tape would have to move at 55 feet per second, or nearly 36 miles per hour. A one-hour videotaped program would require approximately 198,000 feet of tape. Obviously, sending tape past stationary **heads** won't do. To overcome this problem, methods have been devised whereby the video heads rotate, placing information on the tape vertically or diagonally instead of horizontally. This enables a great deal more information to be packed on the tape, especially if the tape is wider than the usual 1/4″ audio tape.

There are two basic types of videotape recorders, **transverse quadraplex** and **helical.** The former is usually used in professional broadcast studios, while the latter usually is seen in nonprofessional closed-circuit systems. However, new helical recorders of broadcast quality have recently been developed and are beginning to appear at stations and networks.

The quadraplex recorders are large and expensive and employ tape that is 2″ wide. Four rotating video heads place the information on the tape vertically, each head taking over where the other leaves off. This enables more information to be placed on the tape per running inch. These recorders also contain stationary audio heads much like those of an audio tape recorder. Usually it is possible to place two audio tracks on the tape, audio 1 being used for the program material and audio 2 being used for information that might be of value to the technicians. For example, beeps recorded on audio 2 can later be used in the editing process. In addition to the video and audio information, there is also a **control track** which is tied to sync information so that the picture remains stable as it is recorded and played back. This sync information is supplied during the interval when the beam is turned off as it is traveling from the bottom of its scan back to the top to begin another scan.

The helical recorders are less expensive than the transverse quadraplex and come in many varieties, some employing 1″ tape and others 3/4″, 1/2″, or 1/4″. All operate on the same principle in that video information is laid down diagonally, or **"slant track."** Tape from a raised supply reel is wrapped around a drum at a slant and then run onto a take-up reel at a lower level. The drum contains two heads (or sometimes just one) which spin at a rapid speed and place the video impulses on the tape. Audio and control track information is laid on the tape in a manner similar to that of the transverse quadraplex recorders.

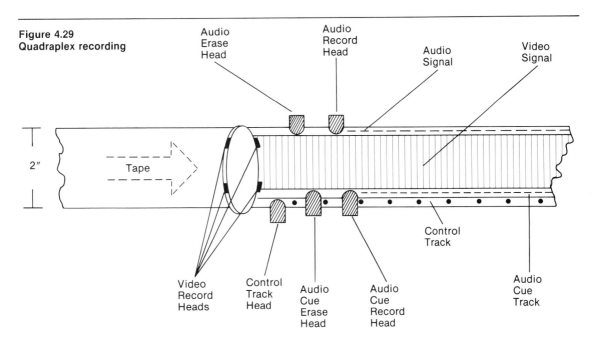

Figure 4.29
Quadraplex recording

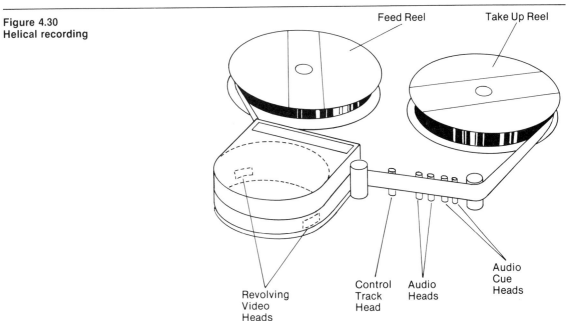

Figure 4.30
Helical recording

VTRs in professional stations are generally reel to reel recorders, but sometimes **cassette** recorders are used, particularly for commercials. Cassette recorders are very popular for educational and industrial uses also.

Figure 4.31
An RCA videotape
recorder using 2″ tape.
Photo courtesy of RCA

Figure 4.32
An Ampex videotape
recorder using 1″ tape.
Photo courtesy of Ampex
Corporation

Figure 4.33
A JVC videotape
recorder using 3/4″
cassette tape.
Photo courtesy of JVC
Industries Company

Figure 4.34
A Sony videotape
recorder using 1/2″
tape.
Photo courtesy of Sony
Corporation of America

Figure 4.31

Figure 4.32

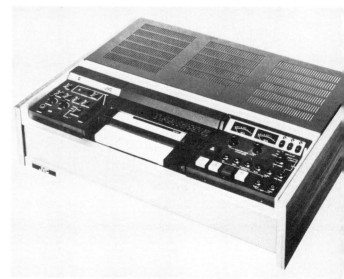

Figure 4.33

Figure 4.34

100

Since the advent of videotape, a great many features have been added to the recorders. Tapes can be edited, pictures can be shown in slow motion or still frame, and instant replay is possible. This latter is accomplished with an entirely different kind of video recorder, a **disc** machine. On a disc, any part of the recording can be accessed without the delay involved in rewinding a tape. Many of the discs used for sports instant replay store only 30 seconds of material at a time.

Editing has become ultra-sophisticated during the past decade, with many programs being taped in bits and pieces and put together later in the editing room. In fact, some programs are now videotaped using "film techniques." In other words, one or two cameras will be used to record a program, but each camera will be connected directly to a tape recorder instead of going through a switcher, in much the same way that a film camera is connected to its reels of film. One camera may take continuous close-ups and another continuous long shots and then the two tapes will be edited with the final result being an intermingling of close-ups and long shots.

Editing is also used for special effects, correction of mistakes, and commercials. Assume that a station wants to make a promotional spot for an already taped series which it will be airing soon. For this spot, it wants to show excerpts from two of the programs. To edit these two bits together, a technician would load a blank tape on one recorder and the tape from program 1 on another recorder. He or she would then **dub** the pertinent material, perhaps 10 seconds of a chase scene, onto the blank tape, would remove the tape of program 1 from the tape recorder and replace it with program 2, and would dub the appropriate material, perhaps a 10-second love scene. However, this is not as simple as it sounds. Sync impulses must be coordinated so that the picture will not roll when the new one appears; both machines must be up to speed when the edit occurs; the timings must be carefully calculated so that the edit takes place at precisely the right

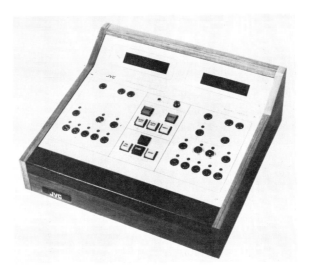

Figure 4.35
A free-standing electronic videotape editor.
Photo courtesy of JVC Industries Company

instant both in terms of audio and video; and there must be an efficient way to find the material wanted on each tape so that valuable technician and machine time is not wasted.

In order to solve these problems, editing equipment has been invented which involves elaborate timers that measure to 1/60th of a second, computer systems to calculate and remember where edits should be made, audio beep systems, and visual frame markers. One presently used editing system first dubs all material to less expensive 1/2″ work tapes. Editing is then planned on these tapes and programmed through a computer-generated dry run to make sure all will produce the desired result. Special markings are placed on the 1/2″ tapes, some visually and some on the audio cue track. These markings are then "remembered" by the computer system, which applies the editing plans to the 2″ master tapes to produce a finished product. Using the 1/2″ tapes saves wear and tear on the masters because all of the back and forth maneuvering necessary to determine the exact edit points is accomplished on the 1/2″ tapes.[11]

Tape editing continues to increase in precision and decrease in expense and time required. This is enabling more people in all facets of television to turn out polished, edited productions.

Portable Video Equipment

Truly portable television equipment has been developed in the 1970s. Equipment was transported from the studio to remote locations as early as the 1930s, but such equipment was usually contained in two trucks and so was a far cry from today's miniaturized equipment.

During the 1950s and 1960s, portable equipment could be contained in one truck. When the truck reached its destination, the cameras were wheeled to the area to be televised and the truck—which contained a switcher, monitors, videotape recorders, audio board, and other gear—was used as a control room. Many station remote trucks contained generators so they could supply their own power. These trucks were used for all types of remote production but were particularly valuable for live or taped sports coverage and for taping events to be shown during news broadcasts.

In the '70s, small portable cameras attached to backpack videotape recorders were developed to the degree that one person could carry both camera and recorder. A person carrying this equipment had much easier access to fast-breaking news than a crew in a truck, so this compact gear was initially used for news gathering and hence was called "electronic news gathering" (ENG) equipment. It wasn't long, however, until many uses were found for this equipment in various areas of informational and entertainment programming. This was coupled with improvements in videotape editing which allowed bits and pieces taped with ENG equipment to be edited into a unified whole.

Remote trucks are still used, however, particularly for complicated shows where switching must occur during the broadcast. It would be impossible, for example, to broadcast a live football game using only cameras connected directly to VTRs since some camera selection or switching must occur as the event is taking place. In this case, large studio-type cameras are

Figure 4.36
A remote truck
Photo courtesy of Video
Innovations, Inc.

Figure 4.37
ENG equipment
Photo courtesy of Ampex
Corporation

Figure 4.38
NBC's master control
Photo courtesy of NBC

located at fixed positions and the maneuverable ENG-type cameras roam the area, but all are connected to a central switching system.[12]

Master Control

Master control of a TV station is usually a bustling place. Often it contains all the videotape recorders so that they can be assigned various duties as the need demands. Recorders may be taping studio productions, rolling pre-taped excerpts into a studio production, airing a program, airing a commercial, editing a program for later viewing, accepting a **network feed** for delayed broadcast, relaying a remote, or any of many other varied functions. No station can afford an unlimited number of videotape recorders, so they are tightly scheduled to conform to highest priority needs. It is from master control that programming fare is sent to the transmitter for airing.

Transmission

As with radio, the transmitter is the place where the information is superimposed onto a **carrier wave.** With television, audio and video are sent separately—the video signal being amplitude modulated and the audio signal being frequency modulated. The two are then joined and broadcast from the antenna.

Each station has a frequency band on which it broadcasts, as with radio. However, a television station uses a great deal more **spectrum** space than a radio station—600 times as much as an AM station. In fact, all AM and FM stations together occupy less spectrum space than four TV stations.

TV channels are placed at various points in the spectrum as follows: Channels 2 through 6 are located between 54 and 88 megahertz; channels 7 through 13 are located between 174 and 216 megahertz. Channels 2 through 13 are in the range designated very high frequency, **VHF**, and 14 through 83 are in ultra high frequency, **UHF.** Both types of waves follow a direct, **line-**

of-sight path, but UHF signals are more easily cut off by buildings and hills and are also more rapidly absorbed by the atmosphere so require higher power.

A television station's signal travels from the station antenna to home antennas. Frequently, though, TV signals must be sent farther than a broadcast signal will reach. Ordinary telephone wire cannot handle TV signals because of the immense amount of information they contain, so a special type of cable called **coaxial cable** has been developed and used when a signal is to be sent a fairly short distance.

For longer distances, such as network programs that must span the entire country, **microwave** relay is used. Microwaves are very short waves much higher in the spectrum than radio or TV station allocations. They are line-of-sight, so relay stations must be in sight of each other and not more than about thirty miles apart. Each microwave station across the nation is mounted on a tower or tall building and receives, amplifies, and **retransmits** the signal to the next station in the chain.

Another system of relay distribution involves satellites. A signal can be sent from a **ground station** to a satellite and from there to ground stations around the world. Three satellites can cover most of the earth's surface. Again, the frequencies used for satellite communication are much higher than those of TV stations. Theoretically, satellites could broadcast directly to homes, but the ground equipment needed to receive these signals is quite complicated and expensive.[13]

Figure 4.39
A microwave tower
Photo courtesy of A.T.&T. Long Lines

At the present time, home TV receivers are not capable of receiving information from satellites or microwave systems. Many are incorporated within a cable TV system and receive pictures via coaxial cable, but generally homes receive signals from conventional broadcast stations.

Reception

The process of displaying the picture on the face of the TV set is essentially the reverse of its creation. The **modulated** impulses are received by the home antenna, **demodulated,** and sent to the TV picture tube and speaker. Audio is, of course, produced very similarly to audio in a radio receiver. Video is produced by electron guns similar to those in cameras.

These guns are located in the rear of the **cathode ray** or picture tube. If the set is black and white, it holds a single gun; if it is color, it contains three guns, one for reds, one for blues, and one for greens. The incoming video signal causes this gun (or guns) to scan the **phosphor** screen in the same manner as the camera gun—left to right, top to bottom, odd lines then even lines—so that it creates what the eye perceives as a moving picture. When the beam strikes the phosphor layer, it causes this layer to glow according to the intensity of the signal, thus creating blacks, grays, whites, and various shades and combinations of color. A television picture is actually small glowing dots blinking very rapidly in various degrees of brilliance.[14]

The picture then has come full circle from the original image picked up by an electronic beam and turned into electronic impulses to electronic impulses turned into a visual representation of the original image.

Figure 4.40
The satellite Intelsat IV
in a test chamber.
Photo courtesy of Com-
munications Satellite Corporation

Figure 4.41
A satellite earth station
in Puerto Rico.
Photo courtesy of Com-
munications Satellite Corporation

Chapter 4

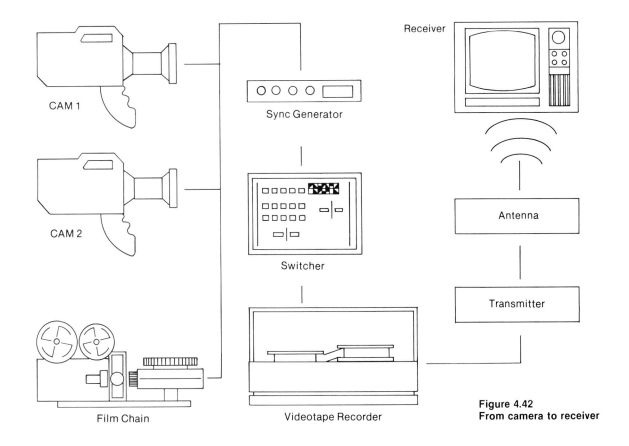

CAM 1

CAM 2

Sync Generator

Switcher

Film Chain

Videotape Recorder

Receiver

Antenna

Transmitter

Figure 4.42
From camera to receiver

The audio portion of TV is similar to radio, while the video portion involves a complex process whereby images picked up by a camera are transmitted through the air to home receivers.

A TV camera generally consists of a *viewfinder, lens,* and *electronic system* which converts an *image* to *electrical impulses* by having a *beam* from an *electron gun scan* a *target* which has received charges from a *photosensitive surface.* Sometimes visual material originates on *35 mm, 16 mm,* or *super 8 mm* film and is projected through a *film chain* to a *vidicon* camera. A *sync generator* is needed to assure that all cameras in a system are scanning in sync. *Monitors* display various pictures which the director can choose. A *switcher* is used to place the proper picture on the air by a *"take," "dissolve,"* or *special effect.* TV studios should have high ceilings, a *grid,* curtains, a large door, air conditioning, camera and mike *outlets,* a *loudspeaker* system, and an *intercom* system. Videotape recorders are *quadraplex* or *helical* and place *audio, video,* and *control* information on tapes. More and more televising is being done remotely by using trucks or *ENG* equipment. *Master control* is the nerve center of a station and usually contains the *VTRs.* TV transmission often employs *coaxial cable, microwaves,* and/or *satellites.* A TV receiver essentially reverses the camera process to cause a *phosphor* layer to glow dot by dot.

Summary

5 The Escape Machine
Entertainment Programming

Watching television is like making love—not a reasoning activity.

Television Quarterly

Cartoon copyrighted by *Broadcasting* magazine

"That's the last place I expected to see violence on TV . . . Romper Room!"

Approximately 75 percent of broadcasting fare is devoted to the cause of entertainment,[1] with shows encompassing music, drama, situation comedy, variety, specials, movies, talk, games, soap operas, children's programs, and hybrids of various entertainment forms.[2] These shows reap their criticism for being inane, violent, boring, insulting, cheap looking, sexually explicit, slapstick, uncultured, obscene, bigoted, exploitive, and unreal. Yet, the average American spends more time "enjoying" them than any other form of leisure activity.[3]

Music

Music is the mainstay of radio, with the disc jockeys' chatter and platters filling the airwaves. A listener who is patient enough can uncover just about every form of music imaginable, but the hit **"top 40"** songs dominate.

Because of the impact radio airings have on record sales, large stations are usually deluged with promotional copies of records so do not need to pay for them. Smaller stations do buy records, but often at reduced rates. All stations, however, do have to pay for the right to air the music through arrangements with ASCAP (American Society of Composers, Authors, and Publishers), BMI (Broadcast Music, Inc.), and SESAC (Society of European Stage Artists and Composers). These are **music licensing** organizations which collect fees from stations based on a formula that includes various factors such as the station's gross income and the amount of music it airs. An all-news radio station pays a small rate just so it can air jingles and station-break music. A TV station pays more for local program theme music and occasional local music specials. A d.j.-oriented radio station pays even more if it has a healthy income.

These three licensers distribute the money to composers and publishers in accordance with the number of times the music has been aired. The top hits, naturally, gain the largest percentage of income. In order to determine which pieces are aired most frequently, each licensing organization surveys a representative sample of stations periodically and asks them for their **play lists.** The information from these lists of records and number of times they were broadcast is then fed into a computer, which determines the pay rate for each piece.

Obviously, one licensing agency rather than three could handle this chore, but three have evolved, mainly to ensure proper competitive practices. In the early days of radio only ASCAP existed. When it raised its fees to an extent that radio stations considered exorbitant, the broadcasters countered by forming BMI. The idea behind BMI was that stations would then play only music by composers and publishers who were represented by BMI, circumventing the need for ASCAP. However, ASCAP ceased its high rate demands, and most stations now play music represented by both ASCAP and BMI and pay licensing fees to both. ASCAP and BMI try to woo successful composers through special financially rewarding contract provisions, so musicians profit from having the two competitive organizations. SESAC represents primarily foreign and religious music; therefore, many stations do not bother to contract with it although in recent years it has captured a few hits and is now seen more frequently on station expense records.

Figure 5.1
A solitary disc jockey
spinning records. Music
is the mainstay of radio,
and perhaps vice versa.
Photo courtesy of KXLU,
Los Angeles

It should be emphasized that ASCAP, BMI, and SESAC pay only composers and publishers, not performers and record companies. Exposure on radio is assumed to increase record demand, from which both performers and record companies profit. However, record companies and performers generally do not feel this way, and sometimes performers compose their own music in order to reap the benefit of the licensing payments. Licensing agencies are nonprofit by nature, so after paying

Figure 5.2
Setup for a local TV music show. This program, called "Times and Tempos," featured nationally known drummer Shelly Manne and local California musicians. Photo courtesy of KOCE-TV, Huntington Beach, California. The various KOCE-TV pictures used throughout this book were photographed by Nraprendra Prasad, Aida Loussararian, Libby Jennings, and George Katzenberger.

expenses connected with surveys, computer calculations, and personnel, they distribute the rest of the money. The largest number of employees are field representatives who handle problems related to collections and also monitor stations which do not subscribe to make sure they are not playing music represented by their licensing organization. The organizations collect not only from broadcasting stations but also from bars, restaurants, concert halls and other concerns which use music as part of their profit motive. This method of payment from stations to musicians, although it has flaws, is far less trouble than each station attempting to contract in some way for each record it wishes to air.[4]

Music as an entity by itself has only a minor role in television entertainment programming. Most shows by prominent musicians such as Andy Williams, Carol Burnett, and the Osmonds, must become variety shows in order to maintain the attention of viewers. Lawrence Welk is one of the few musicians who has been able to survive for a long period with a primary product of music. "Your Hit Parade" lasted from 1950 to 1956 but was stomped out by rock 'n' roll, and Dick Clark's "American Bandstand" has periodic revivals with teenagers. Public broadcasting regularly airs concerts of classical music. Leonard Bernstein was successful with his "Young People's Concerts," and "Voice of Firestone" maintained a small but appreciative audience from 1949 to 1963, when it was canceled because it could not deliver a large enough audience to serve as a lead-in to other network programs.

The miniscule role of classical music on both radio and TV is decried by broadcasting critics. Only about a dozen classical music stations are left on the AM band; most of the rest blast with top 40, twang with country-western, or reminisce with yesteryear's top 40. Even when classical music, or any other music for that matter, is presented on TV, the quality of TV speakers is such that the music grates on the ears of those accustomed to FM and hi-fi systems.

Overall, music has proved to be a profitable form of entertainment for radio stations and is enjoyed by millions as they drive, study, work, and play.

Drama Dramatic programs have changed greatly over the decades. Radio was replete with them until TV took over, at which time radio drama essentially disappeared. Recently radio has initiated a limited revival in an attempt to reawaken public interest and acceptance.

The TV anthology drama of the '50s ("Marty," "Patterns," "A Man Is Ten Feet Tall," "Requiem for a Heavyweight," "Killer") probed character and motivation and emphasized the complexity of life. Although these plays were popular with the public, they became less acceptable to the advertisers, who were trying to sell instant solutions to problems through a new pill, toothpaste, deodorant, or coffee. The sometimes depressing drawn-out relationships and problems of the dramas were inconsistent with advertiser philosophy and largely led to their demise by the 1960s.

What replaced them were episodic serialized dramas with set characters and problems that could be solved within thirty minutes. With series such as "Gunsmoke," "Route 66," "The Defenders," "Marcus Welby, M.D.," "Police Woman," and "The Six Million Dollar Man," plot dominated character, and adventure, excitement, tension, and resolution became key factors. Westerns, detective stories, mysteries, science fiction thrillers, and medical shows all tended to have good guys and bad guys. Although the main characters were the same week after week, they rarely seemed to profit from lessons learned on previous programs and were as pristine at the end of the episode as at the beginning. Problems of individual episodes could be solved, but never the overall motivation for the series because that would mean that the series itself would have to end.

Various forms of dramatic programs show cycles of popularity, with doctor shows being big one year, police shows dominating the next, and westerns holding the limelight a year later. Most of these forms had precursors in style and content within novels, films, and radio, where danger, panic, pursuit, and climax had held sway for years. However television called for changes in concept, because the small screen demanded intimacy rather than spectacle, few characters rather than many, and reliance on close shots rather than long or imagination-induced shots.

The more probing type of drama has surfaced occasionally with network single presentations such as "Death of a Salesman" and "The Glass Menagerie" and public broadcasting series such as "Hollywood Television Theater" and "Visions." Dramas of longer duration became popular with the 1975 serialization of Irwin Shaw's "Rich Man, Poor Man" and the 1977 docudrama "Roots," Alex Haley's saga of his slave ancestors which was aired eight straight nights to the largest TV audience up to that time.

Most TV drama is designed for escapism rather than thought and contains predictable chase scenes and predictable plot ideas designed for high ratings. However, there are shows which attempt to deal with social and humanistic problems.[5]

One of the main problems encountered by TV writers and networks revolves around the fact that, of all forms of entertainment, drama has the greatest capacity to evoke strong and even disturbing emotional responses in its audience. For this reason TV drama is particularly susceptible to criticism and censorship within and without the industry. Examples of network or sponsor management deleting or rejecting controversial content are numerous, but probably even more numerous are outcries from pressure groups, government agencies, and the public at large.

Although presentations regarding sex, bigotry, religion, and similar topics have come under fire, the subject of violence on TV drama conjures up the hottest arguments. Violence is a phenomenon that, like heat waves, seems to recycle in a predictably unpredictable manner. A hue and cry will emerge from various segments of society followed by a TV impoundment of guns, crashing cars, knives, and fists. But to some viewers, nonviolent programming seems bland and does not draw the audience that its more violent counterpart does. So gradually the guns and knives reemerge until they are so prevalent that a hue and cry once again surfaces.

As far back as 1950 Senator Estes Kefauver posed the question before the U.S. Senate whether or not there was too much violence on TV. The first major outcry arose in 1963 after the assassination of President Kennedy. Claims were made that all the violence on TV had led to the possibility of assassination. In 1967 an antiviolence crusade led to an investigation by the Senate communications subcommittee chaired by John

Figure 5.3
Preparations for a television drama. Producer Frank O'Connor (*right*) discusses with his talent a scene from "The Man Who Came to Dinner," presented by Hallmark.
Photo courtesy of Frank O'Connor

O. Pastore. A gradual protest against violence crescendoed in 1976-77 and led to network program changes.[6]

Both quantitative and qualitative problems plague the violence debate. Measuring violence is not like measuring cups of sugar. Is pushing someone in front of a runaway cactus the same violent act as pushing someone in front of a car? Should the humorous "pie in the face" slapstick comedy be considered violent? Is it violent for one cartoon character to push another off a cliff when the one pushed soars through the air and arrives at the bottom with nothing injured but his pride? Should a heated argument be treated the same as a murder? Is it worse to sock a poor old lady than a young virile man? Should a gun fight be considered one act of violence, or should each shot of the gun be counted? Should a bona fide news item about a kidnapping be considered?

Despite all these measurement pitfalls, indices abound which attempt to tell whether violence on TV is increasing or decreasing. One of the oldest was developed by Professor George Gerbner of the University of Pennsylvania. For over ten years he has had trained observers watching one week of TV fare a year to count acts of violence according to his complicated formula. Since his count includes just about everything remotely violent, the networks take offense at his calculations, and CBS and ABC have developed their own violence indices.[7] The National Citizens' Committee for Broadcasting, somewhat with tongue in cheek, developed a "violence index" that calculated how many years each network would have to spend in jail if convicted of all the crimes it portrayed in one week—the range was from 1,063 to 1,485 years.[8]

Measurement is not the only pitfall connected with violence. The effect of TV violence on society is also debated and hard to determine. Many research projects and surveys have been conducted, the findings of which have generally been severely (perhaps even violently) challenged by both friends and foes of TV fare. Some of the results which have surfaced are as follows. (1) People who watch killings and woundings on TV show a greater immediate tendency toward aggressive behavior than do those who watch chase scenes and arguments. (2) People who watch violence on a large screen show greater tendencies toward aggressive behavior than those who watch on a small screen. (3) The inclusion of humor in a program dampens the tendency toward aggressive behavior on the part of the viewer. (4) There is little difference between news programs containing only nonviolent news and ones containing both violent and nonviolent items in terms of increased inclination toward aggression. (5) The more children identify with violent characters in a program, the greater is their inclination toward aggression. (6) There is little correlation between what children consider to be violent acts and what mothers consider violent acts. (7) People think there are more bloody scenes on TV than there actually are. (8) Four out of ten people feel that violence is harmful to the general public and to children in particular. (9) Four out of ten people say they avoid watching violent shows. (10) Hardly anyone believes that watching violence hurts him or her personally.[9]

Innumerable organizations have joined the battle to curb violence. The PTA held hearings on the issue in eight cities in 1977. The American Medical Association wrote a letter to advertisers urging them to refrain from advertising on violent programs. The National Citizens' Committee for Broadcasting distributed a list of the advertisers who most frequently advertise on violent shows. Consumers' groups have boycotted products advertised on violent programs. And even inter-industry groups such as the National Association of Broadcasters and the Screen Actors Guild have at times called for a halt to violence.

The entire violence issue tends to generate heat and may be a subject which will rear its ugly head in future decades.[10]

Situation comedy shows are perhaps the purest form of entertainment in that their aim is to make people laugh. This is not an easy task. It takes strong-penned writers and strong-willed actors and actresses to crank out humorous lines and actions week after week.

The grande dame of situation comedy is Lucille Ball, whose antics will probably live forever in reruns. Others who have made their mark in this form of programming are Robert Young in "Father Knows Best," Gertrude Berg in "The Goldbergs," Phil Silvers as "Sergeant Bilko," and Dick Van Dyke and Mary Tyler Moore, first together and then on separate shows.

The general successful format for a comedy show is the development of characters who are placed in a situation that has infinite plot possibilities, the creation of complication, the reign of confusion, and the alleviation of the confusion. The problems encountered are usually the result of misunderstanding rather than evil, and the audience can relax because it knows the problem will be solved.

The early situation comedies made an attempt to be based on believability, but the necessity to crank out programs accelerated a trend toward paper-thin characters and canned laughter. One of the mainstays became the idiotic father ruling over his patient and understanding wife and kids. The advent of "The Beverly Hillbillies" was cited as evidence of the decadence of TV and perhaps the depth of silly exaggerated situations, slapstick corny plots, and unbelievable characters.

A breakthrough in comedy series occurred with the debut of Norman Lear's "All in the Family," whose bigot lead was replete with a long list of prejudices. This series, unlike any previous comedy series, dealt with contemporary relevant social problems and even with politics, heretofore taboo for comedy series. This program and subsequent similar ones raised the status of situation comedy in the eyes of critics and the public alike.

Situation comedy still comes in for its share of criticism, though, because of too much emphasis on sex, improper portrayal of members of minorities, too slavish obedience to ratings, and outlandish financial demands of the stars. Situation comedy, like its dramatic counterpart, is criticized for making it appear that all problems can be solved in thirty minutes. This concept was particularly pursued during the '60s when the

Situation Comedy

first television-weaned generation began demanding wholesale reforms. There were those who felt that these young people had been exposed to so much TV that their view of reality was a simplistic one that believed all problems could be solved easily and quickly and did not allow for real world complexity.

But the producers of situation comedy shows are still concerned with making people happy. As Norman Lear has said, "I would hope—at least that's the intention—that people turn off these shows and feel a little better for having seen them."[11]

Variety

Variety shows are a hard act to follow—especially for the variety performers themselves. In the days of **vaudeville** a stand-up comedian, juggler, or musical group could survive years by keeping on the move and performing for new audiences in each town. Not so with television. In one prime-time hour a comedian will have exhausted his supply of jokes before an unseen audience of twenty million. Now what does he do to stave off unemployment? Because variety shows absorb jokes faster than writers can write them, and juggling acts faster than performers can learn new ones, and music faster than singers and orchestra can rehearse, very few such shows have enjoyed longevity.

The longest running variety show was Ed Sullivan's "Toast of the Town," which was seen on CBS every Sunday evening at 8:00 p.m. for sixteen years. Different talent appeared each week, with Mr. Sullivan giving straight-laced and straight-faced introductions to each. None ever accused him of being a stand-up comedian, so he did not run out of funny material, but he did know how to put together a first-rate weekly show with wide audience appeal that frequently included such coups as The Beatles and the Singing Nun.

One of the most controversial of programs was the variety show hosted by the Smothers Brothers, who rose from obscurity in the '60s to become a top-rated show in their first season. In a period of political division caused by the war in Vietnam, the Brothers leaned heavily on political satire. Constant battles raged over the censorship which the two brothers felt CBS used to stifle their creativity. Amid arguments over edited segments of programs and lawsuits, the Brothers were relieved of their show.

The list of other entertainers in the variety category is long and should include at the top such names as Jackie Gleason, Sid Caesar, Imogene Coca, Dinah Shore, the recyclable Andy Williams, Flip Wilson, Carol Burnett, Sonny and Cher, and Donny and Marie.

Variety shows are a prime user of studio time in the networks. Most of the drama and situation comedy shows are produced by independent production companies and sold to the networks, but variety shows are usually a product of the network itself. Part of the reason for this is that these programs lend themselves more easily to videotape than to the film techniques often employed for drama and situation comedies. The spontaneity of the acts can be best maintained if it can be captured by a bevy of cameras simultaneously, and rarely is there a need for a car chase or outdoor scene that cannot be taped within the confines of a studio. Variety programs are among the more expensive shows to produce because of the lavish costumes and sets as well as the highly paid talent.

Figure 5.5
Donny and Marie, from the variety show of the same name. These two members of the talented Osmond family often included other members of their family as well as a host of guests on their weekly show.
Photo courtesy of Osmond Enterprises

One criticism of variety shows is that there are too few of them and they have a sameness in that they generally revolve around singers and comedy skits, some of which are overly risque. However, most of them provide wholesome family entertainment, and they do offer variety within the television diet.[12]

Specials

Special is a word used to designate a program that is not within the regular network schedule. Frequently variety shows start and/or end as specials. A performer may be brought on to do a special and be such a hit that he or she is given a weekly berth. Or a star that has been performing for a weekly variety show and has run out of material and/or energy may "retire" to an occasional special. Many of radio's outstanding stars opt for TV specials, as also do stars whose primary medium is records, film, or the stage.

Some of the major names associated with outstanding specials are Barbra Streisand, Frank Sinatra, Bob Hope, Red Skelton, Jack Benny, Mary Martin, Ethel Merman, Fred Astaire, and Elizabeth Taylor. Broadway plays, restaged for TV, are occasional specials, as in the case of *Peter Pan, Annie Get Your Gun,* and *Kiss Me Kate.* There are also old standby specials that have lasted over the years, such as beauty pageants, holiday parades, and entertainment awards shows.

Specials are often aired in order to boost sagging ratings. The regular show scheduled to be aired at that time is canceled and the star-spangled special replaces it, usually walking away with the ratings race if the other two networks stay with their regular programming. What happens often, though, is that networks will schedule competing specials at the same time, particularly if it happens to be an important ratings week. This often leaves the viewer irritated by feast and famine.

Figure 5.6
A scene from a Bob Hope Christmas special. Bob, Peter Leeds (*center*), and Steve McQueen (*right*) televised this from the Air Force Academy in Colorado.
Photo courtesy of Peter Leeds

Specials, like variety shows, are usually produced at network facilities and are, if anything, more expensive to produce since sets and props can only be used once. However, the cost usually seems justified to the networks, for they feel they are getting more holler for the dollar.[13]

Movies

Movies on TV is another evolving area. Many of the regular drama and comedy series are produced on film, so could be considered movies for TV, but they are not generally placed in this category. All movies which are first shown in the theater and then released to TV fall into the movie category, as do films without continuing characters that are made specifically for TV.

In the early days of television, theatrical films were the mainstay of local independent stations. With a twenty-year backlog of films just sitting on the shelf, the film studios were happy for this new source of revenue. No union contract had envisioned this bonanza, so there were at first no **residuals** to be paid. But as the use of movies on TV became popular, both the **guilds** and **unions** negotiated contracts with producers calling for the payment of residuals. With costs thus greatly increased, the producers turned to the networks, which obviously had larger pockets than independent TV stations. The phenomenon of movies on TV caught hold in a big way, and by 1968 there were movies on at least one network each night of the week. Soon the twenty-year backlog of movies was depleted.

The networks, led by ABC, then began contracting for movies made especially for TV. These still are being produced in fair abundance. Many of these made-for-TV movies are low-budget, quickly produced, grade B-

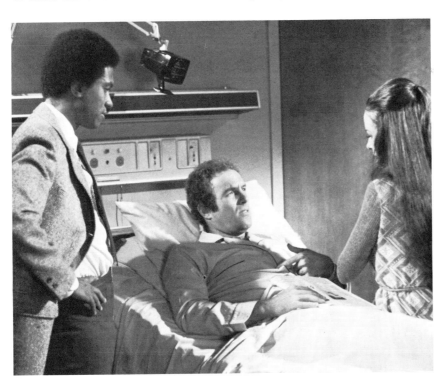

Figure 5.7
Billie Dee Williams (*left*), James Caan, and Shelley Fabares in the made-for-TV movie "Brian's Song." This 1971 movie dealt with the deep friendship of football players Gale Sayers and Brian Piccolo, ending with Brian's fatal illness. It was such a success that it was shown in theaters after being shown on TV.
Photo courtesy of Columbia Pictures Television

The Escape Machine   119

movies, but occasionally one emerges that is good enough to make the rounds at movie theaters after its TV debut.

Of course, big box office movies still find their way onto TV, but the cost per film to a network is generally in the millions. Such film contracts usually stipulate that the films cannot be shown on TV for two years after their release—to try to insure that the TV showings will not divert revenue from the movie theaters.

At present there are three categories of movies seen on local and network TV: the oldies making the rounds for the umpteenth time, the made-for-TV movies, and the two-year-old releases hitting the airwaves for the first time. Overall, movies do not account for as large a percentage of time as during the '60s but they still make their presence known.

Controversies have arisen concerning the content of some of the movies. On one hand, there are complaints that the violence and sexual material present in the movies is much too explicit and that films dealing with homosexuality, rape, prostitution, and similar subjects should be kept off TV. On the other hand, there are complaints that the movies shown on TV are so heavily censored that they are edited beyond recognition or sensibility. The need to edit them, not only for content but also for commercial interruptions, is also irritating to many viewers. The quality of many of the made-for-TV, thin-on-plot, heavy-on-action films has also received criticism. Occasional cries are heard from theater owners, who say that movies on TV hurt their business. But movies in some form or other will no doubt continue to be a staple of television.[14]

Talk Shows

Talk shows capitalize on the average person's desire to know what makes celebrities tick. The shows constantly parade names in the news past hosts or hostesses who attempt to bring out the unusual or peculiar in the guest. The late night talk shows are probably the best known, with Johnny Carson being the dean of talk show hosts. Other well known hosts through the years have included Jack Paar, Steve Allen, David Frost, Merv Griffin, and Dinah Shore.

The cost of talk shows depends primarily on the quality and demand of the guests and host. Some talk shows are virtually free for they are beset with requests from aspiring authors, dog acts, one-man bands and the like who wish to appear gratis on the program for the free publicity. Other shows pay top price to obtain "hot properties" of the show business and political worlds.

Naturally, not all guests on talk shows turn out to have scintillating personalities, so the shows are occasionally criticized for being boring. Some hosts capitalize on abrasiveness in order to get a rise out of guests, and this too is criticized. Some of the subject matter discussed on talk shows seems out of the bounds of propriety to elements of the public.

Talk shows run the gamut of network-produced, station-produced, and independent-produced. Although they have never sustained top ratings, they regularly draw consistent audiences.[15]

Figure 5.8
**Merv Griffin as host of
his talk show. Here he
is interviewing Starsky
and Hutch—David Soul
(*left*) and Paul Michael
Glaser (*right*).**
Photo courtesy of Merv
Griffin Productions

Audience participation shows have always been popular. Early radio had its quiz shows for both children and adults, and today many radio stations have call-in programs on which listeners can express their views on various subjects.

TV took over the quiz-game program idea early in its history with a 1942 simulcast on both radio and TV of "Truth or Consequences." The 1947 season saw several such shows, including "Juvenile Jury," "Break the Bank," and "Leave It To the Girls." Other notables through the early years were "Beat the Clock," "Queen for a Day," "Strike It Rich," "Stop the Music," "What's My Line?" "I've Got a Secret," "Name That Tune," and "Double or Nothing." Excitable game show hosts included Bert Parks, Dennis James, John Daly, and Ralph Edwards.

Most of these early shows had modest prizes for the winning contestants, but during the mid-50s the stakes began to increase as such programs as "The $64,000 Question," "The $100,000 Surprise," "The $64,000 Challenge," and "Twenty-One" made their debut. Of course, the 1958 quiz scandal gave the quiz-game show area a temporary blow. For a while no chance-oriented shows dared touch the airwaves, but gradually additional innocent low-stakes programs emerged, such as "The Dating Game," "Hollywood Squares," "Match Game," "The Newlywed Game," "Family Feud," "Shoot for the Stars," and "Liar's Club."

The gamut of opinion regarding game-quiz shows ranges from those who think the games are educational because of the information contained in the questions to those who think the games feed on avarice and gambling instincts and make fools of all the contestants who participate while at the same time wasting the time of those who watch.

**Audience
Participation
Shows**

The Escape Machine   121

Figure 5.9
Host Jack Narz and contestants tackling the game show "Concentration" with fun and vigor. Correctly matched prize squares yield pieces of a puzzle which serve as a clue to a saying which, in turn, enables the winning contestant to try for the car.
Photo courtesy of Goodson-Todman Productions

Game shows are among the least expensive to produce. All talent except for the host is free, the set can be used over and over, program after program, and the prizes are donated by companies in exchange for mention on the show.

The degree of commercialization inherent in these programs is often questioned. Some programs appear to be one long commercial as the merits of the various prizes are revealed. The games themselves are criticized for being inane and childish and for a sameness which seems to permeate most of them. However, many viewers compete or empathize with both winners and losers, and there is never a lack of people lined up to try their luck or skill on big time TV.

Most game shows are produced by production companies, the most notable of which is Goodson-Todman. They are generally aired during daytime hours, although a few have wedged their way into the evening hours, particularly during the early evening when local stations have control of the programming fare before the network shows start. The syndication and rerun circuits for game shows also flourish.[16]

Soap Operas

Soap operas arose during the heyday of radio and succeeded in dominating the afternoon hours with stories dealing mostly with the housewife struggling against overwhelming adversity—sick and dying children, ne'er-do-well relatives, weak husbands.

Television adopted the soaps at about the same time other programs switched from radio to the new medium. Many of the original traits were retained: each program is serialized in such a way that it entices the viewer to "tune in tomorrow"; the plot lines trail on for weeks; music is used to designate transition; very little humor is included in the dialogue, as adversity is the common thread; soap opera characters, unlike their evening dramatic and comedy counterparts, live with their mistakes and are constantly affected by events which happened on previous programs; they also grow old and have children who grow older.

What has changed from the old radio soap opera days is the program content. Although there are still some housewives struggling against overwhelming adversity, the emphasis is now much more on male-female sexual relationships. Infidelity, premarital sex, artificial insemination, mate swapping, impotence, incest, venereal disease, frigidity, and abortion have been added to nervous breakdowns, sudden surgery, and missing wills. Subject matter is often tried first on soap operas to determine if it will be fit for evening hours. In fact, versions of soap operas have moved to nighttime on occasion, with such programs as "Peyton Place," "Mary Hartman, Mary Hartman," and "Soap."

Sometimes soaps are produced by the networks and sometimes they are produced by independent companies. They are among the most profitable TV ventures, for production is cheap and ads are plentiful. The same paper-thin scenery is used day after day, and since soaps are a world of words and close-ups with very little action, hardly anything is consumed or destroyed. Soap opera stars are paid much less than prime-time talent, a fact which they often decry, since they work at a much more hectic pace. While the nighttime stars are working to crank out one program a week, the talent of the soaps must produce one program a day. Understandably, this leads to some production sloppiness where blown lines are left intact in the aired product. Such incidents are remarkably rare, however, if one considers the time pressures under which the actors are performing.

Figure 5.10
A mother-son scene from "The Young and the Restless." Jeanne Cooper (*left*) plays Kay Chancellor and Beau Kayser plays Brock Reynolds.
Photo courtesy of Columbia Pictures Television

Soap opera regulars, if they can take the pace, can be fairly sure of long-term employment, for many soaps have survived while there have been dozens of turnovers in the prime-time area. Among some of the longest running are "Search for Tomorrow," "The Guiding Light," "Days of Our Lives," "General Hospital," "Love of Life," "All My Children," and "The Young and the Restless."

For the most part, soaps are put in a second-class stepchild position by critics and the broadcasting industry alike—mainly because of their air time, cheap production, and maudlin story lines. However, there are those who feel that from a literary point of view soaps are superior to nighttime programs. Relieved of the chore of solving all problems in thirty minutes, the soap writers can explore character and probe motivation and in that way provide viewers with more realistic, albeit exaggerated, situations.

It was assumed for many years that only middle-class housewives and shut-ins comprised the audience for soap operas. But in recent years many "closet case fans" have emerged including baseball players, nighttime TV stars, politicians, and many men and women who work nights. In fact, a small weekly magazine, *Soap Opera Digest,* which prints capsule plots of each soap on the air that week, has been very successful marketing its product to those who must miss an episode of their favorite but do not want to fall behind the story line.

So, despite the fact that Heather has been jilted at the altar by John, who has discovered that his father is impotent and he is the love-child of an affair between his mother and Dr. Winton, thus making him a first cousin of Sharon, who is in love with Tom, the husband of Tricia, who has just had an abortion in order to cover up her affair with Richard while Tom was out of the country searching for his child of a previous affair who had been put up for adoption—soap operas will no doubt continue.[17]

Children's Programs

Never could Sky King, The Lone Ranger, The Green Hornet, Howdy Doody, Kukla, or Mickey Mouse envision the furor which has arisen over children's programming.

The air time for children's programming has not changed since the 1930s. Saturday morning and after-school hours were the domain of the young in early radio days and still are today. However, radio, by virtue of its aural nature, emphasized imagination and sound effects, whereas TV emphasizes sight and action.

TV networks started children's programming early with an emphasis on puppets, such as Howdy Doody and his real-life friends Clarabell the Clown and Buffalo Bob, and Kukla and Ollie with their real-life friend Fran Allison. The longest running kiddie show on network has been "Captain Kangaroo," which has been on CBS Monday through Friday since 1955 and still enjoys great success with children, plus the approval of parents.

Children's programming was important on early local TV stations too. Most programs consisted of a host or hostess whose main job was to introduce cartoons and sell commercial products. During the '60s, networks too overwhelmingly adopted the likes of "Felix the Cat," "The Roadrunner," "The Flintstones," "Daffy Duck," "Popeye," "Heckle and Jeckle," "Jabber Jaw," "Tom and Jerry," and "The Jetsons"—and therein began the controversy.

For many years these cartoons dominated Saturday morning TV, making for one of the most profitable areas of network programming. The cartoons were relatively inexpensive to produce, and advertisers had learned that small fry can be very persuasive in convincing their parents to buy certain cereals, candies, and toys. The result was profits in the neighborhood of $16 million per network just from Saturday morning TV.

But gradually the bubble burst. Parents who managed to awaken for a cup of coffee by 7:00 a.m. Saturday noticed the boom-bang violent noneducative content of the shows along with the obviously cheap mouth-open/mouth-close animation techniques. A group of Boston housewives became upset enough to form an organization called Action for Children's Television (ACT), which began demanding changes in children's programs and commercials. Scholastic Aptitude Test scores started going down as the first television generation sat to take the tests. Researchers realized that children under five were watching 23.5 hours of TV a week and that by the time they graduated from high school they would have spent 15,000 hours before the tube. Government agencies began to discover that those nutritious cereals weren't so nutritious after all. The Children's Television Workshop developed "Sesame Street," and its successful airing on public TV proved that education and entertainment could mix.

Figure 5.11
The successful children's program "Sesame Street." Luis, played by Emileo Delgado, has a few words with Big Bird.
Photo courtesy of © Children's Television Workshop

All of this led to a long, hard look at children's TV. Research studies were commissioned, which sometimes conflicted in results but overall seemed to indicate that changes did need to be made in children's TV. Studies have shown that children do learn reading and vocabulary from TV but that the children who watch TV the most are the ones who do poorly in reading in school. Watching TV generally cuts down on book reading, but certain TV programs which refer to books actually increase book reading. Children three and under understand very little of what they watch on TV, and yet they will sit mesmerized before the set. Nine out of ten children between the ages of seven and eleven understand social messages when these are present in programs. Some studies show that children predisposed to violence are more apt to increase violent behavior after seeing it on TV than are so-called normal children; other studies show exactly the opposite. It has been determined that watching TV is an activity involving mainly the brain's right hemisphere, which contains nonverbal, nonlogical, visual and spatial components of thought; from this it is theorized that watching TV may hamper development of verbal and logical abilities. One study conducted on highly creative children found that their creativity dropped significantly after three weeks of intensive viewing.[18]

Led and cajoled by ACT, a number of other organizations began demanding reforms in children's TV. They took note of the fact that there were some fine children's programs on TV, such as "The Wonderful World of Disney," "Lassie," and "Mr. Rogers' Neighborhood," but they were after changes in the cartoons, slapstick comedy, and deceptive commercials. In 1974 the FCC issued guidelines for children's television. They stated, among other things, that stations would be expected to present a reasonable number of children's programs to educate and inform, not simply entertain, and that broadcasters should use imaginative and exciting ways to further a child's understanding of areas such as history, science, literature, the environment, drama, music, fine arts, human relations, other cultures and languages, and basic skills such as reading and mathematics. ACT was also largely responsible for getting the National Association of Broadcasters to include in its 1973 code an amendment reducing the number of commercial minutes in children's programs from 16 per hour to 12; this was later further reduced to 9 1/2 minutes.

By the mid-70s most stations and networks had acquiesced, at least in part, to the reform demands. Programs with names such as "Kids' News Conference," "What's It All About?," "Let's Get Growing," "Something Else," "The Big Blue Marble," "Villa Allegre," and "Friends" hit the airwaves. Many of these shows attempt to teach both information and social values. Advertising is more low-keyed than before.

But problems still remain. Reform groups feel that much of what has been done is tokenism and that some of the most popular programs still contain too much violence and slapstick. Broadcast executives eye their sinking children's TV profits with fear. With commercial time cut and production costs soaring for these more creatively produced programs, network profits from them are now only $2 million and falling. The basic problem of the quantity of TV watched by small children has been barely dented. Broadcasters and psychologists alike point out that children, like adults, need entertainment as well as education and that, given a choice, they will still choose "The Flintstones" over "Young People's News" in the same way that adults choose to watch an old movie rather than a sterling documentary.[19] Broadcasters maintain, and probably rightly so, that this is a problem which is beyond their realm. Parents are the ones who must control the set, and as long as parents use it as a cheap baby-sitter, children's viewing hours will not be curtailed and their habits will not be changed.

Summary

Three-fourths of radio and TV programming is entertainment, primarily *music, drama, situation comedy, variety, specials, movies, talk shows, games, soap operas,* and *children's programs.*

Music is most important on radio, but both radio and TV stations must pay fees to *ASCAP, BMI,* and *SESAC* in order to air music. Drama has changed greatly over the years from *anthology* drama of the '50s to *series* drama, with various themes dominating for short periods. Great bursts of controversy arise concerning the *violence* on dramatic shows. Trend-setting situation comedies include "I Love Lucy," "The Beverly Hillbillies," and "All in the Family," with the primary aim of this type of program being to create laughter. Variety shows are hard to maintain because they are so demanding of talent; one of the longest running was "Toast of the Town." Specials are not within the regular network schedules and are often used to boost sagging ratings; generally they are expensive to produce. Movies began on early local TV, then spread to the networks in such abundance that the backlog supply was largely exhausted, and *movies made especially for TV* became popular. Talk shows generally feature provocative hosts or hostesses talking with celebrities. Audience participation shows were abundant on early radio and early TV, then disappeared after the *quiz scandals* to reemerge primarily as daytime game shows. Soap operas are also broadcast primarily during the day and feature serialized stories with increasingly adult content. Children's programs have been highly criticized, particularly by *ACT,* for their violent, slapstick, poorly produced, noneducative content and recently have been undergoing reforms.

6 A Mirror of the World?
Informational Programming

Television has learned to amuse well; to inform up to a point; to instruct up to a nearer point; to inspire rarely. The great literature, the great art, the great thoughts of past and present make only guest appearances. This can change.

Eric Sevareid, in his final commentary

Cartoon copyrighted by *Broadcasting* magazine

" 'No news is good news' may have been your mother's motto, but it doesn't apply around here."

As more and more people turn to broadcasting as their major source of information about what is happening in the world,[1] the programming that generally falls within the news and public affairs area[2] develops more social significance. However, it is often an uphill fight for those committed to informational programming to see their program ideas reach fruition. Not only is such material likely to envelop a station or network in controversy, it is also generally expensive to produce.

Informational programming is not watched by nearly as many people as entertainment programming and hence cannot sell high-priced ads—in fact, sometimes cannot sell ads at all. Since public service programming generally costs three times as much as entertainment programming per **rating** point, it must depend on the profits of its more glamorous sisters to support it.

News

The Americans declared their independence on July 4, 1776, but it wasn't until many months later that the British learned of the declaration. In the War of 1812, the Battle of New Orleans was fought weeks after the war was actually over, for word had not gotten to New Orleans. Today the slightest little rift between countries can be reported, analyzed, and even blown out of proportion within a matter of minutes. More people today are aware of what is happening in the world than ever before, and it is basically radio and television which can take credit for this. The greatly increased worldwide communication of the past few decades is also painless to the viewer or listener. A mere flick of a dial can bring one up to date on current events, or at least ensure that no great disaster has occurred.

In times of disaster it is the electronic media which become the main source of help and information—directing victims to sheltered areas, seeking help from outside sources, communicating vital health and safety information, and calming jangled nerves. The advent of portable equipment for both radio and TV allows news to be reported rapidly and allows for first-hand reports through actuality interviews.

Gathering news is generally a complex process, with stations and networks depending on a variety of sources for news. Basic sources are the news **wire services,** AP (Associated Press) and UPI (United Press International), which furnish major national and international stories collected by a bevy of reporters stationed at strategic points around the world. These reporters have regular **beats,** such as government offices and police stations, which they cover to gather news, and of course they zero in on unusual events which occur in their territories.

The stories they gather are sent, usually by wire or phone, to central AP or UPI offices where they are assembled and often rewritten. Then the stories are typed into a special machine and sent by **teletype** to stations and networks where they are printed out on a machine specially made to receive the signals. Stations and networks, along with other subscribers such as newspapers and magazines, pay the wire services subscription fees for both machine and news.

**Figure 6.1
A radio station's UPI
machine.**
Photo courtesy of KXLU,
Los Angeles

**Figure 6.2
A television news
cameraman covering an
accident story.**
Photo courtesy of KOCE,
Huntington Beach,
California

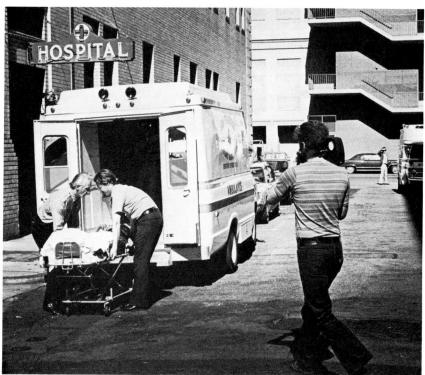

Stations in major markets have their own wire services to help them keep track of local news events, and television stations sometimes augment the news wire service with UNIFAX, a news wirephoto service which furnishes pictures of events reported on the wires. The use made of this wire service news is largely up to the organization which receives it. Some radio stations simply rip the news from the wire service machines each half hour or hour and read the writing on the yellow paper verbatim over the air. Other stations select news items and rewrite them in ways they feel will appeal to their audiences.

At other times the wire service copy may simply serve as a lead to a story that a broadcasting organization, particularly a network, wishes to cover itself. News, therefore, is also collected by the networks or stations themselves. Networks have correspondents stationed throughout the nation and around the world at places where news is likely to occur. If a big news story happens to break in Edinburgh, Scotland, the correspondent stationed in London might be sent to cover it. Radio prides itself on being first and fastest because a single correspondent can cover the story. With television, a crew must accompany the reporter in order to film or tape the visual elements. Once the news is "**in the can,**" a complicated system of airplanes, helicopters, and telephone lines delivers it to network news headquarters.

Usually radio and TV stations do not have reporters assigned permanently to any particular place but rather on a day-to-day basis at places where major stories are likely to break. For example, Monday morning a reporter may cover a picket line, in the afternoon a city council meeting, and the next day a local fair, a ribbon-cutting ceremony, and a protest march. Of course, some reporters are kept on deck or are pulled from routine assignments to cover fast-breaking stories such as fires, murders, and robberies. Some radio stations collect news primarily by telephone by calling police stations, fire stations, and other likely sources to gather information. They can tape the people involved in the news over specially equipped phones and include these taped statements within the broadcast.

Stations and networks also utilize newspapers like the *New York Times, Washington Post,* and *Wall Street Journal* and information called in by listeners as sources of news. Obviously stations depend on networks for news, but to a lesser degree networks depend on stations. If a big fire breaks out in Wichita and the network's nearest correspondent is in Chicago, the network may utilize film footage and information gathered by its affiliated station in Wichita.[3]

While correspondents and reporters are gathering worldwide, nationwide, and local news, news writers and producers remain at network and station facilities reading wire service and newspaper stories, viewing filmed stories prepared in advance, drafting opening and closing copy, ordering phone and satellite lines, rewriting stories, and making decisions regarding the value and importance of the various news items so that the top stories reach the audience. There are almost always more stories being fed in than can be used in broadcast time.

With radio, this selection process is ongoing because news is broadcast many times throughout the day. Radio networks generally feed stories to their stations as they occur and also provide several news programs throughout the day. Thus the news producer of a station **affiliated** with the Mutual network might decide that the 8:00 a.m. news should consist of five minutes of Mutual news as broadcast by the network; a story on a fire in Delhi which is on the UPI wire but which Mutual did not cover; an update of the condition of a hospitalized city official which the producer obtained himself by phoning the hospital; the report on a liquor store robbery gathered by one of the station's reporters and including a brief interview with the victim; a report of a murder received from the local wire service; and the weather as received over the phone from the weather bureau. For the 9:00 a.m. news, the stories of the Delhi fire and liquor store robbery may be included again slightly rewritten, accompanied by two stories excerpted from the 8:00 Mutual news broadcast, a report phoned in live by a station reporter covering a school board meeting, and updates on the hospitalized official and the weather.

Television news has a more defined countdown since the major effort is devoted to the evening news. Throughout the day news producers at station and network facilities are assessing the multitude of news items received to decide which twenty or thirty will be included on the evening news. Communication transpires frequently between producers and correspondents— "There's a hurricane warning in Florida. Should I cover it?" "Yes, forget the Georgia peanut contest and get there right away."/ "Forget the vice-president's luncheon and cover the French embassy picketing. Try to film an interview with the ambassador."/ "The prime minister just resigned and I lined up an interview with his son. Can you give me five minutes of the show?" "Not five, but maybe two."/ "Got the interview with the ambassador." "Send it down the line. We'll use it."/ "The Senate just confirmed the president's nominee for the FAA. Should I try to interview him?" "Don't bother, we have too much other news. Get over to the Secretary of State's news conference."/ "Rewrite this story on the earthquake prediction so it only takes thirty seconds. We have to have time for the ambassador's interview." This type of decision exchange goes on at TV networks and local stations until close to air time when the "final" stories are collected, written, and timed. But last minute changes can still occur, for the news is sometimes changed even as it is being aired—"Just got a damage report on the Florida hurricane. Substitute that for the earthquake prediction."[4]

Presentation of news is another important area. For radio, the days of the dulcet tones are gone; news is generally read by disc jockeys or reporters. However, stations do vary both content and presentation of news broadcasts in relation to their audience. The ABC radio network has four different services (american contemporary, information, FM, and entertainment) to suit the format and style of different affiliates. Since TV news is actually a money-maker for local stations, they are particularly anxious to lead the ratings and therefore attempt to find newscasters who will appeal to

Figure 6.3
A television news setup
for covering a local
meeting for which there
was plenty of advance
notice.
Photo courtesy of KOCE,
Huntington Beach, California

viewers. The networks hope to establish trustworthy, congenial newscasters who will maintain a loyal audience.[5]

Special elements in addition to the daily news fall under the jurisdiction of the news department. Some of these—such as presidential news confer-ences, Congressional hearings, and astronaut launchings—can be predicted in advance so that adequate preparations can be made. Others—such as riots, earthquakes, and assassinations—must be handled as well as possible by reporters and crews who happen to be close at hand covering other assignments. Often stations interrupt their regular programming to broadcast these special events.

Broadcast journalism is proud of its service function. As early as 1932 New York area stations conducted around-the-clock operations to cover the Lindbergh kidnapping case. In 1937 radio provided the main communica-tions for the flood-stricken Ohio and Mississippi Valleys, and in 1938 it did likewise for southern California. Many times since then radio has acted as the main communication conduit during disaster. Radio and TV have brought the world the stories of the Hindenberg explosion, the declaration of World War II, the invasion of Normandy, the surrender of Germany, presidential news conferences, deaths of presidents, political conventions, the visit by Soviet Premier Khrushchev, space orbits, blackouts, riots, President Nixon's trip to China, Watergate hearings, and most other major events. For most of this coverage, broadcasting has been praised for its decorum and service to the nation.

And yet, broadcast journalism is one of the most criticized institutions in our country today. It is blasted by government officials, liberals, conservatives, middle Americans, and members of its own fraternity.

The criticism centers primarily on what broadcast news presents and how it presents it. It is generally conceded that radio and TV bring important events to their audiences, but many critics claim that those media have not yet learned how to make the prime issues of our time understandable. The broadcast media are good at covering wars and shootings but inadequate in dealing with subjects such as inflation, unemployment, and economics. Television, particularly, is obsessed with visual stories and sometimes may down play an important story simply on the grounds that there are no exciting visuals to accompany it. Both radio and TV are good at reaction stories that cover results of events past, but they all too rarely cover major issues that will affect the future. Both media must, of necessity, provide capsulized news. The thirty-minute evening network news programs, when all commercials have been added, boil down to twenty-two minutes of news—approximately the equivalent of three newspaper columns. Obviously, this cannot be the day's news in depth, explained and analyzed. And yet, the news that is chosen is often trivial. Greater coverage is given to the president eating a taco than to his views on the nation's economy. If a station or network has achieved a scoop, it will dwell on that story even though the story itself is relatively unimportant.

The "happy news" chatter among newscasters regarding their weekend plans and their day's activities wastes precious news minutes. In fact, the whole emphasis on newscasters is sharply criticized. At some stations it appears that the major factor is not what news is presented but who is presenting it, so that anchorpersons, sportscasters, weather forecasters are chosen not for their ability to deal with news but for their good looks, pleasing smiles, rapport, and general show biz personalities. If all this still does not muster top ratings, consultants are hired to glamorize the news further by designing eye-catching sets, writing dramatic opening stories, and perhaps firing one "glamour cast" to hire better-looking, bigger-smiling, show biz personalities. All of this tends to bring more attention to the form of the news than to its substance and makes news broadcasting a trendy, fad-filled operation—talkative weathermen this month, abrasive snarling ones next month, and beautiful females the month after. There are even those cynics who hope that perhaps the next trend in local news will be news. They maintain that the intensive competition for ratings causes news, like entertainment programming, to be directed to the mass audience and programmed to provide maximum income with minimum thought given to raising the cultural level.

Radio and TV stations are accused of creating or altering news by their very presence; certainly it was true, especially in the 1960s, that "spontaneous" protests began when the TV remote truck arrived and stopped as it pulled away. Many people feel that violence in the news is overplayed and sometimes appears on the news as violence for violence's sake. Similarly, TV is sometimes held responsible for the evil effects of publicity given to violent lawbreakers. Murderers, kidnappers, skyjackers, and the like receive so much news coverage that they are boosted almost to a celebrity status. At times broadcasters have been encouraged simply to ignore such crimes in the hope that the perpetrators will stop when they see that no one is paying attention to them. Tasteless coverage of the victims of violent acts is also a problem. There are reporters who attempt and often succeed in interviewing people who have just seen a close relative killed or have just lost all their possessions in a disastrous flood. The interview answers given by victims under these circumstances are often not rational and further sensationalize the news event. In their sensationalizing, news media are often accused of judging the guilt of a suspect before he or she has had a chance to receive a court trial. "Trial by the press" is a frequently used ploy of lawyers who think that their clients do not have a chance because of adverse radio and TV publicity. In many types of stories, broadcast journalists accentuate the negative—unemployment going up is reported more frequently and with more fervor than unemployment going down. Because of the speed of radio in particular, news is sometimes reported inaccurately just so it can be first. With the advent of the **minicams,** pictures of events can be shown before the reporter has had time to gather the facts.

Another hue and cry which some individuals have raised, particularly against network broadcast journalism, is that it is a biased product of the "liberal eastern establishment." The criticisms range from charges of outright purposeful distortion of facts to editorializing by exclusion. Politicians and businessmen who are often targets of news darts are particularly prone to cry bias. They bemoan not only what is reported but how it is reported and what is left out of what is reported. For a period of time there was particular objection to the "instant analysis" by network commentators immediately after presidential speeches and other major political pronouncements.[6]

Some criticisms of the news process come from those working within the news industry itself. They are constantly pleading for more air time for news so that they can correct the flaws brought about by the short capsulized treatments. But their cries have been unheeded mainly because the network entertainment programming supplies more dollars. Some reporters criticize their co-workers for lacking an inquisitive edge that prevents them from undertaking serious investigative reporting. They point out that Watergate was uncovered by newspaper reporters, with radio and TV causing barely a ripple. They fear that their cohorts are overcome by a press conference mentality and report only stories handed to them by press agents. Those who do engage in investigative reporting sometimes have to battle government committees to keep their sources confidential.[7]

Reporters also resent the fact that they are rarely allowed to cover events within courtrooms. This is not because of any law but because of an American Bar Association (ABA) rule known as canon 35, which states that no broadcasting or photography should be allowed in the courts. Most judges have voluntarily complied with the ABA canon on the grounds that broadcast coverage would be disruptive to the court proceedings because of the equipment setup and because of possible show-off performances by people involved with the court case who want publicity. However, with radio equipment consisting of little more than a tape recorder and alligator clips, and with miniature TV cameras that can operate in available light, the equipment setup problem is greatly mitigated. As a result, a few judges have allowed broadcast reporters into the courtroom, with generally favorable results.

Criticism is bound to be a permanent irritant to broadcast journalism. For one thing, most of the critics are members of the upper-middle class who don't get most of their information from television and are therefore not part of the mass audience to which broadcasting is attempting to relate. Also, broadcasters, despite their power, can in no way control world affairs, and much of the criticism of broadcast news is closely tied to news events themselves. Perhaps most important, broadcast news is caught squarely between the two purposes of the broadcast industry. The first, as stated in the 1934 Communications Act, is to serve the public interest, convenience, and necessity. The second, as stated by broadcasting's management and stockholders, is to make a profit.[8]

Documentaries

Documentaries are designed to give in-depth coverage of subjects that can be dealt with only superficially in news programs. They require extensive research and expensive production.

Radio documentaries were not uncommon on early radio and occasionally are produced today by radio networks or local stations. Local TV stations also produce documentaries of local issues, but the best known and most controversial documentaries of today are produced by the TV networks. Ed Murrow and Fred Friendly invented the TV news documentary in the early 1950s with "See It Now," which presented bold, strong programs on controversial issues. The series was cancelled in 1958 because it lost its sponsor, its production costs increased, the network was tired of fighting the problems it caused, and Murrow and Friendly got tired of fighting the network. Since then documentaries have gone through phases of varying emphasis, depending largely on the degree to which the networks are pressured into presenting public interest programming. Sometimes documentaries appear only during the Sunday afternoon "intellectual ghetto" hours, and sometimes they enter prime time.

Documentaries are usually divided into "hard" and "soft" based on their subject matter. The "hard" documentaries, by far the more controversial, are usually the result of investigative research of current topics. Examples include "The Selling of the Pentagon," "Harvest of Shame," and "The KKK." "Soft" documentaries give depth information regarding less controversial subject matter, such as "The Louvre," "The White House Tour with Jacqueline Kennedy," and "Lyndon Johnson's Texas." Instantaneous documentaries occur when a well known statesman dies or a riot breaks out. Others involve planning and preparation begun long before the air date.

Documentaries cause innumerable problems for the networks with respect to both expense and content. If a dramatic program set in the 1800s employs words not in the vernacular of the time, it may be criticized, but with none of the severity that occurs when a public official is misquoted in an unfavorable light. Documentaries also have traditionally low ratings so

Figure 6.4
An NBC film crew in
India gathering material
for a documentary on
the world food shortage
called "And Who Shall
Feed This World?"
Photo courtesy of NBC

barely recover their costs. Stations are required by law to give varying points of view for all controversial issues; hence, if some individual or group can prove its point of view was not fairly represented, it can demand free time to present information. Obviously, this adds further cost. A network frequently finds itself in difficulty after airing a controversial documentary. In some instances network executives have been called to testify before Congressional committees regarding the content of shows. Documentaries have been known to cause internal dissension within the network family. Producers argue with network executives who want to censor material, and stations within the affiliate family sometimes refuse to carry a program because of the subject matter.

Documentaries are subject to some of the same criticisms that attach to news—a liberal bias, an emphasis on the negative, editorializing by exclusion, unnecessary sensationalizing. In addition they are criticized for appearing too infrequently on the program schedule and for being aired essentially all at one time—during "black weeks," the weeks when ratings are not taken. Network executives, of course, counter these arguments with dollars and cents and an appeal that perhaps what is needed in this country is less advocacy and less material that will divide the nation into fragmented groups.[9]

Editorials

Radio and TV stations are not mandated to editorialize, and many choose not to. This is due in part to fear of the controversies which may ensue and in part to the difficulty of complying with the strings attached to editorializing. Whenever a station does editorialize about a controversial subject, it must make an attempt to find opposing points of view. If it is going to endorse a political candidate, it must notify all of the candidate's opponents in advance. If it is going to say something negative about a

**Figure 6.5
Editorial Director Paul
Dallas of KABC, Los
Angeles, researching
material for a station
editorial.**
Photo courtesy of Paul
Dallas

person, it must give the person advance notice and an opportunity to reply. Small stations generally do not have the staff to handle these requirements and sometimes do not even have the staff to write the original editorials.

Ideas for editorials are usually conceived by a station management team and then presented by a member of top management. Some editorial material comes from networks or syndicators in the form of commentaries. Occasionally these consist of a series of programs designed to present a spectrum of opinion on a particular subject and in that way cover all points of view which might be considered in the controversy. Commentaries are personal viewpoints, while editorials express the viewpoint of the station management.

Editorializing is itself a controversial subject. Some critics feel that since the number of frequencies is limited, radio and TV stations should not be allowed to editorialize at all because editorializing gives these broadcasters an unfair advantage over others in the community. Others feel that editorializing is guaranteed by the first amendment and that, in fact, broadcasters who do not editorialize are shirking their public duty. Broadcasters often argue that they should not need to seek out opposing points of view because newspapers do not need to do this for their editorials. Methods of editorializing are also debated. If editorials are presented within news programs, they may be mistaken as news, but if they are presented at other times, they can be a jarring interruption to program continuity.

Editorials that are aired are often criticized for their blandness. The subjects covered—such as public parks, automobile safety, and school crosswalks—are often so noncontroversial as to be hardly worth the status of editorial. Presentations are generally dry and nonvisual and are considered boring if they last very long. As a result, editorials are generally the least glamorous of radio and TV programming elements.[10]

Sports

Sports programming is a hybrid of information and entertainment programs. It involves actuality material broadcast from the scene generally in real time and of real events, but most people watch it for entertainment purposes.

Sports and broadcasting enjoy an unprecedented economic relationship. The Dempsey-Carpentier boxing match gave early radio its first big boost, and early TV had its wrestling matches. In recent years sports have become almost totally dependent on television networks' largess. In 1960 CBS brought rights to the winter Olympics for $50,000; for 1980 NBC negotiated $100 million for the Russian Olympics. Rights to televise NCAA football jumped from $3.1 million in 1962 to $12 million in 1970. During approximately the same period, network payments for major league baseball rose from $3.2 million to $16.6 million, for AFL-NFL football from $7.6 million to $34.7 million, and for professional golf from $150,000 to $3 million.[11] Without these television fees, salaries of athletes would probably be cut in half and many teams could not remain solvent. However, sports also benefit broadcasting by being a huge audience drawing card. At times in excess of 60 million people settle themselves in front of their TV sets to watch a highly rated sports game. Ads for such an event can run over $300,000 per minute.[12]

This marriage for money is not always a happy one, however, for some sports suffer from overexposure and broadcasters suffer from overpayment. One of the first sports to be negatively affected by broadcasting was boxing, which was one of the most popular events on early television, with fights virtually every night of the week. But while everyone was watching boxing on TV, no one was supporting club boxing, so about 250 of the 300 small boxing clubs in the U.S. closed up shop between 1952 and 1959. The result was no fresh talent and a boxing lethargy that was not restored until the coming of Muhammed Ali. Baseball was affected, too, for while baseball club owners were greedily grabbing every golden nugget TV offered for the rights to their games, attendance at these games fell 32 percent between 1948 and 1953. Similarly, attendance at college football games dropped almost three million between 1949 and 1953. Eventually teams began restricting the number of games telecast, but it is a long hard pull to coax the sports fan back into the stadium.

Meanwhile the networks were caught in their own upward spiral. Each year networks bid on the various sports events, with broadcasting rights going to the highest bidder. Since sports broadcasts are a plum desired by affiliates and sponsors, networks are eager to get broadcasting rights and often find themselves bidding outlandish prices. The amount of intrigue, one-upmanship, suspense, and avarice that goes into the bidding sometimes outdoes the drama of the most exciting sports events themselves.[13]

To some extent the sports world has created a voracious monster which it expects the broadcasting world to feed. And the monster does eat, consuming most of Saturday, most of Sunday and occasional evenings but without apparently satiating the super spectator's appetite for sports.

Aside from paying for the broadcast rights, networks must pay production and transmission costs, making sports broadcasting one of the most expensive forms of programming stations or networks can undertake. Obviously, the sport cannot be brought to the TV station's studio, so the studio must go to the sport. It is not uncommon for a network to gather twenty cameras, thirty microphones, ten remote trucks, and one hundred technicians to cover a sporting event. Even local stations find it expensive and complicated to cover the local high school football games.

The actual broadcast of a game can be ulcer gulch for those involved. The announcer must attempt to be clever and articulate about plays while listening through a headphone to instructions being barked at him by the producer and director—"After this play remember to do the promo for next week's game and mention the sponsor's name. Tell the audience that Governor Flupadup is here because we want to get a shot of him."—and trying to comprehend messages being passed under his nose—"That was Schlocks's fourth time for hitting three triples in twelve games. Attendance is 27,982. Station break time." The director must choose the best picture from among the twenty or so displayed before him, usually with the help of assistant directors watching particular monitors, e.g., one assistant director watching only the isolated **instant replay** cameras and another watching for interesting crowd scenes. The camera operators must exercise common sense between following the action and following the director.

Sports is big business, not only with the TV networks, but also with independent TV stations and radio stations. There is such a high degree of emphasis on sports that independent networks have been formed to handle the overflow of sports programs which the networks cannot manage. Hughes Sports Network and Television Sports Network have prospered as competition to CBS, NBC, and ABC sports by selling commercial time nationally and paying independent stations to carry the shows. Independent TV stations could not compete with network operations and found themselves out of sports until the advent of the independent networks. Throughout the country, local radio and TV stations manage to have their own sports programs, usually through the local college or university, which often requires full coverage of events with limited appeal in addition to the football and basketball games. Obviously, these local events do not reap the financial rewards of big league sports, but they are often among the most popular programming fare of the stations.

There are those who feel that the sports world has sold its soul to television. It is true that there were two kick-offs during the 1967 Super Bowl because NBC was in the middle of a commercial during the first kick-off. It is true that the 1968 heavyweight title elimination fight was scheduled at the ridiculous boxing hour of 2:30 p.m. in order to fit ABC's programming needs. But it is increasingly difficult for people in sports to register moral indignation, for sports itself is largely show biz, and the athletes seem to have adjusted their adrenalin to fit the needs of the television world. Besides, it seems a small price to pay when the result is that millions of spectators can enjoy the game who otherwise would not have had the opportunity.[14]

Another selling-of-the-soul aspect of the sports-broadcasting relationship involves the frequent commercials which feature top athletes. Ara Parseghian plugs cars, Billy Martin extols light beer, and Joe Namath tells the virtues of panty hose. Part of the controversy revolves around whether or not sports stars should stoop to peddling, but the money earned for such work is certainly intriguing. Large sports salaries plus money from commercials have turned many athletes into company presidents and entrepreneurs. Another aspect of the controversy revolves around the probable duping of the American public when they see sports idols extol the virtues of a product without, in most instances, any expertise or credentials in the area. In order to limit this phenomenon somewhat, athletes and others engaged in testimonials must now at least use the product they advertise. Sorry about the panty hose, Joe![15]

Even if athletes do not perform for commercials, TV still tends to require that they be actors as well as athletes. The number of interviews they must submit to is enough to make the shyest ones glib, and those who want to keep their private lives private find they are hounded just like movie stars.

Probably the most controversial of all aspects of sports and broadcasting involves blackouts. Sports owners realized that they were cutting their own throats when they televised all their games. As a result, a bill was passed by Congress that states that no professional football, baseball, basketball, or hockey games can be broadcast within ninety miles of the origination point unless the game is sold out seventy-two hours in

Figure 6.6
A cameraman from Channel 11 in New York covering a Yankees' baseball game.
Photo courtesy of RCA

advance of game time. The biggest critics of this policy are the fans who are deprived of seeing the game on TV.[16]

There are occasional outcries from the sports world against the TV equipment, mainly that it is a nuisance to have it on the field and that it occasionally blocks spectators' views. Some feel that the instant replay equipment is too sophisticated, out-umpiring umpires and out-refereeing referees.

Whatever the problems are with the sports-broadcasting relationship, it is not likely that either party will initiate divorce proceedings. Broadcasters like what sports does to the profit and loss sheet, and so many sports organizations have built their entire budgets around television that if television were to withdraw the money, the sports structure would collapse. The fans would not approve of that.

Educational Programming

Educational programming is not something America counts as a pride and joy. Most countries exceed the U.S. in both quantity and quality of such programs. In many countries both radio and television stations broadcast direct instructional material to school children as a matter of policy, and although this is done by many American public TV stations, it is generally not utilized to its fullest extent. College credit and adult education courses are programmed in various sections of the country over both public and commercial stations, and a number of universities allow credit for a network series of courses called, "Sunrise Semester." Commercial and public TV also broadcast programs about the activities of the schools as well as self-help, how-to programs.

Generally, educational programming is on commerical stations at the least popular times—6:00 a.m. weekdays or Sunday mornings. The reason is that educational programming is rarely sponsored because, even if it were on at a better time, it would not draw a significant audience. Part of this is due to the nature of the subject matter of the programs and part is due to the fact that these programs are generally low-budget so do not include all the production elements of more expensive entertainment shows.

In many instances TV stations do not produce educational shows themselves but purchase them from syndicators or allow local school districts to handle content and basic production using the facilities and crew of the TV station. Very little is done educationally on radio even though many of the concepts of educational TV programs could be presented quite adequately by audio only.[17]

Religious Programming

Religious programming is another stepchild usually broadcast during the early morning or Sunday morning time slots on both radio and TV. This form of programming is generally quite inexpensive for the stations because it is supplied, on film or tape, free of charge by the various religious sects. Some religious organizations even buy air time for their programs, in that way becoming essentially their own sponsors. More often stations give the air time for these programs, and some stations even pay the production costs involved in broadcasting a service from a local church.

Figure 6.7
Preparations for the filming of an educational program titled "Becoming Me." The program, aimed at the primary grade school level, dealt with self-identity.
Photo courtesy of Great Plains National Instructional Television Library

Figure 6.8
An episode from the syndicated religion series "Insight" called "For the Love of Annie." Regular host, Father Ellwood E. Kieser (*right*) interacts with John Astin and Patty Duke Astin.
Photo courtesy of Paulist Productions

One of the earliest "hits" on network TV was Bishop Fulton J. Sheen, who preached each Tuesday night opposite Milton Berle's "Texaco Star Theater" and who once commented that he and Berle worked for the same sponsor—Sky Chief. Other network TV religious programs have included "Lamp Unto My Feet," "The Eternal Light," and "Frontiers of Faith." Generally religious programming is within the domain of the local station, however.

There are also religious radio and TV stations which broadcast nothing but religious programming. Some of these are devoted to the teachings of one faith and are completely underwritten by that faith, while others sell time to groups of different faiths which wish to present programming.

One problem that confronts commercial stations airing religious programs falls in the area of **fairness.** Theoretically, a station is supposed to allow all major religious sects within its community to present their views. In reality, it is difficult to accomplish this, particularly in a metropolitan area where many religions exist.[18]

Public Affairs

Public affairs programming is a general term for informational programming that does not fall into other categories. Primarily, it consists of interview, discussion, and on-site programs that deal with issues of concern to the citizenry. Some long-running network programs like "Meet the Press" and "Face the Nation" have featured prominent names in the news being interviewed (or grilled) by top journalists.

Most public affairs programs, however, are local productions dealing with community problems and are very important at license renewal time. All stations are licensed by the Federal Communications Commission to serve in the public "interest, convenience, and necessity," which has been interpreted, in part, to mean the airing of programs dealing with issues that concern the listening or viewing audience. Under the present license renewal processes, stations must survey the leaders of their community in order to ascertain the major problems of the area and then develop programming to deal with those issues. Stations generally do this but often try to skimp on

Figure 6.9
A genesis of public affairs material. KFI radio's Jim Todd (*right*) interviews James F. Collins, who won first and second class of a holstein heifer class at the local county fair.
Photo courtesy of KFI, Los Angeles

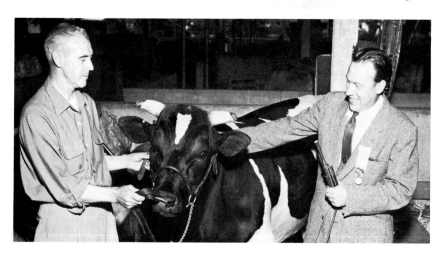

the actual production of these programs because costs generally cannot be recouped through commercials.

Although stations are criticized by the public for their lack of good public affairs programming, they find that when they do air quality material, very few people watch, hence making that programming an unattractive buy for advertisers.

These programs, like the more detailed documentaries, also raise fairness issues, and frequently a station finds itself needing to give time and facilities to a group whose point of view was not represented on a public affairs program dealing with a controversial topic.

Finding adequate issues and program participants is generally not a problem faced by stations since all communities seem to have adequate spokespeople with opinions to air. There are many instances where public affairs radio or TV programs have been instrumental in helping to correct injustices or problems within the community, thus constituting a worthwhile public service. But, like religious and educational programs, they are plagued with poor air times, low ratings, low budgets, and generally uninterested station managers.[19]

Sometimes all of a station manager's other problems seem dwarfed upon entering the area of political broadcasting. The biggest problems come during the years when there are major elections. It is then that political candidates fill the airwaves in their attempts to become elected or reelected. According to **Section 315** of the Communications Act, stations must give **equal time** to all political candidates running for the same office. Although this may sound delightfully simple, it is actually a very complex subject. If the president is running for reelection and delivers a routine Labor Day speech over radio and TV, must his opponents be given equal time? If an ad is sold to a candidate for the Republican Party, must one also be sold to a candidate for the Restoration Party? If one candidate for senator appears on a **syndicated** talk show, must all stations which carry that show allow equal time to all other candidates opposing him? If a TV station airs some old movies starring an ex-movie star candidate, must the station give equal time to the opposition candidates? If a station editorially endorses one candidate, must it allow all other candidates to reply?

The answer to all the above questions is a qualified yes—qualified because somewhere within the reams of material published to help broadcasters wade through Section 315 ramifications there are probably exceptions to exceptions under particular circumstances that can occur for each of these situations. Section 315 has been amended several times and, for one thing, no longer requires that stations give equal time for material presented on bona fide news broadcasts. Therefore, if the president's Labor Day address were on the six o'clock evening news, it would not be subject to equal time. Section 315 has also been temporarily waived so that debates between Republican and Democratic presidential candidates can take place, but generally the law requires broadcasters to treat all candidates equally, regardless of their party or present occupation. This applies whether the air

Politics

time is given away or sold. If a station of its own accord endorses a candidate for mayor in a two-minute editorial, then all opposing candidates would have to be given free two-minute blocks of time to reply. If a candidate for supervisor buys a thirty-second commercial, then all other candidates must be sold similar commercial time if they request it. Offhand, it appears that this would please stations, but in reality it does not since, by law, political candidates must be sold spots at bargain rates. Stations must often refuse ads from regular, high-paying advertisers in order to fit in all the political ads.

Some stations have attempted to avoid pitfalls of Section 315 by broadcasting absolutely nothing political during election campaign time, but they have found that this is difficult to do. What's more, it does not endear them to the FCC, politicians, or their community because it represents a shirking of public service. Each election season broadcasters try to do the best they can with Section 315, but there are always new situations arising, some of which wind up being decided in the courts—sometimes in ways that further muddy the waters.

There have been cries to eliminate the equal time provisions altogether so that broadcasters would have the same freedom of choice as newspapers. This is staunchly opposed by the smaller minority parties and the nonincumbent candidates on the grounds that the incumbents could perpetuate themselves by getting an overabundance of coverage and that stations could influence elections to suit their biases.[20]

Other issues than equal time also arise at election times. One is the overriding role of broadcasting in the election process. Television particularly has become the most potent force a candidate has at his disposal, especially one running for a national office. No whistle-stop campaign can get a face and views in front of as many people as can one television commercial. But there are those who complain that in order for a candidate to win an election, he or she must project as a TV personality, and that maybe the country should not be run only by the glib and the glamorous. Candidates must rely on their public relations firms and media advisors more than on their political views and philosophies.[21]

Broadcasting's coverage of political events is also criticized for giving too much emphasis to frilly baby-kissing events and too little to the issues that divide the candidates. Most of the spots that stations sell to potential office holders are thirty seconds long—hardly time enough to tell how one would run major aspects of the government. There are also complaints that too much money is spent on broadcast advertising, making running for office a game for the rich. Devious methods used for obtaining campaign money have led to some public financing of presidential campaigns and other reforms, but it still is extremely expensive to seek office, and television time is one of the greatest expenses.[22]

Coverage of political conventions is also a thorny topic, for network coverage of the Republican and Democratic nominating conventions has changed the political structure. In some ways this has been an advantage, for the delegates now tend more to business than to partying since they

know they are under a watchful eye. But because the conventions are on TV, they have become show business, with major actions being programmed for **prime time** and with contrived suspense building so viewers won't flip the dial to a cop show. The actual cost to the networks of covering a convention is in the neighborhood of $3 million, and this has led them to pool resources.[23]

Coverage of election results, whether they be national, statewide, or local, also offers controversies. No longer do networks predict the outcome of the elections before the polls close, but they still do make predictions which are fallible. The networks and the wire services share the cost of operating a cooperative agency, News Election Services (NES), which feeds them the results of ballot-counting. NES has reporters at each of the key precincts who call vote results to a centralized computer as soon as they are available. The computer analyzes this information in relation to past results for each precinct and, although it does not actually predict, it passes to the networks and wire services analyzed information about the voting. Each network and wire service then makes its own prediction decision. Sometimes the predicting is wrong or the computer has not been fed all the necessary information to churn out accurate data. Of course, both networks and stations also have reporters stationed at various key points to provide on-the-scene reports.[24]

Between election campaigns, politics is still evident in broadcasting as the media air press conferences and intermural political disputes that may arise between election years. The press tries not to come too close to the

Figure 6.10
Setup for a political broadcast. Local candidates are invited to the station to present views and answer questions posed by reporters.
Photo courtesy of KOCE-TV, Huntington Beach, California

politicians it covers, but there have been complaints that broadcasters do have their political darlings and are in a position to foster the careers of those they like.

Despite its imperfections, broadcasting brings to the people more information about candidates than they could gain by themselves while at the same time it simplifies the campaigning process for the candidates.

Summary

Informational programming, which includes *news, documentaries, editorials, sports, educational programming, religious programming, public affairs,* and *politics* can create for stations and networks controversy, expense, prestige, and goodwill.

News gathering is a complicated process involving *wire services, network correspondents, station reporters,* newspapers, and the public at large. Broadcast journalism is praised for its coverage of special events but criticized for oversimplifying, oversensationalizing, overvisualizing, over-glamorizing, overpublicizing law breakers, creating news by its presence, interviewing tastelessly, and biasing the news. Documentaries are generally classified as "*hard*" or "*soft*" and cause external and internal dissension. Editorializing can place stations in a "damned if you do, damned if you don't" situation involving controversy, public service, and free air time for opposing views. A unique financial relationship has evolved between sports and broadcasting that has led to changes in the games, commercial *testimonials* by sports stars, and *blackouts.* Educational programming, while aired frequently on public broadcasting, is generally relegated to undesirable times on commercial TV and is virtually nonexistent on commercial radio. Most religious programming is handled by local stations, and there are stations which program only religious material. Public affairs programs generally serve community interests and often deal with controversial topics. Political broadcasting is affected by *Section 315* of the Communications Act and is also criticized for being too potent a force in politics and for emphasizing nonimportant political elements.

7 Time on Our Hands
Programming Decisions

Imitation is the sincerest form of television.

Fred Allen, performer

Cartoon copyrighted by *Broadcasting* magazine

"I like the hand-shaking, but I keep running into soreheads whose favorite TV program I've pre-empted."

Radio and television stations are as individual as people in their handling of programming. However, for purposes of simplification, programming techniques will be broken down into the processes undertaken by the different kinds of broadcast entities as follows: an **independent** radio station; a network-**owned** or **-affiliated** radio station; a radio network; an independent TV station; a network-owned or -affiliated TV station; and a TV network.

To understand how radio programming is developed, it is best to look at a newly licensed small independent station faced with the need for something to fill its air time. Generally a management team will decide what type of material the station will air. In some small stations this "team" may consist of one person. In larger stations it may be the general manager, program manager, sales manager, business manager, and chief engineer. Inputs from all are necessary to determine whether the costs of the programming decided upon can legitimately be borne by the revenue which the station will generate.

Independent Radio Stations

Radio station programming decisions revolve around two main elements—**format** and special features. Some of the overall formats used by radio stations include agricultural programming, soul music, beautiful music, classical music, contemporary music, country-western, ethnic programming, golden oldies, jazz, middle-of-the-road music, news, progressive rock, public affairs, religion, music by request, rhythm and blues, rock, talk shows, and top-40 hits.[1]

Some of the special features stations may include programming for the blind, children's programs, comedy, live concerts, boating reports, drama, editorials, farm reports, government meetings, homemaking advice, personality interviews, public discussions, local special events, and local sports.[2]

Many factors affect these format and feature decisions. One consideration is the programming already available in the station's listening area. For example, an overall format of country-western music may be decided upon because no other station in town offers that type of music. However, if there are only a few country-western music fans in the local area, this format will probably not be adequate for drawing an audience. Therefore, the composition of the listening audience is another important factor. A rural audience will probably be more interested in frequent detailed weather reports than will a city audience. The interests of the community and the interests of the station management can also affect programming. If the town has a popular football team, the station might choose to broadcast football games.

Once the general format and features are decided upon, it becomes the program manager's responsibility to execute this programming. Since most radio stations opt for some type of music format to constitute the bulk of their programming, the program manager must find disc jockeys whose talents fit the station format. For example, rock music disc jockeys must be capable of fast, lively chatter, while a classical music host must be more

Figure 7.1
A disc jockey show
from an independent
top-40 radio station.
Photo courtesy of KHJ,
Los Angeles

subdued and capable of pronouncing foreign works. For an audience call-in show the on-the-air talent must have good rapport with people.

The program manager must also begin building a station record library. This is usually just a matter of making sure the station is on the right mailing lists. Since record companies are eager to have their selections aired, sometimes the program manager finds he must fend off salespeople wanting to give him records they want him to plug.

The special features must be handled by the program manager as the need dictates. If local college news is to be aired, a communication system for obtaining the news must be set up. If public affairs discussions are to be held, participants must be contacted and coordinated. If a local fair is to be covered, the details for a remote coverage must be cleared. If an editorial is to be aired, people and organizations with opposing viewpoints must be notified. If city council meetings are to be covered, arrangements must be made with the proper government officials.

News demands particular attention at many radio stations. Those with an all-news format devote most of their energies to this area. Generally they will combine network news, **wire service** news, and news stories obtained by their own local reporters out in the field. They take care to write and rewrite and update stories in order to present them in as interesting a form as possible.

A station with less emphasis on news might subscribe to a wire service and augment this with a small news department of several people. These people will search out stories as best they can, given their limited numbers and, in most instances, limited resources. Once they have gathered local information, they will write the stories and will probably also be in charge of rewriting or editing wire service stories. In a station where news has minimal emphasis, the entire news "department" may consist of a UPI or AP machine from which the announcer rips and reads.

Most of the programming of a small independent radio station is produced locally. There are music suppliers who produce large reels of taped music used mainly by automated stations, and there are a few **syndicators** who supply feature-type programs, documentaries, religious programs, and jingles. Generally, though, music is selected and introduced by a disc jockey operating from a radio station. News, sports, editorials, and public service programs originate from the studio or a local remote location.

Most of the country's 7,000 commercial radio stations are independent; i.e., they do not have formal association with NBC, CBS, ABC, or Mutual.[3] Some stations are network-owned, which means that a network organization has financial ownership of the station and supplies some programming. Other stations are affiliated with networks. In this case, the station receives programming from the network but the network has no financial control over the station.

Since no organization can own more than seven AM and seven FM stations, the number of owned stations is very limited. Usually only one station per listening area is affiliated with each network. The rest of the stations are independent, the management that owns them generating their program content.

In reality, there is very little programming difference between independent radio stations and affiliated or owned stations. The owned and affiliated ones are often larger, more powerful, more influential stations and hence have more employees. The general manager and the program manager's job are subdivided into such positions as news producer, sports producer, and public affairs producer. However, like the independents, the stations must select a format and produce programs.

Network-Owned or -Affiliated Radio Stations

Figure 7.2
Recreation of an old radio drama by a station long affiliated with NBC.
Photo courtesy of KFI, Los Angeles

Figure 7.3
Lowell Thomas, no doubt network radio's longest lasting personality. Thomas began in 1929 with one of the earliest programs, called "Headline Hunters," and remained on the radio regularly until after his 80th birthday. For many years he preceded "Amos 'n' Andy" with the news, prompting him to say of himself, "Here is the bird that everyone heard while they were waiting to hear 'Amos' 'n' Andy.'"
Picture courtesy of Lowell Thomas

Radio Networks

Radio networks have changed greatly over the years. During the 1930s and 1940s they supplied most of the popular programming of the time—soap operas, children's programs, drama, comedy. When this programming moved over to television, the radio networks became basically news services.

Each network has reporters throughout the world and supplies its affiliates with up-to-date news. The networks broadcast news periodically throughout the day, and stations merely tap into the network feed and **retransmit** the news the network is broadcasting. The networks also provide some special feature programs and recently have attempted a limited revival of radio drama.

The method of payment for this programming varies from station to station. Generally, the network secures ads for its news and then pays large-market affiliates a token amount for airing the news or features while smaller-market stations usually do not receive reimbursement for the airing and sometimes have to pay line charges to the nearest market. Sometimes the stations secure local ads to insert in the news.

The development of TV programming can also be understood by looking at a newly licensed independent station faced with the need for something to fill its air time. As with radio, the program manager is only one member of a team that determines which programs the station will air. Here too, others are needed to decide whether the costs can be covered by the income and still leave a reasonable profit margin for the investors. TV stations do not generally have a specific format as such, although they may emphasize certain types of programming, such as sports, movies, or foreign language programming.

Since most TV stations are on the air over 100 hours a week, the program department has a large chore. It must not only develop programs which will attract an audience from within its signal range, but it must acquire rights to air products which are preproduced and syndicated throughout the country.

Some of the material which independent stations can air comes from program syndicators who distribute and sometimes produce programs. Motion picture companies are one source of material. They package a number of theatrical pictures and sell license rights to stations on a yearly basis with no limit to the number of air dates used. Usually these packages contain 25 percent good titles, and the remaining are either mediocre or just plain bad. To determine the value of a given package, the program department must examine the pictures offered and decide the suitable air time for each, the number of runs for which an audience can be successfully generated and which features cannot be aired at all.

Motion picture companies also offer packages of two to five excellent titles that have been aired on the network and therefore can reasonably be expected to attract many people who have either not seen them or wish to see them again. This type of package is more expensive and offers fewer rerun possibilities.

Old network programs are usually the greatest source of program material for independent stations. They are sold through syndication companies, not by the networks directly. All three networks program motion pictures for TV, and after they are aired on the network, they are available to local stations in packages similar to theatrical products. Again, larger packages contain some less than spectacular titles. Many of the best TV features are shelved by networks for play only once yearly, which limits the material available for independent stations.

The syndicators also offer packages of episodes of continuing ex-network series in the half-hour, one-hour, ninety-minute, and two-hour range. These are usually the most profitable product offered to local stations. Where the network aired the series on a once-a-week basis, the local station usually offers it on a **strip** of Monday-through-Friday schedule in a time period selected because of viewer interest and availability. The series package is offered on a yearly license with no limit on reruns by the station. Some of the series that are on—and on—and on—the rerun circuit are "I Love Lucy," "Gilligan's Island," "I Dream of Jeannie," and "Star Trek."

Still another source of programs is the independent syndicator who has acquired TV rights to productions of small theatrical film companies, independent TV producers, foreign film companies, and foreign television stations either government or privately operated. They offer packages of movie titles, specials covering yearly events, and dramatic programs not usually seen on U.S. networks. Some examples are Shakespearian drama, world cup soccer, and rugby.

Several independent networks offer live sports events such as golf, football, basketball, and soccer, and one offers special dramatic and variety programs and several beauty contests. Usually the independent network will sell ads for the program and offer it to the station with all the ads included. This means that the station cannot generate its own revenue when it airs the program, so the network will pay the station to air the program. Sometimes even under this arrangement the special network will leave several commercial open spots in the program for the station to sell. This sweetens the pie.

Programs are also available directly from independent television production companies. For example, the Merv Griffin Company has been the syndicator of his show along with several game shows offered for a price based on the market value of the shows or simply what the market will bear.

Religious programs are available sometimes free and sometimes for purchase, depending on the policy set by the station's management. In order to control the type of religious programming, some stations accept only nonpaid material. Once they sell religious time to any group, they must sell it to any other such group who can pay for air time. Sometimes this leads to requests from offbeat religious groups that the station does not wish to allow on its airwaves.

Wire services and independent news bureaus offer news programs to stations for a fee.

So much for outside sources. While they will fill many hours of air time, no TV station can be really profitable unless it produces some of its own programs. How does one start to develop programs? This can be answered by looking back to the program manager who started all of this and following the steps he or she takes.

To assist in putting together local programs, the program manager normally hires an executive producer for the station. This person will have a successful track record in developing and producing programs. When the program manager has decided on the number of hours to be locally produced, he or she will, in concert with the general manager and sales manager, allocate funds for the productions needed.

The executive producer then must find several experienced people to act as producers for news, sports, entertainment, and public service programming. In smaller stations one producer will wear several hats. The best sources of experienced people to become producers are those with whom the executive producer has worked in the past and those from local stations in the area. Through observation and recommendation, the executive producer will be able to choose people who are ready to move up to a more responsible post and those who have reached a dead-end at their present positions.

In the news area, the executive producer and producer must select the on-air talent which they feel will draw the greatest audience by being different enough from other local talent, and they must acquire field reporters, camera people, and sound technicians to handle local news.

The news producer must act as or hire an assignment editor to assure complete coverage of news events with an eye to economy. The news producer must also develop a format for presenting the news in the most interesting and informative manner possible. This involves working with the station's art department to design distinctive sets and graphics as a means of attracting larger audiences. When a team is operative, the news producer must constantly evaluate performance and recommend changes which will improve ratings.

An additional assignment of the news producer may be sports programming. He or she must survey the community for interest in professional and school team activities and develop shows around these interests. If no local team sport will generate enough audience, an option is to produce sports interview programs which feature local coaches and sports personalities along with professionals who might be in town for other reasons. The biggest problem is competing with the top sports events in the country which the networks offer.

The news producer might also be head of public affairs programming, being constantly aware of community news happenings. Elected officials and candidates for office who can discuss community problems are good sources for this type of program. Citizens airing opinions about upcoming legislation as it will affect the community are another good source.

In the news area also falls the station's editorial policy, which is usually set by the general manager in committee with sales, business, program, and news departments. Station editorials are discussed and approved by this group, then turned over to the legal department, which evaluates the terminology from the standpoint of possible legal actions. As with radio, the station is obligated to present all sides of issues which it airs, so the news producer must contact people and organizations which are likely to oppose the editorial in order to allow them to prepare rebuttals.

Another area of program concern is entertainment programs produced by the station. The producer and executive producer must develop program ideas which will attract the local audience away from network programs. This is no easy chore. A local station typically has a very small budget and limited access to talent. Sometimes variety shows or dramas will be produced, and some stations feature dance shows, usually hosted by a popular local disc jockey who brings in well known musical personalities and groups to **lip sync** currently popular recordings while young people dance in the studio. A man or woman hosting a children's program that featured cartoons was a popular source of local television programs for many years. They now tend to feature more live action.

Religious, instructional, and other public service programs are selected

**Figure 7.4
Bruce Fitzpatrick
presenting part of an
astronomy series called
"Surveying the Uni-
verse," produced at an
independent TV station.**
Photo courtesy of Bruce
Fitzpatrick

and produced to fulfill the license requirement while serving the community which constitutes the audience.[4]

Unlike radio, there is in TV a great deal of difference between independent stations and affiliated or owned stations. Legally the difference is the same. A network has financial and programming control over its owned stations, simply supplies programs to its affiliates, and has no formal relationship with independents. However, since there are only about 700 commercial TV stations compared with about 7,000 commercial radio stations, the percentage of owned or affiliated TV stations is much greater than in radio. There are only about 100 independent TV stations in the country.[5]

Networks are allowed to own five **VHF** and two **UHF** stations. All three networks try to take advantage of this and own stations, particularly VHF ones, to the allowable limit in as many of the larger markets as possible. Networks also try to affiliate with stations in as many markets as possible. In markets that have only three stations, independents are usually nonexistent. If a market has only one or two stations, those stations will share networks. In other words, they will affiliate with more than one network. In a four-station market, the lone independent will usually be a strong station because it can select from all nonnetwork programming. By the time a market has five or six stations, the point of diminishing returns sets in for the independent stations.

Programming procedures differ greatly between independents and affiliates. Whereas independents must obtain much programming from syndication sources, the affiliates receive the bulk of their programming from the network. This is done through a network-affiliate contract which is a rather complicated document.

This contract states that the network will pay the station for the network programs which the station airs. This may at first seem backward, since the station is the one receiving the goods. However, it is the network that sells most of the ads connected with the program, so it receives its revenue that way. The more stations that air the program, the larger the audience, and hence the higher price the network can charge for the ads.

The amount the network pays the station is decided by a complicated formula that considers the amount the station charges for ads, the time of day, the length of the program, and the number of commercials which the network plans to include in the program.

The network pays the station at a percentage of what the station could have earned had it filled the time with local ads. In prime time this percentage is about 33 percent, and at other times it is less. Of course, the network will pay the station a larger total for a one-hour than for a half-hour program. Usually the network will not fill one or two commercial minutes in a program so that stations can sell local ads. It then pays the station less than it would if all the commercial time had been filled. For example, a network pays a station more for airing an hour program Monday at 8:00 p.m. in which the network places four minutes of ads than it pays the station for airing an hour program Monday at 1:00 p.m. in which the network places ten minutes of ads.

There are many other details in the network-affiliate contract. A station can refuse a network program if it feels the program is unsuitable for its audience or if it has material of greater local importance which it wishes to air. The station must indicate its acceptance or rejection of regularly scheduled network programs within two weeks of the time they are offered and must indicate the same for special network programs within seventy-two hours of offering time. If an affiliated station rejects a network program, the network is free to offer that program to another station within the market area.

The network pays the station less if the program is aired on a delay basis—later than the network suggests it be aired. The network holds liability responsibility for lawsuits which may arise from any network program. If a station changes ownership, the network has the right to decide if it wishes to offer continued affiliation to the new owners.[6]

At first glance it appears that the affiliated station program manager has an easier job than the counterpart at the independent station. The network provides most entertainment shows and some news and public affairs. This means that the program manager needs to oversee only the local news, public affairs, instruction, and other programs necessary for the station to keep its license. Needing to find programs for a fraction of the program day permits the program manager of an affiliated station to be more selective. The added advantage of viewer habit in watching the network station provides more money to bid for and obtain the best available talent in the local market.

Owned and operated station program managers have the added advantage of help from the network organization. Each of the networks has a stations division which produces additional programs for all owned stations at a greatly reduced cost. This is possible because money provided by each is pooled and the station pays its share based on the number of people which its station reaches. Most of the instructional programming is handled by this method.

Less obvious are the program manager's problems of finding good air time for the required programs. A network may program every day from 7:00 a.m. until 10:00 p.m. with the exception of several hours in the late afternoon and some time on the weekend. This means that the program manager's selections must air at times when the audience is minimal or when children constitute the major portion of viewers. Such limitations tend to stifle the program manager's creativity and make the station vulnerable to challenge by local community groups. The vulnerability is aggravated by the fact that the affiliated or owned station usually commands the larger share of the available audience than does an independent station, and hence more local groups seek its air time to tell their message to the public.

An affiliated station manager also has the problem of making sure the network offerings are meeting the particular station's **license** application. The license application has been filed with the Federal Communications Commission and outlines the policies which will be followed by station management. The application states the number of hours which the station will operate daily and the total cumulative weekly time. It sets forth the percentages of each category of programming and the amount of air time which will be devoted to locally originated programs. A typical breakdown which might face the program decision-maker is as follows:

Type of Program	Nonlocal Origination	Local Origination
Entertainment	75 percent	6 percent
News	3 percent	5 percent
Public Affairs	2 percent	3 percent
Farm Reports	1 percent	1 percent
Instruction	2 percent	1 percent
Religion	0 percent	1 percent

This type of outline is a part of the application of all stations licensed to broadcast whether they be owned, affiliated, or independent. However, the independent program manager can keep this foremost while planning programming whereas the owned or affiliated program manager must evaluate this against network offerings and justify a stand if he or she does not want to accept network offerings.

Program planning must follow these limits very closely for very good reason. Every three years the station must apply for license renewal. To determine whether the stations have adhered to the previous application

**Figure 7.5
Coverage of a criminal suspect who contacted affiliated TV station WIIC to seek help in surrendering.**
Photo courtesy of WIIC-TV, Pittsburgh

Chapter 7

percentages, the FCC chooses seven days at random from the three-year period and has the station submit this **composite week** as proof of performance. This problem is always uppermost in the program manager's mind when asked to preempt regularly scheduled programs in order to present a timely special.

Another problem of the affiliated station program manager is the need to review constantly network programs as they relate to the morals and mores of the community the station serves. Programs which seem perfectly innocent in Los Angeles and New York and other larger markets may offend many people in smaller towns. This can be a costly and time-consuming problem at best and can cost the station its license at worst. So network affiliation is not a cure-all for the program department.[7]

Television Networks

Network prime time TV programming is the most viewed, most controversial, and most maligned of all broadcast programming. Ideas for network shows come from personnel within the networks, production companies, and, on rare occasion, from the public at large. Usually the first material developed is a written **story line** for the series. If this turns out well, a **pilot** will be produced—one program will be taped or filmed as it might appear in the series.

In the early spring of each year a committee of network executives begins making decisions regarding the next fall's program lineup. They consider all the programs presently in the lineup as well as new ideas submitted to them, basically from independent production companies, in the form of pilots accompanied by series story projections.

These decisions are compounded of such factors as **ratings** of present programs, fads of the time, production costs of the series, the overall program mix the network hopes to attain, ideas that have worked well or poorly in the past, the kind of audience the program will appeal to, and the type of programs the other networks may be scheduling. The final schedule is determined after a great deal of jiggling of time sequences and programs. Usually about one-third of the programs from the previous season will be killed and replaced by new shows. And many continued programs will have their time slots changed.[8]

Once the series is selected, production begins with an eye toward costs. These costs have risen every year of television's short history. Where a producer's exceeding the budget was cause for little more than a mild rebuke in the early days, it has become serious enough to destroy careers in the current era. Budget construction is a serious business which depends on the entire production team.

The budget is broken down into two main categories, **above-the-line** costs and **below-the-line** costs. The first covers the team hired to handle the show from inception to completion and includes talent, producer, director, and secretaries. The second involves crew, facilities, and physical elements such as scenery, videotape, film, and graphics.[9]

Budget costs begin almost at the time of approval of an idea. The producer must be hired and he or she, in turn, starts immediately to

Sample Budget Worksheet

Name of Show _____

	Show Budget			Show Actual	
Above the Line	No. of People	No. of Hours	$	No. of Hours	$
Talent					
Staff Announcers	____	____	____	____	____
Free Lance Announcers	____	____	____	____	____
Other AFTRA Fees	____	____	____	____	____
Other Talent	____	____	____	____	____
AFTRA P & W	____	____	____	____	____
Miscellaneous	____	____	____	____	____
Producer/Director	____	____	____	____	____
Total Above the Line	____	____	____	____	____
Below the Line—Labor					
Technical—In Shift	____	____	____	____	____
Overtime	____	____	____	____	____
Stagecraft—In Shift	____	____	____	____	____
Overtime	____	____	____	____	____
Film Dept.—In Shift	____	____	____	____	____
Overtime	____	____	____	____	____
Miscellaneous	____	____	____	____	____
Contingency	____	____	____	____	____
Total Labor	____	____	____	____	____
Below the Line—Production Facilities					
Technical Facilities—Standard in House				____	____
Extra				____	____
Stagecraft—Standard in House				____	____
Extra				____	____
Stagecraft Sets and Props				____	____
Original Construction Cost				____	____
Weekly Continuing Construction Cost				____	____
Raw Stock Tape and Film				____	____
Film Processing				____	____
Misc. Equipment Rental or Purchase				____	____
Contingency				____	____
Total Facilities				____	____
Total Below the Line				____	____
Grand Total				====	====

Figure 7.8
Sample budget worksheet for TV production

assemble a team. The writers, associate producers, assistants, director, and secretaries are needed first. Then come scenic and graphic artists, lighting director, makeup artists, hairdressers, and, of course, talent.

The director, lighting director, and scenic artist must survey and select several facilities capable of handling the production. This gives the producer some bargaining power in coming to terms on facilities. Settings must be approved by the creative teams and contracts let for their construction. Many preproduction meetings will be necessary before the show is ready to go into final production. The company then moves into facilities for taping or filming.

Costs are broken down into three phases in final production. The first is setup and rehearsal. Full FACS (facilities) is the second, and occurs when all systems are ready to complete the show. The third is **strike,** which is the breaking down and putting away of all sets and props. Now the show is ready for post-production editing, the final phase before airing or release. Here the producer, director, and editor team up to polish the finished product to a luster which will insure success, they hope.

Usually programs are produced in blocks to fill a thirteen-week season. If the series is successful, another block of programs will be prepared. However, not all programs last even thirteen weeks. Those with the poorest ratings are usually pulled early in the **season** and replaced by a series that was an also-ran during the spring meetings or by a summer replacement which drew good ratings. Some years networks cancel so many series during the fall that they actually have the equivalent of several seasons during one year.

The cancellation of programs is often controversial, regardless of when it occurs. In a few instances write-in campaigns by viewers have saved series, but generally the network follows through on its cancellation plans. Usually shows are cancelled because of poor ratings, but sometimes there are other reasons. Production costs may soar beyond the revenue that can be generated. Writers may run dry of plot ideas for a particular series. Or one network may decide to change its type of programming in some time slot in order to counter-program another network.[10]

This **counter-programming** is another controversial area. Sometimes one network will select a program specifically to draw an audience away from another network. For example, if an NBC children's program is receiving significantly higher ratings than a CBS drama at 8:00 Sunday evening, CBS may change to a children's program just to attract some of the audience away from NBC. Likewise, if a 9:00 p.m. CBS variety show is outdrawing an ABC western in the same time slot, ABC may switch to a variety show to attract some of CBS's audience. This leaves the viewer faced with the dilemma of choosing between two similar programs at 9:00. The variety show fan would prefer to have one variety show at 9:00 and one at 10:00, but the networks usually don't comply with this reasoning.

Preemptions annoy some TV viewers, who become upset when their favorite program is not shown because of a special news event or special entertainment program which the network feels it should air. Often there is not unanimity among the TV executives who make the decisions regarding whether or not an event is important enough to pre-empt a regularly scheduled program.

Another bone of contention concerning network programs centers around reruns. The recent trend has been for networks to fund fewer and fewer program productions each year and instead begin the "summer" reruns in the spring. Network executives claim this is necessary in order to have a profitable organization. Since production costs continue to climb, the only way to make the money stretch is to produce less. There are costs involved with reruns, such as the **residuals** that must be paid to some of the people involved in the original production, but the overall cost of a rerun is much lower than the cost of producing a new program.[11] Since networks are so profitable, actors, technicians, and some members of the public at large claim that they have no need to reduce production and, hence, the number of jobs available within the industry.

Networks program a great deal of material in addition to their prime time series, such as news programs, documentaries, sports, soap operas, children's programs, and specials. Many decisions must be made regarding these programs, too. Sometimes they are canceled because of poor ratings. Sometimes they are altered because they are too expensive. Sometimes they are keyed down because they are too controversial. This latter category receives the most publicity.

Producers of documentaries frequently find themselves in a squeeze between reporters who wish to expose injustices and managers who do not wish to alienate any of the hands that feed them. For example, during the era when cigarette companies advertised heavily on radio and TV, documentaries about the hazards of smoking were touchy, to say the least.

Those making program decisions in both radio and TV live a fishbowl existence. If their decisions are popular as well as financial successes, they will ride high. If not, there are always others waiting in the wings.

Figure 7.9
A network documentary dealing with juvenile justice entitled "This Child Is Rated X."
Photo courtesy of NBC

Summary   Programming decisions can be discussed in terms of *independent* radio stations, network-*owned* or -*affiliated* radio stations, radio *networks*, independent TV stations, network-owned or -affiliated TV stations, and TV networks.

A management committee at independent radio stations makes *format* and *special feature* decisions; then the *program manager* hires talent, secures records, and oversees public affairs and news. Network-owned or -affiliated radio stations operate in much the same way as independents but are often larger and more powerful. Radio networks supply news primarily, with the method of payment varying from station to station. Independent TV stations obtain programming from *motion picture companies, off-network program and series packagers, independent syndicators, independent networks, independent television production companies, religious organizations,* and *wire services.* They also produce news, sports, public affairs, editorial, and entertainment programs in-house. Network-owned or -affiliated TV stations receive most of their programming from networks under terms of a *formal contract* and then plan locally produced programs to air at nonnetwork times. TV networks consider *story lines* and *pilots* from many sources and then commit to production those they wish to air. *Cancellation, counter-programming, preemptions,* and *reruns* are controversial elements of TV networks' programming decisions.

8 The Tenuous Relationship

Broadcasting and Government

A broadcast license is a license to print money.

Lord Roy Thompson

Cartoon copyrighted by *Broadcasting* magazine

"Hey, Ed. Fella wants to know if we're authorized to broadcast from Mars."

There are few countries of the world where the government has such a hands-off policy toward broadcasting as in the United States. Nevertheless, the United States has many governmental bodies which affect and regulate the radio and television industry in one way or another. While the primary government body concerned with broadcasting is the Federal Communications Commission, other agencies that have influence include the Federal Trade Commission, Congress, and the courts.

Organization of the Federal Communications Commission

The Federal Communications Commission (FCC) was created because of the mass confusion and interference that had arisen when early radio stations broadcast on unregulated **frequencies** and at unregulated power. First Congress passed the Radio Act of 1927, which created the Federal Radio Commission (FRC) to deal with the chaos. Then in 1934 Congress wrote a new law, the Communications Act, which formally established the FCC with powers similar to its predecessor, the FRC.

The FCC is composed of seven commissioners appointed for seven-year terms by the president with the advice and consent of the Senate. The president designates one commissioner to be chairperson, but generally no president has the opportunity to appoint many commissioners because their seven-year terms are staggered. Each commissioner must be a U.S. citizen with no financial interest in any communications industry, and no more than four of the seven commissioners are supposed to be from one political party. Usually commissioners have backgrounds in engineering or law.

The commission maintains central offices in Washington and field offices in thirty districts. Its staff of approximately 1,800 civil service employees is organized into seven administrative offices (executive director, plans and policy, general counsel, chief engineer, opinions and review, administrative law judges, and review board) and five bureaus (common carrier, broadcast, cable television, safety and special services, and field operations).

Figure 8.1
FCC organization chart

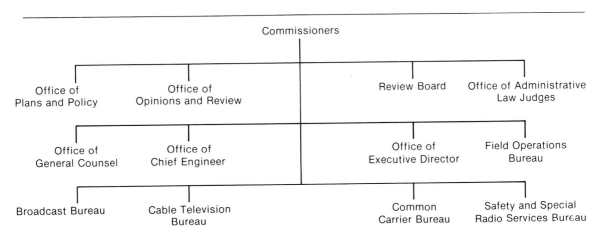

Policy determinations are made by all the commissioners, with the chairman then being responsible for the general administration of the commission's affairs. Most of the day-to-day work such as handling interference complaints, public inquiries, and station applications is undertaken by the staff.[1]

The FCC has myriad functions, many of which are not related to commercial radio and television broadcasting. For example, it has jurisdiction over airplane communications, ship-to-shore radio, police and fire communications, telephone and telegraph common carrier services, **"ham"** radio operations, military communication, satellite transmission, and **citizens' band** radio. It also advises the State Department in negotiating international radio and television agreements so that other countries will not interfere with American communications. In wartime it coordinates the use of radio and TV with the national security program and may set up a service to monitor enemy propaganda. It is constantly encouraging new uses of radio waves, particularly those that will promote safety.

All of this makes for an increasingly heavy work load on the commission, particularly as new uses for **radio waves** surface. The sudden popularity of citizens' band radio in the mid-1970s swamped the commission with problems of interference and channel reallocation.[2]

Technical Functions of the FCC

A great deal of what the FCC does in regulating radio and TV stations involves engineering. The FCC assigns frequencies to individual stations, determines the power each can use, and regulates the time of day each may operate. It then polices to make sure the broadcasters stay within the frequency, power, and time regulations and to make sure unauthorized persons do not use the airwaves. In fact, about one-fourth of all FCC employees are employed in this fieldwork.

The FCC makes overall regulations to prevent interference between stations, and it regulates the location of station transmitters and the type of equipment used for transmission. It also administers tests by means of which station personnel are licensed, which are usually referred to as the third-class license test and the first-class license test. A third-class license must be obtained by most radio and some TV station personnel. It allows them to turn a station on or off and perform some of the simple electronic functions. The test is fairly easy to pass, especially if the study guide which the FCC provides is read carefully. It consists of questions relating to such subjects as antenna lighting, station identification, operating power, and responsibilities of licensed operators. The first-class license requires a fairly detailed knowledge of electronics and generally cannot be passed without formal training. The operator who possesses a first-class license can handle complicated electronics and maintenance, including that of the station transmitter.[3]

The FCC also sets up broad policies. It controls the general allocation of frequencies, deciding which frequencies go to ship-to-shore communication, which to TV, which to FM radio, and so forth. Within the frequencies

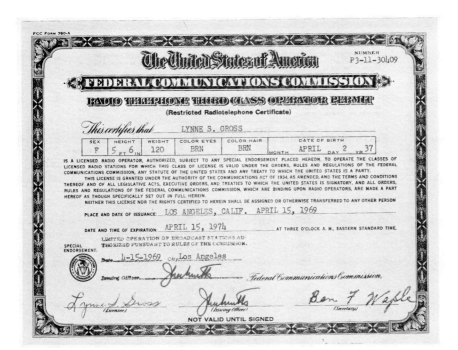

Figure 8.2
An FCC third-class broadcasting license.

it allocates to radio and TV, the FCC creates a table designating the power and times of stations that can exist in each section of the country and on each frequency.

The commission designates **call letters** of all stations. Those stations west of the Mississippi begin with K and those east of the Mississippi begin with W (except for some of the early stations such as KDKA in Pittsburgh which had call letters before the ruling went into effect.) A station can select or change the other letters of its call letters so long as the letters it chooses are not already in use by another station.[4]

The FCC also requires stations to keep engineering and programming records, usually referred to as **logs.** The engineering logs are records of readings made periodically at the transmitter covering such technical matters as **power deviation, frequency deviation, plate current,** and **plate voltage.** Program logs show such information as the title of each program, the time it begins and ends, the type of program (e.g., entertainment, news, religious), the source of the program (e.g., local, network, recorded), the names of the advertisers, the amount of time given to advertisements, the times when station identifications are given, the names of organizations for which public service announcements are made, and the name and political affiliation of political candidates appearing.

The Emergency Broadcasting System is also under the jurisdiction of the FCC. This is a national hook-up which ties together all radio and TV stations so that information can be broadcast from the government to the citizenry during a national emergency. All stations are required to maintain

PROGRAM LOG

Time Scheduled Hr. Min. Sec.	Title or Sponsor	Length	Source	Type	Announcer Initials	Actual Time Hr. Min. Sec.
12: 00: 00	Noon News	15 min.	LS	N	B.T.	12:00:00
	Miracle Soap	30 sec.	TR	C		12:02:10
	Handy Dandy Openers	30 sec.	TR	C		12:06:20
	Hairline Shampoo	30 sec.	TR	C		12:10:35
12: 15: 00	Heydown Time	15 min.	LS	M	D.W.	12:14:30
	Ball Game Promo	30 sec.	TR	PR		12:19:30
	Vet's Asso.	20 sec.	T	PS		12:25:05
12: 30: 00	Station Break	60 sec.	TR	SI		12:30:30
	Colst Toothpaste	20 sec.	LS	C	B.T.	12:30:35
	Henry's Hardware	20 sec.	TR	C		12:30:55
12: 31: 00	The Jeff Jeb Show	3 hours	LS	M	J.J.	12:31:20
	Echo Gas	30 sec.	TR	C		12:36:15
	Everybody's Airline	20 sec.	LS	C	J.J.	12:39:05
	Sweeties Deodorant	30 sec.	TR	C		12:45:10
	Cancer Society	30 sec.	T	PS		12:50:55
1: 30: 00	Station Break	60 sec.	TR	SI	B.T.	1:30:00
	Colst Toothpaste	20 sec.	LS	C		1:30:20
	Feline Cologne	20 sec.	TR	C		1:30:40
1: 31: 00	News Break	5 min.	LS	N	B.T.	1:31:00
	Pete's Photo	20 sec.	TR	C		1:33:10
	Hexatall Drugs	20 sec.	TR	C		1:33:30
1: 36: 00	Tom and Jerry Show	3 hours	LS	M	T.R./J.F.	1:37:10

Figure 8.3
Sample page of a program log

172   Chapter 8

the equipment necessary for receiving emergency notification and to test this equipment regularly. If a state of emergency is declared, some stations will remain on the air broadcasting common information and others will shut down and remain off the air until the emergency is over.

Most of the technical responsibilities of the FCC are noncontroversial, and broadcasters generally appreciate the FCC's role in this regard.

Station Licensing by the FCC

The most controversial and publicized functions of the FCC center around the power to issue, revoke, renew, and transfer **licenses.** It is through this power that the FCC makes regulations which directly and indirectly affect the entire broadcasting industry.

Any citizen, firm, or group wishing to be issued a radio or TV license must file a written statement of qualifications with the FCC. One category of qualifications is character, which includes obvious matters such as felony convictions, participation in community organizations, and desire to be involved in the day-to-day operations of the stations. Other stipulations are that aliens and foreign companies cannot own U.S. stations except in unusual circumstances; not more than one AM, one FM, and one TV station serving the same listening area can be licensed to the same applicant; and no more than seven AM, seven FM, and seven TV stations (only five of which can be VHF) serving different areas can be licensed to the same applicant. These provisions apply to networks as well as other companies, so NBC, although it may have **affiliates** in many cities, cannot own more than one TV station in a particular city and cannot own more than a total of seven TV stations.[5]

The relationship between newspaper ownership and broadcast ownership is particularly controversial and fluctuating. The FCC, in an effort to diversify media control, has ruled that an owner should not control newspapers and broadcast operations in the same city. This ruling has been hotly contested and dragged through the courts by those in the media business. Whenever compromise or resolution of the issue appears imminent, new aspects of the problem are brought to the fore and the entire problem recycles. However, in recent years newspapers applying to buy stations for the first time have not been favorably considered by the FCC.[6]

Applicants for licenses must describe their financial and technical qualifications. Financially, they must have access to enough capital to build and begin operation of the station, and they should show that commercial support for the station is possible.

Applicants applying for a new AM station must arrange for an engineering investigation to establish that the station will not interfere with other stations because of its frequency, power, or hours of operation. An applicant for an FM or TV station can consult the **allocation tables** already set up by the FCC to find a place for a station. Obviously, all of the best frequencies have been taken, so nowadays it is more common for a company to buy an existing station than to try to start one.

The applicant must also set forth a full statement for its proposed program service which the FCC can take under cautious consideration. The FCC has no power to censor program materials; in fact the Communications Act specifically prohibits censoring by stating:

> Nothing in this Act shall be understood or construed to give the Commission the power of censorship over the radio communications or signals transmitted by any radio station, and no regulation or condition shall be promulgated or fixed by the Commission which shall interfere with the right of free speech by means of radio communication.[7]

This indicates that the FCC cannot refuse a license to a financially, technically, and morally qualified candidate simply because it plans to broadcast some form of programming that the FCC finds objectionable. However, there is another section of the Communications Act which states:

> The Commission, if public convenience, interest, or necessity will be served thereby, subject to the limitations of this Act, shall grant to any applicant therefore a station license provided for by this Act.[8]

This "public convenience, interest, or necessity" has become the keystone through which the FCC involves itself in programming regulation.

In order to define "convenience, interest, and necessity," the commission in 1946 issued the so-called "Blue Book," which set forth program criteria it felt stations should abide by. It was strong on the need for **sustaining** public service programs and the evils of overcommercialization. Over the years the commission softened its tone, and in 1960 it issued a much briefer statement of policy which listed fourteen elements usually necessary to meet the public interest:

1. Opportunity for local self-expression	8. Political broadcasts
2. Development and use of local talent	9. Agricultural programs
3. Programs for children	10. News programs
4. Religious programs	11. Weather and market reports
5. Educational programs	12. Sports programs
6. Public affairs programs	13. Service to minority groups
7. Editorializing by licensees	14. Entertainment programs

It also warned broadcasters to avoid abuses with respect to the total amount of time devoted to advertising as well as the frequency with which programs are interrupted by commercials, but it did not specifically define what constituted abuses.[9] Armed with the public "convenience, interest, and necessity" clause, the FCC can refuse to grant a license to an organization because of the programming plans.

Once an applicant has filed a written statement of its character, financial, technical, and programming qualifications with the FCC, it asks the FCC for a **Construction Permit** (CP) and gives public notice of its intentions to start a station. The FCC then holds the application for thirty days to give parties a chance to object. The most common objections come from other groups who wish to apply for the same station, but occasionally a neighboring station may object because it believes it will experience technical interference, or stations within the same listening area may object because they feel the area cannot support another station financially. If there are objections, staff members of the FCC hold hearings to attempt to resolve the difficulties. If more than one group wishes to apply for the station, FCC staff members will make the award to the group which appears more qualified. Often applicants are equally qualified from a character, financial, and technical viewpoint, so the award will go to the group that proposes the most acceptable form of programming for serving the public convenience, interest, and necessity. Hearing decisions can be appealed through various levels of the FCC and the courts, so a station applicant faced with hearing possibilities must be able to weather several years of legal maneuvers.

If the applicant survives the hazards along the way and receives a CP, then building the station can begin, but only after construction has been completed can the license and permission to begin conducting program tests be granted.[10]

Once a station receives a license, it usually experiences little supervision from the FCC over its programming until license renewal time. Licenses come up for renewal in groups by states every three years. For example, if all New York stations are up for renewal in 1977, they are again all up in 1980. Prior to the mid-1960s, license renewal was basically a private affair between the FCC and the broadcaster. The listeners and viewers had very little to say about the matter. Letters from the viewers to the FCC complaining about a station went into the station's renewal file and, if numerous enough, were considered by the FCC at license renewal time, but citizen testimony and evidence were not allowed because it was felt that viewers had no legal standing or vested interest in broadcasting.

During this period stations did receive rebukes for such violations as failure to make proper entries in logs, failure to broadcast station identifications frequently enough, failure to have engineering instruments calibrated properly, failure to authenticate sponsorship of programs, failure to present controversial issues properly, and failure to give **equal time** to political candidates. For these violations stations were fined, issued **cease and desist** orders, and issued short-term probationary licenses of less than three years, but over a thirty-five year period only forty-three licenses were denied renewal out of approximately 50,000 renewal applications.[11]

In 1964 a black group from Jackson, Mississippi asked the FCC if it could participate in the license renewal hearing of station WLBT-TV because the group felt that the station was not serving its viewership properly and was presenting racial issues unfairly. When the group was turned down by the FCC, it took the matter to the courts, and in 1966 obtained a reversal opening the door for citizens groups to be heard concerning license renewal.

In 1969 a group of Boston businessmen challenged the renewal of TV station WHDH, which had been operated by the *Boston Herald Traveler* for twelve years. The businessmen claimed that they could operate the station more in the public interest than the Herald Traveler and hence should be given the license. The FCC agreed, revoked the *Herald Traveler's* license, and transferred it to the Boston businessmen. This decision sent shivers through the entire broadcasting community. Never before had a station license been transferred involuntarily unless the station licensee had first been found guilty of excessive violations. In the Boston case, although there were charges of concealment of interests, the FCC had not actually stated that the *Herald Traveler* was an undesirable licensee but rather based its decision on the opinion that the businessmen were better. Broadcasters immediately began pounding on the doors of Congress to urge passage of legislation that would prohibit license challenges. Meanwhile, citizen groups by the score began challenging licenses in cities across the country. Legislation has not been passed, but the FCC has not repeated its WHDH action, appearing to take the point of view that a license should first be revoked before competing groups can apply. However, the situation is still very much up in the air.[12]

In 1970 the Alabama Educational Television Commission applied for what it assumed would be routine renewals for its public television stations. However, the FCC refused renewal because of citizen petitions stating that the commission had systematically deleted all Public Broadcasting Service programs dealing with blacks or Vietnam. The Alabama commission was allowed to reapply for its stations with the understanding that it would mend its ways. Nevertheless, the case marks the first time such harsh action was taken against any public broadcasting stations.[13]

These actions, and others, served to make broadcasters aware of the power of the public so that citizen groups throughout the country are now at least listened to by the broadcasters. Occasionally they have significant impact. Such groups now have the power to file a "petition to deny" with the FCC—a document that formally asks the FCC to deny a particular station's license and lists the reasons the denial is requested. Such petitions are considered very seriously by the FCC.

Citizens have also been incorporated into license renewal procedures through a process called **ascertainment.** In order to obtain license renewal, stations are required to survey people in the community periodically to ascertain citizens' views on the major needs of the community. The stations must first establish their viewing or listening demographics so that they know the composition of their audience and the percentages of various minorities and age groups that listen to or view their programs. They then interview leaders of the various groups which comprise their audience and also randomly selected regular audience members, asking each to identify what he or she considers the major issues and problems facing the community. Stations then evaluate the material they obtain from the interviews and propose a plan to air programs dealing with the various issues and problems.

This material, along with information about station operation for the previous three years, is submitted to the FCC by each station at license renewal time. Before it goes to the FCC the material is available in a public file so any citizen can inspect it. Each license renewal application is somewhat circular. The station proposes a program service which it plans to offer for the next three years, which the FCC usually approves. However, to see whether the station adhered to its proposal, the FCC requires that three years later, at the next license renewal time, the station submit a list of programming for a **composite week**—seven days from the previous three years selected at random by the FCC. The FCC's main concern here is whether the program service adhered to what was proposed three years earlier. If it did, and if there are no major complaints against the station, the license will be renewed for another three years.

If, however, there is a big discrepancy between the type of programs the broadcast licensee said it would air and the type it actually did air; if it broadcast many more commercials than it said it would; if there were numerous complaints about the station; or if there were numerous technical citations—then a hearing may be held. During this hearing the applicant bears the burden of proving that renewal of its license will serve the public interest. Obviously, these hearings are expensive and create poor public relations, so stations generally try to avoid them, often by compromising with citizens groups so that the groups approve of the programming proposal and do not complain to the FCC.[14]

The FCC can also revoke a station's license at a time other than when it comes up for renewal. In such a case the burden of proof is on the commission. The rare cases when the FCC has taken such action involved concealment of a station's real ownership, unauthorized transfer of control of a station, excessive technical violations, and abandonment of the station by the owners.

The FCC also becomes involved when a station is sold and the license is therefore transferred from one party to another. It is the station management's prerogative to set the selling price and select the buyer, but the FCC does check on the character and financial, technical, and programming qualifications of the buyer. The FCC also holds hearings if a station is going to change owners in less than three years—this to prevent people from buying stations simply for speculative purposes without concern for the service function of broadcasting.

It should be noted that the FCC has no direct control over networks but can control them indirectly through the owned and operated and affiliated stations. For example, when the FCC limited the number of hours of network programming a station could air during **prime time,** in effect, a half-hour was chopped off network programming. But the networks themselves are not licensed. Consequently, they go through the license-renewal process only vicariously by way of the stations carrying their programs.

Another federal body which becomes involved in broadcast regulation from time to time is the Federal Trade Commission. This commission was established by the Federal Trade Commission Act and the Clayton Act. Both acts were passed in 1914, basically to prevent unfair competition

The Federal Trade Commission

**Figure 8.4
Federal Trade Commis-
sion building in
Washington, D.C.**
Photo courtesy of the
Federal Trade Commission

resulting from the giant corporate trusts. In 1938 the Wheeler-Lea Amendment to the FTC act was passed declaring that "unfair or deceptive acts or practices in commerce are also illegal."[15] This opened the door for the FTC to look into matters where consumers were being deceived, and it served as the takeoff point for the FTC's involvement in broadcasting.

This involvement concerns mainly fraudulent advertising, which is deceptive to consumers. If the FTC feels that a company's ads are untruthful, it has the power to order the company to stop broadcasting the ads. In some instances it can make the company broadcast a message publicly disavowing the false claims in the untruthful ad. Needless to say, this is distasteful to advertisers.

Five FTC commissioners are appointed for a term of seven years each by the president with the consent of the Senate. The president appoints the chairperson, who in turn handles most of the management and personnel aspects of the commission. Working directly under the chairperson is the executive director, who as the commission's chief operating officer oversees day-to-day operations of the FTC offices and bureaus. The commission organization includes people to advise the commissioners on legal matters, policy planning and evaluation, competitive practices, consumer education, scientific and technical matters, and national television advertising. The commission staff also includes hearing officers to undertake the initial fact-finding for cases coming before the commission, an office of public

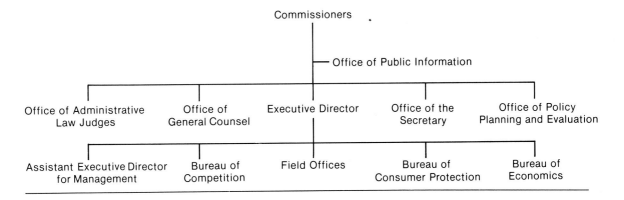

Commissioners

Office of Public Information

| Office of Administrative Law Judges | Office of General Counsel | Executive Director | Office of the Secretary | Office of Policy Planning and Evaluation |

| Assistant Executive Director for Management | Bureau of Competition | Field Offices | Bureau of Consumer Protection | Bureau of Economics |

Figure 8.5
FTC organization chart

information to inform the media of commission activities, and a compliance division to make sure that the orders of the commission are followed. Throughout the country there are regional FTC offices to handle local complaints and problems and refer them to Washington, if necessary.

The FTC attempts as much as possible to be preventive rather than punitive in its relationships with broadcasting as well as other forms of business. In other words, it tries to disseminate its philosophies to businesses in the form of written statements known as Trade Regulation Rules, Industry Guides, and Advisory Opinions so that businesses know how to avoid incurring the wrath of the FTC. If, for example, the commission decides to issue guidelines on toy advertising, it will inform all toy companies that it is planning to create rules in their area. Executives of toy companies as well as members of the general public then have a chance to express opinions about what these rules should include. After the members of the FTC have heard the various opinions, they write the guidelines and publicize them as widely as possible among toy companies, related trade associations, and consumers. The Trade Regulation Rules, Industry Guides, and Advisory Opinions do not have the force of law; they are suggestions to businesses which the FTC hopes will be followed in order to avoid trouble.

If a company violates one of these guides or engages in other practices which the FTC feels hurts competition or deceives consumers, then the FTC can bring action against the company.

Obviously, the FTC staff cannot act as a constant watchdog over every company in the country. Although the staff does occasionally bring charges, it depends greatly on the public at large and businesspeople in general to bring complaints to it.

Often investigations are initiated by letters from consumers sent to the Washington FTC office or to one of the regional offices. These letters are first reviewed to make sure that the complaints expressed actually come under the jurisdiction of the FTC. If so, the investigation begins with FTC personnel questioning officials of the company involved in the alleged misdeed. Usually the FTC wants proof from the company that its ad is

accurate. For example, if the complaint is against a car manufacturer who says its car is 50 percent quieter than any competitor's car, the FTC will require scientific proof of this claim. At the end of the investigation, the FTC may close the case for failure to find a violation or it may issue a formal complaint and cease and desist order to the company involved. If the company does not feel it should have to stop its alleged violation, it can appeal to an FTC hearing examiner, then to the FTC commissioners, and from there to the U.S. District Court of Appeals and eventually to the Supreme Court. Very few cases actually go to the Supreme Court; most are reconciled at the lower levels.[16]

**Major Court
Cases Related
to Broadcasting**

The courts of the United States have had a significant impact on broadcasters, mainly because both FCC and FTC cases can be appealed through the court system, but also because of direct court cases which have influenced the course of broadcast history and regulation.

Two of the earliest court cases involved revocation of station licenses. One concerned Dr. J. R. Brinkley, who in the 1920s and early '30s broadcast medical "advice" over his Milford, Kansas, station. He specialized in goat gland operations to improve sexual powers and in instant diagnosis over the air for medical problems sent in by listeners. These problems could always be cured by prescriptions obtainable from druggists who belonged to an association Dr. Brinkley operated. The other culprit was the Reverend Robert Shuler, who used his Los Angeles station to berate Catholics, Jews, judges, pimps, and others in his personal gallery of sinners. He professed to have derogatory information regarding unnamed persons who could pay penance by sending him money for his church. The Federal Radio Commission decided not to renew either of these licenses and, although both defendants cried censorship, the Court of Appeals and U.S. Supreme Court sided with the FRC on the grounds that with only a limited number of frequencies available, the commission should consider the quality of service rendered. In ruling on the Shuler case, the court wrote that if stations were possessed by people

to obstruct the administration of justice, offend the religious sensibilities of thousands, inspire political distrust and civic discord, or offend youth and innocence by the free use of words suggestive of sexual immorality, and be answerable for slander only at the instance of the one offended, then this great science, instead of a boon, will become a scourge, and the nation a theater for the display of individual passions and the collusion of personal interests. This is neither censorship nor previous restraint.[17]

Since that 1932 decision, the courts have ruled on many other issues pertinent to broadcasters. Some, like the Brinkley and Shuler cases, have dealt with censorship and are based on the guarantee of freedom of speech and press of the First Amendment to the Constitution. Obscenity and indecency rulings are generally in this area and become controversial because of the evolving definitions of "obscene" and "indecent"; e.g., what is considered obscene in one decade passes as acceptable in another. Other free speech court cases have dealt with defining what actually constitutes **slander** and **defamation of character** and what is censorship as opposed to clear and present danger to the country.

Conducting **lotteries** on radio or television is not permitted, as distinguished from reporting winners of a lottery, but there have been some cases brought before the courts to determine whether or not a station is, in fact, conducting a lottery. Monopolistic media concentrations have also been subject to court cases, especially as related to newspaper-broadcasting combinations. Copyright suits have been brought by those who feel such rights were violated by a station or network. Cases have also come to the courts regarding fraudulent advertising, rights to privacy, and station contests and games.

The areas that have probably seen the most significant and prolific actions by the courts, however, involve editorializing, equal treatment of political candidates, and fair presentation of issues.

Editorializing was first ruled on in 1941 in a case involving WAAB, a Boston radio station which for several years had been expressing its views on political candidates and controversial issues. This case became known as the Mayflower Decision because the Mayflower Broadcasting Corporation had applied for the channel occupied by WAAB but its application was rejected on grounds having nothing to do with editorializing. During the course of license renewal hearings, the FCC ruled that editorializing was not in the public interest and hence should be halted on WAAB.

This decision, although resented, was not challenged by broadcasters because few of them were interested in editorializing. However, during the 1940s several top members of the National Association of Broadcasters became interested in the issue, and the Cornell University radio station petitioned the FCC to reconsider the Mayflower Decision. As a result, after hearings held from 1947 to 1949, the FCC finally reversed itself, stating that stations should be encouraged to editorialize.

This decision did not have any immediate impact on broadcasting. Stations did not immediately rush into editorializing since they traditionally had not engaged in it, and they were unsure about exactly what the FCC meant by editorializing. Over the years editorializing guidelines have been defined and refined by court cases and FCC rulings. Now it is generally accepted that stations are not required to broadcast opposing views for every editorial aired, but if the character or integrity of a group or person is going to be attacked, that person or group must be notified and given reasonable opportunity to reply. Also, if the station plans to endorse a political candidate editorially, it must notify the opponents within twenty-four hours and provide opportunity for reply.[18]

Closely related to editorializing are equal time and **fairness** provisions. Equal time refers to the fair treatment of political candidates and is in effect only during election campaign periods. Fairness involves presenting pros and cons of controversial issues whether these issues be presented in editorials, documentaries, talk shows, or other programming forms.

Equal time stems from Section 315 of the 1934 Communications Act, which states:

If any licensee shall permit any person who is a legally qualified candidate for any public office to use a broadcasting station, he shall afford equal opportunities to all other such candidates for that office in the use of such broadcasting station, and the Commission shall make rules and regulations to carry this provision into effect: Provided. That such licensee shall have no power of censorship over the material broadcast under the provisions of this section. No obligation is hereby imposed upon any licensee to allow the use of its station by any such candidate.[19]

A number of interesting cases resulted from Section 315 which have led to its amendment. In 1956 WDAY-TV in Fargo, North Dakota granted time to a splinter candidate running for the Senate. In keeping with the regulation of Section 315, the station did not censor the candidate's speech, which later became the subject of a successful **libel** suit against both the candidate and the station. The state supreme court declared that the station should be immune from damages because it could not, by law, censor the speech, but the U.S. Supreme Court ducked the issue, so no real decision was rendered regarding the broadcaster's liability in such a situation.

In 1959 Lar Daly, a candidate for mayor in Chicago protested that the incumbent mayor, who was running for reelection, had been seen on a local news show, and Daly demanded equal time on that station. Had he been an ordinary candidate, he might have been granted time and the issue dropped. However, he was an eccentric who dressed in an Uncle Sam outfit complete with red, white, and blue top hat, and he ran, unsuccessfully, for some office in every election. As a result, Daly was granted his equal time, but Congress amended Section 315 so that the equal time restrictions would not apply to candidates appearing on newscasts, news interviews, news documentaries, and on-the-spot coverage of news events.

Although Section 315 has become known as the "equal time" clause, it actually states that candidates should be given "equal opportunity." This has led to challenges resulting in policies stating that if one candidate is given free air time, all the others must be allowed free time. If the candidate purchases the time, other candidates must be able to purchase it at the same rate. The time given to all candidates must approximate the same time period so that one candidate is not seen during prime time and another in the wee hours of the morning. And the facilities the first candidate was able to use must be available to the opponents.

Each election year the courts are hit by new cases regarding Section 315, for many of its ramifications are still largely uncharted despite thick booklets on political broadcasting issued by the FCC and NAB.[20]

The fairness doctrine is an outgrowth of the equal time clause. When Congress amended Section 315 in 1959, it stated that nothing in the news exemptions should be construed as relieving broadcasters "from the obligations imposed upon them under this chapter to operate in the public interest and to afford reasonable opportunity for the discussion of conflicting views on issues of public importance." This phrase, which seemed harmless at first, brought trouble for broadcasters as cases reached the courts.[21]

One creative application of this fairness doctrine was a case brought in 1967 by John F. Banzhaf III, who asserted that cigarette commercials presented only one side of a controversial issue of public importance and that stations should be obliged to air commercials opposing cigarette smoking. The Supreme Court upheld Banzhaf, and, until cigarette commercials were banned, stations had to provide spots for antismoking ads.

Another fairness doctrine decision rendered by the Supreme Court in 1969 arose over actions at Pennsylvania station WGCB operated by the Red Lion Broadcasting Company. This station had broadcast a talk by the Reverend Billy Hargis which charged Fred J. Cook, author of books critical of Barry Goldwater and J. Edgar Hoover, with Communist affiliations. Cook demanded that WGCB give him the opportunity to reply. The station said it would if Cook would pay for the time, but Cook objected and contacted the FCC, which ordered the station to grant Cook the time whether or not he was willing to pay for it. The decision was appealed through the courts and upheld by the Supreme Court on the grounds that free speech of a broadcaster does not embrace the right to snuff out the free speech of others.

In 1970 the Friends of the Earth tried to ditto Banzhaf's case in the ecology area by requesting that ads for automobiles and gasoline be countered by antipollution ads. However, they were not successful, and the FCC stated that the cigarette ruling was not to be used as a precedent because that case was unique.[22]

Figure 8.7
Lar Daly campaigning on Chicago TV in his Uncle Sam suit.
Photo courtesy of *Broadcasting* magazine

Other government bodies besides the FCC, FTC, and courts are at least tangentially concerned with broadcasting. For example, Congress passes on FCC and FTC commissioners and budgets and sometimes conducts special investigations into broadcasting activities, such as the quiz scandals. Some congressional laws such as the copyright bill and the Educational Broad-

Other Government Influences

casting Facilities Act have great bearing on broadcast operations. And, of course, the 1934 Communications Act was passed by Congress, and it may be revamped by Congress.

The president can suspend broadcasting operations in time of war or threat of war and call into action the Emergency Broadcast System.

The Federal Aviation Authority becomes involved with antenna towers and lighting so that planes will not crash into antennas. The Food and Drug Administration occasionally becomes concerned with misbranding or mislabeling of advertised products. The surgeon general's office became a party to the ban of cigarette advertising on radio and TV. Certain international treaties affect particularly stations near the Mexican and Canadian boundaries. The list can go on, but overall government influence and control over broadcasting in the U.S. is significantly less than in most other countries.

Government Broadcasting Agencies

The government operates several broadcast networks, one of which is the Armed Forces Radio and Television Service (AFRTS) broadcasting to American servicemen overseas. It was originally set up in 1942 by the Army, with later full cooperation of the Navy, as the Armed Forces Radio Service (AFRS) to provide a "tie with home" for military personnel wherever the necessities of war took them. While the initial service was only by short wave, AFRS broadcast stations began to be established early in the conflict. All of these stations were troop-operated. While most were in fixed locations where the troops were stationed, a number of the stations actually moved along with the advancing armies. All of them, fixed or mobile, provided an invaluable morale factor to the men and women whose normal lives had been dislocated by war. AFRS produced and provided to these stations many programs, such as "Command Performance" and "Mail Call," which featured prominent Hollywood stars. In addition, network programs were supplied with all commercials deleted. At one time AFRS was the largest network in the world. Although it has shrunk from its World War II size, it has added troop-operated television and still continues programming to overseas military personnel.[23]

Another government-operated broadcast facility is the Voice of America, which beams radio and television programs around the world via shortwave transmission. VOA is presently an arm of the United States Information Agency, although proposals are under consideration to change its organization. It has in the past been part of the State Department and at one time was run primarily by NBC and CBS.

The directive which serves as the philosophy of the Voice of America is as follows:

The long range interests of the United States are served by communicating directly with the peoples of the world by radio. To be effective, the Voice of America must win the attention and respect of listeners. These principles will guide VOA broadcasts:
1. VOA will establish itself as a consistently reliable and authoritative source of news. VOA will be accurate, objective, and comprehensive.

Figure 8.8

Figure 8.9

Figure 8.10

Figure 8.8
True Boardman, pro-
ducer and writer of the
AFRS World War II pro-
gram "Mail Call." The
program featured stars
reading letters that
might have come from
home.
Photo courtesy of True
Boardman

Figure 8.9
Arthur Shields (*left*) and
Gary Cooper perform for
"Mail Call" about 1943.
Photo courtesy of True
Boardman

Figure 8.10
The control room of the
Armed Forces Radio
and Television Services
facilities located in
Rosslyn, Virginia.
Photo courtesy of the U.S.
Army Audio-Visual Activity

2. VOA will represent America, not any single segment of American society. It will therefore present a balanced and comprehensive projection of significant American thought and institutions.
3. As an official radio, VOA will present the policies of the United States clearly and effectively. VOA also will present responsible discussion and opinion of these policies.[24]

VOA programs emanate from transmitters in the United States and various parts of the world supplemented by radio facilities in friendly nations which rebroadcast the programs over their own stations. Most of the radio programs originate from studios in Washington, D.C., where twenty-six programs using one hundred different sources can be produced simultaneously. VOA broadcasts about 800 hours of programs a week in thirty-six languages. These consist of news, features, commentaries, and special events as well as music programs. It is impossible to know the effect of VOA, but it is estimated that 43 million adults around the world listen to the broadcasts each week.

In addition, the United States operates Radio Free Europe, which beams programs to Communist satellite countries such as Czechoslovakia, Hungary, Poland, and Rumania, and Radio Liberty, which beams programs to the Soviet Union.[25]

The Case for Government Regulation

The relationship between broadcasters and the government is a forced marriage that has never enjoyed a honeymoon atmosphere. Broadcasters are ever fearful that their privileges will be regulated to oblivion, and government agencies are afraid that broadcasters will take advantage of their privileges to the detriment of the entire system. The upper hand is attached to a constantly swinging pendulum seeking a middle ground.[26]

Sometimes government regulation protects the broadcaster. Obviously the technical regulations fall into this category, preventing the interference and chaos that reigned in the 1920s. Also, the system generally insures that stations are licensed only to people of proper character so that one or two bad apple stations cannot ruin the entire broadcasting barrel.

Licenses are also refused to station applicants who might promote unfair competition, and antitrust suits are filed against station owners who tend to monopolize. This protects the free marketplace and helps all broadcasters stay in business once they have obtained a license.

The rules that have been established to limit the number of stations which any one company can own are an example of the government's attempt to prevent large companies from taking over all broadcasting, thus eliminating opportunities for smaller companies and individuals. The government's constant concern over newspaper-broadcasting cross-ownership is an example of its attempt both to provide communities with varying points of view and to provide broadcasting as a whole with diverse ownership.

Government regulations generally attempt to protect station owners from being overpowered by the networks. The ruling that limits to three

Figure 8.11
Voice of America's
master control board.
Two technicians on duty
around the clock can
feed twenty-six pro-
grams to VOA's U.S.
transmitters at the same
time and can switch all
channels at every sta-
tion break.
Photo courtesy of United
States Information Agency

Figure 8.12
Antennas at VOA's
Greenville, North
Carolina relay station.
Photo courtesy of United
States Information Agency.

hours per night the number of hours of prime time programming which networks can supply was an example of an attempt in this direction, as was the ruling which disallowed one company from owning two networks, thus separating NBC Red and Blue into NBC and ABC.

The checks and balances function of the government works to protect the freedom of the press and support the First Amendment, a vital need for broadcast journalism.

Government regulation also protects the public. In personal ways it protects the individual against slander and invasion of privacy. On a more general plane, it attempts to protect the public at large from one-sided presentations of controversial or political issues, from obscenity, and from intentional distortion of fact in both programs and commercials.

Regulatory agencies generally take the point of view that the airwaves belong to the people and should serve those people. Since broadcasting is basically a business intent on profit, it would probably offer no public service if left to its own devices but rather would concentrate only on types of programs which ensure large audiences. By structuring in such a way that stations must provide public affairs, educational, and religious pro- gramming, the regulatory agencies feel they are serving the people.

Regulation also protects against rapid irreversible change. Both the FCC and FTC are criticized for laxness and slowness, but by setting down only vague guidelines and deciding most issues on a case-by-case basis, both organizations prevent cataclysmic changes which would jar the systems of individuals and companies. There is usually a great deal of advance warning and discussion before any sort of policy is set, and even what is set can easily be overturned if it does not work as intended. The net result is moderation and the kind of policy that survives a host of tests. This indirect method of regulation allows for compromises that can resolve conflicting points of view and for new interpretations of the Communications Act.

The Case Against Government Regulation

Criticism of government regulation abounds, particularly within broad- casting circles. A loud cry of anguish against the evils of paperwork can be heard each year as stations attempt to have their licenses renewed. Station owners argue that the government forms are too long and the red tape too tangled, that license renewal applications digest reams of paper which just might happen to be read by some government employee, and that the time and energy that goes into renewal applications could be better spent prepar- ing the public service programs which the government is advocating. At the very least, broadcasters think that licenses could be renewed for five years rather than three to help cut down on the needless work.

Regulation is condemned because it drifts, stalls, and vacillates. Terms such as "interest, convenience, and necessity" on which lifeblood decisions are made are inadequately defined. Semantic problems plague the definition of "public service." Guidelines issued by the various agencies are often muddled to start with, altered frequently, and then reversed by the courts. The broadcaster trying to abide by the law becomes confused and befuddled and must wade through thick books which attempt to explain broadcast rules, regulations, and policies.[27] FCC and FTC commissioners often have widely disparate views as to the extent to which their agencies should regulate, and many of their decisions are by a one-vote margin.

The snail's pace of decision-making is a constant frustration to broadcasters. The length of time needed to obtain a construction permit or to secure permission to alter a technical device can try souls and pocketbooks. The long, drawn-out hearings, almost always held in Washington, are a great personal and financial inconvenience to the broadcasters involved. Some of the slowness is attributed to the ineptness of the bureaucracy involved and some to the overdeliberation of commissioners and judges. All government agencies suffer from an overload of work which not only slows the process but also prohibits thoroughness. The size of the FCC staff, for example, is much too small to allow for thorough analysis of the license applications it receives each year. There are so many problems inherent in broadcasting that the FCC can do little more than put out fires. Neither commissioners nor staff members have time or opportunity to develop policy or do long-range planning. Hence, many decisions are based on the facts of today without consideration for the plans of tomorrow.

Even in areas where the FCC and FTC claim to regulate in a systematic manner, they are often accused of being ineffective. The FCC, for example, is supposed to see that stations broadcast in the public interest. But educational, religious, and public service groups do not feel really helped because the material they do get to air is low-budget and broadcast at undesirable times. The FCC does not regulate airing time or production cost for these groups, so in effect it is not aiding their cause significantly.

Asking broadcasters to predict their programming strategies for three years in advance is often called unrealistic, from both a regulatory and a broadcasting point of view. Constant changes in society make it necessary for broadcasters to react and cover problems that were not cited at license renewal time, and make it necessary for the commission to overlook unfulfilled promises by broadcasters at the next license renewal period.

Some claim that in an attempt to allow for a multitude of broadcast ownership possibilities, regulators are preventing large companies which own multiple stations from growing. These companies are generally the ones that can undertake the most innovative broadcasting because they have capital to back them up and do not need to be overly concerned with the short-term dollar. For example, newspaper owners are especially efficient at owning broadcasting stations because news functions can double up.

Federal Trade Commission rulings against false advertising can be particularly ineffective. By the time the FTC conducts an investigation and issues a cease and desist order for a particular commercial, the commercial has run its course anyhow and sold many products, so the company is quite willing to remove it from the airwaves. Sometimes legal proceedings concerning a type of advertising may go on for ten years and all during that time the advertising continues. About the only real clout the FTC has regarding any particular ad is the bad publicity which might arise for the company involved. This effect can be unfortunate too, for if the company is innocent, it still suffers from the bad publicity.

Many people feel that the regulating agencies overstep their bounds and tread on the wrong side of the thin line that separates watchdog and dog watched. The primary criticisms are against the FCC's incursions into programming decisions. The Communications Act specifically prohibits censorship, but some of the actions taken by the FCC in the name of "public interest" are controversial enough to raise cries of censorship.

Regulation suffers from people problems that often seem unsolvable. Commissioners who come to the FCC have little prior experience with broadcasting, and yet some of them use their FCC position as a stepping stone to high-paying executive positions within broadcasting. Senators and congressmen depend on the support of broadcasters to become elected and hence are often heavily influenced by broadcasting lobbies.

Despite all the pros and cons of regulation, broadcasters have managed to exist with it through periods of growth and rapid change, and it is likely to remain with them in the years to come.

Summary

The U.S. government exercises less control over radio and TV than do most governments, but many federal agencies are involved.

The *FCC* handles a great deal besides radio and TV, but within the broadcasting areas it oversees technical and licensing functions. Technical functions include preventing *interference, licensing* personnel, allocating *frequencies,* designating *call letters,* and requiring *logs.* The FCC licenses in accordance with the character, financial, technical, and programming qualifications of the license holder; it *renews licenses* taking citizen opinion into account; it *revokes licenses;* and it oversees *license transfers.* The *FTC*'s jurisdiction relates to deceptive advertising, which it both prosecutes and attempts to prevent. The courts have issued many decisions involving censorship, freedom of speech, *lotteries,* editorials, *equal time,* and *fairness.* Limited control of broadcasting is also exercised by Congress, the president, and other federal agencies. In addition, the government operates *AFRTS* and *VOA.* Regulation is a highly controversial subject with some of the major disputes involving newspaper-broadcasting cross-ownership, possible regulation of networks, program regulation, license renewal procedures, semantic problems, and the slowness and ineffectiveness of regulation.

9 **Unto Thyself Be True**
Self-Regulation

*The NAB reminds me of a dead mackerel in the moonlight—
it both shines and stinks.*

James Fly, former FCC Commissioner

Cartoon copyrighted by *Braodcasting* magazine

"The chamber of commerce is on our necks again . . . They want us to say 'partly sunny' instead of 'partly cloudy.' "

While the FCC represents the most formidable external regulation force of broadcasting, the codes of the National Association of Broadcasters (NAB) represent an internal source of self-regulation—an attempt by broadcasters to keep their own house in order.

In addition to the NAB codes, there are other written, oral, and subtle forms of self-regulation, such as advertiser, network, and individual station standards; personal convictions of people within the industry; opinions expressed in journals and organization meetings; and awards for excellence.

If there were no FCC, there would no doubt still be some form of regulation of the radio and TV industry because the nature of broadcasting is so public and omnipresent that outside criticism is bound to have its impact. In order to maintain a positive image and an audience, to say nothing of a **license,** a broadcaster must subscribe to some standards. The credibility of all broadcasting suffers when quacks use the airwaves to promote goat gland operations claimed to enhance male virility, or when the public discovers that disc jockeys are being paid under the table to plug certain records.

Forces for Self-Regulation

Self-regulation is a phenomenon dating from the early days of broadcasting. In 1929 the NAB established a morally upright list of standards little adhered to and soon ignored, but it was a beginning for what became the NAB code. The code was revised a number of times, and in 1952 a second code was drafted to cover TV.[1] Throughout the years the NAB codes, as well as other codes and standards, have been altered, strengthened, weakened, and deleted in an attempt to balance outside forces and the realities of the broadcasting business. In some instances the codes have, admittedly, only locked the barn door after the horse was stolen. For example, not until it was discovered that quiz shows were rigged did the NAB code include a provision against such collusion.

Many forces are at work helping to set the standards of self-regulation which broadcasters adopt. Probably the most formidable is government. Broadcasters are ever fearful of increased federal regulation from both FCC rules and regulations and congressional laws. Therefore, their own regulations are often attempts to "head them off at the pass." If they feel the government is close to mandating certain actions, they will incorporate those actions into one of the nonmandatory codes, thus reducing the government's need to act.

Community and national citizens' **pressure groups** can alter broadcasters' behavior. Organizations such as the NAACP and NOW have been successful in changing both program fare and hiring practices as they relate to minorities. Action for Children's Television and similar community action groups have had an important role in changing children's programming. Consumer groups have frequently organized boycotts against products advertised on certain programs, and recently broad consumer groups have established a power base to affect overall programming. The groups, such as the National Association for Better Broadcasting and the American Council for Better Broadcasts, consider that their members are consumers of television programs and are thus qualified to campaign for

Figure 9.1   **Figure 9.2**

better television programming in the same way that other consumer groups campaign for accurate ingredient listings on food products.

Professional critics occasionally serve as a catalyst for establishing self-regulation. Their individual influence is small because television programs live and die by ratings rather than by critical review, but their columns are sometimes used to substantiate points being made by other groups. Occasionally critics have been instrumental in saving a news or documentary show which might have been dropped for poor ratings.

Broadcasters are often the brunt of comments by national opinion leaders. It is hard to tell whether either Newton Minow's "vast wasteland" speech or former Vice President Agnew's blast at broadcast journalism led to any self-regulation, but both certainly caused a stir within the industry.

Both economic forces and current events can shape self-regulation policies. During the depression years the amount of commercial time allowable by the NAB code increased. And more restrictions were placed on violent programming after the King and Kennedy assassinations.

The Structure of NAB Code Regulation

The National Association of Broadcasters was formed in 1923, not to act as a self-regulation agency, but to counter demands from the American Society of Composers. Artists, and Publishers (ASCAP) regarding increases in the amount ASCAP was planning to charge radio stations for airing music. In fact, the first managing director of the NAB was a veteran of ASCAP battles with the piano roll industry.[2] Since the resolution of the ASCAP issue, the NAB has acquired many other purposes. It lobbies in Washington for congressional actions favorable to broadcasters. It holds conventions and workshops to facilitate communication and professional growth among industry members. It supports and conducts broadcast-related research. It acts as a public relations arm for all of broadcasting. And it encourages and implements self-regulation.

This last task is accomplished primarily through "The Television Code" and "The Radio Code," booklets which spell out do's and don'ts for television and radio stations. However, abiding by the codes is entirely voluntary—broadcasters are not in any way forced to do so. Stations which subscribe to one of the codes can display the code's "Seal of Good Practice" and are generally looked upon favorably by the FCC for complying with the standards.

Only about 30 percent of the nation's radio stations and 50 percent of the TV stations subscribe to the codes.[3] Reasons vary. For one thing, it costs money. A radio station subscribing to the code must pay 75 percent of its highest minute rate per month up to a maximum of $27 per month. A TV station's rate is based on market size, status, and the station's affiliation, with the amount paid yearly ranging from approximately $100 to $5,000.[4]

Many stations are unwilling to live within the restrictions of the code, particularly those dealing with the amount of time devoted to commercials. Conversely, some stations have discontinued subscribing to the code because they think the programming and advertising standards are too lenient.

The procedures for establishing the radio and television codes differ slightly. In both instances members of the code board are appointed by the president of the NAB from individuals representing stations or networks that subscribe to the code. The radio code board consists of no more than eleven members, with no more than two representatives from each network. The TV code board consists of no more than nine members, with no more than one representative from each network. All are appointed for three-year terms. There are slight differences between radio and television regarding how many consecutive terms one individual can serve. Of course, if a station or network resigns from the code or has its affiliation withdrawn for violation, a member from that station or network can no longer serve on the board.

Both the radio and television code boards meet at least twice a year to review the code with an eye toward making recommendations for changes. They also consider cases brought to their attention which may involve code violations. The actual day-to-day work involved with code regulations is handled by a code authority director and his staff. This director is responsible for reviewing programming and commercials presented over the media, reviewing and screening complaints, interpreting words and phrases of the codes, maintaining liaison with governmental agencies, recommending amendments to the codes, and handling the procedures taken against alleged violators. The latter involves informing the station or network by registered mail of the charges against it and then setting up hearing procedures with the appropriate code board.

The code boards report to either the NAB television board of directors or the NAB radio board of directors, which are the bodies that have the authority to alter the codes or suspend subscribers. In practice, they usually accept the recommendations of the code boards.

Several thousand programs and commercials are submitted to the code authority director each year for screening before they are aired. The code authority does not review every commercial and program appearing on a subscriber's station—to do so would require an enormous staff and budget. Rather, subscribers may submit material to the code authority for an opinion, and usually do if they feel the material may be controversial. Producers thereby add the ounce of prevention needed to waylay criticisms after the fact. This procedure mitigates the chances of a station or network being expelled from the code—an action rarely taken. It is not uncommon, however, for stations to resign from the code because they disagree with certain new provisions.

Syndicators, film companies, independent production houses, and others involved in the production, distribution, sale, or lease of recorded programs can become affiliate subscribers to the code. Buyers of their material are thus assured that they meet the requirements of the NAB code. However, the buyers too can submit material for review.

A station or other organization remains a subscriber to the code permanently unless the group resigns, is expelled, or does not pay its yearly fee. There is no formal review procedure of all stations to make sure they are adhering to standards. They are assumed to be doing so unless some complaint or monitoring shows otherwise.[5]

The Television Code

According to the regulations and procedures of the television code, its purpose is "to maintain a level of television programming which gives full consideration to the educational, informational, cultural, economic, moral and entertainment needs of the American public to the end that more and more people will be better served."[6]

Typical code provisions are that narcotic addiction should not be presented except as a destructive habit; material should not be broadcast which is obscene, profane, or indecent; special sensitivity is necessary in the use of materials relating to sex, race, color, age, creed, religious functionaries or rites, or national or ethnic derivation; the use of liquor and the depiction of smoking in program content should be deemphasized; any technique that attempts to convey information to the viewer below the threshold of normal awareness is not permitted; contests may not constitute a lottery; news reporting should be factual, fair, and without bias; morbid, sensational, or alarming details not essential to news should be avoided; commentary and analysis should be clearly identified as such; the television broadcaster should seek out and develop programs relating to controversial public issues; requests for time for public service announcements should be carefully reviewed with respect to the character and reputation of the group; the advertising of hard liquor is not acceptable; acceptability of ads for personal products should be determined with emphasis on ethics and canons of good taste; personal endorsements should be genuine and reflect personal experience; no children's program personality or cartoon character should deliver commercials within or adjacent to programs in which the person or character regularly appears; and the television broadcaster should not accept medical advertising which offensively describes or dramatizes distress or morbid situations involving ailments.[7]

Over the years certain portions of this code have been surrounded by controversy. The standards on violence and obscenity have been changed a number of times and are considered too ambiguous and lenient by some. Likewise, there is debate over what constitutes "morbid, sensational and alarming details" in a newscast. Some broadcasters feel that the code places too great an onus on them for screening out undesirable organizations and advertisers wishing to present messages on TV. Provisions regarding medical advertising and advertising to children have caused dissension in the ranks.

Perhaps most of all, time standards for advertising cause a great deal of controversy both within and without the industry because this is a bread and butter issue. If a station thinks it cannot break even using the NAB standards, it will not subscribe to the code. Recently the TV code board established different standards for **independent** stations than for **affiliates** because so many independents felt they had greater financial hardships than other stations. The time standards are rather complicated, but some of the basics can be summarized as follows:

Total minutes of nonprogram material allowed per hour:

Prime time, affiliated stations	9:30
Other time, affiliated stations	16:00
Sat. & Sun. children's programs, affiliated stations	9:30
Mon-Fri. children's programs, affiliated stations	12:00
Prime time, independents	14:00
Other time, independents	16:00

Total number of interruptions per hour:

Prime time, affiliated stations	4
Other time, affiliated stations	8
Sat. & Sun. children's programs, affiliated stations	4
Mon-Fri. children's programs, affiliated stations	8
All time, independents	7

However, there are many exceptions to these basics. For example: (1) Sixty-minute variety programs may have five interruptions. (2) News, sports, and similar programs can be interrupted any number of times depending on program format. (3) Only three consecutive announcements can be made during station breaks (this is why many stations return very briefly to program material after three commercials and a station break; it is then all right for them to present three more commercials). (4) Single sponsors can present more than three or four ads at a time if doing so cuts down on interruptions. (5) An independent station which carries commercials at station breaks can have only six interruptions per hour program. (6) Sometimes independents can run seven announcements consecutively in order to cut down on clutter.

Another confusing area of time standards relates to the definition of nonprogram material since this involves not only standard commercials but also billboards (brief ads usually consisting of a slide with a picture or name and phone number), announcements about other programs which the station airs, and credits of any sort that are longer than thirty seconds. Excluded from the definition of nonprogram material are public service announcements and announcements about the program presently being shown. When game shows extol the virtues of a product awarded to a contestant as a prize or give credit to a hotel or airline for services rendered, this is considered program material unless it exceeds the thirty-second time limit. Praise for an airline that lasts sixty seconds counts as thirty seconds of nonprogram time.

Sometimes special reports are issued by the NAB to expand advertising standards for troublesome products such as toys, personal products, alcoholic beverages, acne products, and nonprescription medicines.

The Radio Code

The NAB radio code is very similar to the TV code with one major difference being the amount of time allowable for commercials. The radio specifications are much less complicated than the TV: "The amount of time to be used for advertising should not exceed 18 minutes within any clock hour. The Code Authority, however, for good cause may approve advertising exceeding the above standard for special circumstances."[8]

For the most part, concepts of the radio programming specifications differ from TV only where peculiar aspects of the aural experience are involved. For example, the radio code states that "without sacrificing integrity of presentation, dramatic programs on radio shall avoid . . . sound effects calculated to mislead, or shock, or unduly alarm the listener."[9] Along the same line, the radio code warns that "broadcasters are responsible for making good faith determinations on the acceptability of lyrics under applicable Radio Code standards,"[10] and that "guests on discussion/interview programs and members of the public who participate in phone-in programs shall be treated with due respect by the program host/hostess."[11]

Advertising Self-Regulation

Advertising is one of the most criticized aspects of broadcasting. It is also substantially affected by outside forces. The businesses and corporations which advertise usually impose restrictions on their ads, as do radio and television networks and stations and the NAB codes. However, despite all these prior restrictions, often ads that are broadcast are considered misleading, exploitive, or offensive by elements of the public. The Federal Trade Commission is, of course, the government agency acting as a watchdog over such ads, but the advertising industry itself in the early 1970s decided to form a policing agency, the National Advertising Review Board (NARB).

This board became an agency to handle complaints about ads from an individual, a group, an advertiser's competition, or the board's own monitoring activities. The board is made up of fifty members—thirty representing national advertisers, ten representing **advertising agencies,** and ten representing the public. The fifty members, all unpaid, never meet as a group but are appointed as needed to serve on five-person panels to consider specific complaints.

Before the complaints reach these panels, they are screened and sometimes resolved by the National Advertising Division (NAD) of the Council of Better Business Bureaus. The overall structure of the NARB and appointment of its members are handled by a committee made up of the presidents of the American Advertising Federation, the American Association of Advertising Agencies, the Association of National Advertisers, and the Council of Better Business Bureaus.

Complaints reviewed by the NAD and NARB involve such matters as the adequacy of substantiation of a product claim, competence of a person making a testimonial, claims with respect to price savings, fair and honest reference to a competitor's product, and proper substantiation for guarantees and warranties. When the NAD receives a complaint, it asks the advertiser for substantiation of its claim. If this substantiation is accepted, the matter is closed. If not, the NAD discusses the matter with the advertiser in the hope of resolving the problem by having the advertiser agree to alter or withdraw the ad. If this is not accomplished, the matter is referred to the NARB, which reviews the matter and makes a recommendation which it hopes the advertiser will accept. If not, the NARB refers the matter to the FTC.

An advertiser's participation in this procedure is, of course, voluntary. The advertiser can simply ignore the request from the NAD, but that would be foolhardy because of the bad press and inevitable government action that would result.[12]

Network and Station Policies

All networks and many stations have their own written or unwritten codes even though they subscribe to the NAB codes, and their codes are usually stricter and more detailed than the NAB codes. For example, some stations will not accept beer and wine ads even though they are approved by the NAB codes. Other stations publish a list of words which they consider obscene or indecent.

At the networks, the business of making sure that all programs and commercials adhere to both NAB code and network regulations falls to the **broadcast standards** department, a group operating independently of programming or sales and reporting directly to top network management. This group reviews all program and commercial ideas when they are in outline or storyboard form and then screens them several times again as they progress through scripting and production. If any of the ideas proposed run counter to standards, the broadcast standards department requests changes before the idea can proceed to the next step. A broadcast standards employee almost always observes program rehearsals and tapings and may request costume or movement changes. The department is also responsible for making sure all copyrighted material used within programs has been cleared and that all advertising claims can be substantiated.

Naturally, all is not roses and honey between broadcast standards and

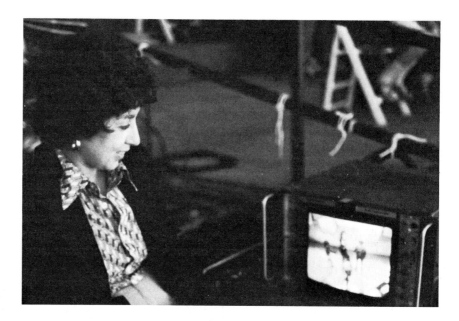

Figure 9.3
Susan Futterman,
manager of children's
programs for ABC's
broadcast standards
department, previews a
proposed children's
show.
Photo courtesy of Susan
Futterman

program or commercial producers. The latter can appeal decisions to top management or try to convince broadcast standards to compromise on certain issues.

At local stations the broadcast standards function may not be as formal. Frequently the general manager performs the function on an "as needed" basis, and sometimes the function is delegated to whatever group or person handles station legal matters or public relations.

Network and station self-regulation occurs constantly and informally at all levels through the actions of individuals employed in broadcasting. A disc jockey who decides not to play a record he considers in poor taste is engaging in self-regulation even though management gives him no direction on the matter. Likewise, writers, producers, directors, actors and actresses, and editors are constantly making decisions based on their own ideas of propriety and appropriateness.[13]

Broadcasting Organizations

Self-regulation is promoted by organizations besides the NAB. Occasionally it takes the form of a formal code, as in the case of the Radio-Television News Directors Association Code of Broadcast News Ethics. More often it is in the form of written or informal guidelines established at meetings. Often it involves matters first discussed in some of these organizations, which eventually wind up as issues for the NAB codes.

Most of the organizations represent subgroups of the radio and TV business, the proliferation of which is often a matter for criticism. For example, broadcast executives can choose to join the National Association of Television Program Executives, the Association of Maximum Service Telecasters, the Institute for Broadcast Financial Management, the Broadcasters Promotion Association, the National Association of Council Broadcast Executives, the Association of Independent Television Stations, the

Daytime Broadcasting Association, and/or the National Association of FM Broadcasters.

For news personnel there are such organizations as the Radio-Television News Directors Association, the Association of Radio Television News Analysts, and the Radio-TV Correspondents Association.

Engineers have available to them the Audio Engineering Society, the Institute of Electrical and Electronic Engineers, the Society of Broadcast Engineers, and the Society of Motion Picture and Television Engineers.

Advertising organizations abound, including the American Advertising Federation, the American Association of Advertising Agencies, the Affiliated Advertising Agencies International, the Advertising Research Foundation, the Association of National Advertisers, the League of Advertising Agencies, the Radio Advertising Bureau, and the Television Bureau of Advertising.

For educators there are such organizations as the National Association of Educational Broadcasters, the Broadcast Education Association, and the Association of Public Radio Stations.

The Academy of Television Arts and Sciences is for those involved in the creative activities of programming; Alpha Epsilon Rho is a national honorary broadcasting society; and Broadcast Pioneers is open to those who were involved in early radio and TV.

Other representative organizations include American Women in Radio and Television, the Association of Black Broadcast Executives, the FM Rock Broadcaster Association, the National Association of Gagwriters, the National Cable Television Association, National Religious Broadcasters, the National Association of Independent Television Producers and Distributors, and the National Association of Farm Broadcasters.[14]

Figure 9.4
A panel discussion on student internships at a convention of the Broadcast Education Association.
Photo courtesy of Livingston Hinckley

Broadcasting Awards

Like the organizations, broadcasting awards have an informal regulatory function. Broadcasters covet awards and use them for personal and station promotion. Therefore, they will frequently air programs which they feel might qualify for awards.

Most famous of the TV awards are the Emmys bestowed by the Academy of Television Arts and Sciences for many categories of national programming. Each year the categories within which awards will be made are hotly disputed by committees of industry representatives. How many westerns should be on TV before an award is given for best western? Is sound mixing on videotape enough different from sound mixing on film to merit separate Emmys? Should writers of short series be placed in the series category or the specials category? These intramural disputes occur to some extent because of the changing nature of TV programs, the huge outpouring of material, and the importance placed on winning an Emmy.

For commercials, the top statuette is the Clio, given annually at the American TV and Radio Commercials Festival Awards for best U.S. radio and TV commercials. The prestigious George Foster Peabody Awards for Distinguished Broadcasting are bestowed annually in news, entertainment, education, youth programs, promotion of international understanding, and public service.

Other awards include the American Optometric Association Public Service Award for outstanding broadcasts on the subject of vision; the Major Armstrong Award for excellence in FM broadcasting; the Freedoms Foundation Awards for programs to bring about a better understanding of America; the Golden Mike Awards for excellence in news writing and

Figure 9.5
The Emmy, awarded for outstanding television programming.
Photo courtesy of the Academy of Television Arts and Sciences

presentation; the International Broadcasting Awards for worldwide radio and TV commercials; the Mortgage Bankers of America "Janus" Awards for excellence in financial news programming; the National Press Photographers Association Awards for best news film; and the Silver Anvil Awards for public service programming.[15]

Radio- and TV-oriented periodicals can act as a platform for discussions of issues pertinent to broadcasters' well-being. While they do not formally—or even informally—regulate, many of the subjects written about will later work their way into forms of self-regulation.

Radio and Television Publications

The "bible" of the industry is *Broadcasting,* a weekly magazine covering the gamut of industry news, such as the latest FCC and Congressional actions, speeches of industry leaders, conventions, executive changes, economic trends and reports, and programming concepts. Once a year the same organization that publishes *Broadcasting* publishes *Broadcasting Yearbook,* which contains a wealth of material grouped under such headings as "Broadcasting in General," "The TV Marketplace," "Facilities of Radio," "Broadcast Advertising," "Equipment and Engineering," and "Professional Services." Within these categories are names, addresses, and facts about all radio and TV stations in the country and all advertising agencies, networks, program suppliers, equipment distributors, and other broadcasting-related groups.

Variety and *The Hollywood Reporter* are trade journals covering news of the entire entertainment field and are heavily subscribed to by those in the industry. Copies of *Billboard* can be found in most radio stations, since this publication covers the record and music scene and lists the top hits in various categories of music. On the scholarly side, *Journal of Broadcasting* is one of several journals to concentrate on historical, statistical, bibliographical, and legal aspects of broadcasting. *TV Guide* is well known to

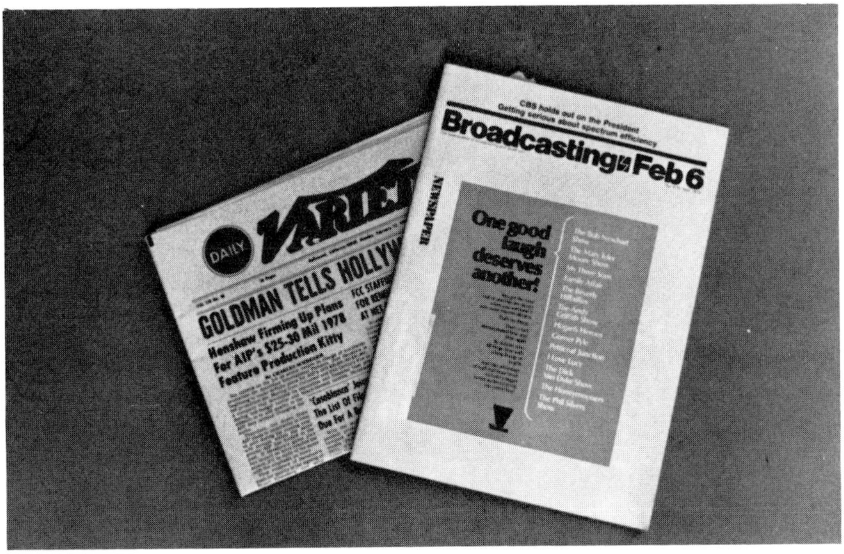

Figure 9.6
Two well known entertainment periodicals, *Variety* and *Broadcasting.*

most people for its list of weekly programs and articles of interest to the general public.

An almost endless, changing list of periodicals aim at subgroups of the radio-TV business. Many are official organs of the professional societies mentioned earlier. The names of these journals are usually indicative of their target audience—e.g., *Broadcast Management/Engineering; Public Telecommunication Review; Cable Report; Educational and Industrial Television; Advertising Age; Journal of College Radio; Journal of the SMPTE; Television/Radio Age; Broadcast Engineering; European Broadcasting Union Review; Journal of Advertising Research; Radio Broadcast.* [16]

An Assessment of Self-Regulation

It is impossible to brand self-regulation as an absolute good or absolute bad. Obviously, because of its voluntary nature, self-regulation does not always work.

Self-regulation does weaken the need for government regulation; but, again, there are those who think that broadcasting should be under a larger federal thumb so that procedures which are now voluntary could become mandatory.

The various forces of self-regulation often have incurable flaws. The NAB code authority budget does not allow for as thorough screening of material as some people would like; and yet, self-regulation is already a more costly activity than many stations are willing to support. Consumers are underrepresented on regulating boards, but how does one find the "typical consumer" to sit in judgment?

The informal vehicles of self-regulation—organizations, awards, periodicals—can be criticized for over-proliferation, wheel-spinning, and inequality, and yet they can point with pride to accomplishments.

Summary

The broadcasting industry has many mechanisms of self-regulation by which it sets standards for serving the public properly in the hope of holding off excessive government regulation.

The government, *consumer groups, critics,* and *opinion leaders* all have a role in helping broadcasters set standards. The primary self-regulation organ is the *NAB code,* which includes a television code and radio code, drawn up and revised by representatives of stations and networks. These codes contain both programming and advertising guidelines. The code authority is an administrative body that screens programs and commercials on request and handles the initial stages of violations. The advertising industry has established the *NARB* to police its own industry. Its effectiveness, like that of the NAB, depends on voluntary cooperation. Networks and stations also engage in self-regulation through their *broadcast standards* departments. More informal forms of self-regulation come from broadcasting's *professional organizations,* such as NATPE, IEEE, AAAA, NAEB, and AWRT; from *awards,* such as the Emmy, Clio, and Peabody; and from *periodicals,* such as *Broadcasting, Variety,* and *Billboard.*

10 The Bottom Line
Advertising and Business Practices

Papa, what is the moon supposed to advertise?

Carl Sandburg, in The People, Yes

Cartoon copyrighted by *Broadcasting* magazine

"The boys in sales may be a little cocky, but they do bring in the bucks."

The root of all broadcasting is money. Simply stated, radio and television stations obtain money from advertisers and use it to produce and transmit programs. However, some of the mechanics of broadcast finances are complicated processes involving rate cards, advertising agencies, station representatives, and profit analysis.[1]

Basic to most broadcast sales is the **rate card** , a chartlike listing of the prices that the station charges for different types of ads. One of the many variables that affect the prices listed on the rate card is the number of commercials the advertiser wishes to air. Stations rarely accept only one ad at a time—it would be too expensive in relation to the time taken by the salesperson to sell the ad. What's more, a buyer would not realize satisfactory results if its product was mentioned only once. Usually a station requires that an advertiser air an ad at least twelve times. It will try to induce the advertiser to buy even more than that by offering lower prices per ad as the number of ads increases. For example, a company which places an ad twelve times on a radio station might be required to pay $25 per ad, or a total of $300. If it bought twenty-four ads, it would pay $20 per ad, or a total of $480. And if its ad ran thirty-six times, each ad would be reduced to $18, for a total of $648.

Another variable is the length of the ad—usually twenty, thirty, or sixty seconds. Obviously, a one-minute commercial will cost more than a thirty-second commercial, but usually not twice as much. For example, twelve one-minute ads might cost $25 each, and twelve thirty-second ads might cost $15 each.

Another major cost variable is the type of facility on which the ad is purchased. A thirty-second ad that costs $25 on a radio station might cost $1,000 on a radio network; $750 on an **independent** TV station; $1,000 on a network-owned TV station; and $60,000 on a TV network. The underlying basis of all rate cards is the number of station listeners or viewers, so a 3,000 watt FM station would not charge as high a rate as a 50,000 watt AM station; and a small town TV station would have a much lower overall rate card than a similar station in a metropolitan area.

Audiences are of varying sizes at different times of the day, so this factor too becomes a variable on rate cards. A radio station or network would probably have the greatest number of people listening from 7:00 to 9:00 a.m. and 4:00 to 6:00 p.m., when people are in their cars commuting. This would be referred to as its Class AA time and would cost the most money. From 9:00 a.m. to 4:00 p.m. and 6:00 to 10:00 p.m. would have a lower fee and be referred to as Class A time. The lowest rate of all would be Class B time, which would be 10:00 p.m. to 7:00 a.m., when people are sleeping. Television stations are a different story, with the most viewers congregated between 7:00 and 11:00 p.m. for its Class AA time. Classes A and B vary from station to station depending on programming. Some stations fine-tune their times to AAA, AA, A, B, and C degrees. Television stations often sell ads on particular programs rather than for particular times, so that an ad bought at 9:00 p.m. Tuesday during "The Tuesday

Rate Cards

Night Movie'' might cost more than an ad bought at 9:00 p.m. Wednesday during ''This Week's Report.'' In this case, the rate card lists programs rather than times. Televison networks usually do not employ a rate card at all but sell ads based on what the market will bear.

Other variables are often taken into account when rate cards are established. Such factors are the number of months or years an advertiser utilizes a particular station; the average age of the audience listening or viewing; and whether an advertiser is willing to be flexible concerning the advertising times or whether a fixed position is wanted to assure that an ad will be run at a particular time. Sample rate cards are reproduced on the opposite page—one for a small station, the other for a large station.[2]

Selling Practices

Theoretically, a station time sales representative approaches a potential advertiser, convinces him to buy a group of ads at the price established on the rate card, and then sees that a bill is sent to the advertiser for the correct amount. However, in the real world of economics, this theoretical case is not always the practiced one.

For example, many radio stations, particularly smaller ones, engage in what is called **barter** or trade-out; they trade an advertiser air time for some service the station needs. Perhaps the station owns a car which needs occasional service; in order to receive this service free from Joe's Garage, the station will broadcast twelve ads a week for Joe's Garage with no money changing hands. Similar barter arrangements are often negotiated with restaurants, stationery suppliers, gas stations, audio equipment stores, and the like.

Some stations sell ads on a per-inquiry basis, which means the station gets paid only if consumers respond to the ad. A typical sales pitch for such an arrangement might be, ''Hurry right down to your nearest Foody Market, buy at least $10 of groceries, mention WXXX to the check-out clerk and receive absolutely free one toothbrush of your choice.'' For each toothbrush given away, the station would receive a set amount of money.

Another unusual advertising buy is called the **timebank.** An advertiser supplies a program to a station in return for an agreed-upon amount of time that can be used as needed. For example, the Wham-Em Sporting Goods Company might produce a cartoon show on bike safety for children and give this to a local station in exchange for twenty-four ads during the home team baseball game broadcasts and twelve ads during the company's special presummer sale week.

Another variation from the rate card is called **run-of-the-schedule. A** salesperson sells time to an advertiser at the lowest rate on the card with the agreement that the station will air the ads at the best time it has available after all other ads are placed. If the station is almost totally sold out, the advertising company gets the short end of the stick, for its ads are placed at the poorest times. However, if the station has some of its best time available, the advertiser can get a better deal than what was paid for.

Co-op advertising involves shared costs, usually by a national and a local advertiser. A commercial for an ''Instant Pleasure'' camera may end,

CLASS "AAA"				CLASS "AA"		
3 PM — 12 MIDNIGHT, Monday - Friday				6 AM — 10 AM, Monday - Sunday		
10 AM — 12 MIDNIGHT, Saturday - Sunday						
	60's	30's			60's	30's
1x	$90	$76		1x	$70	$60
6x	$80	$68		6x	$65	$55
12x	$70	$60		12x	$60	$50

CLASS "A"				CLASS "B"	
10 AM — 3 PM, Monday - Friday				12 Mid — 2 AM, Monday - Sunday	
	60's	30's		Flat Rate:	$25
1x	$60	$50		CLASS "C"	
6x	$55	$45		2 AM — 6 AM, Monday - Sunday	
12x	$50	$40		Flat Rate:	$15

Figure 10.1
Rate card of a small radio station.

FREQUENCY ANNOUNCEMENTS

Announcement rates are based on the number used during an established twelve-month period, and become effective from the beginning of service on firm contracts or as earned.

60-Second Announcements

(150 Words, Live)

Times	AAA	* AAA Combo	AA	A	B	** C
1	$320	$250	$205	$131	$100	$44
15	309	247	194	124	95	42
50	296	237	179	116	89	39
150	275	220	166	107	84	36
300	261	209	159	100	79	34
500	253	202	154	97	77	33
750	246	197	151	95	75	32
1000	240	192	149	93	74	31

30-Second Announcements

(75 Words, Live)

		*				**
1	$256	$205	$164	$105	$80	$35
15	248	198	155	99	76	34
50	238	190	143	92	71	31
150	220	176	132	86	67	29
300	209	167	127	80	63	28
500	203	162	124	78	61	27
750	195	156	121	76	60	26
1000	193	154	120	75	59	25

10-Second Announcements

(25 Words, Live)

		*				**
1	$160	$130	$103	$66	$50	$22
15	155	124	98	62	47	21
50	148	118	89	58	45	20
150	138	110	83	54	42	19
300	130	104	80	50	40	18
500	126	101	78	48	39	17
750	124	99	76	47	38	16
1000	121	97	75	46	37	15

*Combo: Rates apply only to the number of AAA announcements that are ordered and broadcast in combination with an equal or greater number of announcements of the same or greater length within other time classifications except Class C.

Frequency Announcements Rate based on total number of announcements used during an established twelve-month period. Rate applies as earned.

Weekly Package Plan Rate based on a consecutive seven-day period.

WEEKLY PACKAGE PLAN

Weekly Package Plan rates apply only to the number of 60-second, 30-second and 10-second announcements broadcast for one product within a consecutive seven-day period on run-of-station schedules. Such announcements are subject to immediate preemption for frequency announcements without notice. Further, without liability to the Station, Weekly Package Plan announcements are subject to omission by Station without charge to Advertiser, or to rescheduling by the Station in a time period considered equivalent by the Station.

Frequency announcements may be combined with Weekly Package Plan announcements to earn lower plan rates, but Weekly Package Plan announcements may not be combined with frequency announcements to earn lower frequency rates.

60-Second Announcements

(150 Words, Live)

Weekly Plan	AAA	* AAA Combo	AA	A	B	** C
6	$291	$233	$176	$117	$94	$40
12	284	227	171	112	89	38
18	275	220	166	107	84	36
24	268	214	161	102	79	34

30-Second Announcements

(75 Words, Live)

		*				**
6	$233	$186	$142	$94	$75	$32
12	226	181	137	90	71	30
18	220	176	132	86	67	29
24	214	171	128	82	63	27

10-Second Announcements

(25 Words, Live)

		*				**
6	$146	$117	$89	$60	$48	$20
12	143	114	86	57	45	19
18	138	110	83	54	42	18
24	135	108	81	51	40	17

TIME SIGNALS

(Flat and not combinable with other announcements)
(12 Words of Commercial Copy or Six Seconds Transcribed)

AAA	* AAA COMBO	AA	A	B	** C
$104	$83	$62	$41	$30	$13

**C May be counted toward Frequency Announcements or Weekly Package Plan, but may not count toward Combo.

Figure 10.2
Rate card of a large radio station.

Figure 10.3

Figure 10.4

Figure 10.3
Preparation for a local ad for a Minneapolis savings and loan association. The ad will run during baseball season but since it must be prepared ahead of time, production takes place in San Diego during the winter so that a warm, sunny climate can be portrayed.
Photo courtesy of Centre Films—George Stupar, photographer

Figure 10.4
The staging of a ten- second station break commercial for a regional doughnut house.
Photo courtesy of Centre Films—George Stupar, photographer

Figure 10.5
Producing a commercial for a nationally distributed beverage. The part of Mr. Kool-Aide had to be performed by a stuntman because of the weight of the costume.
Photo courtesy of Centre Films—George Stupar, photographer

Figure 10.5

"To purchase this sensational camera, make a short trip to Lou's All-You-Need Photo Shop at 160 Main Street." The cost of this ad would be divided on an agreed-upon formula between Instant Pleasure and Lou's.

Some stations offer rate protection to their constant buyers so that even if the station's rate card costs increase, these good customers can still buy ads at the old prices.

Although it is poor business practice, some salespeople, in order to obtain business, simply cut the prices on the rate card and offer ads at lower prices than those indicated.

Another important difference in selling practices revolves around whether an advertiser wants to run a national, regional, or local radio or television campaign. To a large extent this is determined by the size and product line of the company wishing to advertise. It would be a total waste of money for Smith's Used Car Lot in Omaha, Nebraska to run a national ad because people from around the nation are not going to fly to Omaha to buy a used car. Much more appropriate would be advertising placed on local Omaha radio or TV. A farm equipment company would also be wasting its money with national ads but might want to advertise on a regional basis covering many of the stations in the Midwest. On the other hand, large companies with such products as automobiles, cereal, clothing, or cosmetics that are distributed throughout the country are ready-made for national advertising.

Regardless whether an advertiser opts for national, regional, or local exposure, there are two primary ways to buy advertising—program buying and **spot** buying. In the early days of radio and television most advertisers bought programs, paying all the costs to produce and air such programs as "Lux Radio Theater," "Colgate Comedy Hour," "Kraft Television Theater," and so forth. The advertiser had the advantage of constant identification with the program and its stars.

Figure 10.6
Producer Frank O'Connor (*left*) and director Patrick Garland discuss a setting along the North Sea for the "Hallmark Hall of Fame" production "The Snowgoose." Hallmark is one of the last companies to be the sole sponsor of occasional TV programs.
Photo courtesy of Frank O'Connor

**Figure 10.7
Compact video equipment being used to tape a carpeting spot.**
Photo courtesy of Centre Films—George Stupar, photographer

Program buying is rarely done anymore, for several reasons. One reason is that costs of television production have soared to the extent that not even the largest companies can afford total underwriting of a program week after week. Also, after the quiz scandals of the late 1950s, the networks were leery of such overriding program control by advertisers and began to take greater control of content. Only occasional specials are now totally paid for by one advertiser. Instead, program participation is common. When one hears, "The following portion of 'Sock It To Em' is brought to you by the Widget Manufacturing Company," several advertisers have joined together to pay the costs of the program. Each airs its ads during a particular portion of the program. This kind of program buying is usual with network TV but rare in local radio except for a few local public service or sports programs.

What is common in the local market and on network radio is spot buying. The advertiser bears none of the cost for or identfication with a particular program but rather buys air time for certain times of day. Hence a disc jockey whose show runs from 6:00 to 9:00 a.m. may present ads from several dozen advertisers, all falling under the umbrella of spot advertising. In radio, spots can be aired at almost any time since essentially all ads are spots. In television, on the other hand, spots are aired at more definite times, especially on **affiliated** stations, where network shows come already brimming with ads. In this case, the TV station sells most of its spots for station break time or for insertion in locally produced shows. Of course, some network shows do leave a few ad spaces available for local spots, which usually sell well in the local market. Independent TV stations have more spots available than affiliated stations, but, again, many of the programs they air come complete with ads. Radio network news is generally sold on a spot basis, but some of the features are purchased through the program buying process. Regardless of the selling practices used, stations must be sure that their programs fill both a station need and an advertiser need.

Sales Staffs

Radio and TV time selling—like insurance, shoes, and stock—needs a salesperson to interact between the product and the customer. Exactly how this function is executed varies greatly from station to station.

How it works in a small radio station is not difficult to follow because most of the advertising comes from the local area. Usually the disc jockeys are also salespeople, spending four hours a day announcing and playing records and four hours going to the local hardware stores, grocery stores, and car dealers selling ads. Often the general manager of a small station doubles as a salesperson too.

Within larger radio stations the selling process is more indirect. TV talent and big name disc jockeys usually do not sell time. Instead, members of a sales force contact local merchants and are generally paid on a salary plus **commission** basis. These salespeople are expected to service ads as well as sell them so that advertisers will repeat their business. Servicing ads includes such things as making sure the ads are run at the appropriate times and facilitating any copy changes that may be needed.

TV stations and larger radio stations are interested in obtaining ads from companies that distribute goods nationally—companies such as Proctor and Gamble, General Mills, and General Motors. It would be very expensive for each station to send salespeople to the headquarters of these companies, so stations generally hire **station representatives** to obtain these ads. Station representatives are national sales organizations which operate as an extension of the stations with which they deal. They are middlemen between the company that wants to buy ads or its agency and the radio or TV stations that want to sell ads. Usually these reps handle national sales for dozens of stations around the country, some representing just radio stations, some just TV, and some a combination of the two. For obvious competitive reasons, a station rep will not service two stations in the same listening area. The network-owned and -operated stations have their own corporate reps, as do some large independent chains such as Westinghouse and Metromedia, but most of the stations of the country utilize station representative companies such as Petry Radio Sales, The Katz Agency, and John Blair and Company.

A station rep earns its income from commission on the sales it obtains for the station. The percentage of commission varies because it is negotiated by each station and rep but generally falls between 5 and 15 percent.[3] TV stations generally pay lower commission since they sell millions each year in ads while radio stations pay a higher percentage since the price per ad is lower. Needless to say, good communication must be maintained between station and rep so that the rep can work for the station's best interest. In addition to selling ads, some station representatives help their stations with programming decisions, audience research, and station promotion.

Radio networks maintain their own sales forces to obtain national ads for news, sports, commentary, and feature programs. Some radio network programs are commercial-free and the station affiliates insert their own spots.

TV networks maintain large sales forces devoted to selling and servicing major national advertisers. The competition among these sales forces is keen. Each network wants to ensure that all its programs sell—but sell at the highest rate possible. The buyers and sellers of TV network time are generally a small, close-knit fraternity, so it behooves a network salesperson to emphasize service. Generally network management is also deeply involved with sales and makes sure that a knowledgeable team presents programs and program ideas to potential sponsors.

Advertising Agencies

When salespeople or station representatives are vying for ads from major advertisers, they generally do not deal only with the company but rather work through the company's **advertising agency.** An ad agency handles overall advertising strategies for a number of companies. It usually advises them about newspapers, magazines, direct mail, and other forms of advertising as well as radio and TV. Ad agencies came into existence over a hundred years ago to act as middlemen between companies who needed to advertise their product in markets where they were distributed and advertising outlets which wanted to obtain as many ads as possible.

Most of the major advertising agencies are what is generally termed full-service agencies. They establish advertising objectives for their clients and determine to whom the product should be sold and the best way to reach these consumers. They conduct research to analyze the audience. They attempt to obtain the best buy for the money available. They test the advertising concept. They design the advertisement or produce the commercial. They determine how long a company should continue a campaign and when it should initiate it. And they handle postcampaign evaluations. In all these processes they work closely with marketing and management executives within the companies they represent.

For its efforts, the advertising agency generally receives 15 percent of the billings. In other words a billing of $1,000 to its client for commercial time on a TV station means that $850 goes to the station and $150 is kept by the ad agency to cover its expenses. Because dollar amounts are fairly constant from agency to agency, the main "product" an ad agency has to sell to its customers is service. Advertisers frequently change agencies simply because one agency has run out of creative ideas for plugging its product and a new agency can initiate stimulating new ideas.

Since agencies generally deal with all media, the broadcast salesperson approaching an ad agency must convince the people handling accounts that broadcasting is the best deal for their clients and that the particular network or stations he or she represents offers an exceptionally good deal.

The largest of the ad agencies is J. Walter Thompson, which generally has billings of about $870 million a year, giving it, at 15 percent, an income of over 130 million.[4] Other large agencies include Leo Burnett; Young and Rubicam; Batten, Barton, Durstine, and Osborne; Grey Advertising; Ted Bates and Co.; Dancer-Fitzgerald-Sample; Benton and Bowles; and McCann-Erickson.[5] Most of these agencies are divided into departmnnts that include account executives, media specialists, TV program buyers, copywriters, art directors, and marketing research specialists. Therefore, a team of people work on the ad campaign of any one company. Not all agencies are large, however. In fact, some are one-person operations with only a few clients who like the overall attention they receive from the person directly responsible.

Not all major advertisers employ an ad agency. Some maintain their own in-house services, which amount to an ad agency within the company. Other companies will not hire a full service agency but will hire what are sometimes referred to as modular agencies. These handle only the specific things a company asks for—perhaps only the designing of an ad or the post-advertising campaign research. Usually this type of work is paid for by a negotiated fee rather than a 15 percent commission. There are also media buying services which concentrate only on buying radio and television spots.

Although there are many variations, the most common procedure is for a company to hire an advertising agency, which then makes the basic advertising decisions and sees that they are carried out. As far as broadcasting is concerned, these ad agencies deal with networks, station representatives, and occasionally individual stations to ensure that the ads of their clients receive the best treatment. Throughout the process both company officials and broadcast executives are informed of the successes and failures of the advertising campaign.

A company buys **time** on a station or network in order to air a commercial extolling the virtues of itself as a company or of one or more of its products. Production of commercials then, is a very important facet of the whole advertising scene.

Commercial Production

Companies rarely produce their own commercials for they simply are not endowed with the equipment or know-how to do so. They are in the bread-making, car-selling, or widget-manufacturing business, not the advertising business.

Small businesses which place ads on small radio stations generally have the stations produce the ad. The people who sell the time to the merchant will write and produce the commercial at no extra cost. If they are good salespeople, they will, of course, spend time talking to the business's management to determine what they would like to emphasize in the ad and will check the ad with them before it is aired. Production is usually quite simple, frequently just written copy that the disc jockey reads over the air. Often the commercial is prerecorded with music or sound effects added, and occasionally the merchant will talk on the commercial. At any rate, the whole process is kept at a simple, inexpensive level.

Large companies that advertise on radio usually have much more elaborately produced ads that include jingles and top-rated talent. The production costs are generally in addition to the cost of buying time.

Television commercials are still more elaborate. Usually they are slick, costly productions which the advertiser pays for in addition to the cost of commercial air time. Local stations sometimes produce commercials for local advertisers and charge them production costs—the cost of equipment, supplies, and personnel needed to make the commercial. But a great deal of local TV advertising and most network commercial production is handled through advertising agencies.

As part of its service to the client, the advertising agency will decide the basic content of the commercial, perhaps trying to come up with a catchy slogan or jingle. Often a **story board** is made which is a series of drawings indicating each step of the commercial.

The advertising agency then puts the commercial out to bid, and various independent production companies state the price at which they are willing to produce the commercial and give ideas as to how they plan to undertake production. The ad agency then selects one of these companies and turns the commercial production over to them.

OPEN ON 7-YEAR-OLD GIRL WEARING
A POTATO RING ON EACH FINGER.
DEMURELY, SHE TAKES ONE OF THE
RINGS OFF HER FINGER ...

MUSIC THROUGHOUT.

SINGERS: "Give a ring..."

PUTS IT IN HER MOUTH, AND
CRUNCHES.

SFX: LOUD CRUNCH.

SINGERS: "Give a crunch,
          Give Crunchi-O's."

CUT TO GORILLA FACE MASK.

SINGERS: "Give a ring..."

MASK IS REMOVED REVEALING
BEAUTIFUL WOMAN. SHE WINKS AT
CAMERA AS SHE BITES INTO
CRUNCHI-O.

SFX: LOUD CRUNCH.

SINGERS: "Give a crunch.
          Give Crunchi-O's."

CUT TO JEWELER LOOKING THROUGH
EYEPIECE AT POTATO RING.

SINGERS: "Give a ring..."

HE DECIDES RING IS GOOD ENOUGH
TO EAT. AND EATS IT.

SFX: LOUD CRUNCH.

SINGERS: "Give a crunch.
          Give Crunchi-O's."

DISSOLVE TO CRUNCHI-O CANNISTER.

MUSIC UNDER.

ANNCR. VO: "Introducing Crunchi-O's.
            The new potato snack from
            Nalley's...."

DISSOLVE TO CU OF PRODUCT.

ANNCR VO: "made in the shape of
           golden bite-size rings ...
           for a crunchy, crisp
           potato taste that's
           really different."

CUT TO TEENAGER REACHING
INTO CANNISTER FOR CRUNCHI-O.

SINGERS: "give a ring..."

HE TOSSES CRUNCHI-O OVERHEAD AND
WAITS TO CATCH IT ON THE WAY DOWN.

SINGERS: "Give a crunch..."

SUDDENLY, HUNDREDS OF CRUNCHI-O'S
POUR DOWN, FORCING TEENAGER TO
COVER UP.

SINGERS: "Give Crunchi-O's."

CUT TO MEDIUM CU OF CRUNCHI-O
CANNISTER.

MUSIC UNDER.

SUPER: AMERICA'S ONLY
       POTATO RING.

ANNCR VO: "Crunchi-O's.
           America's only
           potato ring.
           New from Nalley's."

Figure 10.8
A commercial story-
board
Photo courtesy of Della
Femina, Travisano

Figure 10.9

Figure 10.10

Some of the production companies maintain their own studios and equipment while others rent studio facilities from companies that maintain them or from stations or networks. It is even possible that a station may lease its facilities for a commercial that winds up appearing on a different station.

The time, energy, pain, and money that go into producing a commercial often rival what goes into TV programs themselves. One commercial often takes days to complete and involves fifteen or twenty people and costs of well over $50,000. Take after take is filmed or taped so that everything will turn out perfectly. Once the commercial is **"in the can,"** it may air hundreds of times over hundreds of stations. Hence the obsession with perfection.

Commercials can take many different approaches. Some attempt to be minidramas that show how the advertised product can solve a problem while others place the accent on humor. In an attempt to establish credibility, the ad agency might decide to have a well known celebrity pitch the product with a **testimonial** of its virtues. Some ads demonstrate products in use. Others involve interviews with satisfied customers. Some ads use no people whatsoever but employ animation, special effects, or unusual design. Most ads try to appeal to some basic human instinct such as security, sex, love, curiosity, or ego inflation.[6]

Commercials have enabled television and radio to create their programs, but the "program content" of commercials has also had an effect on the vernacular and life-style of American society. Remember— "LS/MFT"— "Use Ajax . . . bum bum . . . the foaming cleanser"— two dancing Old Gold cigarette packs— "Why don't you pick me up and smoke me sometime?"—"How are you fixed for blades?"—Betty Furness for Westinghouse—"Schweppervescense"—"You'll wonder where the yellow went"—"Leave the driving to us"—"Take tea and see"— "Does she or doesn't she?"—Mr. Clean—"Look ma, no cavities"—"Everything's better with Blue Bonnet on it"—Stan Freberg's chow mein—the li'l

Figure 10.9
A client representative and advertising agency representative giving final instructions to Winter Horton (*center*), the head of the production company producing the commercial.
Photo courtesy of Centre Films—George Stupar, photographer

Figure 10.10
An early commercial for a grocery chain, set up to be broadcast live.
Photo courtesy of KFI, Los Angeles

Figure 10.11
The Bing Crosby family doing a spot for Minute Maid orange juice.
Photo courtesy of The Coca-Cola Company

Figure 10.12
Johnny Philip Morris, who was part of the "Call for Philip Morris" radio ads.
Photo courtesy of KFI, Los Angeles

Figure 10.13
Betty Furness advertising live for Westinghouse during the 1952 nominating conventions.
Photo courtesy of Betty Furness

Figure 10.11

Figure 10.12

Figure 10.13

old winemaker—greasy kid stuff—"Double your pleasure, double your fun"—"Put a tiger in your tank"—"Is this any way to run an airline?"—"ring around the collar"—"You've come a long way baby,"— "Mama mia, that's-a some-a spicy meat-a-ball"—"Try it, you'll like it"— "I can't believe I ate the whole thing"— Marlboro country—"the land of sky-blue waters"—"the asked-for motor oil"— and "Let your fingers do the walking."[7]

Advertising revenue is by far the largest source of income for radio and TV stations and networks. However, there are other minor forms of income, mainly the renting of facilities to independent producers who wish to use them for taping programs or commercials and the money recouped from selling programs produced. Radio stations and networks do not rent facilities or sell programs as often as do TV operations, but there are occasions when outside organizations need audio recording capabilities and a station has a studio free so is willing to rent. Since most radio programs

Income and Expenses

Figure 10.14
Balance sheet for a TV network.

Balance Sheet

Assets		Liabilities and Shareholders' Equity	
Current assets:		Current liabilities:	
Cash and cash equivalents	$335,086	Current maturities of long term debt	$ 2,984
Notes and accounts receivable	387,727	Accounts payable and accrued liabilities	348,023
Inventories	151,880	Income taxes	63,165
Program rights	94,214	Total current liabilities	$414,172
Prepaid expenses	32,860		
Total current assets	$1,001,767		
		Amounts due after one year:	
		Long-term debt	96,666
Investments	20,990	Liability for program and talent rights	12,556
		Other	52,063
Property, plant, and equipment:		Total	$161,285
Land	25,226		
Buildings	148,139	Deferred income taxes	30,280
Machinery and equipment	235,969		
Leasehold improvements	25,508	Shareholders equity:	
	432,842	Preference stock	544
		Common stock	72,472
		Additional paid-in capital	219,651
Less accumulated depreciation	206,794	Retained earnings	480,872
Net property, plant, and equipment	$228,048		773,539
		Less common stock in treasury	27,666
Excess of cost over net assets of businesses acquired	53,376	Total share	745,873
		Shareholders equity	$1,351,610
Other assets	47,429		
	$1,351,610		

Figure 10.15
Profit and loss sheet for
a small radio station.

Monthly Profit and Loss Sheet

Income

Local time sales		$8,451.87
Agency sales		829.90
Political sales		30.00
	Total income	$9,311.77

Expenses

Payroll and payroll taxes		$4,010.55
Commissions to employees		588.04
Licenses and taxes		57.80
Office supplies and expenses		174.19
Travel and entertainment		97.48
Advertising		230.85
Sales promotion		147.61
Audience measurement		170.20
Agency commissions and talent fees		206.36
Utilities, office		37.06
Power, transmitter		58.55
Telephone, office		314.62
Telephone, broadcasting		150.73
Rent		725.00
Interest		328.83
Royalties		465.85
Music programs		50.00
Dues and subscriptions		38.90
Operating supplies		100.36
Insurance		102.06
Professional services		145.00
Automobile expense		108.21
Repairs and maintenance		28.25
Miscellaneous		75.00
	Total expenses	$8,411.50
	Excess of income over expenses	$900.27

are live disc jockey shows or news, they do not lend themselves well to **syndication.** However, occasionally a special public service series which one station produces can be sold to other stations.

TV facilities are frequently rented for use, both within the facility and on remote location. Program matter too can be sold for rerun purposes or for airing in foreign countries—probably the most lucrative market of all for program syndication. In fact, most network-run programs do not make expenses when they are aired initially on the network but must wait until they are rerun in this country or aired abroad before they turn a profit.

The sources of income for broadcasting entities are fairly clear-cut—advertising plus some supplemental income from facilities and programs. However, stations and networks have a large variety of expenses. Over half the expenses of radio stations are for salaries of disc jockeys, newscasters, salespeople, management, and staff personnel. The rest of the outgo is for such things as rental of studio space, equipment maintenance, new equipment, office supplies, taxes, **music license** fees to ASCAP and BMI, travel and entertainment of potential advertisers, station promotion, fees paid to obtain **rating** reports on the size of the station's listenership, commissions to advertising agencies and station representatives, utilities and power, interest on loans, insurance, automobile expenses, and audio tape.

The general types of expenses of TV stations are similar to those of radio stations. About one-third of a TV station's expenses are for personnel, the dollar amount of which is larger than for radio stations. The TV station expenses for equipment, utilities, and power are much higher than those of radio.

Network expenses are somewhat different because large amounts of money must be paid for transmitting program material via leased phone wires, **microwave** facilities, and satellites. Programs purchased from independent producers constitute another major expense, as do payments to affiliates for airing programs.[8]

Stations and networks keep track of their income and expenses as do most businesses, through **balance sheets** and **profit and loss** statements. Representative financial accountings for broadcasting facilities are shown in figures 10.14 and 10.15.

Determination of Profit

Although profit and loss statements show whether or not a station is making a profit, they do so after the fact, when it may be too late. It would be sound policy to know before embarking on a project whether or not it will make money. Often an accurate projection cannot be made because of the fickle tastes of the public, but often merely the arithmetic of assessing profitability is difficult.

The most direct connection between expenses and income can be seen in a small radio station. Since disc jockeys are usually also salespeople, they must, in effect, pay for their own salaries and part of the overhead. Therefore, if a d.j. is earning $250 a week and the average station ad is $20, he or she will be helping the station maintain a profitable position by selling $300 in ads a week, or approximately fifteen ads. Likewise, the station manager must earn salary plus overhead in order to operate a profitable station.

The connection is not so direct in television. The nature of the programming it airs and the complexity of the expenses make it difficult for a TV station to know when it is making money.

As an example, assume that an independent station in a large city has bought seven ninety-minute Elvis Presley films, each costing $20,000, for a total of $140,000. The contract stipulates that for the $140,000 the station can air the programs as often as it wants for one year. So the station decides to have an Elvis Presley week and air each program three times—9:00 a.m., 3:00 p.m., and 7:00 p.m. In effect, each program now costs $20,000 divided by three, or approximately $7,000. According to station policy, each ninety-minute show can have twenty minutes of commercials; however, the ad rates are going to be different for each showing.

A typical one-minute ad rate for 9:00 a.m., when very few people are watching TV, would be $250. In the afternoon more people are watching, so the rate might be about $400. In the evening the whole family is available to watch, and the rate might jump to $800. Therefore, twenty minutes of ads at 9:00 a.m. would be $5,000—not yet break-even for the $7,000 cost. At 3:00 p.m., twenty minutes of ads would yield $8,000; at 7:00 p.m., twenty minutes of ads would yield $16,000.

Since the total revenue is $5,000 + $8,000 + $16,000 (or $29,000) the station has seemingly made $9,000 on each $20,000 program. However, 15 percent of the collected $29,000 (or $4,350) goes to the advertising agency and another 10 percent (or $2,900) goes to the station representative. Overhead will run at least 15 percent of the $20,000 program cost (or $3,000). So $4,350 + $2,900 + $3,000 = $10,250, which must be added to the $20,000 cost, bringing it to $30,250. Since only $29,000 was collected, the station actually lost money.

The station is now faced with the problem of how to recoup its money and make some profit. It could have another Elvis Presley week later in the year without paying anything for the programs, but this would probably not sell very well because it would be such a recent rerun. The station could change its mind and air the programs four times a day instead of three, but this might not be too popular with viewers. Or it might air six or seven of the best programs later in the year and try to collect a little additional revenue this way.

This type of financial analysis must become second nature to broadcast managers if they are to make sound decisions which prevent the flow of red ink.

The Economy of Broadcasting

Broadcasting's direct effect on the national economy is minimal. It is an approximately $5 billion industry—$3.5 billion in advertising on TV and $1.5 billion on radio.[9] Since the gross national product (GNP) of the United States is about $1.4 trillion, this means that broadcasting accounts for little more than .3 percent of the GNP. In fact, more money per year is spent on buying and repairing TV sets than is spent on advertising. Needless to say, the social and political impact of broadcasting's approximate 8,000 radio stations and 1,000 TV stations[10] far outweighs their economic dent.

In fact, there are more TVs than bathtubs in the United States. The U.S. Census Bureau reports that 97 percent of American homes have TV sets while only 92 percent have tubs or showers, and only 87 percent have telephones.[11] Radios are even more pervasive, for 98.6 percent of homes and 99 percent of cars have radios.[12] Radios outnumber people 1.7 to 1.[13] More important, people don't just own these devices, they use them. The average household TV is on six hours and forty-four minutes a day,[14] with the average person watching about three hours of that time.[15] Children spend more time watching TV than they spend in the classroom.[16] The average person also tunes in radio three hours a day,[17] and during the course of a week radio reaches 92 percent of all people and 99 percent of all teenagers.[18] A majority of people utilize TV as their primary source of news and rank it high in believability.[19] Watching TV is the third most time-consuming activity of Americans, preceded only by sleeping and working, and followed closely by listening to the radio.[20]

For all these reasons networks can consider a prime-time show a loser if it does not play to a "house" of over twenty million, and they can look askance at any advertiser who might suggest paying less than $35,000 for a thirty-second commercial.[21]

About half the television advertising money goes to the networks and the remainder to local and regional ads. For radio, about 75 percent of advertising money is designated for local spots and most of the rest winds up at the radio networks.

The bulk of broadcasting enterprises are profitable. TV networks and network-owned stations almost invariably wind up well in the black. Affiliated and independent stations do well too, especially if they are VHF, and recently more and more UHF stations are reversing their earlier trend and winding up in the profit column. Radio networks often lose money, but their owned stations do so well that the overall network operation shows a profit. AM stations almost invariably show profit, and FMs are becoming more profitable each year, closing the gap between AM and FM stations.[22]

Because of the enormous social impact of broadcasting, the price at which radio and television stations sell is far greater than their tangible assets. For example, a powerful AM station in a large city which may have $1 million in equipment, buildings, and land may sell for $5 or $6 million. A small FM grossing $100,000 in ads per year may sell for $300,000. The first TV station sold in 1949 went for only $300,000. Now it is not uncommon for TV stations to sell for $20 million. The reason for this apparently inflated price is that what is actually being bought is a right to use the airwaves and "good will," a catch-all industry term that underscores the fact that broadcasting is related more to socio-political power than to economic gain.[23]

Advertising Under Fire

Despite the fact that advertising achieves its purpose—i.e., it sells products and it provides the money for program production—its very existence is highly controversial.

The overall structure of the broadcasting-advertising relationship is frequently questioned. Most countries depend on government tax money to operate their broadcasting systems; commercials, if they exist at all, provide only supplementary income. Of course, this leads to greater government control, since he who pays the piper picks the tune. There are those who claim the piper analogy holds for American TV too, but the heads of large companies and advertising agencies instead of the government control program content. They point to specific instances of advertiser censorship and to the overall censorship that occurs simply because advertisers refuse to sponsor certain types of programs.

There are also many criticisms about the way commercials are aired. The most frequent is that there are simply too many commercials. With the profit margin that most stations enjoy, they should be able to air fewer ads and still please stockholders. Since broadcast advertising is usually a sellers' market because there are more companies wishing to advertise than there are available spots, by raising the cost of ads, stations and networks could air fewer commercials, cut down on demand, and still maintain a profit. The frequency with which commercials interrupt programs is another gripe often voiced. In some countries commercials are grouped only between programs or all at one specific time of day. Of course, rates cannot be as high for clustered commercials because they lose impact under that sort of airing situation. For that reason, advertisers are generally opposed to the clustering that now occurs. Ads appear to be more numerous than they actually are because most commercials are much shorter than they used to be. Where one minute used to contain one advertisement, it now contains three twenty-second commercials. The frequency with which certain commercials are aired also grates on some people's nerves, and they become irritated with the repetitious sales pitches.

In some instances the type of products advertised on TV is seriously questioned. There are those who claim that advertising nonprescription medicines encourages people to use them to excess. Likewise, beer, wine, and personal sanitary products are considered by some groups to be inappropriate TV fare. Cigarettes, of course, have been banned from radio and TV, but their consumption has not decreased; in fact, it has increased.

There are those who see advertising as having an overall negative effect on the structure of our society. It makes our society dominated by style, fashion, and "keeping up with the Joneses" while at the same time it retards savings and thrift. It fosters materialistic attitudes which stress inconsequential values and leads to waste of resources and pollution of the environment. It leads people way beyond what they need and want into purchases of total frivolity and waste and creates a society where soft drinks and sugary snacks are considered prerequisites for health and vigor. Advertising also fosters monopoly because the big companies which can afford to advertise can convince people that only their brands have merit.

A large number of criticisms of broadcast advertising are aimed at the commercials themselves. They are accused of being misleading, insulting, abrasive, and uninformative. Because twenty seconds, thirty seconds, or even a minute is not enough time to explain the assets of a product in an intelligent manner, commercials frequently try to gain attention so that the listener or viewer will remember the name without really knowing any more about the product. Of course, just as liabilities of a product or service are never discussed, so a writing school will discuss its successful graduates but never its unsuccessful ones.

Words such as "greatest," "best," and "most sensational" may make for good copy, but they have very little concrete meaning. Worse yet are terms such as "scientifically tested" and "medically proven," which are not followed by any description of what constitutes the test or proof. Sometimes advertisers claim that "our product is guaranteed to give 50 percent more satisfaction" or "ours is whiter and brighter"—50 percent more than *what?* whiter and brighter than *what?* Statistics can lie too: "three out of four doctors'' might represent a total sample of four doctors. ''Secret ingredients'' such as ''DXK'' and ''KQ108'' are thrown about without indication of what these ingredients contain.

Sometimes demonstrations are not what they appear to be. One classic case involved a Rapid Shave commercial where the shaving cream appeared to shave sandpaper. Actually, what was being shaved was a sheet of plastic covered with sand. Likewise, a Campbell's soup commercial once had marbles at the bottom of the bowl so that the vegetables would rise to the top and make for a richer looking soup. This practice was quickly outlawed—no one puts marbles in soup. Even when demonstrations are valid, they may not be applicable. For example, a watch put through a hot and cold temperature test may operate perfectly at 110 degrees and −20 degrees but not be satisfactory at normal temperatures.

Testimonials come in for their share of criticism because frequently the well known stars employed for the commercials have no way of knowing whether what they are reading from the cue cards is correct or not. Sometimes the implications given by or about the stars are misleading—''John Q. Superstar runs ten miles a day and eats Crunchies for breakfast.'' The implication, of course, is that the Crunchies enable him to run ten miles—in all probability a false premise.

Commercials have also been criticized for fostering stereotypes of women and minorities—the dumb housewife who can't get her wash clean without help from a detergent genie, or the lazy Mexican who doesn't want to do his work. Many times commercials are accused of exhibiting poor taste by being loud, repetitive, or ugly. However, because they attract attention, albeit negative, they often succeed in selling products.

Commercials on children's programs have been particularly controversial in recent years. Children are much more vulnerable than adults to sales pitches. They usually cannot distinguish truth from exaggeration or fact from fiction. If a favorite cartoon character or program host says Crackle Bars should be eaten every day for breakfast, young tots will become believers and badger parents until Crackle Bars are served for breakfast. A child seeing a close-up of a small truck on TV will think the truck is as large as the TV screen but will be disappointed to discover its actual size. Other aspects of children's advertising that have been decried are the quantity of ads on children's programs and the deceptive special effects (quick cuts, sound effects, exaggerated camera angles) that have been employed to make products, toys in particular, appear exciting and irresistible. Advertising to children has been both reduced and improved in recent years due largely to the efforts of Action for Children's Television as well as guidelines from the various advertising organizations, from the NAB, and from the FCC. The FCC's 1974 guidelines, for example, state, among other things, that stations should take special measures to provide auditory and/or visual separation devices between program material and commercials; that program hosts should not sell products; and that the display of brand names and products should be confined to commercial segments.[24]

Although advertising is severely criticized from many quarters, it has its positive elements. It spurs the economy, it supports program costs so that the public can receive radio and television without paying for it directly, and it enables people to become informed about products available to them.

Summary

Advertising money pays for programming through a series of complicated processes that include *rate cards, ad agencies,* and *station reps.*

Rate cards are based on the number of people watching or listening to a station and take into account the number of ads, the length of the ads, the time of day, the type of facility, and other factors. Sometimes in selling ads stations engage in *barter, per-inquiry advertising, time-bank processes, run of schedule, co-op advertising,* and *price cutting.* Ads can be *national, regional,* or *local* and *program* or *spot.* To sell ads, stations rely on sales forces and station representatives. Ad agencies work for companies wishing to advertise and usually earn a 15 percent *commission.* Commercials can be simple and produced free by a radio station or complicated TV productions that may cost as much as programs to produce. Advertising is the main station income; expenses include payroll, rent, maintenance, new equipment, taxes, license fees, and commissions. Stations generally try to determine the *profitability* of a program before committing themselves to it. Broadcasting's effect on the economy is much less than its effect on the social and political aspects of society. Advertising is criticized for its overabundance, frequency, tastelessness, negative effect on society, and misleading nature. Ads on children's programs particularly have come under attack.

11 The Rating Game
Audience Measurement

There are only two rules in broadcasting: keep the ratings as high as possible and don't get in any trouble.

An anonymous television executive

Cartoon copyrighted by *Broadcasting* magazine

"We were ahead at 4:28; second at 4:29:55; first at 4:31:02, third at 4:46; second at . . ."

Few aspects of broadcasting are criticized as vehemently as **ratings,** and yet they are all but worshipped within the executive realms of broadcasting.

Ratings have arisen because of the desire of various broadcasting groups to know how many people are watching or listening to programs. Companies invest a great deal of money in advertising and want to know that their messages are reaching an audience. The only way for them to believe they are getting their money's worth from the ad is to be told the size of the audience. Stations generally charge advertisers at a rate based on the number of viewers or listeners. In addition, the broadcasters themselves want to know public reaction to their programs. Often this will help them anticipate changes in trends or tell them when a program has passed its prime.

Frequently both broadcasters and advertisers want to know public reaction before investing a great deal of money. Overnight ratings early in the season will help them determine whether or not to continue producing a show.

When companies advertise in print media such as newspapers and magazines, they are also interested in knowing the audience size. With print media, though, this is easier to calculate because it is possible to count the number of copies sold. It is much harder to count the number of people watching TV or listening to the radio in the privacy of their homes or cars. As a result, the rating system has been developed.

Early Rating Systems

Systems for determining audience size began very early in radio history, the first "rating method" being fan mail. Research showed that one person in seventeen who enjoyed a program wrote to make his feelings known. This "system" was effective enough while the novelty of radio lasted, but it was never representative of the entire audience.

When radio became more commonplace, stations would offer a free inducement or prize to those sending in letters or postcards. This "system" was not considered an accurate measurement of the total number in the audience, but it could give comparative percentages of listeners in different localities. For example, if two stations in two different cities made the same offer, the number of replies to each station would tell which station had the larger audience.

Early in the 1930s, advertising interests joined together to support ratings known as the Crossleys (Cooperative Analysis of Broadcasting). This was a **recall** type of rating—people in about thirty cities were telephoned and asked what programs they had been listening to at various times in the past. Crossley ratings were discontinued in 1946 when commercial companies offered similar services.

Hooper ratings were also started in the early 1930s and were similar to Crossley ratings except that respondents were asked what programs they were listening to at the time the call was made—a methodology known as **coincidental telephone technique.** Part of Hooper was purchased by the A. C. Nielsen Company in 1950, and part still exists, providing services to local radio stations.

Figure 11.1

Figure 11.2

Figure 11.1
A 1936 audimeter utiliz-
ing punch tape
Photo courtesy of
A. C. Nielsen Company

Figure 11.2
A 1956 audimeter
Photo courtesy of
A. C. Nielsen Company

Figure 11.3
Installation of a modern
audimeter.
Photo courtesy of
A. C. Nielsen Company

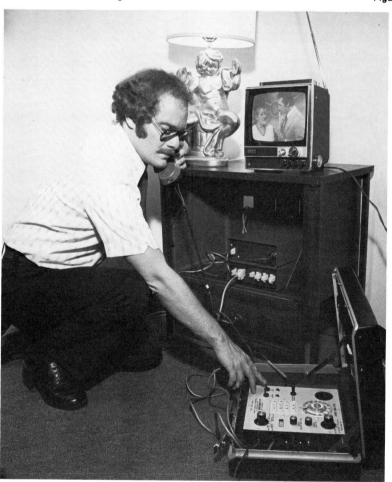

Figure 11.3

Another radio rating service, The Pulse, Inc., that began in 1941 utilized face-to-face interviewing. Interviewees selected by **random sampling** were asked to name the radio stations they had listened to over the past twenty-four hours, the past week, and the past five midweek days. If they could not remember the stations they had heard, they were shown a roster containing station call letters, frequencies, and identifying slogans. This was generally referred to as the **roster/recall** method. The Pulse was a dominant radio rating service for many years but went out of business in 1978.

In 1946 Broadcast Measurement Bureau (BMB) was started, supported by the stations themselves. It used postcard questionnaires to obtain county-by-county information about the audiences of each station. It published two reports before going out of business for lack of station support.[1]

Nielsen

The name most readily associated with ratings today is the A. C. Nielsen Company. It was established in 1942 as the Nielsen Radio Index but did not come into prominence until after World War II. It no longer deals with radio ratings but is a major television rating system of particular value to the networks.

Nielsen uses the **audimeter,** an electronic device that is attached to the TV set and records viewing characteristics. In earlier days it was attached to radio sets. It registers when a set comes on, what station it is tuned to, and exactly when the dial is changed to another station. Because it is set-oriented, Nielsen's statistics are based on households, not individual people. Audimeters have changed over the years. Some have recorded on paper punch tape, some on film, and some are wired directly to a Nielsen office.

The audimeter is placed in about 1,200 American homes which are supposedly representative of the 71,000,000 television homes in the U.S. with respect to such **demographics** as age, income, occupation, ethnic background, and geographic location. Nielsen does not, of course, reveal the identification of its homes, and it pays each household a small fee in order to use it in the sample. The sample homes are periodically updated to conform to changing national norms.

Nielsen publishes several types of reports. One is the **overnights,** which are available only in Los Angeles and New York. In those cities a number of sets are wired directly to computers at a Nielsen center and results are recorded immediately so that in the morning the results of the previous day's programming are known. The overnights give only quantity details involved with the number of households viewing and do not take into account qualities such as age, sex, or income. Nielsen plans to initiate national overnights, but presently is providing national quantity-only data thirty-six hours after broadcast.

Another Nielsen report is the Multi-Network Area Report, or MNA. This reports on the seventy leading population centers of the country—those cities with at least three stations so that all three networks are

Figure 11.4
Sample Nielsen over-
night
Courtesy of A. C. Nielsen
Company

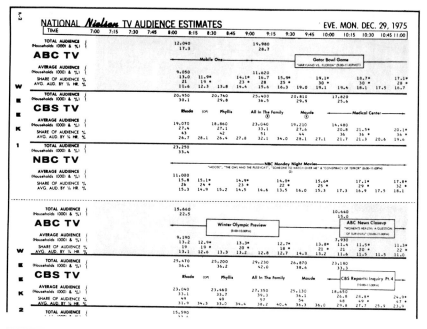

Figure 11.5
Sample Nielsen MNA
Courtesy of A. C. Nielsen
Company

broadcasting simultaneously. These seventy population centers comprise approximately 66 percent of the national viewing audience, hence, 66 percent of the Nielsen sample, which is the result of about 800 audimeter readings. In order to obtain this rating, the recording device is removed from each audimeter and taken or mailed to a local Nielsen office to be analyzed. MNAs give demographic breakdowns by such factors as age and

Figure 11.6
Sample Nielsen Television Index (NTI).
Courtesy of A. C. Nielsen Company

NTI/NAC AUDIENCE DEMOGRAPHICS REPORT
November 1975
(4 Weeks Ending November 23, 1975)
TABLE 5 - TELEVISION USAGE AND NETWORK PROGRAM AUDIENCE ESTIMATES BY HALF-HOURS

DAY NETWORK PROGRAM NAME	NY TIME	WEEKS	HOUSE-HOLDS	WORKING WOMEN	WOMEN 18+	15-24	18-24	18-34	18-49	25-54	55-64	55+	TEENS TOTAL	FEMALE	MALE
MONDAY 9.00PM - 9.30PM TVU		1234	69.3	52.4	54.1	45.7	43.3	45.5	50.1	54.8	62.0	59.2	42.2	39.6	44.7
A ABC NFL FOOTBALL GAME		1234	18.4	8.5	8.3	5.5	6.5	8.3	8.0	8.2	11.5	9.2	11.5	5.7*	17.2
C ALL IN THE FAMILY		1234	29.1	22.5	25.4	22.7	22.8	23.4	23.5	24.6	25.0	26.3	19.7	21.8	15.8
N NBC MONDAY NIGHT MOVIES		12 4	19.9	18.1	16.2	1C.7	13.4	15.3	16.1	17.6	18.8	15.4	7.0	4.5*	9.4
N HALLMARK HALL OF FAME(S)		3	22.4	18.9	18.7	12.6+	10.0+	15.7	17.2	20.7	18.4+	20.3	12.6	19.0+	6.3+
MONDAY 9.30PM - 10.00PM TVU		1234	67.9	50.4	52.9	45.5	41.5	47.9	49.3	53.7	60.0	57.0	39.5	36.8	42.2
A ABC NFL FOOTBALL GAME		1234	22.1	9.6	9.3	6.8	7.8	8.8	9.1	9.6	13.2	9.7	12.6	5.9*	19.2
C MAUDE		1234	24.2	18.5	21.6	20.6	21.2	21.2	23.4	20.8	20.7	23.4	15.5	19.6	11.5
N NBC MONDAY NIGHT MOVIES		1 4	21.1	16.0	16.7	7.6*	8.6+	13.6	15.3	18.8	21.7	17.8	6.6+	2.8*	10.4+

NTI/NAC AUDIENCE DEMOGRAPHICS REPORT
November 1975
(4 Weeks Ending November 23, 1975)
TABLE 5 - TELEVISION USAGE AND NETWORK PROGRAM AUDIENCE ESTIMATES BY HALF-HOURS

DAY NETWORK PROGRAM NAME	NY TIME	WEEKS	TOTAL PERSONS	LADY OF HOUSE	MEN 18+	15-24	18-24	18-34	18-49	25-54	55-64	55+	CHILDREN TOTAL†	6-11	2-5
MONDAY 9.00PM - 9.30PM TVU		1234	47.0	56.8	49.4	35.7	36.1	42.6	45.9	50.0	52.9	57.6	30.5	36.3	21.1
A ABC NFL FOOTBALL GAME		1234	11.4	8.9	16.7	11.3	5.6	8.3	15.6	18.7	19.3	17.5	8.0	9.4	5.6
C ALL IN THE FAMILY		1234	20.5	26.7	17.5	13.5	14.7	16.3	15.9	16.4	18.0	22.0	16.0	18.6	11.8
N NBC MONDAY NIGHT MOVIES		12 4	11.4	16.9	12.2	11.1	10.7	10.9	11.3	11.8	13.9	14.1	2.9	2.8*	3.2+
N HALLMARK HALL OF FAME(S)		3	14.8	19.3	12.6	7.0*	7.7*	11.1	10.4	11.8	15.3+	17.9	12.5	16.2	6.3+
MONDAY 9.30PM - 10.00PM TVU		1234	45.1	55.4	48.6	35.1	35.0	42.9	45.9	50.2	51.2	54.8	26.0	30.4	18.8
A ABC NFL FOOTBALL GAME		1234	13.4	10.0	20.9	14.8	13.9	19.5	21.0	23.1	25.0	21.3	8.3	9.8	5.9
C MAUDE		1234	16.5	22.4	13.6	10.5	11.3	12.8	12.7	13.0	13.9	16.6	11.9	15.5	9.5
N NBC MONDAY NIGHT MOVIES		1 4	11.3	17.6	11.8	8.7*	7.1*	9.3	10.4	11.5	13.5*	15.7	2.2*	2.0*	2.3*
N HALLMARK HALL OF FAME(S)#		3	16.1	21.7	13.4	7.4*	9.0*	12.2	11.2	12.9	16.2+	17.3	12.5	17.7	4.0*
MONDAY 10.00PM - 10.30PM TVU		1234	39.5	50.1	45.7	34.2	35.3	42.4	44.7	47.9	46.6	48.5	17.1	20.0	12.3
A ABC NFL FOOTBALL GAME		1234	14.1	11.1	23.0	16.0	15.6	21.8	23.3	26.0	25.1	21.8	6.8	8	
C MEDICAL CENTER#		1234	11.2	16.6	9.1	7.8	8.4	8.5	9.0	8.8	7.5+	10.			
N NBC MONDAY NIGHT MOVIES		4	15.8	23.1	17.6	14.9	15.6*	17.4	16.8						
N DEAN MARTIN CELEB. RCAST(S)		3	13.1	17.9	13.7										
MONDAY 10.30PM - 11.00PM TVU															
A ABC NFL FOOTBALL															

sex and are based on a week's worth of data which arrives on subscribers' desks a week after broadcast.

The national data called the NTI, or Nielsen Television Index, is published every two weeks and covers a two-week period. It is a very detailed report of data collected from all 1,200 audimeters. It provides a multitude of statistics, including ratings for each fifteen-minute time period, breakdowns by various categories of people, statistics to compare present ratings with those of a year earlier, and rankings of the programs covered.

Another service provided by Nielsen is called the **sweeps.** The previously mentioned reports are of value primarily only to the networks. The sweeps are more ambitious. Three times a year—one week in February, one week in May, and one week in November—Nielsen conducts research to elicit comprehensive ratings of all time periods for each individual station in the country. These ratings are then used by local stations to sell their ads. For the sweeps, Nielsen does not use its audimeter sample, which is not extensive enough to cover all stations. Rather, it utilizes an entirely different group of about 190,000 households, who fill out **diaries** indicating what shows were watched at what time, on which channels, and by which family members. Nielsen field representatives collect the diaries and interview viewers further about programs and advertisements.

Advertisers, **advertising agencies,** stations, and networks subscribe in advance on a yearly basis to the Nielsen ratings. The amount they pay depends on a variety of factors, such as the number of ratings they want to

Figure 11.7
Sample Nielsen sweep
Courtesy of A. C. Nielsen Company

LOS ANGELES, CA

STATION TOTALS (000)								DMA RATINGS																	STATION	START TIME	NUMBER OF QUARTER HOURS AVERAGED			
PERSONS	ADULTS	WOMEN	MEN	FEM	MALE	TNS	CHD	PERSONS		WOMEN						FEM	MALE	MEN					TNS	CHD			WEEKS			
2+	18+	25-64	25-64	15-24	15-24	GIRLS	6-11	2+	18+	18+	18-34	18-49	25-49	25-54	WKG	15-24	15-24	18+	18-34	18-49	25-49	25-54	12-17	2-11			1	2	3	4
23	24	25	26	27	28	29	30	31	32	33	34	35	36	37	38	39	40	41	42	43	44	45	46	47						
67	*48*	*27*	*28*	*34*	*33*	*33*	*46*	*1*	*4*	*1*	*2*	*1*	*2*	*1*	*2*	*4*	*4*	*1*	*2*	*1*	*2*	*1*	*4*	*3*						
17	*12*	*7*	*7*	*9*	*9*	*8*	*12*	*LT*	*1*	*LT*	*LT*	*LT*	*LT*	*LT*	*1*	*1*	*1*	*LT*	*1*	*LT*	*LT*	*LT*	*1*	*1*						
929	721	256	223	73	80	20	70	8	9	9	8	8	8	8	6	7	8	9	7	8	8	8	8	6	KTLA	7:00PM	2	2	2	2
904	678	236	236	59	76	36	70	8	8	8	6	7	8	7	8	6	8	9	9	8	9	9	10	6		7:00PM		2	2	
890	708	269	251	56	63	22	71	8	9	9	7	8	9	9	7	5	6	9	7	9	9	10	5	6		7:00PM	2	2	2	2
713	535	192	168	63	56	15	79	6	6	7	6	6	6	6	5	6	5	6	5	6	6	6	5	6		7:00PM		2	2	2
863	667	242	221	63	68	22	72	8	8	8	7	8	8	8	6	6	7	8	7	8	8	8	7	6			4	8	8	6
1028	391	173	102	91	79	100	323	9	5	5	9	8	8	7	6	9	8	4	7	5	5	4	14	26	KTTV	7:00PM	2	2	2	2
1226	481	201	113	153	82	130	336	11	6	7	11	10	10	8	6	14	6	5	6	6	5	5	18	29		7:00PM	2	2	2	2
1106	392	170	101	111	83	128	333	10	5	6	8	8	8	7	5	11	8	4	7	5	5	4	18	27		7:00PM	2	2	2	2
916	345	128	100	114	66	132	265	8	4	5	7	6	6	5	5	11	6	4	4	5	4	4	17	19		7:00PM	2	2	2	2
762	278	101	71	78	70	97	210	7	3	4	6	5	5	4	4	7	7	3	4	4	3	3	14	17		7:00PM	2	2	2	2
1005	376	154	97	109	76	117	293	9	5	5	8	7	7	6	5	10	7	4	6	5	4	4	16	24			10	10	10	10
831	763	228	164	16	11	3	37	7	9	11	3	4	5	6	6	2	1	8	2	3	3	4	1	3		7:00PM	4	4	4	4
524	430	161	115	40	24	21	28	5	6	6	4	5	5	5	6	4	2	5	2	3	3	4	5	2	KABC	7:30PM	2	2	2	2
912	768	301	225	69	52	35	53	9	10	11	8	9	10	10	10	7	5	8	7	7	8	8	6	4		7:30PM	2	2	2	2
726	604	250	201	73	44	23	51	7	8	9	8	9	9	9	10	7	4	7	7	7	8	8	5	4		7:30PM	2	2	2	2
1089	828	295	281	140	115	56	72	10	11	10	14	13	12	11	12	14	11	11	12	12	11	11	11	8		7:30PM	2	2	2	2
861	740	264	220	68	46	27	48	8	9	10	7	8	8	8	8	7	5	9	7	7	7	8	4	4		7:30PM	2	2	2	2
885	753	283	222	68	49	31	51	8	10	11	8	8	9	9	9	7	5	8	7	7	7	8	5	4			4	4	4	4
678	524	194	196	31	45	20	64	6	7	6	5	6	7	7	5	3	5	7	4	6	6	7	6	5		7:30PM	2	2	2	2
142	79	15	41	18	9	12	29	1	1	1	1	1	1	1	1	2	1	1	3	2	2	2	2	3	KBSC	7:30PM	2	2	2	2
60	23	7	9	5	4	3	16	1								1							1	1		7:30PM	2	2	2	2
84	47	15	22	10	2	7	14	1	1	1	1	1	1	1	1	1		1	1	1	1	1	1	1		7:30PM	2	2	2	2
82	39	11	24	3		3	27	1	1									1	1	1	1	1	1	2		7:30PM	2	2	2	2
42	13	4	9			6	19																1	1		7:30PM	2	2	2	2
81	40	10	21	7	3	6	21	1			1					1		1	1	1	1	1	1	2			10	10	10	10
608	491	178	152	40	42	14	34	5	6	6	5	5	5	5	5	4	4	5	3	4	5	5	5	3	KHJ	7:30PM	2	2	2	2
543	432	168	114	28	20	16	44	5	5	6	4	5	5	5	4	3	2	4	2	3	3	4	4	4		7:30PM	2	2	2	2
560	424	157	106	37	22	20	52	5	5	6	3	4	4	5	3	3	2	4	2	3	3	3	4	5		7:30PM	2	2	2	2
627	503	200	127	39	21	22	54	6	6	7	5	6	6	7	5	4	2	5	2	3	4	4	3	5		7:30PM	2	2	2	2
578	450	172	119	35	29	19	40	5	6	6	4	5	5	6	5	3	3	5	2	3	3	4	5	4		7:30PM	2	2	2	2
583	460	175	123	36	27	18	45	5	6	6	4	5	5	6	4	3	2	5	2	3	4	4	4	4			10	10	10	10
122	101	35	42	5	14	3	4	1	1	1	1	1	1	1	1	1	1	1	1	1	1	1	1			7:30PM	6	6	6	6
837	770	306	245	25	25	11	24	8	10	11	7	8	9	9	12	2	2	9	6	7	8	8	2	2	KNBC	7:30PM	2	2	2	
545	449	158	140	35	38	16	17	5	6	6	4	4	4	5	6	3	3	6	4	4	4	4	4	2		7:30PM	2	2	2	2
512	435	169	120	17	24	5	29	5	5	6	4	4	5	5	4	2	2	4	2	3	3	3	2	3		7:30PM	2	2	2	2
449	430	152	122	16	11	8	6	4	5	6	2	2	2	4	5	1	1	5	2	2	3	3	1			7:30PM	2	2	2	2
450	384	121	118	14	23	4	25	4	5	5	3	3	3	3	3	1	2	5	3	3	3	4	2	2		7:30PM	2	2	2	2
773	550	214	223	35	60	32	91	7	7	7	5	6	7	8	5	3	6	7	6	7	8	7	9	6		7:30PM	2	2	2	2
324	206	91	65	4	12	11	51	3	3	3	2	2	3	3	3		1	2	2	2	3	2	4	5	KNXT	7:30PM	2	2		2
349	279	90	61	24	16	9	25	3	3	4	2	2	2	2	1	2	1	3	1	2	2	2	2	2	KTLA	7:30PM	2	2	2	2
264	204	88	56	9	6	8	20	2	2	3	1	2	3	2	3	1		2		1	1	1	2	1		7:30PM		2	2	
371	318	91	66	14	14	7	21	3	4	4	1	2	2	3	2	1	1	3	1	2	2	2	2	1		7:30PM	2	2	2	2
294	246	78	81	19	13	11	14	2	3	3	2	2	2	2	2	2	1	3	1	2	2	3	2	1		7:30PM		2	2	2
328	271	87	66	17	13	8	20	3	3	4	2	2	2	2	2	2	1	3	1	2	2	2	2	2			4	8	8	6
1147	382	178	101	106	65	120	391	11	5	6	9	8	8	7	7	10	6	4	6	5	5	4	16	33	KTTV	7:30PM	2	2	2	2
1286	401	169	109	145	65	150	429	12	5	6	10	9	9	8	6	14	6	4	5	5	5	5	20	37		7:30PM	2	2	2	2
1125	373	158	89	119	82	135	352	10	5	6	8	7	7	7	6	12	8	4	5	5	4	4	19	30		7:30PM	2	2	2	2
1032	344	137	89	92	63	122	339	9	4	5	7	6	6	5	5	9	6	3	4	4	4	4	16	27		7:30PM	2	2	2	2
856	245	97	61	75	67	103	293	8	3	4	5	5	5	4	3	7	7	2	3	3	3	2	16	25		7:30PM	2	2	2	2
1088	348	148	90	107	68	126	361	10	4	5	8	7	7	6	5	10	7	3	5	4	4	4	17	30			10	10	10	10
1463	977	385	318	179	106	135	180	14	13	14	15	15	15	15	15	18	11	12	12	12	13	13	20	15	KABC	8:00PM	4	4	4	4
2728	1604	643	492	356	254	263	445	26	21	23	31	29	28	27	24	35	26	19	25	23	22	21	42	38		8:00PM	2	2	2	2
2123	1250	519	390	220	170	146	391	20	16	18	24	22	24	22	17	22	18	14	18	17	17	16	27	34		8:00PM	4		4	
1990	1259	478	366	274	223	182	266	19	16	18	25	22	20	19	20	27	23	15	19	17	16	15	29	23		8:00PM	2	2	2	2
1715	1051	405	292	161	98	125	314	16	14	16	16	16	16	16	14	16	10	11	12	11	12	12	18	28		8:00PM	4	4	4	4
1503	913	353	273	138	149	109	235	14	12	12	12	13	13	13	12	13	15	12	12	12	11	11	21	20		8:00PM		2	2	2
2124	1304	469	473	168	180	116	390	20	17	17	19	19	20	19	16	17	19	18	20	20	21	20	25	32		8:00PM	4	4	4	4
9	6	3	3		2																				KBSC	8:00PM	6	8	8	8
9	9	4	2																							8:00PM	4	4	4	4
3	3																									8:00PM	8	9	9	8
13	9	4	5																							8:00PM	4	4	4	4
6	5	2	2																							8:00PM	8	8	8	8
6	5	2	2																								26	29	29	28
2	2	1																								8:00PM	3	3	3	3
3	3	1	2																							9:00PM	4	4	4	4
5	4	2	2																								33	36	36	35
246	231	72	65	6	13			2	3	3	1	1	1	2	1	1	1	2		1	1	1	1		KCOP	8:00PM	4	4	4	4
251	229	68	56	13	7	4	3	2	3	3	2	2	2	2	2	1	1	2		1	1	2	1	1		8:00PM	4	4	4	4
215	208	85	57	11			1	2	2	3	2	2	3	3	2	1		2		1	1	1				8:00PM	4	4	4	4
321	311	132	89	23	16			3	4	5	2	2	2	3	3	2	2	3	1	1	1	2	1			8:00PM	4			4
92	85	21	39	4	12		1	1	1	1				1			1	1	1	1		1				8:00PM		8	8	
180	177	54	43	8		3		1	2	2		1	1	1	1	1		2		1	1	1				8:00PM	4	4	4	4
234	222	77	59	11	6	1	1	2	3	3	1	2	2	2	2	1	1	2		1	1	1	1				20	16	16	20
34	32	7	16	1	3		1																			8:00PM	2	6	N8	
107	102	29	21	6	5	1		1	1	1		1	1	1	1			1				1				8:00PM	2			2
219	212	37	25	1		1	6	2	2	3					1			2								8:00PM	4	4	4	4
23	24	25	26	27	28	29	30	31	32	33	34	35	36	37	38	39	40	41	42	43	44	45	46	47						

PROGRAM AVERAGES

FEBRUARY 1977

receive, the type of service they are, and the market where they operate. Generally it costs each network about $1 million a year if all it subscribes to is the main rating, the NTI. Stations and advertisers pay less.[2]

Arbitron

A second rating service is Arbitron, formerly called American Research Bureau, or ARB, which measures both television and radio audiences. Its main rating service is similar to and competitive with the Nielsen Station Index in that it establishes audiences of local TV stations. Arbitron's primary research technique is diaries, by which it surveys for the whole

MARKET	RANK	MARKET	RANK	MARKET	RANK	MARKET	RANK
NEW YORK	1	WICHITA-HUTCHINSON	56	MONROE-EL DORADO	113	JONESBORO	172
LOS ANGELES	2	TULSA	57	CHARLESTON, SC	114	LAKE CHARLES	173
CHICAGO	3	RICHMOND	58	JOPLIN-PITTSBURG	115	ARDMORE-ADA	174
PHILADELPHIA	4	SHREVEPORT-TEXARKANA	59	LAFAYETTE, LA	116	GREAT FALLS	175
BOSTON	5	KNOXVILLE	60	COLUMBUS, GA	117	CHEYENNE	176
SAN FRANCISCO	6	SYRACUSE	61	WICHITA FALLS-LAWTON	118	MARQUETTE	177
DETROIT	7	DES MOINES	62	MONTGOMERY	119	GAINESVILLE	178
WASHINGTON, DC	8	MOBILE-PENSACOLA	63	SANTA BARBARA-SANTA MARIA-		PANAMA CITY	179
CLEVELAND	9	JACKSONVILLE	64	SAN LUIS OBISPO	120	EL CENTRO-YUMA	180
PITTSBURGH	10	OMAHA	65	LA CROSSE-EAU CLAIRE	121	BILOXI-GULFPORT-PASCAGOULA	181
DALLAS-FT. WORTH	11	ROCHESTER, NY	66	BINGHAMTON	122	ROSWELL	182
ST. LOUIS	12	GREEN BAY	67	BEAUMONT-PORT ARTHUR	123	ST. JOSEPH	183
HOUSTON	13	ROANOKE-LYNCHBURG	68	ROCHESTER-MASON CITY-AUSTIN	124	EUREKA	184
MINNEAPOLIS-ST. PAUL	14	DAVENPORT-ROCK IS-MOLINE		ERIE	125	CASPER-RIVERTON	185
MIAMI	15	(QUAD CITY)	69	WAUSAU-RHINELANDER	126	PALM SPRINGS	186
ATLANTA	16	FRESNO	70	TRAVERSE CITY-CADILLAC	127	TWIN FALLS	187
TAMPA-ST. PETERSBURG	17	SPRINGFIELD-DECATUR-CHAMPAIGN	71	CORPUS CHRISTI	128	MANKATO	188
SEATTLE-TACOMA	18	SPOKANE	72	EUGENE	128	GREENWOOD-GREENVILLE	189
BALTIMORE	19	CEDAR RAPIDS-WATERLOO	73	LUBBOCK	130	JACKSON, TN	190
INDIANAPOLIS	20	PORTLAND-POLAND SPRING	74	YAKIMA	131	TUSCALOOSA	191
DENVER	21	JOHNSTOWN-ALTOONA	75	WILMINGTON	132	GRAND JUNCTION	192
HARTFORD-NEW HAVEN	22	SOUTH BEND-ELKHART	76	COLUMBIA-JEFFERSON CITY	133	LIMA	193
SACRAMENTO-STOCKTON	23	PADUCAH-CAPE GIRARDEAU-		BLUEFIELD-BECKLEY-OAK HILL	134	LAFAYETTE, IN	194
PORTLAND, OR	24	HARRISBURG	77	TOPEKA	135	ANNISTON	195
CINCINNATI	25	YOUNGSTOWN	78	LAS VEGAS	136	HARRISONBURG	196
MILWAUKEE	25	ALBUQUERQUE	79	SAVANNAH	137	BELLINGHAM	197
KANSAS CITY	27	WEST PALM BEACH	80	QUINCY-HANNIBAL	138	BOWLING GREEN	198
BUFFALO	28	JACKSON, MS	81	ALBANY, GA	139	PARKERSBURG	199
PROVIDENCE	29	CHATTANOOGA	82	BOISE	140	OTTUMWA-KIRKSVILLE	200
SAN DIEGO	30	BRISTOL-KINGSPORT-JOHNSON CITY	83	MACON	141	PRESQUE ISLE	201
NASHVILLE	31	SPRINGFIELD, MO	84	COLUMBUS-TUPELO	142	SAN ANGELO	202
COLUMBUS, OH	32	LINCOLN-HASTINGS-KEARNEY	85	MCALLEN-BROWNSVILLE (LRGV)	143	ZANESVILLE	203
CHARLOTTE	33	SPRINGFIELD, MA	86	FT. MYERS	144	LAREDO	204
PHOENIX	34	GREENVILLE-NEW BERN-		MINOT-BISMARCK-DICKINSON	144	SELMA	205
MEMPHIS	35	WASHINGTON	87	BANGOR	146	FARMINGTON	206
NEW ORLEANS	36	LEXINGTON	88	ODESSA-MIDLAND	147	FLAGSTAFF	207
GREENVILLE-SPARTANBURG-		FT. WAYNE	89	CHICO-REDDING	148	NORTH PLATTE	208
ASHEVILLE	37	PEORIA	90	UTICA	149	HELENA	209
GRAND RAPIDS-KALAMAZOO-		EVANSVILLE	91	MISSOULA-BUTTE	150	ALPENA	210
BATTLE CREEK	38	HUNTSVILLE-DECATUR-FLORENCE	92	BAKERSFIELD	151	MILES CITY-GLENDIVE	211
OKLAHOMA CITY	39	TUCSON	93	RENO	152		
ORLANDO-DAYTONA BEACH	40	LANSING	94	TALLAHASSEE	153		
ALBANY-SCHENECTADY-TROY	41	SIOUX FALLS-MITCHELL	95	ABILENE-SWEETWATER	154		
WILKES BARRE-SCRANTON	42	FARGO	96	MEDFORD	155		
CHARLESTON-HUNTINGTON	43	COLUMBIA, SC	97	DOTHAN	156		
SALT LAKE CITY	44	AUSTIN, TX	98	TYLER	157		
LOUISVILLE	45	BATON ROUGE	99	FLORENCE, SC	158		
NORFOLK-PORTSMOUTH-NEWPORT		COLORADO SPRINGS-PUEBLO	100	ELMIRA	159		
NEWS-HAMPTON	46	BURLINGTON-PLATTSBURGH	101	FT. SMITH	160		
SAN ANTONIO	47	EL PASO	102	CLARKSBURG-WESTON	161		
BIRMINGHAM	48	WACO-TEMPLE	103	ALEXANDRIA, MN	162		
DAYTON	49	ROCKFORD	104	WATERTOWN-CARTHAGE	163		
HARRISBURG-YORK-LANCASTER-		MADISON	105	IDAHO FALLS-POCATELLO	164		
LEBANON	50	SALINAS-MONTEREY	106	LAUREL-HATTIESBURG	165		
RALEIGH-DURHAM	51	AUGUSTA	107	SALISBURY	166		
FLINT-SAGINAW-BAY CITY	52	AMARILLO	108	BILLINGS	167		
GREENSBORO-WINSTON SALEM-		SIOUX CITY	109	RAPID CITY	168		
HIGH POINT	53	WHEELING-STEUBENVILLE	110	ALEXANDRIA, LA	169		
TOLEDO	54	DULUTH-SUPERIOR	111	ANCHORAGE	170		
LITTLE ROCK	55	TERRE HAUTE	112	MERIDIAN	170		

**Figure 11.8
Arbitron's ADI (Area of Dominant Influence) list.**
Courtesy of The Arbitron Company

nation one week each February, May, and November, the same as Nielsen. Surveys are made more frequently for larger markets.

Arbitron calls the geographic areas it surveys Areas of Dominant Influence, or ADIs. To determine ADIs, Arbitron has divided the nation into over 200 nonoverlapping viewing areas. Counties are placed in an ADI based on the stations most listened to in that county. Population size does not determine ADIs. In other words, a large area like Chicago is considered one ADI while a small area like Peoria, Illinois, is another. Sometimes very small areas are combined, such as Albany-Schenectady-Troy, New York. The largest ADI is New York City, with over six million households, and the smallest is Miles City-Glendive, with under 7,000. ADIs of sparsely populated areas may cover several states. For example, the Salt Lake City ADI covers not only all of Utah but part of Wyoming and Idaho.

Potential diary keepers in each ADI are chosen by computer and then contacted by Arbitron personnel to solicit their cooperation. A diary is given for each TV set in the home, for recording the viewing of each individual by quarter-hours. Information about the viewers, such as family size and ethnic background, and information about the TV sets, such as capability of receiving UHF and color, is collected.

Diary information is processed by computer and printed for each of the ADIs. The booklets printed contain a great deal of information broken down into numerous subcategories such as age, sex, and time of day.

Arbitron estimates that its costs are $20 to $50 per sample household. It

Figure 11.9
A sample page from an
Arbitron diary.
Courtesy of The Arbitron
Company

PLEASE START RECORDING YOUR LISTENING ON THE DATE SHOWN ON THE FRONT COVER.

THURSDAY

TIME		STATION		PLACE	
(Indicate AM or PM)		WHEN LISTENING TO FM, CHECK HERE (✓)	FILL IN STATION "CALL LETTERS" (IF YOU DON'T KNOW THEM, FILL IN PROGRAM NAME OR DIAL SETTING)	CHECK ONE (✓)	
FROM —	TO —			AT HOME	AWAY-FROM-HOME (INCLUDING IN A CAR)

PLEASE CHECK HERE ⬭ IF YOU DID NOT LISTEN TO RADIO TODAY.

sells the information it gathers at different prices to different stations, the price based on sample size, market size, and number of reports desired. A network affiliate in a large market such as Philadelphia might pay over $50,000 per year for seven reports, while a station in a small area such as Madison, Wisconsin might pay only $8,000 a year for three reports.

Arbitron has recently launched a metered television service to compete with Nielsen in Los Angeles and New York by providing overnight ratings.

Arbitron also surveys radio by the diary method, having each household member twelve years old or older keep a diary of radio listening. Again, Arbitron divides the country into markets and provides more frequent reports for large markets than for small ones. In this case, Arbitron determines Metropolitan Survey Areas (MSAs) and Total Survey Areas (TSAs) for each market. The TSAs are larger than MSAs and often do not receive stations as clearly as the MSAs.

Data are analyzed for radio slightly differently than for TV. The results are two different booklets, Arbitron Radio primarily for the radio stations and Arbitron Radio Demographic Buyer for time buyers.

The price a radio station pays for a report depends on such factors as the size of the market, whether the station is AM or FM, and the highest price the station charges for ads. In general, radio ratings are less important in small markets with only a few stations than they are in large markets with many stations.[3]

Figure 11.10
An example of one of the many reports Arbitron furnishes to subscribing radio stations. This report estimates the number of different persons who, when listening to the radio, tune in to only one station during the time period.
Courtesy of the Arbitron Company

Exclusive Cumes

Exclusive Cume listening estimates identify the number of different persons who, when they are listening to the radio, tune in to only one station during the time period.

The day-parts are:
 Monday-Sunday, 6AM-Midnight
 Monday-Friday, 6-10AM
 Monday-Friday, 10AM-3PM
 Monday-Friday, 3-7PM
 Monday-Friday, 7PM-Midnight

The demographics are:
 Total Persons 12 +
 Men 18 +
 Women 18 +
 Teens 12-17

APRIL/MAY 1977

Exclusive Cume Listening Estimates— Metro Survey Area, In Hundreds

MON.-SUN. 6:AM -MID.

STATION CALL LETTERS	TOTAL PERS. 12 +	MEN 18 +	WOMEN 18 +	TEENS 12-17
WAAA	756	337	396	23
WBBB	46	33	13	
WCCC	247	158	89	
WDDD	83	83		
WEEE	435	188	247	
WFFF	12		12	
WGGG	531	136	130	265
WHHH	54		29	25
WIII	40	23		17
WJJJ	154	104	50	

MON.-FRI. 6:00AM -10:00AM

STATION CALL LETTERS	TOTAL PERS. 12 +	MEN 18 +	WOMEN 18 +	TEENS 12-17
WAAA	2362	920	1320	122
WBBB	61	33	13	15
WCCC	414	267	147	
WDDD	121	108	13	
WEEE	885	442	445	
WFFF	76	11	65	
WGGG	912	144	362	406
WHHH	165	39	62	64
WIII	241	44	157	
WJJJ	254	163	81	10

MON.-FRI. 10:00 AM -3:00 PM

STATION CALL LETTERS	TOTAL PERS. 12 +	MEN 18 +	WOMEN 18 +	TEENS 12-17
WAAA	1615	675	859	81
WBBB	74	49	25	
WCCC	323	206	117	
WDDD	156	105	51	
WEEE	1299	557	730	12
WFFF	41	22	19	
WGGG	885	220	227	438
WHHH	183	21	61	101
WIII	291	92	176	23
WJJJ	213	103	110	

MON.-FRI. 3:00 PM -7:00 PM

STATION CALL LETTERS	TOTAL PERS. 12 +	MEN 18 +	WOMEN 18 +	TEENS 12-17
WAAA	1253	709	459	85
WBBB	90	65	25	
WCCC	394	230	164	
WDDD	225	170	55	
WEEE	1450	505	892	33
WFFF	134	73	61	
WGGG	948	162	330	456
WHHH	234	14	94	126
WIII	222	67	155	
WJJJ	135	50	75	10

MON.-FRI. 7:00 PM - MID.

STATION CALL LETTERS	TOTAL PERS. 12 +	MEN 18 +	WOMEN 18 +	TEENS 12-17
WAAA	2532	1299	1130	103
WBBB	46	33	13	
WCCC	183	149	34	
WDDD	181	103	78	
WEEE	1287	599	673	15
WFFF				
WGGG	825	144	299	382
WHHH	195	49	45	101
WIII	208	43	142	23
WJJJ	331	139	182	10
	632	221	378	33

Excl Cume

Footnote Symbols: (*) means audience estimates adjusted for actual broadcast schedule (+) means AM-FM Combination was not simulcast for complete time period.

ARBITRON

The Rating Game 237

Other Measurement Services

In addition to Nielsen and Arbitron—usually thought of as the "big two"—there are about fifty measurement organizations with specialized purposes.

For example, TVQ researches attitudes and opinions which people have about specific television programs and personalities. Its method is to mail a questionnaire to different families each month to determine the degree to which they are aware of particular shows or people and how much they like the shows or personalities.[5]

Trendex, Inc. was the first company to offer instantaneous overnight TV ratings, beginning way back in 1950. It did this by using the coincidental telephone technique—1,000 telephone calls every evening half-hour in twenty-five cities asking people what they were watching at the moment. As the other rating services developed overnights, Trendex's service dwindled and now it makes reports only on special order.[6]

The four radio networks cooperate in the annual Radio All-Dimension Audience Research (RADAR) to gather information to supply an overall view of radio listening throughout the United States.[7] A research organization called Trace measures radio listening by checking automobiles as they are stopped for traffic lights.[8] Sindlinger and Company, using the telephone interview method, matches information about audience makeup with probable buying patterns.[9]

Other companies research such characteristics as brand name recall, attitude change, unconscious motivations that affect product buying, viewer involvement, station images, before and after advertising and program effectiveness, audience loyalty, and news content and personalities.

Pretesting

Another fairly large area of research is pretesting. Both advertisers and programmers like to know the probability of success of an idea before they invest in it heavily. Companies such as ASI Market Research, Inc., which operates Preview House, a 400-seat theater in Los Angeles, or McCollum/ Spielman and Co., Inc., which operates Preview Studios in three sections of the country, show both proposed programs and commercials to sample audiences and elicit their reactions by questionnaires, various button-pushing techniques, or electronic techniques that measure perspiration. Sometimes audience members are given products that might be associated with certain programs in order to obtain reactions.[10]

CBS has its own pretesting activity, the CBS Program Analysis Unit. The company invites small groups of people to a studio to preview program material. Each person is seated next to buttons indicating 'like' and 'dislike,' and as the program proceeds, the person pushes the appropriate button to express his or her opinion. Reactions are recorded on IBM cards and polygraphs so that the session coordinator can obtain an immediate readout of reactions. CBS uses all of this information to aid in such decisions as casting changes, news program formats, and new program ideas.[11]

Several companies such as Burke Marketing Research, Inc. and Gallup and Robinson, Inc. test commercials while the participants remain in their homes. They see that the ads are placed in a set period of programming on cable TV, a UHF station, or a willing VHF station. Potential testees are then telephoned and invited to watch the programming of the particular channel. The following day the same people are called again and asked their opinions of the commercials.[12]

Several different types of statistics are reported by audience research companies. The main one, of course, is the rating, which is basically a percentage of the households watching a particular TV program or listening to a particular radio station.

Measurement Calculation

Assume that the pie in the figure represents a sample of 500 television households drawn from 100,000 TV households in the market being surveyed. The rating is the percentage of the total sample. Thus, the rating for station WAAA is 80/500, or 16 percent; the rating for WAAB is 50/500, or 10 percent; and the rating for WAAC is 70/500, or 14 percent. Usually when ratings are reported, the percentage sign is eliminated, thus WAAA has a rating of 16. Sometimes ratings are reported for certain stations and sometimes for certain programs. If WAAA were airing network evening news at the particular time of this rating pie, then this news would have a rating of 16 in this particular city. Of course, national ratings are drawn from a sample of more than just one market. There are approximately 71

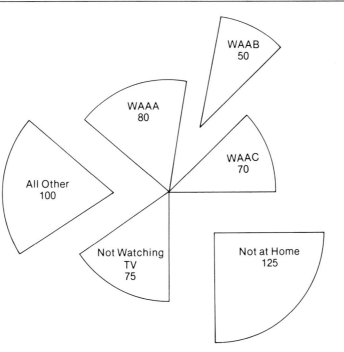

**Figure 11.11
Ratings pie**

million households in the United States, so the number of households watching national programs can be determined by multiplying the rating times 71 million. For example a rating of 20 is 20 percent times 71 million, or 14.2 million. National **prime time** ratings in the 20s are considered acceptable.

A different measurement based on a **universe** defined as all TV households using TV at the time is called **share** of audience. In the pie shown above, 300 homes had the sets on—80 to WAAA, 50 to WAAB, 70 to WAAC, 100 to all others. In the other 200 homes, either no one was at home or the TV was off, so they do not count in the share of audience total. Therefore, WAAA's share of audience would be 80/300, or 26.7; WAAB's share would be 50/300, or 16.7; and WAAC's share would be 70/300, or 23.4. A share-of-audience calculation will always be higher than a rating unless 100 percent of the people are watching TV—an unlikely phenomenon.

Another calculation is homes using TV (**HUT**). This is the percentage of TV households that have the set tuned to anything. In the above example, the HUT figure is 60; 300 out of 500 households had the sets tuned to something (300/500 = 60 percent).

Another way to look at these three statistics is by their formulas:

$$\text{Rating} = \frac{\text{homes tuned to station}}{\text{total TV homes}}$$

$$\text{Share} = \frac{\text{homes tuned to station}}{\text{homes using TV}}$$

$$\text{HUT} = \frac{\text{total TV homes}}{\text{sets turned on}}$$

Several other less important measurements are taken from time to time. One is a **time-period measurement,** which is usually calculated for radio. It shows the average proportion of homes in which sets are tuned to each station during each half hour period of the day. If ten homes out of 100 are tuned to station KAAA from 8:30 to 9:00 a.m., then its time-period measurement is 10 for that half hour. If five out of 100 homes are tuned to station KAAB from 6:00 a.m. to 6:30 a.m. and seven out of 100 are tuned from 6:30 to 7:00 a.m., KAAB would have gained two time period points during the latter half-hour.

Coverage is another term often used in audience measurement. It refers to the number of homes that could be reached if all conditions were ideal. In other words, it is the number of homes that can see or hear the station's signal. Obviously, stations in a large city like New York will have greater coverage than stations in a small town like Cody, Wyoming. Coverage is also divided into A coverage and B coverage, depending on how clearly and reliably a station is received in an area.

Another measurement, **circulation,** refers to the number of homes that tune in a station over a set period of time. Usually circulation figures are given in terms of one week and represent a station's drawing power as opposed to the drawing power of one particular program. Circulation is calculated as the number of homes that tune in to a station at least once a week. Therefore, if over the course of a week 90 households out of 1,000 tune in radio station KZZZ, its circulation would be 9. This is an arbitrary type of count which came into being because advertisers wanted some way to compare radio station effectiveness with newspapers. It is easy to calculate a newspaper's circulation by counting the number of papers sold. There is no comparable calculation for radio and TV stations, but the number of people tuning in per week is considered to be fairly equitable.

There are also **instantaneous measures** and **average measures.** An instantaneous count is the number of households tuned in to a program at a particular moment. For example, Nielsen could take a reading of its meter at 8:06 p.m. and give an instantaneous reading for that moment. An average measure gives the average number of households tuned in to a station over a period of time. For example, NBC might want to know the average number of households watching the network between 9:30 and 10:00 p.m. on Sunday. If it obtained instantaneous counts of 20 at 9:30, 15 at 9:40, 17 at 9:50, and 12 at 10:00, its average for the 9:30 to 10:00 period would be 16.

A cumulative measure, often called a **cume,** gives an estimate of the number of different households tuned in for two or more periods of time. For example, Pete's Car Lot might be interested in knowing the total number of households that heard its KXXX ad on Tuesday at 9:00 a.m., 1:00 p.m., and 5:00 p.m. Pete's might hire Trendex to call the same 1,000 households at each of these times. Perhaps at 9:00, Trendex would find that 30 of the 1,000 households were tuned to KXXX, for a count of 3. At 1:00, 32 households might be tuned in, but only 5 of those households would be ones that were not tuned in at 9:00, so the additional number would be 5/1,000, or .5. At 5:00, 40 households might tune in, 20 of which were not tuned in at either 9:00 or 1:00, so the additional would be 20/1,000, or 2. The cume would be 3 + .5 + 2, or 5.5. An ad that ran at 9:00 Monday, 9:00 Tuesday, 9:00 Wednesday, and 9:00 Thursday might have data as follows based on a sample of 100:

Monday   — 10 households tuned in
Tuesday   — 7 households tuned in, 3 of which are new
Wednesday   — 6 households tuned in, 2 of which are new
Thursday   — 10 households tuned in, 1 of which is new

The cume would be 10 + 3 + 2 + 1 = 16

One more statistic that is very important to advertisers is the cost per thousand, or **CPM** (M stands for the Latin term for thousand). This is an indication to the advertiser of how much it is costing him to reach 1,000 households. For example, if an advertiser pays $30 for a radio spot and the ratings show that that spot is reaching 5,000 households, then it is costing the advertiser $6.00 for each 1,000 households. Generally advertisers want

CPMs between $2.00 and $5.00. An advertiser who buys a national TV ad for $50,000 would be happy with a rating of 20, for that means over 14 million households are receiving the message. A price of $50,000 for 14,000,000 households equals $3.57 as a CPM. Of course, CPMs for subgroups will be much higher than $4.00. An advertiser wishing to reach working-age men at 2:00 p.m. might find the CPM for that group is about $50, since very few would be tuned to TV.

Ratings Under Fire

Criticisms surrounding ratings do not snipe at the core of their existence. Ratings are needed in order for broadcasters and advertisers to know how widely their programs are being received. Criticisms of ratings stem, not from their basic being, but more from their methodology and interpretation.

All ratings are based on samples rather than the entire population. Therefore, it is the viewing and listening tastes of a very small percentage of people who are representing the tastes of the entire audience. It is simply too expensive and impractical to survey the whole population, so **samples** must be used for audience measurement, just as they are for scientific research. A frequent criticism of audience research methodology is that the sample size is not large enough. Nielsen's audimeters placed in 1,200 homes out of a total of 71,000,000 represent a percentage of .00169, often decried even by those who revere the ratings most as too small to prove anything.

Rating companies provide critics with a wealth of authoritative "proof" that their sample, though small, is statistically sound. Also, they point to their continuing attempt to make their sample representative of the entire population so that within the sample group there are the same percentages of households with particular demographic characteristics as in the population of the entire United States. Some of the characteristics considered are age, education, race, sex, family size, place of residence, and income. A rating sample would attempt to have the same percentage of households headed by a thirty-year-old high school educated black woman with three children living in the city and earning $8,000 per year as in the population of the whole United States. But just which of these characteristics are important to audience measurement can be avidly debated. So, too, can one debate the extent to which changes in population data should be incorporated into samples. Because of the cost involved in installing meters, only 1/5th of the sample is changed each year, leaving Nielsen open to the criticism that it does not represent present moment demographics.

Once a company has determined the type of sample it wishes to compose, it can find population percentages from readily available government data. Some companies then gather samples to meet these percentages by contacting people listed in telephone books, a technique criticized because it does not include those with unlisted numbers. Others draw samples by canvassing designated neighborhoods, a procedure criticized because neighborhoods are not necessarily homogeneous.

Even after determining the ideal households to include in a sample, the companies are faced with the problem of uncooperative potential samples.

About 30 percent of the people contacted refuse to have machines installed on their sets and about 50 percent do not want to keep diaries. Substitutions must be made for uncooperative people, and this may bias the sample in two ways—the substitutes may have characteristics that unbalance the sample, and uncooperative people, as a group, may have particular traits that bias the sample.

Problems with ratings methodology do not cease once the size and composition of the sample have been decided and the people selected. There is also the problem of receiving accurate information from these people. Each rating method has its drawbacks in this regard.

A certain number of Nielsen machines develop mechanical malfunctions, further reducing the sample size in an unscientific manner. The machines record only that the set is on; they do not reveal whether or not anyone is watching it. Some people turn the TV set on to entertain the baby—or the dog. Some people attempt to appear more intellectual by turning on cultural programs but not actually watching them, or they may react in other ways unlike their normal behavior simply because they know they are being monitored.

Diaries are subject to human deceit also, for people can lie about what they actually watched. Or, more innocently, they can simply forget to mark down their viewing or listening and then attempt to fill in a week's worth of programming from memory—perhaps aided by *TV Guide*. Arbitron generally finds it can use only about half the data it sets out to collect because people do not fill out the diaries, do not fill them out correctly, or turn them in too late.

Interview techniques can also contain bias—one form being the bias of the interviewer. If the person doing the interviewing has certain preferences toward programs or stations, he or she may influence a person who is unsure of what actually was seen or heard, to respond toward the interviewer's preferences. Many interviewers are inexperienced and unskillful and are working only as temporary employment. Telephone interviews are biased by unanswered phones, and door-to-door by unanswered doorbells. House-to-house interviewing is becoming increasingly difficult because interviewers refuse to canvass unsafe neighborhoods, and people refuse to admit interviewers to their homes, again because of safety factors. Lack of memory or purposeful inaccuracies can affect interviews based on recall, while calls made to determine what a person is viewing or hearing at the moment are unable to supply data involving late night or early morning programs without greatly alienating many citizens.

Stations, too, can influence ratings. Those aware of rating periods sometimes engage in the practice called "**hypoing**." They broadcast their most popular programming, hold contests, give away prizes, and generally attempt to increase the size of their audience, usually only temporarily.

There are those who contend that the whole rating structure is hopelessly out of date, operating as though a family unit still sat hushed at night around the parlor radio set. This criticism evolves mainly because ratings are generally based on households rather than individuals. In modern society the household structure has lost much of its impact and, with multiple sets and outside-the-home listening and viewing, both programming preference and purchasing are in many instances individual rather than household decisions. Hence, the basic household structure of audience measurement can lead to invalid results.

Another overall criticism of ratings has been that they are too secretive; that the rating companies keep methodology and sampling techniques too close to the vest. This opens the door for corruption and incompetence.

Even after rating material has been collected, it is still subject to computer error, printing error, and, even more important, flaws in interpretation. Although rating company methodology is often criticized, management interpretation is the area most criticized. Rating companies publish results and really cannot be held responsible for how they are used. This area of error is the domain of broadcasting and advertising executives.

The main criticism is that too much emphasis is placed on ratings, especially the Nielsen network ratings. Despite the fact that rating companies themselves acknowledge that their sampling techniques and methodology yield imperfect results usually not accurate to one percentage point, programs are sometimes removed from the air when they slip one or two rating points. Actors and actresses whose careers have been stunted by such action harbor resentment. Trade journals will headline the ratings lead of one network over the others when that lead for all programs totaled may be only two or three points. National executives anxiously, perhaps even religiously, await the Nielsen overnights and make daily decisions based on them, only to find that the nationals, received later, reverse the standings of many programs. Nielsen and Arbitron sometimes do not agree, and yet some programmers will ''believe'' only one service's figures. Ratings should be an indication of comparative size and nothing more, but in reality their shadow extends much further.

The overdependence on ratings leads to programming concepts often deplored by the critics. In a popularity contest attempt to gain the highest numbers, stations and networks neglect programming for special interest groups. All programming tends to become similar, geared toward the audience that will deliver the largest numbers. During the '60s, programming to attract youth predominated, for that age group was the largest portion of the population. Programmers place emphasis on viewer quantity often to the neglect of such factors as creativity, station image, public access, flexibility, availability to the community, and station services to advertisers.

Dependence on ratings tends to perpetuate the imitative quality of programming. When one show receives a high rating, many similar shows are spawned. Ratings indicate what people liked in the past but give no clue as to what people will like in the future.

Advertisers too are guilty of being slaves to quantity. Often a small but select audience might be best for a specific purpose—e.g., estate planning insurance might be better advertised on a classical music station with a low rating than a top-40 station with a high rating. Audience measurement barely touches on qualitative factors such as opinions and attitudes of people toward programs and products, brand name recognition in relation to program identification and purchasing decisions, and level of audience attention to selected material such as commercials. Advertisers are not prone to demand such research. They, like broadcasters, seem content to assume that quantity is the primary goal and that cost-per-thousand—regardless of the composition, attitude, or attention of the thousand—will move goods from the shelf. With the present audience measurement structure, ratings should be used as an aid, not an end, but all too often this is not the case.[13]

Because of the numerous loopholes that can be found in audience measurement procedures, various groups have been formed to test the reliability of the rating company data. Most of this activity grew out of a House of Representatives committee hearing on ratings held in 1963. The Federal Trade Commission had previously issued **cease and desist** orders to several rating companies telling them to stop misrepresenting the accuracy and reliability of their reports. The FTC charged the rating companies with relying on hearsay information, making false claims about the nature of their sample populations, improperly combining and reporting data, failing to account for nonresponding sample members, and making arbitrary changes in the rating figures. The House picked up on these charges and, as a result of its investigation, issued a congressional committee report entitled *Broadcast Ratings: The Methodology, Accuracy, and Use of Ratings in Broadcasting.*[14]

Research on Research

While the House inquiry was in progress, the broadcasters themselves formed the Broadcast Rating Council to monitor, audit, and accredit the various rating companies. This organization serves as a watchdog over-seeing the rating companies. Among its duties are checking the sample design; checking the implementation of the samples and the extent to which the predesignated sample is achieved; checking the interviewers and the controls placed on them; verifying the fieldwork of interviewers; checking the procedures for handling questionnaires from the time of receipt through final data processing; and checking published reports and procedures to ascertain the reliability of printed output. The BRC has developed minimum standards in each of these areas and awards its own accreditation to the companies which meet or exceed the standards. Submitting to accreditation is voluntary, but most rating companies do it because broadcasters are their major customers.[15]

In 1963 the National Association of Broadcasters and the networks also set up the Committee on Nationwide Television Audience Measurement (CONTAM), which undertook several basic research projects. One dealt with the effect of sample size on accuracy in rating estimates. For the study, CONTAM used 56,000 completed diaries which had already been processed so that ratings results were known. CONTAM selected various sized samples from this 56,000 ranging from 100 samples of 50 each to 100 samples of 2,500 each to see if sample size affected the probability of the sample having the same rating as the 56,000 total. CONTAM concluded that the larger the sample, the greater was the probability of accuracy, but, at best, samples could be only an indication of the true value. Another study investigated the significance of the differences in rating methods and found that Nielsen and Arbitron agreed in their program rankings 94 percent of the time—a fairly large percentage of agreement.

An investigation of the effect of no-answer phone calls revealed significant differences. CONTAM, through determined follow-up calls, found that many people who did not answer their phones were in fact home and watching TV but for various reasons did not answer the phone. The difference was enough to change the viewing from 52.5 to 57.5. CONTAM also found that interviewer technique can bias ratings.[16]

A Committee on Local Television and Radio Audience Measurement dealt with the problem of unlisted households and found that the larger the city, the larger the percentage of unlisted phone numbers, but the committee concluded that the effect of leaving out people with unlisted phones from survey samples was minimal.[17]

Another industry group investigated people who had refused to cooperate in ratings surveys and compared them with people who had cooperated. It found that the cooperators generally watched more TV, had larger families, and were younger and better educated than the noncooperators. This is a factor that could tend to inflate all ratings, making it appear that broadcasting permeates society to a greater extent than it does.

This cooperation factor was borne out in 1966 by the Politz research organization, which telephoned 12,000 households to check their viewing habits. It found 41 percent of households using TV at night while Nielsen found 55 percent during the same time period. This would indicate that ratings favor broadcasters over advertisers, for they artificially increase the thousands, thus increasing the CPM.[18]

The All-Radio Methodology Study (ARMS) was formed by the NAB and the Radio Advertising Bureau in 1963 to perform several studies to determine the best procedures for gathering radio rating data. This group found that the coincidental telephone method was the most accurate and that diaries tended to be more accurate if they were collected in person than if they were mailed.[19]

NBC network radio undertook a three-year study of Cumulative Radio Audience Method (CRAM), which paid particular attention to the effect of sample nonresponse. NBC augmented the coincidental telephone technique by calling back at a later time and by interviewing everyone in a household over thirteen years of age rather than just one person. It found by these methods that radio listening was usually higher than that reported by rating companies. Another part of the CRAM project utilized daily phone calls to the same sample for an entire week. This method realized about 13 percent higher cooperation rate than the diary method.[20]

The intangibles associated with broadcast listening and viewing are enormous. Unlike newspapers, the consumption of which is spread out over time, broadcasting vanishes as soon as it has been presented. In addition, radio waves refuse to obey political or geographic boundaries, making the concept of a **market** a muddled one at best. Networks and stations themselves cannot survey their own audience totals, for the numbers would be suspect. Then, too, the desired result is thrice removed from the original stimulus. Programs are produced to attract a large audience to watch the commercials, which, it is hoped, will induce people to buy products. No wonder, then, that it is difficult to supply meaningful ratings. And yet something is needed, because millions of dollars and decisions are involved. Given these parameters, ratings are the best method devised as yet.

Rating companies can defend their methodology by declaring that conscious manipulation of the truth by sample participants will average out. While one person is inflating his diary to improve the rating of his favorite rock station, another is exaggerating to an interviewer the number of hours for a middle-of-the-road station.

To the critics of sampling procedure, the rating companies can reply, "All right, you come up with a better idea." No two people in the country are exactly alike, so sampling procedures must do the best they can. In general, the methods used by rating companies are as good as any yet devised.

The size of the Nielsen nationals are such that no one claims they are accurate to more than three points. Diary and telephone methods are generally more reliable depending on sample size. Larger, more refined sample sizes could be easily accommodated if subscribers were willing to pay the cost.

Likewise, more qualitative data could be gathered, interviewing techniques could be improved, education about ratings could be more widespread—but someone must pay. There has been no hue and cry for these improvements because subscribers—broadcasters and advertisers—have not been willing to foot the bill.

Hypoing can affect ratings, but it is outlawed by the FCC. That agency has never prosecuted any stations for this violation, which is difficult to prove, but rating companies' hands are tied in relation to this issue.

Rating companies claim they must be somewhat secretive, particularly in regard to identification of the sample households. If any significant number of households were bribed, this could severely endanger rating validity. The formation of the Broadcast Rating Council serves to keep rating companies honest.

As to the fact that some ratings in all probability inflate the overall use of radio and TV, the rating companies can state that this may be true, but since it is done uniformly, no one suffers. Broadcasting is a choice advertising medium, and if the numbers watching or listening were reported as slightly smaller, all stations could simply increase their CPMs and advertisers would wind up paying the same total dollars. Besides, there are other ratings that deflate the use of radio and television.

The effects which ratings have on program content are simply the result of the democratic process. Audience members get what they vote for. If stations were to use another criterion, say creativity, as the basis for advertising rates, the situation would be far more unjust than the present quantitative rating system. Creativity is an abstract which really has not been defined, let alone counted.

We can hope for refinement of techniques and more intelligent exercise of interpretation, but audience measurement is presently and no doubt will continue to be a vital part of the broadcasting process.

Summary   Ratings are calculated to determine the number of households watching TV or listening to radio so that advertisers will know the audience size for their commercials.

The earliest rating method was *fan mail*, followed by ratings of *Crossley, Hooper,* and *BMB*. The name most associated with ratings today is Nielsen, a company which uses *audimeters* and *diaries* and publishes *overnights, MNAs, NTIs,* and *sweeps*. Another rating service, *Arbitron,* divides the country into *ADIs* and uses diaries and *meters* for its reports. *The Pulse,* Inc., specializes in radio and uses the *roster/recall* interview technique. Other measurement services include TVQ, Trendex, RADAR, Trace, and Sindlinger and Co. *Pretesting* groups include Preview House, Preview Studios, and CBS Program Analysis Unit. Audience measurement companies calculate various statistics. The *rating* is the most important and represents the percentage of homes viewing or listening to a particular station. Other measurements are *share, HUT, coverage, circulation,* and *cume. CPM* is very important to advertisers. Ratings are criticized for small *sample* size, unrepresentative samples, bias, reflection of *"hypoing,"* antiquated basics, inadequate interpretation, and overdependence of management on them. Attempts to improve ratings have been undertaken by the FTC, House of Representatives, *BRC, CONTAM, ARMS,* and *CRAM*. Despite all their flaws, ratings are necessary to the broadcasting industry.

12 What! No Commercials?

Noncommercial Radio and Television

I think public television should be the visual counterpart of the literary essay, should arouse our dreams, satisfy our hunger for beauty, take us on journeys, enable us to participate in events, present great drama and music, explore the sea and sky and the woods and hills. It should be our Lyceum, our Chatauqua, our Minsky's and our Camelot. It should restate and clarify the social dilemma and the political pickle.

E. B. White, writer and philosopher

Cartoon copyrighted by *Broadcasting* magazine

"It's for a good cause. We're raising funds for our local noncommercial television station."

Struggling beside its more glamorous commercial cousin has been the noncommercial radio and television system of the United States— floundering and fluctuating, arguing and achieving, staggering and starring. Its history is scarred with defeat and victories and its present is replete with insecurity, but it has nonetheless emerged as a viable aspect of American broadcasting.

Broadcasting was born noncommercial, and, in fact, many of the early stations were started by educational institutions. For example, in 1919 Professor Earle M. Terry established a station at the University of Wisconsin which sent weather bulletins to several hundred listeners in farm areas around Madison. The professor and his students experimented with other forms of communication and particularly favored Hawaiian music because its twang carried well.[1]

A History of Educational Radio

The early twenties witnessed a radio rush by colleges and universities around the country resulting in seventy-four such institutions broadcasting by the end of 1922.[2] The colleges used these stations primarily to aid extension activities, raise funds, and offer college credit courses which people could listen to in their homes. The main problem facing these stations was the same one which plagued other early stations—they all had to broadcast on the same frequency, 360 meters. As more and more stations added their signals to the air waves, home-study students often could not hear their lessons because of interference, faculty members became disillusioned with the effectiveness of radio, and many colleges ceased their broadcasts. In 1925 thirty-seven educational stations left the air and only twenty-five new ones began.

As commercial stations became more firmly entrenched, they overpowered the educational stations both in wattage and dollars. During the '20s radio stations generally shared time with each other, so it was not uncommon for an educational and commercial station to alternate hours. If the commercial station decided it wanted a larger share of the time, it would petition the Federal Radio Commission and both it and the educational station would need to go to Washington for the appeal. This was an expensive and time-consuming process which the educational station could not afford. Usually the educational stations found themselves coming away with the short end of the stick on disputes involving time, power, and position to the extent that they were unable to use their broadcasting facilities effectively for any type of continuing programming.

After 1925 the secretary of commerce strongly urged people who wished to enter broadcasting to buy an existing station rather than add one to the already overcrowded airwaves. As a result many educational facilities were propositioned by commercial ventures that wished to buy their stations. Frequently they succumbed because the financial drain of the stations outweighed the dwindling public service value.

The result was a downward spiral for educational radio. In 1928 thirty-three educational stations gave up, followed by thirteen more the following year.[3]

In 1929 the National Committee on Education by Radio organized and suggested that 15 percent of all radio stations be reserved for non-commercial educational use. The group tried to establish this reservation policy in the 1934 Communications Act. It was unsuccessful largely because commercial interests so touted their own cultural contributions as to negate the need for strictly educational stations.

Despite defeat, educational organizations such as the National Association of Educational Broadcasters (NAEB), the National Education Association (NEA), and the U.S. Office of Education (USOE) kept this issue alive while the educational stations continued to dwindle to approximately thirty.[4]

With the advent of FM broadcasting, educators, through perseverance, began to taste victory. In 1945 the FCC reserved the twenty FM channels between 88.1 and 91.9 exclusively for noncommercial radio. These channels at the lower end of the FM band are reserved for educational use everywhere across the country, so it can be assumed that any stations heard below 91.9 on the FM band are noncommercial.

By the end of 1945 there were six FM educational stations on the air.[5] The number grew to 48 by 1950 and passed 800 by the mid-70s.[6] Part of this FM increase was due to a 1948 ruling authorizing low-powered ten-watt educational FM stations which generally reach only two to five miles and are easily and inexpensively installed and operated. Approximately half the FM educational stations are of the ten-watt variety, generally operated by educational institutions as training grounds for students.[7]

As the number of educational radio stations increased, the need for some form of network grew. Actually, the need had been evident as far back as the '30s. Several attempts were made to exchange program material so that stations would not be burdened with producing all their program fare themselves. However, the attempts were not overly successful, and little was accomplished except for a few isolated instances of station program exchange.

The National Association of Educational Broadcasters, organized in 1934 as a spokesgroup for the educational radio field, formed the first workable duplication and distribution operation. This so-called "**bicycle network**" begun in 1949 was not a network in the same sense as the commercial networks because programs were not sent through wires to all stations simultaneously. Rather, programs were taped and then sent from one station to another by mail on a scheduled round-robin basis.[8]

When the Corporation for Public Broadcasting (CPB) was formed in the late 1960s, primarily to serve the needs of public television, radio was also included under its umbrella, and the NAEB ceded its radio networking duties to National Public Radio (NPR), an arm of CPB. In succeeding years many of the radio stations were interconnected by phone wires.[9]

Radio Ownership and Financing

The majority of noncommercial radio stations are owned by educational institutions—colleges, universities, high schools, public school systems, boards of education. Some are owned by state or municipal authorities or religious groups, and a few are owned by private groups, such as the Pacifica Foundation.[10]

The bulk of the financing comes from the budgets of the institutions which own the stations. Indirectly, this is frequently tax money, since taxes form the basis for the income of public schools. Other forms of financing are **endowments,** grants, and public donations. Endowments sometimes come from alumni of a university donating a substantial sum of money with the stipulation that the interest earned from the money be used to operate a radio station. Special grants from individuals, companies, or government agencies, including the Corporation for Public Broadcasting, are usually used for specific purposes, such as buying new equipment or producing a series of programs. Some stations, mainly those owned by private groups, attempt to subsist on donations from listeners and the limited funds they bring in by selling ads in a program guide.

Owning and operating a noncommercial radio station is far from financially rewarding, but the organizations which own them find them worthwhile in terms of recognition, prestige, and service. It was recently reported that 13 percent of the adult population is aware of public radio and 4 percent listen regularly.[11]

Programming concepts vary greatly from one educational station to another. Some program primarily music, but usually not the top-40 format popular with commercial radio stations. In fact, it is within the educational stations that most of the vestiges of classical music broadcasting reside. Other educational stations devote most of their daytime hours to programs designed for schoolchildren. Some have a potpourri format that may include varying combinations of information, news, consumer education, public health, children's programs, drama, music, and local sports.[12]

Stations depend to varying degrees on programming from National Public Radio. Only the large, well-staffed stations qualify to receive the programs sent over NPR's leased-line interconnected network service. According to NPR's policies, only public radio stations with at least five full-time professional employees, eighteen hours a day of programming every day of the year, and an annual nonduplicated nonfederal budget of $75,000 can qualify to receive programs over network lines. This eliminates over 600 of the approximately 800 stations, leaving a network of some 170 stations. Generally it is the 10-watt stations that do not qualify, but since they are mainly for training, they are interested in producing their own programming in any event. These nonqualifying stations can receive NPR material by ordering tapes of specific programs at a nominal cost.

For a fee of about $100 a year, the qualifying stations receive approximately fifty hours of programming per week sent over the interconnected phone wires. Some of these programs are produced by NPR itself; others originate at the stations and are sent by wire to NPR headquarters for national distribution.

The program fare of the network covers a wide gamut of cultural and informational material—news, senate hearings, concerts, dramas, self-help

Radio Programming

**Figure 12.1
National Public Radio's
control room.**
Photo courtesy of National
Public Radio

**Figure 12.2
The original facilities of
KETC, the St. Louis
public television station,
which went on the air in
1954.**
Photo courtesy of KETC,
St. Louis

material, documentaries, and foreign features, especially from the British Broadcasting Corporation and Canadian Broadcasting Corporation.[13]

Early television was dominated by commercial interests, with a little activity from educational institutions. Several universities offered college credit courses over local commercial channels, and in 1950 the University of Iowa built a TV station which it ran as a partially commercial venture.[14]

Educators, while recognizing the value of television, also realized that they would face a losing battle akin to the early radio experience if they attempted to compete with commercial companies for stations. As a result, the same groups that fought for the allocation of noncommercial FM radio stations attempted to convince the FCC that there should be channel reservations for noncommercial television stations. This time the battle was somewhat easier, thanks largely to the support from FCC Commissioner Frieda Hennock. When the freeze was lifted in 1952, the FCC had authorized the reservation of 242 noncommercial channels—80 VHF and 162 UHF.[15] Unlike FM, these channels were scattered around the dial in that different channels were reserved in different cities—e.g., channel 13 in Pittsburgh, channel 11 in Chicago, channel 28 in Los Angeles.

Obtaining the channels and activating the stations were two different matters, mainly because of the huge sums of money which television stations demand. Fortunately for educational television, the Ford Foundation became interested in its cause and provided much of the money for the early facilities and programs. In 1953 the nation's first educational TV license was granted to the University of Houston in Texas. By 1955 there were nine stations on the air, and by 1960, 44 stations.[16]

The Ford Foundation also became involved in programming by helping to establish the National Educational Television and Radio Center in Ann Arbor, Michigan, which acted as a distribution "bicycle network" center. This center gradually dropped some of its functions, including radio, changed its name to National Educational Television (NET), started producing programs, moved to New York, and allied itself with the New York public TV station for production.[17]

Ford also funded general programming concepts such as Chicago TV College, a fully accredited set of televised courses which enabled students to earn two-year college degrees through at-home viewing or a combination of at-home viewing and on-campus class attendance.[18] Another Ford-funded experiment of the late 1950s was the Midwest Program on Airborne Television Instruction (MPATI) by which programs for schoolchildren were broadcast onto two UHF channels by an airplane that circled two states.[19]

Despite its largess, the Ford Foundation could not **underwrite** all of educational television, so educators turned to the government to seek additional funds for building stations. In 1962, after a year of debate, Congress passed the Educational Broadcasting Facilities Act, which authorized $32 million for five years to be made available to states to assist in the construction of educational television facilities on a **matching fund** basis.

A History of Public Television

Figure 12.3
Professor Harvey M.
Karlen conducting a
lesson on national
government for
Chicago's TV College
during the mid '60s.
Photo courtesy of Great
Plains National Instruc-
tional Television Library

At this point government funds could be used only for facilities and not programs—a satisfactory arrangement to the educators, who were leary of strings which the government might attach to programming money. This act led to an increased interest by many groups in establishing educational TV stations. Because of the many requests, the FCC in 1966 revised its assignment table upward and set aside 604 channels in 559 communities. By the end of 1965, the number of stations on the air had doubled from the 1960 number of 44.[20]

Educational TV was not without its growing pains. In many cities the channel allocation for the educational television station was in the UHF band, making it difficult for the station to gain either audience or community financial support. What's more, overall, educational programming was, in a word, dull, so that it did not attract large audiences even in VHF cities. The Ford Foundation, feeling that it alone was supplying too much of the support for educational television, began withdrawing some of its financial support. Innumerable educational broadcasting organizations and councils appeared and disappeared, some because of financial problems and some because of lack of clear focus or political infighting. The result was a system so loosely organized that it impeded the impact of the medium.

The Carnegie Foundation therefore set up the Carnegie Commission on Educational Television. This group of highly respected citizens spent the better part of two years studying the technical, organizational, financial, and programming aspects of educational television. In 1967 it published its report, "Public Television: A Program for Action."

The Carnegie Commission changed the term "educational television" to "public television" to overcome the pedantic image the stations had acquired. It also recommended that "a well-financed and well-directed

Figure 12.4
Bill Nixon conducting a
science lesson used by
MPATI.
Photo courtesy of Great
Plains National Instruc-
tional Television Library

system, substantially larger and far more pervasive and effective than that which now exists in the United States, must be brought into full being if the full needs of the American public are to be served."[21]

Most of the commission's many recommendations were incorporated into the Public Broadcasting Act of 1967 passed by Congress. Title I of this act authorized an additional $38 million for the construction of facilities; Title II provided for the establishment and funding of the Corporation for Public Broadcasting (CPB) to provide national leadership for public broadcasting and to make sure that it would have maximum protection from outside interference and control; Title III authorized the secretary of health, education, and welfare to make a comprehensive study of educational and instructional broadcasting.

The heart of the bill, Title II, stipulated that the fifteen members of the board of the Corporation for Public Broadcasting be appointed by the president with consent of the Senate and that this corporation was in no way to be considered an agency or establishment of the U.S. government. The main duties of the CPB were to help new stations get on the air, to obtain grants from federal and private sources, to provide grants to stations for programming, and to establish an interconnection system for public broadcasting stations.[22]

The Corporation for Public Broadcasting was specifically forbidden from owning or operating the interconnection system. Therefore, the corporation created the Public Broadcasting Service (PBS), an agency to schedule, promote, and distribute programming over a wired network interconnection. This system was not to produce programs itself but rather was to obtain them from such sources as public TV stations, production companies, and foreign countries. Hence, a three-tiered operation was established: (1) the stations produced the programs; (2) PBS scheduled and

What! No Commercials?   257

distributed the programs; and (3) CPB provided funds and guidance for the activities.

This arrangement has not been without its internal disputes. During 1972-73 a feud developed between CPB, headed by its lay board, and PBS, headed by a board of public broadcasting station managers. The primary issue was which of these boards should have final say regarding what programs should be transmitted on the PBS network. A compromise was worked out which changed the structure of PBS slightly to include lay people on its board and which created monitoring committees to resolve disputes whenever PBS or CPB felt that particular programs or series were not balanced or objective.[23]

Under the CPB-PBS tenure, public broadcasting has grown in numbers of stations and scope of influence. By the mid-1970s over 200 stations were on the air, and an estimated 23 million households were watching public television at least once a week.[24] The stations voted to construct a satellite interconnection system to replace the wired network.[25]

Television Ownership and Financing

Ownership of public television stations is akin to radio station ownership in that educational institutions own many stations. However, many more public TV than public radio stations are owned by states and community groups. State ownership is common particularly in the South. Alabama, the first state to build and operate TV stations, owns nine stations which cover the state in a mini-network. About fifteen other states followed Alabama's lead by owning one or more stations. About one-fourth of public television stations are licensed to nonprofit community corporations. These corporations are usually formed by leaders in the community and obtain their support from the communities they serve.[26]

Financing public television is much more complicated than financing public radio because of the greater expense. As already mentioned, early TV financing came primarily from the Ford Foundation, followed by the federal government.

As of the late 1970s, support of public television was costing approximately $250 million a year. In general, about 24 percent of public TV's money comes from state boards of education and governments and 23 percent from the federal government. Most of the federal government money goes to the support of CPB and its activities, which often turn out to be some form of grant to local stations. For example, each year most stations receive community service grants from the corporation for purposes of their own choosing. Some stations also receive program development grants to produce **pilot** programs for proposed network series. Corporation money also pays for the network interconnection and for selected research and information projects. Other federal money goes directly to stations for facilities or special programs funded by other government agencies.

About 12 percent of financial income comes from state colleges, another 11 percent from local schools and governments, and 8 percent from foundations such as the Ford Foundation. Community subscribers who pay a yearly fee to the station and usually receive for that a magazine listing the station's programs account for 7.5 percent of income. Underwriting of programs by businesses accounts for slightly over 3 percent, as do station auctions.[27] When companies such as Xerox, Mobil, or 3M underwrite programs, they usually pay all or part of the production costs for a particular series and receive a short credit line before and after the program. Auctions, which have become an institution, particularly at community-owned stations, involve donations of unusual objects from members of the community which are then auctioned off over the air to people calling in to place their bids.

Although subscribers and auctions combined account for only about 11 percent of the income, many stations devote a great deal of effort to encouraging people to contribute to the station in one way or another by holding promotional campaigns or "get a friend to join" campaigns. Community-owned stations particularly emphasize subscription drives because they do not have support from specific educational organizations and must secure a larger percentage of their income from the public. Often funds from sources such as foundations or the federal government are given as matching funds, so contributions from members of the community provide an excellent base of funds to be matched. Subscriber campaigns also tend to assure that people in the community will become involved with the station.

Television Programming

Programming on public television has changed greatly over the years. Most early programming was produced on a shoestring budget and usually consisted of local free talent discussing issues or information. As a result, educational television became known for its "talking heads." As funds increased, quality increased, but it was a long, slow road. The program exchange from NET helped somewhat, but to a large extent the stations just exchanged mediocrity.

The advent of the Corporation for Public Broadcasting and its accompanying funding allowed public television to embark upon innovative programming of high quality. The first series to arouse interest in virtually every public TV station was the successful 1970 children's series "Sesame Street," produced by a newly created and newly funded organization, the Children's Television Workshop (CTW). This series helped strengthen PBS as a network because it was in demand throughout the country. In the same year the public television drama "The Andersonville Trial" won the Emmy for Best Program of the Year. Other public broadcasting series which have met with sustained popularity are "The French Chef," Julia Child's cooking show produced in Boston; "Mr. Rogers' Neighborhood," a children's program produced in Pittsburgh; "The Advocates," a cultural program placing issues on trial, produced partially in Boston and partially in Los Angeles; "Black Journal," a public affairs series dealing with news and issues of importance to blacks produced in New York; "The Way It Was," nostalgia filmclips and interviews with former sports heroes produced in Los Angeles; and "The Ascent of Man," Jacob Bronowski's view of humanity produced by the British Broadcasting Corporation.

Figure 12.5

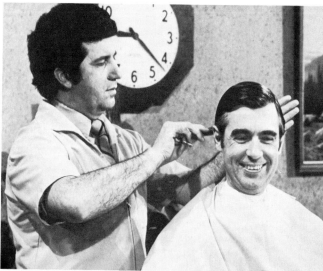

Figure 12.6

Figure 12.7

Figure 12.8

Figure 12.5
The "Sesame Street" gang posing for a group picture. Some of the most famous, longest-running characters of this show have included Big Bird, Oscar the Grouch, the Cookie Monster, Mr. Hooper, Bob, Susan, and Ernie and Bert.
Photo courtesy of © Children's Television Workshop

Figure 12.6
Fred Rogers (*right*) getting a haircut on "Mr. Rogers' Neighborhood." Since a visit to the barber can be a frightening experience for very young children, Mr. Rogers assures them that haircuts don't hurt at all.
Photo courtesy of Family Communications, Inc.

Figure 12.7
Governor Michael J. Dukakis of Massachusetts moderating a special preview edition of "The Advocates." The subject debated on this program was whether or not the United States should expand its nuclear power program.
Photo courtesy of WGBH Educational Foundation

Figure 12.8
The French chef, Julia Child, about to prepare an unusual dish.
Photo courtesy of WGBH Educational Foundation— Paul Child, photographer

In 1974 PBS established a Station Program Cooperative, a unique method by which many of the PBS programs are selected. First PBS conducts an audience research survey to determine national program needs; then it solicits program proposals from stations and production companies which, it is hoped, will meet the needs determined from the survey. These proposals are catalogued and sent to the various stations, which begin voting on those programs they would like to carry. The first few rounds of voting allow stations to express their interest in certain programs but do not bind the stations to purchase the programs. After a number of proposals have been eliminated for lack of interest, actual purchase rounds are conducted, and stations are required to help pay the production costs of those programs they wish to air. This process results in each program produced for PBS under the Station Program Cooperative having a slightly different group of stations paying for and airing it. Often the money which stations contribute to production costs comes from the CPB community service grants by following the route: CPB to local stations to PBS to producing stations.[28]

Not all PBS programs come through the station cooperative. Some are underwritten by foundations, corporations, or the government, and some are purchased from foreign governments. In fact, there are those who claim that PBS stands for "primarily British shows" because of the large amount of fare produced by the BBC.

Programming formats do differ from one public television station to another. One station may be much heavier on direct instruction than another, which emphasizes general cultural programs. Or one station may produce more local shows than another, which relies heavily on pre-produced programs.

A typical programming day, if such a thing exists, might be as follows. From 7:00 to 10:00 a.m. the station would air children's programs which it obtained through PBS; then from 10:00 a.m. until noon, it would air programs designed to be used in schools as part of the curriculum. Some of these might have been locally produced while others would have been produced at other stations or by production companies. From noon to 1:00 p.m. the station would program local news, locally produced, and 1:00 to 3:00 p.m. again would be taken up with classroom instruction. Children generally are out of school about 3:00, so from then until 6:00 p.m. would be a repeat of the PBS children's programs aired in the morning or programs designed for after-school viewing by teachers so they can improve teaching methods or learn new material. The hours of 6:00 to 7:00 might be devoted to college credit courses, and the evening hours until sign-off could consist of a locally produced documentary and programming from PBS that might include a cooking show, a drama, and a symphony.[29]

Public broadcasting has found that the price of success is abundant criticism. In its early days, when it was a minor element of broadcasting, it was usually criticized only for its dull programming. Now that it has overcome the "talking head" era and has both publicity and audience, its programming and organization have begun to receive some sharp blasts.

Public Broadcasting Controversies

Figure 12.9
A documentary called "Winners and Losers: Poverty in California" produced by public television station KOCE. Producer-director David Fanning films a scene from a housing development in East Oakland.
Photo courtesy of KOCE-TV, Huntington Beach, California

Figure 12.10
A locally produced program, "Film's Flying Ace." Frank Tallman (*right*), Hollywood stunt pilot, chats with George Peppard, one of the stars Tallman has worked with in over thirty years of making aviation films.
Photo courtesy of KOCE-TV, Huntington Beach, California

It is criticized for appealing to too large an audience and too small an audience; for being overly pro-government and overly anti-government; for being pro-business and anti-business; for being too centralized and too localized; and for spending too much money and too little money. In short, it seems that whatever direction public television turns, it finds itself between a rock and a hard place.

With the founding of the Corporation for Public Broadcasting and its government funding, programming improved to the extent that public television stations gradually entered the world of the Nielsens and even made a substantial showing on occasion. This brought about a philosophical dilemma. Should public TV develop programs which would appeal to large audiences under the umbrella of bringing culture to the masses and probably along the way compromise its standards to some degree, or should it program specialized material in order to maintain itself as an alternative service to fill the void left by ABC, CBS, and NBC? Obviously, this question hasn't been answered, but various shades of opinion exist, and controversies erupt when public television trespasses over what certain groups consider the fine line of audience size.

Commercial broadcasters are naturally uneasy with the thought that public TV might dent their audiences and hence their rate card, so they want public broadcasting to refrain from programming material similar to commercial network fare. A hue and cry arose when public television hired two commercial network commentators at high salaries. There are conflicts within the public TV structure too. People involved with producing programs for in-school or formal education use feel they are unfairly upstaged by the more glamorous cultural programming, which of course attracts the larger audience.

On the other hand, many people argue that public broadcasting appeals to much too narrow an audience, generally only to the highly educated. They point out that very few members of racial minorities or low-income areas watch public TV, thus creating a situation where public TV is responsible for the culturally rich becoming richer and the culturally poor becoming poorer. A programming philosophy geared more toward the masses could rectify this. Also, some people fear that when public broadcasting becomes too specialized, it loses impact.

Public television's relationship with the government is also a source of controversy. A large number of people, including many government officials, have criticized public television for being an arm of liberal left-wingers. This situation came to a head a number of years ago when members of the Nixon administration spoke out strongly against public broadcasting's political views, culminating with the Nixon veto of a CPB funding bill.

Other people feel that public broadcasting does far too little muckraking, being fearful of biting the hand that feeds it in its welfare of the airwaves state of existence. Since public broadcasting must regularly return to Congress for its funds, it is not likely to alienate this body.

This two-edged argument has been the center for external criticism from politicians and the public at large as well as the seed for the internal battle that arose between the Corporation for Public Broadcasting and the Public Broadcasting Service. When Henry Loomis, the Nixon-appointed head of CPB, set a policy of less public affairs programming and more entertainment, the station managers on the PBS board began their rebellion. Negotiation and the reorganization of the PBS board have softened the schism, but there is bound to be intermittent controversy surrounding the issue of subtle government censorship.

For similar reasons, public broadcasting has been condemned as both pro-business and anti-business. Companies that underwrite programs do not want offensive, controversial fare, and it has been rumored that public broadcasters oblige, perhaps even to the extent of softening criticism on a program against oil companies because one came through with a sizable grant.

Businesses, however, state that they really cannot intimidate public television even if they wanted to because they provide only one of the many sources of income. With no one income source, public television has programming freedom, which it sometimes uses to denigrate business.

With the formation of CPB, public broadcasting took on a more national stature, leading to fewer strictly local programs. Some critics argue that public broadcasting stations have thereby forsaken their local communities in order to cash in on the glamour and audience of the nationally distributed programs. To a larger extent than sits well with some people, PBS programs foreign shows, especially from the BBC, curtailing potential jobs and influence of Americans. For example, a furor was raised when CPB decided to grant some of its money to the BBC in order to co-produce a Shakespeare series.

To many people, this centralization is a healthy phenomenon because it ensures better programming, including the BBC series, than would ensue if the same money were used for local programs. In their argument against localism, they point out that local stations will not tackle national problems and frequently are less adventuresome than PBS because they refuse to carry national programs involving racial controversy, criticism of business, coarse language, or criticism of foreign policy.

Public broadcasting proponents still poor-mouth and point out that their system operates on 10 percent of the income of one commercial network. Public radio, particularly, feels that it receives far too little of the federal pie. On the other hand, there are those who wonder whether public broadcasters are not too extravagant in spending $40 million for a satellite system. As public broadcasting asks for increasingly more tax dollars the ranks of those who feel that it is beginning to be overfed are swelling. Commercial broadcasters who try to halt public broadcasting's expense curve sometimes complain that corporate underwriting is robbing their system of advertising dollars.

All these controversies make for interesting debate and allow public broadcasters to share some of the outrage registered toward their commercial brethren.[30]

Many schools, medical facilities, businesses, and government agencies utilize television in instructional ways without actually broadcasting over either public or commercial broadcasting stations.

Some institutions transmit over Instructional Television Fixed Service (ITFS), a specialized type of television transmission. An ITFS facility is licensed by the FCC and broadcasts through the air much like a regular TV station, but its signal travels above 2,500 megahertz, which is much higher than the signal of regular TV. Regular home TVs cannot, therefore, receive the program material; it can only be received where a special receiving antenna and **down converter** have been installed. There are about 100 ITFS facilities being utilized for various purposes. Some send medical update information from a central facility to local hospitals so that doctors can be brought up to date without having to travel to a classroom. Others beam in-service courses in engineering, marketing, finance, and other business subjects to local corporations, again allowing the employees to receive education without leaving the premises. School districts use them for such purposes as in-service teacher training and repeat broadcasting of programs for schoolchildren so that a teacher may use the same program each class period during the day.

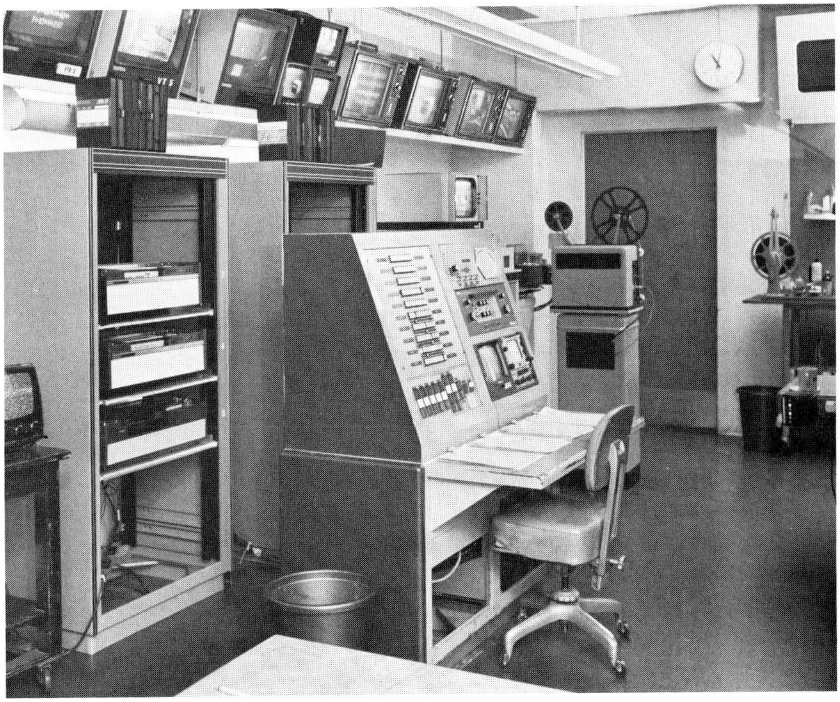

**Figure 12.11
An ITFS facility. The various cassettes and monitors allow for broadcasting a number of different programs at once on various channels.**
Photo courtesy of KZH-31, Long Beach Unified School District

Some schools and businesses utilize **closed-circuit** facilities, the signal being sent by wire through a building or several buildings. A company may have a central studio wired to receivers in various offices and assembly line areas so that executives of the company can speak to all the employees, or stories about employee achievements can be circulated to everyone via company news programs. Several elementary school districts wired all their schools during the '60s so they could produce classroom lessons and send them to all schools. Likewise, colleges, instead of having ten sections of one course taught by ten different instructors would have one instructor lecture over closed-circuit TV to students sitting in ten different classrooms viewing the material. These closed-circuit systems occasionally involve talkback systems so that students in the various classrooms can question the instructor.

Sometimes video material is available on an **information retrieval** system. For example, a company with an assembly line might prerecord instructional sequences showing how to perform the necessary duties at each point in the line. These tapes would be placed on a bank of tape recorders in a special information retrieval area. When new employees are hired or old employees moved from one point on the line to another, they simply go to the information retrieval area, dial the tape for their particular job and watch it. Teachers in schools may buy or make tapes that deal with certain concepts so that a student who is absent or who wants to review may dial the tape in the information retrieval area, often located in the school library.

Video is also used self-contained within a room. A teacher may prerecord in a studio a sequence that is particularly difficult to show in a classroom, such as the making of a hospital bed or the reaction of certain chemicals. When it is time to teach that lesson, the teacher plays the tape over a television set, usually by operating a **cassette** videotape recorder in the classroom. Hospitals or doctors' offices sometimes have TV sequences playing in waiting rooms to show patients symptoms and cures of various diseases, methods of caring for babies, hospital procedures, or care of dental braces.

Many companies have elaborate facilities where they produce programs used at many different locations to update employees on company products or processes.

Self-contained units that include a camera are often used for performance improvement. A swimming coach may tape swimmers and play the tape for them so each swimmer can improve upon faults. Or a business may tape salespeople so they see how they actually communicate. Sometimes a self-contained unit is used simply for magnification. A science teacher dissecting a frog in front of a class of thirty students may place a camera above the frog with the output going to several TV monitors so that all students can see the procedure clearly. Hospitals mount cameras above operating tables so interns can watch a doctor operate by looking at a TV set.[31]

New educational applications for video are being found daily. Some wend their way into public broadcasting stations for the public at large to view. Some are shown only to selected groups. And some are limited to very

What! No Commercials?

Figure 12.15
A portable TV unit being used to tape a basketball game so players can assess their strengths and weaknesses.
Photo courtesy of Orange Coast College

small groups or perhaps only one individual. In any case, the importance of TV as an educational medium is beyond question, and its expansion to even wider applications is virtually assured.

Summary   Public broadcasting has undergone fluctuations of financing and programming but has now come into its own as a significant broadcasting service.

Many early radio stations were operated by colleges, but gradually they were overpowered by commercial interests. It was not until *FM* was established that some radio stations were reserved for noncommercial educational uses. Most such stations are owned by educational institutions and are financed by these institutions, by *endowments,* by *grants,* and by *public donations.* Radio programming varies greatly but many of the larger stations feature *NPR* programs. Noncommercial educational TV allocations were reserved early, and initial expenses were underwritten largely by the *Ford Foundation.* In 1962 Congress passed the *Educational Broadcasting Facilities Act* to help with funding. In 1967 the *Carnegie Commission* recommended renaming and restructuring "public" television. The result was establishment of the *CPB* and its network organization, *PBS.* Public television stations are owned by educational institutions, states, and community groups. They receive funding from state and federal governments, educational institutions, foundations, *subscribers, underwriters,* and *auctions.* Programs are instructional and cultural and often come from the *Station Program Cooperative* and the *BBC.* Public broadcasting has been caught up in controversies that involve charges of being pro-government, anti-government, pro-business, anti-business, too centralized, too localized, too big, too small, too tight, and too extravagant. Nonbroadcast television is used by many schools and businesses for generally instructional purposes. Methods include *ITFS, closed-circuit TV, information retrieval,* and *self-contained* TV units.

13 A Wired Nation?

Cable Television

Cable television should be the supermarket of the mind.

Milt Gelman, TV writer

"From now on, ask where they live *before* you give them the free trial offer!"

Cable television began as an offshoot of the fledgling television communications medium. It is a system for receiving TV by wire rather than through the open airwaves. Conventional television is dependent upon antenna systems in **"line of sight"** with the transmitter or with a clean **reflection** of the signal from a hill or building. If the receiving antenna cannot be lined up with the station transmitter, then TV reception is poor or nonexistent. However, cable reception is not dependent on placement of an individual antenna in relation to the transmitter. Rather, a **master antenna** is erected for one community and the signal received is strengthened and distributed by wire to any home in the area which subscribes to it. For this reason, cable TV is also referred to as Community Antenna Television (CATV). Of course, a fee is charged to the consumer for the service. Usually there is an initial installation fee of approximately $15 and a regular monthly service charge based on the number of TV sets in the house. Many additional channels can be added with cable because there is no need to worry about interference: each channel is carried on wires so does not need **spectrum** space.

Figure 13.1
Cable TV technical setup.

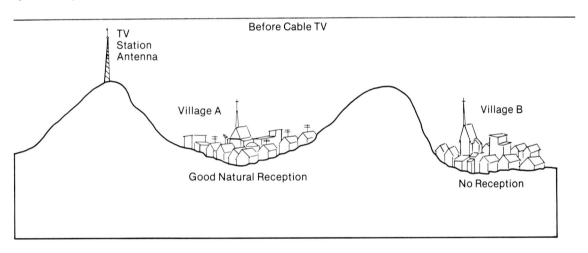

Before Cable TV

TV Station Antenna

Village A

Good Natural Reception

Village B

No Reception

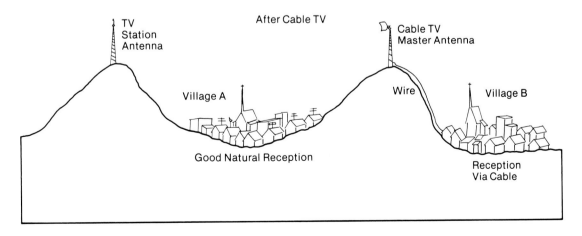

After Cable TV

TV Station Antenna

Cable TV Master Antenna

Village A

Wire

Village B

Good Natural Reception

Reception Via Cable

The Beginnings of Cable

There are many different stories about how cable TV began. One is that it was started by a man in a little appliance shop in Pennsylvania who was selling television sets. He noticed that he was selling sets only to people who lived on one side of town. Upon investigation, he found that the people on the other side of town could not obtain adequate reception, so he placed an antenna at the top of a hill, intercepted TV signals and ran them through a cable down the hill to the side of town with poor reception. When people on that side of town would buy a TV set from him, he would hook their home to the cable.

Another story is that cable service was started by a **"ham"** radio operator in Oregon who was experimenting with TV just because of his interest in the field. He placed an antenna on an eight-story building and ran cables from there to people's homes. The initial cable subscribers helped pay for the cost of the equipment, and after that was paid off, they charged newcomers $100 for a hook-up.

Whether or not these stories represent the true beginning of cable TV is hard to say. But there were many remote or mountainous places where friends and neighbors gathered together with the intent of providing television reception for themselves.

**Figure 13.2
A cable TV antenna to receive UHF, VHF, and radio.**
Photo courtesy of Storer Cable TV

One factor that helped cable TV in its beginning was the **freeze** on television stations from 1948 to 1952. The only way for people to receive TV if they were not within the broadcast path of one of the 108 stations on the air was to put up an antenna and, in essence, catch the signals as they were flying through the air.

Most of the early cable TV systems were capable of handling three signals. As early as 1949 a multi-channeled antenna system was developed in Lansford, Pennsylvania as a money-making venture. With no local signal available, the system carried the three network signals imported from nearby communities. Fourteen such companies were in operation by the end of 1950, and the number swelled to seventy by 1952.

At this point the FCC was convinced that as the number of stations increased, the need for CATV would diminish and gradually vanish entirely. The one factor which eluded their attention was that many communities were too small to support the expense of station operation. If the basic philosophy of "mass communication for an informed public" was to be a reality, CATV would have to grow. Signals would have to be imported from cities where stations could find support for their operations.

However, even with 65,000 subscribers and an annual revenue of half a million dollars in 1953, cable TV was still only a minor operation. Most broadcasters felt no concern about this business which was growing on the fringes of their signal contour. Some, however, were becoming alarmed by the feeling of permanence growing in some cable systems. **Coaxial cable** was replacing the open line wire of early days; space was leased on telephone company poles for line distribution instead of the house-to-house loops augmented by a tree here and there.

As it grew, cable TV became a little more sophisticated, and, in addition to importing signals into areas where there was no television, began importing signals into areas where there was a little television. For example, a small town might have one TV station and the cable system would import the signals from two TV stations in a large city several hundred miles away. This is when objections to cable TV first began. The existing TV stations in the area would find that their audience had shrunk because people were watching the imported signal. As a result, they could no longer sell their ads for as high a price as they had before the importation.[1]

Some of the stations in areas affected by the cable TV appealed to the Congress and the FCC to help them with their plight. In 1959 the Senate Commerce Subcommittee suggested legislation to license CATV operators. The actual extent of CATV operations, even at this late date, was impossible to identify because the operators were not required to report to any governmental agency—in spite of the fact that in many areas of the country the audience served by CATV ran as high as twenty percent of the available viewers. The attempts to draft legislation were littered with arguments and debates lasting into 1960 and ending with the defeat of a bill proposed by Senator John Pastore.[2]

Political Rumblings

With the failure of federal intervention came a rash of state and local attempts to assert jurisdiction over CATV. In most areas the local city council became the agency which issued cable **franchises** and placed stipulations on how the cable system was to conduct business. Competing applicants for a cable franchise would present to the council their plans for operation of the system to include such items as the method of hookup (e.g., telephone poles or underground cable), the speed with which hook-ups would be made, the amount to be charged to the customer for the installation fee and for the regular monthly service fee, and the percentage of the profit which the company was willing to give to the city council for the privilege of holding the franchise. Based on this information, the council would award the franchise to the company it felt was most qualified.[3]

Between 1961 and 1965 the number of cable systems doubled. In 1964 the average system served only 850 viewers and earned less than $100,000 annually. **Multiple system ownership** was less than 25 percent because of the lack of economic incentives.[4] On the surface CATV seemed to be run by small businessmen. However, the opposite was actually true. Large companies such as Teleprompter, Reeves, and TV Communications Corporation were buying the systems and maintaining them as individual rather than combined operations. One reason was that the favorable cash flow created by monthly subscriber payments could be invested in other business activities.

Cable's Muddled Growth

From 1959 through 1965 the FCC maintained a policy of nonintervention in cable TV matters. It was hoping that the problems between the operators and broadcasters would be settled by court decision. Unfortunately, the situation only became more confused as court cases piled upon court cases. The main theme of the TV broadcasters was that the cable systems were infringing on copyright materials by rebroadcasting material created by networks and stations. Decisions were rendered in many diverse cases, but the situation remained unclear.

In 1965 the FCC was finally prodded by Senator Pastore to issue rules governing cable operation. This precipitated a congressional debate between the Senate Communications Subcommittee, which oversees the FCC, and the House Commerce Committee under Chairman Oren Harris. Harris demanded that the FCC only recommend rules which would be debated and enacted as new legislation on the subject. This lack of congressional guidance only added to the confusion caused by a lack of consensus on the part of broadcasters.

The FCC Acts

In April of 1965 the FCC issued a "Notice of Inquiry and Notice of Proposed Rulemaking." In its "First Report and Order" it covered only two main areas. (1) All CATV linked common carriers from this time forward would be required to carry the signal of any TV station within approximately sixty miles of its system. (2) No duplication of program material from more distant signals would be permitted fifteen days before or fifteen days after such local broadcast.

The rule of local carriage caused little or no problem. Most CATVs were glad to carry signals of local stations. But the thirty-day provision caused bitter protest from cable operators, for it limited their right to import distant signals. In May of 1966, the FCC in a second order reduced the thirty-day provision to only one day.

Figure 13.3
A cable TV channel converter to place UHF signals on the VHF band.
Photo courtesy of Storer Cable TV

Chapter 13

As background to this conflict, one must visualize the frustration of broadcasters who had spent large sums of money. Many were barely able to survive on the revenue generated by their station while cable operators with far less invested were realizing profits by carrying the broadcaster's signal and importing distant signals. During this period there were on file and pending applications for cable coverage of areas both urban and rural which would account for at least 85,000,000 people. It is easy to understand the fears of station operators. Their basic desire was for the FCC to provide them with full administrative protection.

The attitude prevailing at the FCC during this time was strongly in favor of local TV stations in every area of the country. The second report issued by the FCC in 1966 restricted cable service in the top 100 markets to existing services. This order came when 119 systems were under construction, 500 had been awarded franchises, and 1,200 had applications pending. All of these systems would be required to prove that their existence would not harm any existing or proposed station in their coverage area. By making no increase in staff to handle this load, the FCC was in essence freezing the growth of cable operations in the top 100 markets. This made station owners very happy.

The effect this ruling had on cable operators during the remaining years of the decade was the reverse of what the FCC had in mind. Long an advocate of local service and ownership, the FCC could not or did not foresee what would happen. Cable systems unable to expand were sold in large numbers to large corporations which could withstand the unprofitability of the freeze period. Broadcasters bought up large numbers and owned 30 percent of all cable operations by 1970.

Local Origination

Over the years cable TV underwent considerable programming changes. At first it was a common carrier similar to the telephone company; i.e., it picked up signals and brought them into homes for a hookup fee and regular monthly fees.

Under this system, there was no **local origination** of programs. But gradually some of the cable facilities began undertaking their own programming. The most common "programming" in the beginning was with unsophisticated weather information. The cable TV operators would place a thermometer, barometer, and other calculating devices on a disc and have a TV camera take a picture of it as it rotated slowly. This would then be broadcast on one of the vacant channels so that people in the area could check local weather conditions. Some systems had news of sorts. This might be just a camera focused on a bulletin coming over a wire service machine, or it might be 3 × 5 cards with local news items typed on them. At any rate, it was simple, inexpensive, one-camera-type local origination.

Gradually studio-type local origination began usually in the form of local news programs, high school sports events, city council meetings, local concerts, and talk shows on issues important to the community. The first regularly scheduled cable local origination was in 1967 in Reading, Pennsylvania, and shortly after that there was local programming in San

Figure 13.4
A simple local organiza-
tion whereby announce-
ments are placed on the
TV screen one after the
other as the drum
rotates.
Photo courtesy of
TeleCable of Overland Park,
Kansas

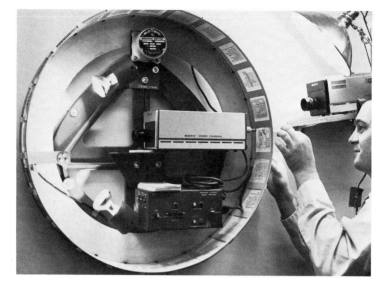

Figure 13.5
A cable TV control room
for studio productions.
Photo courtesy of
TeleCable of Overland Park,
Kansas

Figure 13.6
A cable TV facility
covering a sports
remote.
Photo courtesy of
TeleCable of Overland Park,
Kansas

Diego, California. The FCC became involved in this and gave the San Diego cable system the authorization to engage in local programming. After that other cable systems began such programming.[5]

In October of 1969 the FCC issued a rule that required all cable TV systems with 3,500 or more subscribers to begin local origination no later than April of 1970. The purpose was to promote local access for the public in areas where no station time existed.

When April of 1970 came along many of the cable TV operators who were not engaging in local origination claimed hardship and told the FCC that they did not have the funds to build studios, buy equipment, and hire crews. As a result, the FCC's order was not enforced. In 1971 the FCC made another attempt to require CATVs to engage in local origination. This too failed, so the FCC decided only to require that systems with over 3,500 subscribers make equipment available to those wishing to produce programs for local origination. By the mid '70s only about 20 percent of the cable facilities were engaging in local origination, and the most popular type of programming was local sports, primarily high school and college events. About 70 percent of these systems were using 3/4″ video cassette machines for recording and playback.[6]

One type of programming that has aroused controversy is Public Access Cable Television (PACT). This enables the public at large to express their views and concerns over one of the cable channels. Cable systems attempting this have faced both apathy and antipathy. In many areas so few people come forth to express their views that it hardly seems worth the cable system's effort to maintain the equipment and hire the personnel needed for the programming. Some of the people who do come forth are from fringe groups wishing to propagate various pressure group causes or even lewd modes of behavior. These individuals or groups make it difficult for the cable operators to present balanced opinions.[7]

More FCC Action

When cable continued to grow, the FCC became more involved and decided it did have jurisdiction and should initiate rules and regulations. Thus, in 1972 it issued a policy which established four different kinds of channels for cable and said each system should provide its subscribers with all four.

The Class 1 channels were retransmission channels which served the function cable TV had been involved in since its inception—merely providing programming already on the air.

Class 2 channels were the local origination channels on which cable systems were to originate programs.

Class 3 channels were coded channels which could not be received unless the subscriber had special equipment installed to unscramble the signal. This was intended for special programs that the viewer would have to pay extra for in order to watch.

Class 4 channels were to provide for two-way communication so that a message could be sent from the subscriber's home to the cable origination point or to some other destination. At first not much evolved from this concept, but there have been experiments involving teaching homebound students, gaining citizen opinion about city council actions, and allowing sports fans to guess the plays coaches will select. For all these activities, subscribers have some sort of button system which allows them to initiate voice contact or to feed input into a computer. Homebound students can ask the in-studio teacher a question while citizens being questioned about city council action can press an "approve" button or a "disapprove" button and have their votes tallied by a computer.

In addition to setting up these four types of channels, the FCC provided retransmission rules regarding how many stations a cable system could import into the area. These were established mainly to protect regular stations already in existence so that they could remain profitable and not be threatened by an overabundance of signals coming from distant places.

One of the basic retransmission rules was that all cable systems had to carry all stations that were within thirty-five miles of their location and all other local stations which, as shown by polls, were viewed frequently by people in the area. This was to ensure that the local stations were on the cables and could profit from the additional viewership. This, of course, had been a basic premise of the FCC rules from the beginning.

Once the cable system was providing all the local channels to its viewers, it could import other signals provided that it met certain criteria. In the top 50 cities of the country, cable systems could import if they were not already carrying at least three network services and three **independent** stations. In other words, if there were not six TV stations within their thirty-five mile radius, then they could bring in stations from elsewhere. In **markets** 50 to 100, they could import if they were not already carrying at least the three networks and two independents. In markets over 100, the rule was three network stations and one independent. In rural areas without local TV, they could import anything they desired.

The FCC made two exceptions to the above rules. One was that any station which broadcasts in a foreign language could be imported into any area. The other was that any public broadcasting station could be imported provided that there was no complaint from the local public TV station.

The FCC's 1972 policy also was strongly in favor of local origination. It did not set any mandatory date as it had done before, but it strongly urged systems to establish access channels for the public at large, education, and government.[8]

The FCC regulations on retransmission have generally been adhered to, but its ideas on classes of channels and local origination have not been overwhelmingly instituted.

By 1976 there were over 3,000 cable systems in the United States serving almost 7,000 communities and approximately 15 percent of the nation's TV households. Some cable systems had fewer than 100 subscribers; the largest had almost 100,000. Most offered between eight and twelve channels, but all newly constructed systems are supposed to offer at least twenty.[9]

The new copyright law which went into effect in January of 1978 resolved one of the major dilemmas that had widened the gap between cable operators and broadcasters for many years. The basic fight began in 1960 when United Artists Productions, holders of license rights to a large library of feature films purchased at a cost of $20,000,000, sued two cable operators for copyright infringement in their performance rights. They cited the 1931 case of a hotel owner who was required to pay royalties for radio music programs piped to rooms of his hotel. This initial ruling handed down in 1966 favored the plaintiff, United Artists. On appeal to the U.S. Supreme Court, the decision was overruled in 1968. This dropped the hot potato of copyright in the FCC's lap.

Further complicating the issue was the fact that the copyright law under which the United States then operated was written in 1909. Congress had been trying for many years to update the copyright situation with new legislation. The many controversies and special interests surrounding the issue made this one of the most lobbied bills of recent history.

The cable TV-copyright controversy was debated by broadcasters and cable operators. The former felt that cable systems should pay copyright fees on programs they retransmit because transmission rights are not included within the broadcast TV package. Cable operators felt that copyright was already taken care of by the TV stations and networks, and cable systems were merely extending coverage.

Finally, in 1976 a new copyright law was passed to be effective January 1978. Under it, cable TVs must pay royalties for transmitting copyrighted works. This money is in the form of a compulsory license paid to the registrar of copyrights for distribution to copyright owners.[10]

Pay TV is not a new idea, but its alliance with cable TV has supplied a new direction. Pay TV (also known as **subscription TV** and **toll TV**) has several features which distinguish it from conventional broadcast TV. One is that it has no advertisements. Another is that it is impossible for people in a household to receive its programs unless they pay money.

The early pay TV systems proposed to transmit programs either through the air or by cable together with a signal to scramble the picture. The viewer could see the program only if a decoding device were activated. For some systems this decoding device was attached to a coin box. When the subscriber placed money in the coin box, the picture was unscrambled. Other systems operated in conjunction with an IBM card or a sealed tape which recorded the fact that the show had been seen. Another system operated much like the telephone. Whenever a set was tuned to the pay TV input, a signal was sent by phone lines to a central location, and the subscriber was then billed in the same way that one is billed for using the phone.

The originators of pay TV proposed to woo viewers with programming superior to that on commercial television. Their plans included first-run movies, cultural programs, Broadway plays, and top sports events.

Experiments with pay TV date back to the early days in TV laboratories. Zenith developed a system called Phonevision which it announced in 1947. In 1950 the FCC first authorized pay TV systems to attempt operation. Several wired experiments were tried in the 1950s in Palm Springs, California; Bartlesville, Oklahoma; Chicago, Illinois; and Etobikoke, Canada. They met with little success and were abandoned. The companies involved could not develop high quality programming without money from subscribers, and subscribers were not willing to pay unless there was high quality programming. Thus the systems became mired in a vicious circle.

The pay system that lasted the longest was begun in Hartford, Connecticut in 1962 and discontinued in 1969. It differed from the earlier experiments in that the programs were sent out through the air rather than by wire. The system was operated by RKO General in conjunction with its Hartford UHF station, WHCT. Most of the time WHCT broadcast regular sponsored programs, but ten hours a week it offered scrambled pay TV programs. These could be received by families with decoding devices attached to their sets. The subscriber inserted a card into the decoding box which both unscrambled the picture and made a billing record. This system used the Zenith equipment and offered movies and sports events. In 1969 WHCT dropped pay TV and broadcast in the usual way for its whole schedule.

An unfortunate page in pay TV's history occurred in 1964. Sylvester L. (Pat) Weaver, a former president of NBC, attempted wired pay TV in Los Angeles. It was in its beginning stages when the voters of California passed a referendum outlawing all subscription TV. This referendum was highly supported by theater owners, who feared that pay TV would threaten their existence. Later the California Supreme Court declared the law unconstitutional, but the system had already been mortally wounded.

During the late 1960s the FCC established regulations for pay TV. Only one pay TV could operate in a community, and then only where there were at least four commercial TV stations. Pay TV could not show feature films more than two years old or sports programs regularly shown in the community over commercial TV. This latter ruling was to protect the established TV stations from the threat of a phenomenon known as **siphoning.** The fear was that the pay TV systems might simply take over, or siphon, the TV stations' programming by paying a slightly higher price for the right to air the events and thus force established TV stations out of business. Many potential pay TV entrepreneurs found these rulings stifling. Furthermore, public apathy left pay TV without a strong foothold.

The merger of pay TV and cable TV into the concept of pay cable has strengthened both entities. Several companies, the first of which was Home Box Office, now beam first-run movies, night club acts of show business headliners, children's programs, and sports events via satellite to cable systems. The systems then pick up the signals with **ground stations** and show them to the subscribers for a fee over and above the monthly service charge. The programs are shown on the cable system's scrambled channel in much the same way previous pay TV systems worked.[11]

Overall, those involved in cable TV find that they have grown in fifteen to twenty-five years from simple reception improvement installations to complex community organizations.

Summary

Cable TV is a system of TV transmission whereby the signal is transmitted by wires rather than through the air. It has grown from a simple *retransmission* service to a complex programming service.

Cable TV was begun in an attempt to supply outlying rural areas with TV programs. At first it supplied programs only to areas with no TV but gradually began entering areas with minimal TV. Established TV station owners felt threatened and appealed to Congress and the FCC for help, which was not forthcoming. Cable's legal position became quite muddled, and in 1965 the FCC issued limited rules regarding cable which generally favored broadcasters. Some cable TV systems began *local origination,* and at one point the FCC required that they all begin local programming but then did not enforce the order. In 1972 the FCC spelled out more detailed regulations on cable which included *four classes of stations* as well as *retransmission rules.* A 1976 *copyright law* required that cable TVs pay copyright fees. Cable TV has joined forces with *pay TV*, which has had an unsuccessful history. Pay cable offers programs to subscribers commercial-free but for a fee.

14 Behind the Scenes
Broadcasting Personnel

I've been fired twice, canceled three times, won some prizes, owned my own company, and made more money in a single year than the President of the United States does. I have also stood behind the white line waiting for my unemployment check. Through television I met my wife, traveled from the Pacific to the Soviet Union, and worked with everyone from President John F. Kennedy and Bertrand Russell to Miss Nude America and a guy who played "Melancholy Baby" by beating his head. With it all, I never lost my fascination for television nor exhausted my frustration.

Bob Shanks, vice president of ABC

Cartoon copyrighted by *Broadcasting* magazine

"I have just been informed that the technicians of this station have started their long-threatened strike."

As of the mid-1970s there were just over 120,000 full-time employees in commercial and public radio and TV stations and networks, distributed as follows:

Commercial TV networks	10,465
Commercial TV stations	42,393
Commercial radio networks	876
Commercial radio stations	56,982
Public broadcasting stations	10,730
Total	121,446[1]

This small number represents about .17 percent of civilian nonagricultural employment, or slightly less than the total employment of Eastman Kodak.[2]

Many broadcasting entities organize their personnel into four categories or divisions—programming, engineering, sales, and business. Many reports which the FCC requires stations to file ask for information regarding these categories, and at most stations such a breakdown represents the main on-going activities of broadcasting.

Programs are the product of radio or TV stations or networks, so the programming departments are roughly equivalent to the manufacturing departments of most companies and, like these counterparts, are the largest departments. They are headed by program managers who oversee the total programming concept of the station or network as well as the production of in-house programs. In other words, they are in charge of everything that goes out over the air whether it is purchased from a **syndicator** or produced by the station or network.

Programming

For most radio stations this is not an overwhelming job because production and programming are very similar since most of the programming is live disc jockey shows. At a typical radio station the disc jockeys will report to the program manager along with the music librarian, who is responsible for cataloging new records and filing old ones. If the station is strong on news and public affairs, the program manager will also oversee coordinators of those areas and their reporters. A radio network program manager has mainly news as a concern.

Handling all of a TV entity's programming and production is not a job for one ordinary mortal, so most program managers have large staffs. They include assistant program managers to help acquire programming material and a studio production coordinator or executive producer to schedule studios and production personnel and determine setup, rehearsal, and **strike** times.

Talent usually falls under the province of the program manager. A station that presents many news programs, talk shows, documentaries, children's programs, entertainment shows, and other local programs will have contracted talent on the payroll. This is usually supplemented by other talent hired to perform on a limited number of programs. The program manager finds the people needed through talent agencies. TV stations also employ announcers. Their job is not nearly so exciting as that of a radio

Figure 14.1
A radio station contest operator. This is the person who takes the calls when disc jockeys make such offers as, "The seventh person to call will win a newly released album."
Photo courtesy of KHJ, Los Angeles

Figure 14.2
This TV news department staff member gathers a story with the aid of portable equipment.
Photo courtesy of RCA

station disc jockey, for the TV station announcer's main duty is to come on the air during a station break and read whatever announcements are necessary. Networks as well as stations hire some talent on contract and some on a **free-lance** basis.

A TV station may or may not have a music librarian, depending on the quantity of music it uses. Generally the only canned music needed is for theme music, since background music for dramas and comedies is created by free-lance composers.

Writers are handled in a manner similar to actors. A station or network may have several writers on staff to handle regular copy and will hire free-lance writers to script programs.

One of a television station's most powerful departments, broadcast standards and continuity, passes on the acceptability of program content. People in this department check all scripts, programs, and commercials to be aired to make sure they do not violate the NAB Code and are acceptable to the local community. This department also often makes sure that copyrighted materials used on programs have received proper clearance.

The production area includes producers, directors, unit managers, stage managers, stage hands, film services, makeup, graphics, and scenery. **Producers** are key people because each producer is responsible for bringing together all the elements necessary for taping a program or series of programs. This includes scripts, graphics, sets, props, and music. Producers are also responsible for seeing that the show does not go over budget. Producers for a complicated show may have assistants; for example, a game show producer may assign to an associate producer the task of obtaining all the prizes.

Figure 14.3
Larry Stewart attempting to add to his knowledge about blindness before writing a PBS documentary, "Out of the Shadows . . . Into the Sun." Larry spent several days blindfolded with only a guide dog for eyes. Here he is pictured with guide dog senior instructor Russ Post.
Photo courtesy of Larry Stewart

TV **directors** have primary authority within the studio. They give directions to the crew members during rehearsal and taping and have responsibility for the artistic composition of the pictures and sound. They are, in essence, the "boss" of the studio during productions. Sometimes they will have associates, perhaps to operate the stopwatch and handle time cues.

Some stations and networks have **unit managers** responsible for seeing that all the necessary equipment is readily available for each taping session. For example, a producer might tell the unit manager that an upcoming show will require three film chains. If the station has only three film chains, and one is usually used for over-the-air station breaks, then the unit manager will have to try to convince the producer to change the script to require only two chains or else convince the people involved with the air schedule to use a different means of station identification while this particular show is being taped.

A **stage manager** (also called a **floor manager**) is responsible for what happens in the studio while the director is in the control room. This person quiets the studio when the taping is to begin, cues the talent when he or she is to start talking, and gives the talent time signals to show how much time is left in the program. Stagehands set up scenery and props before and during a show and strike them afterward.

The film department becomes important for any programs that employ filmed sequences. A film crew will shoot the necessary footage, and editors will cut and splice it so it is in the proper form needed for the program. Preproduced "**canned**" film is stored by the film department and edited for airing as needed.

Makeup artists apply basic makeup for most performers and also create character makeup when needed. The graphics department supplies charts and slides for programs, and the scenery department includes people who design, build, and paint sets.

There are many variations within stations and networks. In some stations programming and production are separate and the program manager has only informal responsibility for production, a production manager having the primary responsibility. Sometimes news is an entirely separate department, or, if one company owns both a radio and TV station in the same city, it may have one combined news department for both stations. Frequently broadcast standards will report directly to the general manager. And, of course, titles vary all over the lot. What one station or network calls a manager another may call a coordinator, director, or vice president.

Engineering

Heads of engineering departments are usually called chief engineers and have reporting to them the engineers who operate the equipment as well as those who design and maintain it. The FCC requires that stations have on their staff at least one person who has passed the FCC-administered first class license test. Only this licensed operator is allowed to make certain adjustments and repairs on the **transmitter.** Small radio stations often

Figure 14.4

Figure 14.5

Figure 14.6

Figure 14.7

Figure 14.4
Producer Melinda Cotton (*center*) conferring with director Gary Greene prior to a news show broadcast. Anchor persons Wendy Wetzel and Arline Radillo look on.
Photo courtesy of KOCE-TV, Huntington Beach, California

Figure 14.5
Director Harry Ratner calling for a camera cut.
Photo courtesy of KOCE-TV, Huntington Beach, California

Figure 14.6
Stage manager Richard Jansen making some script notations.
Photo courtesy of KOCE-TV, Huntington Beach, California

Figure 14.7
A camera crew setting up to film a commercial.
Photo courtesy of Centre Films—George Stupar, photographer

Figure 14.8
Graphic artist Carl
Glassford preparing
some title cards.
Photo courtesy of KOCE-TV
Huntington Beach,
California

Figure 14.9
A radio station engineer
at a large station where
disc jockeys do not
handle their own
engineering.
Photo courtesy of KHJ,
Los Angeles

Figure 14.10
Technical director Toby
Baker at the switcher.
Photo courtesy of KOCE-TV
Huntington Beach,
California

Figure 14.8

Figure 14.9

Figure 14.10

operate with just one engineer, making him or her the chief engineer. Disc jockeys may then operate the turntables, audio boards, and tape recorders as they produce their shows. Other radio stations have engineers playing the material for the disc jockeys as well as planning for new equipment, repairing old equipment, and deciding on equipment setup for ease of operation.

In television stations or networks it is possible that the chief engineers, although they have a first class license, seldom touch the equipment because they have so many engineers under them that their total time is taken up with scheduling and supervising. Sometimes this makes for unhappy chief engineers because their background and interests lie with schematics, levers, buttons, and knobs but they must deal with paper and people.

The nature of television, as distinct from radio, makes it impossible for the talent to operate equipment as a disc jockey can. Numerous engineers work on any particular TV program—camera operators, audio engineers, technical directors, projectionists, videotape recorder operators, video shaders, and the lighting director and crew. Certain people may develop specialities, but all engineers should be able to handle most positions. For example, the people who run cameras should know enough about audio to be able to set up microphones and operate the audio board.

The **technical directors** of shows are the people who operate the switcher to change the picture being aired from one source to another. They execute the aesthetic decisions of the director regarding what should be sent over the air when and in what manner by pushing the appropriate buttons and levers. The technical directors, however, are responsible for the overall engineering aspects of a show and would be the ones to decide whether or not a taping session should be stopped because of a minor problem with the videotape recorder. They are in charge of the technical crew of a particular show and work with the directors to make sure the crew receives appropriate break time and meal time.

The technical directors' crew includes the camera operators, who obviously are responsible for obtaining the shots the directors want; the audio engineers, who place microphones in the studio for best possible pick-up, move boom microphones during the show, and operate the audio console and other audio sources such as tape recorders and turntables in order to achieve the sound that the directors specify; the projectionists, who operate the film chain when film or slides are to be inserted into the program; the videotape recorder operators, who record the program as it is being performed and later edit it as necessary; and the video **shaders,** who operate remotely located camera controls to obtain the best picture possible from the cameras.

The lighting directors and their crews set up lights before the show and handle any lighting changes during a production session. In some stations these people report to the production manager rather than the chief engineer so they can be in on production meetings and contribute their aesthetic expertise about lighting effects to create time or mood.

These engineers not only help produce programs, they also keep the station on the air. Videotape recorder operators and projectionists together see that the proper tapes and films of programs and commercials are aired at the scheduled times. And, as with radio, engineers design and repair equipment and keep abreast of the latest technological advances so they can advise management on equipment purchases.

Sales

The sales department is mainly responsible for obtaining commercials for the station or network. At a small radio station the general manager and/or disc jockeys may double as salespeople. Larger stations will have salespeople and perhaps a national sales manager to coordinate with the **station representative** or **advertising agency.** Obviously, the networks deal only with national advertising. Some salespeople pound the pavement to make their deals and others sit in smoke-filled rooms. Their success and

Figure 14.11
A challenging assign-
ment for a couple of
camera operators.
Photo courtesy of KOCE-
TV, Huntington Beach,
California

Figure 14.12
Engineer Al Lugo
threading a videotape
recorder located in a
remote truck.
Photo courtesy of KOCE-
TV, Huntington Beach,
California

Figure 14.13
Video shader Gary Metz
making adjustments on
the camera control
units.
Photo courtesy of KOCE-
TV, Huntington Beach,
California

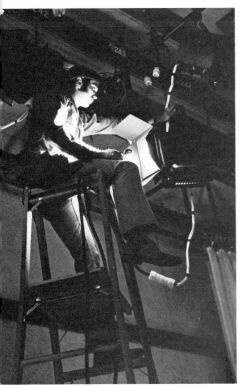

Figure 14.14

Figure 14.15

Figure 14.16

Figure 14.14
A lighting assistant setting the lights for a studio production.
Photo courtesy of KOCE-TV, Huntington Beach, California

Figure 14.15
Engineer Jeri Shepard performing master control switching during a station break.
Photo courtesy of KOCE-TV, Huntington Beach, California

Figure 14.16
A maintenance engineer checking a camera's electronics.
Photo courtesy of General Telephone Company

perseverance are rewarded, however, for most of top management has risen through the sales ranks.

Another area frequently placed in the sales department is **traffic.** Here is generated the station **log,** which lists all programs and commercials to be aired each day. Traffic is often found in the sales department because the most important coordinating job involved with the log is scheduling the various commercials. As time sales are made, someone must make sure that the ads are actually scheduled to air under the conditions stipulated in the sales contract. However, traffic also involves the scheduling of program content, so sometimes it is in the programming department, and sometimes it is even found in the business area.

Public relations, promotion, and research are all sales-oriented aspects of broadcasting that are extremely important—in fact, so important that some chief executives have these functions report directly rather than through a sales department. The public relations function of a station or network is to try to build general goodwill between the broadcaster and the general public, a service particularly essential at license renewal time. Promotion involves all methods used to encourage people to listen to a particular station or program such as special contests, billboards on buses, ads in newspapers, and feature stories in magazines. Those working in research mainly coordinate with the **rating** services and analyze data for their own purposes, but sometimes they conduct station- or network-generated research projects.

Public broadcasting stations do not, of course, have sales departments as such. However, they usually have people in charge of obtaining grants, community contributions, and other funding, which in many ways resembles a sales function.

Business
Broadcasting, like any other business, must distribute paychecks, sort mail, balance the checkbook, and sweep the floor. Such housekeeping functions are essential to smooth operation and generally reside in the domain of a business manager who reports to the chief executive, such as the station manager or president.

Accounting and bookkeeping functions fall under this business manager, with the records of payroll expenditures, equipment and supply purchases, inventories of supplies, cash receipts, cash expenditures, and the like. Stations regularly compile **balance sheets** listing all assets and liabilities of a station or network at a specific point in time and **profit and loss statements,** which show how much the company received and spent over a period of time so it can tell whether its expenses are exceeding its income. At large, sophisticated broadcasting operations, accountants may keep track of unused facilities, idle time of personnel, budgeted costs of specific programs, and efficiency factors of various departments. The job of the business department is to keep all records needed for FCC reports, income tax returns, social security reports, and insurance claims.

General office management, also in the business area, may include overseeing the janitorial services, distributing work to a secretarial pool, making sure the mail is handled efficiently, arranging for public tours of the facility, and establishing security regulations. Purchasing and stockroom procedures constitute another function of the business office. Legal matters, involving advice to keep a station out of trouble as well as actual lawsuits, are handled under the business department, as are personnel matters such as hiring, firing, promoting, reprimanding, mediating and negotiating with unions. Of greatest importance to most broadcasting employees is the payroll department, which issues the paychecks.

How all these functions are distributed depends on station or network size, market, format, success, and top management philosophy. Very few radio stations have personnel departments because it is unjustified for a total staff of ten to twenty people, but TV networks have eight to ten people whose full-time job is to interview job applicants. A TV network will have several staff lawyers, and they may even report directly to the president if a problem seems particularly sticky. A station, however, will probably hire a lawyer from a law firm as needed. Many small stations have a policy of no visitors simply because there is not physical space for the extra bodies; hence, they have neither public tour nor security needs. Networks, on the other hand, have guards at every gate and regular formal tours conducted by hired pages. Many stations are lucky to have one secretary, let alone a secretarial pool, and in some instances the station manager is also the janitor.

No two broadcasting entities are organized in exactly the same way, but theoretical organization charts of a medium-sized radio station and a TV station might be like the following figures.[3]

Organization Charts

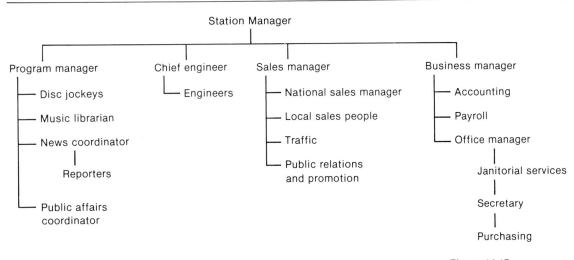

Figure 14.17
Medium-sized radio station theoretical organization chart.

Figure 14.18
Television station
organization chart.

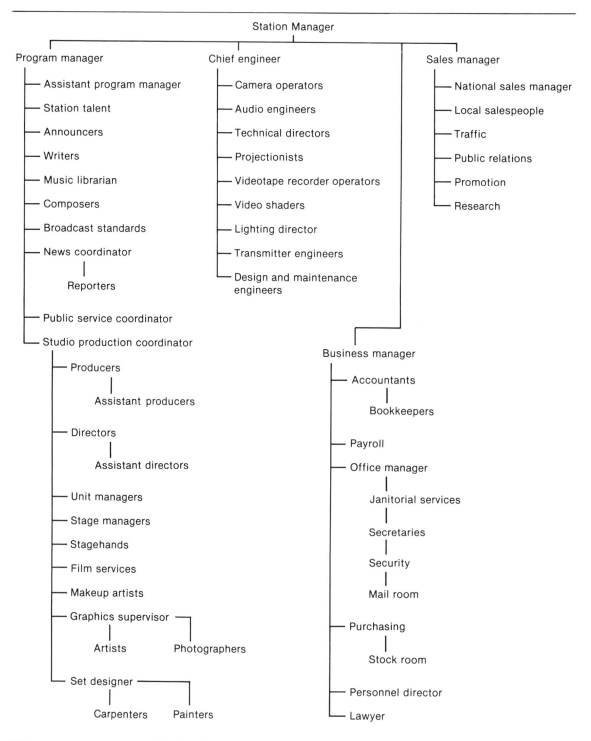

Chapter 14

Below are some actual organization charts from various types and sizes of stations.[4]

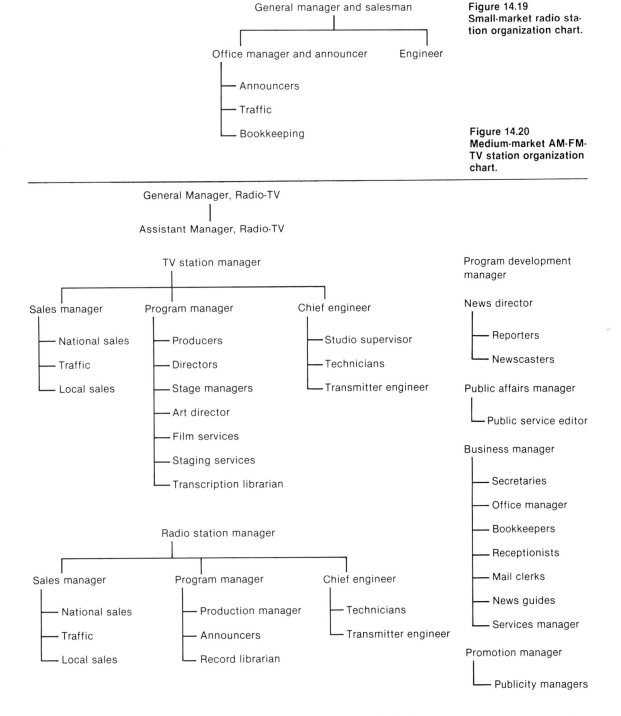

General manager and salesman

Office manager and announcer   Engineer

— Announcers

— Traffic

— Bookkeeping

Figure 14.19
Small-market radio station organization chart.

Figure 14.20
Medium-market AM-FM-TV station organization chart.

General Manager, Radio-TV

Assistant Manager, Radio-TV

TV station manager   Program development manager

Sales manager   Program manager   Chief engineer   News director

— National sales   — Producers   — Studio supervisor   — Reporters

— Traffic   — Directors   — Technicians   — Newscasters

— Local sales   — Stage managers   — Transmitter engineer

— Art director   Public affairs manager

— Film services   — Public service editor

— Staging services   Business manager

— Transcription librarian   — Secretaries

— Office manager

— Bookkeepers

Radio station manager   — Receptionists

— Mail clerks

Sales manager   Program manager   Chief engineer   — News guides

— National sales   — Production manager   — Technicians   — Services manager

— Traffic   — Announcers   — Transmitter engineer   Promotion manager

— Local sales   — Record librarian   — Publicity managers

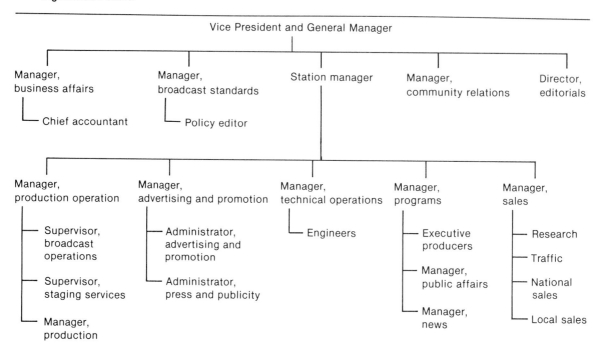

Figure 14.21
Large-market TV station organization chart.

Vice President and General Manager

- Manager, business affairs
  - Chief accountant
- Manager, broadcast standards
  - Policy editor
- Station manager
- Manager, community relations
- Director, editorials

- Manager, production operation
  - Supervisor, broadcast operations
  - Supervisor, staging services
  - Manager, production
- Manager, advertising and promotion
  - Administrator, advertising and promotion
  - Administrator, press and publicity
- Manager, technical operations
  - Engineers
- Manager, programs
  - Executive producers
  - Manager, public affairs
  - Manager, news
- Manager, sales
  - Research
  - Traffic
  - National sales
  - Local sales

Allied Organizations

The 120,000 people employed in broadcasting represent only those working directly for a station or network. There are many others who spend all or part of their time engaged in broadcast-related work: 539 television program producers, distributors, and program services; 261 radio program producers and distributors; 298 television commercial producers; 154 radio commercial and jingle producers; 224 advertising agencies; 229 station representatives; 60 rating companies; 55 brokers; 18 station finance companies; 107 management consultant firms; 79 public relations, publicity, and promotion services; 35 talent agencies; 85 employment services; 880 broadcast attorneys; 3,500 cable TV systems; 347 equipment manufacturers; 12 microwave and satellite services; 42 TV processing labs; 281 consulting engineers; 6 music licensing groups; 52 unions; 42 news services; and 290 broadcasting departments of colleges and universities.[5]

These figures do not give an accurate count of the actual number of people in broadcasting because the activities of many of these categories extend well beyond broadcasting. For example, advertising agencies are concerned with print media as well as broadcast media; their job is to find an advertising mix for their customers, not just arrange commercials for radio or television. Nevertheless, it is interesting to note the extent to which broadcasting, itself a service, is served by other organizations.

There may appear to be a great many employment opportunities within companies which produce radio or TV programs or commercials. To some extent there are, but appearances are deceptive. A few very successful production companies—such as MTM, Tandem Productions, Universal, Viacom, and Columbia Pictures Television—supply large numbers of programs to the TV networks. However, most production companies are small groups hoping to hit on something that will bring financial reward. Many of them never make it and collapse, although perhaps they reappear some years later with a new name and the same people involved. For the most part, independent production companies cannot afford to own their own facilities, so they rent regular station or network facilities and personnel in order to produce their programs. Therefore, the camera operator who works on the channel 5 noon news may at one o'clock begin working an entertainment show to be aired on CBS. Independent production, therefore, does not necessarily create a large number of jobs for new people.

Most of the allied organizations are dealt with in other sections of this book, but a few bear describing in a little more detail. **Brokers** aid in the buying and selling of radio and television stations in much the same way real estate agents do for homes. Individuals or organizations wishing to sell a station may list it with a broker, who then tries to find a suitable buyer under the guarantee of a commission on the station sale price. Since stations represent basically a sellers' market, the real problem a broker has is finding enough stations, not enough buyers. Of course, stations can be sold without the aid of a broker. Banks generally will not finance purchase of broadcasting facilities, but there are companies which specialize in such transactions.

Consulting engineers, management consultants, promotion services, and attorneys are usually hired by stations on a short-term basis. A new station will hire a consulting engineer for an engineering survey. Or a station that has been given permission to increase its power will hire such a consultant so that all the technical procedures are properly accomplished. A station having personnel problems may hire a management consultant to suggest a new organization, or a station wishing to execute a spectacular two-week promotion for a particular program might hire a promotion service. When a legal problem surfaces, an attorney is hired to handle the case.

Microwave and satellite services are very expensive specialized communication services from which the networks rent time in order to send signals across the country or around the world. TV processing labs are specialized film processors many of whom **dub** videotape to film.

Agents

A word should be said about agents since they are generally controversial in a "needed by all, resented by all" role. Their function is to find work for creative people in return for a percentage—usually 10 percent—of the amount earned. The largest talent agency is William Morris, founded in 1898 to represent talent in the **legitimate theater** and **vaudeville.** It has grown steadily, adding representation for motion pictures, radio, phonograph records, and television. In its earlier days it was all but eclipsed by MCA, which was founded in 1924 as the Music Corporation of America to represent dance bands and orchestras. MCA grew rapidly, representing not only musicians, but actors, writers, producers, directors, composers, and others in the creative fields. It also began packaging shows with its own talent, for which it collected fees for the entire shows, and it acquired Universal Studios as its production house. In 1962 this situation came to the attention of the Justice Department, which invoked the **antitrust act** on the grounds that one company should not represent talent on one hand and produce programs with that talent on the other. Since MCA made more money collecting on its shows than on its individual stars, it kept the Universal production unit and gave up the talent agency business, thus leaving William Morris as the largest agency.

It is virtually impossible for an actor or actress or a free-lance writer, director, producer, or other creative person to become successful without an agent because networks and most production companies deal only through agents and not directly with talent.

In some ways this can be advantageous to the person. An agent can present a client in glowing terms that the client could not make about herself or himself. An agent is constantly out in the field representing people, so possesses a wealth of information about what jobs will be available. The agent can also negotiate salary and contract, leaving the talent "above it all." And many agents can give sound professional advice to help a person improve. On the other hand, agents who are so inclined can abuse their power. Critics of agents sometimes contend that the agent receives 10 percent of everything the talent earns and sometimes does nothing to deserve it; that because an agent represents a large number of people, he or she will not always have one particular client's interest at heart and sometimes will even sell out a client or make an undesirable deal for the client in order to continue doing business with a particular production company; and that sometimes an agent will get a client involved in a disastrous project simply to obtain the 10 percent commission.

Networks and production companies have ambivalent feelings toward agents too. They would rather deal with agents than with hordes of aspiring actors, but once an actor becomes known and desired by the production houses, they would rather the agent disappeared so they could deal directly with the person.[6]

Unions

Another broadcasting phenomenon very important to the production scene are **unions**. Like agents, they are much more important in the large cities than in small towns. Unions operate only where they are voted in by the employees, and that is much more likely to happen where there is a concentration of activity. At present about 33 percent of the TV stations and 8 percent of the radio stations deal with one or more unions.[7] Of course, all the networks are unionized. Unions negotiate wages and working conditions. They also prosecute members of management who violate provisions of the union contract and union members who work for less than union scale or otherwise violate contract agreements.

One of the most prominent of the broadcasting unions is the American Federation of Television and Radio Artists (AFTRA), a union for performers in live and videotaped programs. AFTRA was begun in 1936 as a union of radio artists in New York, Chicago, and Los Angeles and was called the American Federation of Radio Artists (AFRA). Today its jurisdiction extends to all fifty states and covers radio transcriptions, phonograph records, and slide-film recordings as well as live and taped radio and TV programs and commercials.

Another performance union, the Screen Actors Guild (SAG), was organized in 1933 by actors discontent with the poor pay of motion picture studios. SAG and AFTRA have had several jurisdictional disputes over the years, the most bitter occurring when videotape was introduced. SAG felt it should have the jurisdiction because the material was being recorded to be kept much as film is kept. AFTRA felt it should have control because taping was accomplished in a TV facility. AFTRA won the battle, but at present SAG has jurisdiction over anything produced at one of the traditional film studios even though the medium used is videotape. AFTRA and SAG have frequently discussed merging, a move which would strengthen the position of performers. Now most performers belong to both unions, paying an **initiation fee** of several hundred dollars to each and monthly dues to each in an amount related to the income earned from acting.[8] Both unions have an extremely high unemployment rate. It is estimated that 80 percent of the members earn less than $2,000 a year from acting.

If a station or network is a signator to AFTRA, it must pay at least the minimum wage negotiated by the union to all performers. Complicated formulas specify that a principal performer is to be paid more than someone who has less than five lines, who in turn is paid more than an **extra.** And, of course, the few stars of the business can demand far more than the minimum wage. AFTRA also negotiates such matters as meal and rest periods, credits, wardrobe, use of stand-ins, travel requirements, dressing room facilities, and **residuals.** This last is a thorny issue for it involves the formula for paying performers when shows or commercials are rerun. Performers feel the residual percentage should be high since reruns eliminate jobs. Networks and stations want to keep the residuals low so that rerun costs are low.

Another performance union is the American Federation of Musicians (AFM), which has jurisdiction over musicians who perform live or taped on radio or TV. AFM is not as important to broadcasting now as it was when radio networks had their own orchestras. During the late 1930s and early 1940s, AFM forced stations to employ musicians even though they had no work for them by making the stations sign contracts stating that they would hire a certain quota of musicians based on the station's annual revenue. These contracts were declared illegal in 1940 and were not renewed, but the AFM threatened networks and record companies with strikes if they supplied music to stations that did not employ musicians, so many of the quotas continued. In 1946 Congress specifically outlawed the use of threats to require broadcasting stations to employ individuals in excess of the number needed to do the job.

The first established union for broadcasting engineers was the International Brotherhood of Electrical Workers (IBEW), which had originally been formed in the late 1880s by telephone linemen. This union successfully struck a St. Louis radio station in 1926 and later obtained network contracts. In 1953 NBC technicians formed their own union which became known as the National Association of Broadcast Employees and Technicians (NABET). Now NABET and IBEW compete, sometimes vigorously, in attempting to convince employees of stations to vote them into power.

A third technical union, International Alliance of Theatrical Stage Employees and Moving Picture Machine Operators of the United States and Canada (IATSE), moved into television from motion pictures. In some stations this union has jurisdiction over only stagehands and in other stations it includes stagehands and some equipment operators.

As with performance unions, members must pay an initiation fee and regular dues. One of the points of frustration to people trying to obtain a first job in broadcasting is that one must have a job to join an engineering union but must join the union in order to get a job. Breaking into that vicious circle is often difficult.

There are several broadcasting **guilds** which do not operate in exactly the same way as unions, but they are involved with setting pay rates and negotiating. Three of the most important are Directors Guild of America (DGA), Writers Guild of America (WGA), and Producers Guild of America (PGA).

In addition, there are many smaller unions for groups such as photographers, film editors, set designers, makeup artists, and carpenters.[9]

Minority Hiring

In recent years broadcasters, along with other businesses, have been under pressure from the federal government to increase their hiring of minorities. A study conducted by the Office of Communication of the United Church of Christ in 1972 revealed that 22 percent of broadcasting employees were women and 10 percent were minorities.[10] During the next few years women employees grew to 27.3 percent and minorities to 13.4 percent.[11] Women and minorities have not been widely assimilated into top management positions yet, but their numbers are continuing to grow in all areas of broadcasting.[12]

Job Preparation

Gaining employment in broadcasting is not an easy task because there are many more people who would like to be so employed than there are jobs. A recent survey conducted by the National Association of Broadcasters[13] showed that almost 300 colleges have programs leading to degrees in radio and television. These schools graduate approximately 10,000 students a year, ostensibly into an industry that employs only 120,000.

Obviously, however, it is possible for the persevering to become employed in broadcasting. Although it is not essential to obtain a college education for most of the entry level jobs, it is generally a wise course.

Stations and networks are interested in hiring people with promotion potential and generally feel that a college education makes people more promotable.

Enrolling in one of the 300 colleges with programs leading to a broadcasting degree is advisable, but it is important to have broad knowledge in other fields too. Someone wishing to enter the news field would be almost valueless if he or she were an outstanding videotape recorder operator but knew nothing about national or international affairs. Political science, history, and journalism courses should be a must for reporters. Likewise, accountants and salespeople should have proper business courses; engineers should know electronics; writers should emphasize composition and literature; directors should be knowledgeable about drama, music, and psychology; and graphics personnel should know art and photography.

Anyone wishing to enter radio has a much better chance of landing the initial job by obtaining a first class license. Although this is in no way necessary to become a disc jockey, small stations need to double-up on personnel in order to be economically sound, so a jack-of-all-trades who can be chief engineer, disc jockey, and salesperson has a much better chance of obtaining a job than someone who specializes narrowly in announcing music.

A student, while in college, should make every attempt to obtain experience in the industry through part-time jobs, internships, or nonpaid fill-in work. Many broadcasting openings have an "experience required" tag attached to them, and persons who have at least made the attempt to rub elbows with the industry can sometimes get a foot in the door for these jobs.

It is also advisable for students to join broadcasting organizations, such as those mentioned in chapter 9 on self-regulation, in order to meet people in the field. It is a truism that frequently "it is not what you know but who you know" that enables you to obtain employment. Many of these organizations have special reduced rates for students.

The first job is the hardest to obtain and usually involves a great deal of letter writing and pavement pounding. Many of the broadcast-related journals contain want-ad sections that provide excellent leads. Letters of introduction and résumés can be sent to broadcast stations, networks, and allied organizations. *Broadcasting Yearbook,* published once a year by the same organization that publishes *Broadcasting* magazine, can serve as an excellent source for names and addresses for these potential employment sources. It is also wise to phone or visit as many facilities as time and money will permit.

The nature of the first job is not nearly so important as getting in the door. Most broadcast facilities promote from within, making it much easier to obtain the desired job from within than without. It is also easier to move from one broadcast facility to another if some experience has been gained, regardless of what the experience was. Patience tempered with aggressiveness and geographic flexibility are traits which are likely to lead to advancement.

Career Compensation

On the average, broadcasting is not an especially high-paying industry. True, there are the superstars who make millions, but they are few and far between. Others earn a decent but not sensational living. Typical mid-1970s weekly pay in television was as follows: salesperson $270; announcer $229; technician $213; newscaster $196; producer/director $189; traffic manager $188; and stagehand $126. Typical weekly pay in radio was: newscaster $160; announcer $150; and traffic manager $115.[14] There is no standard pattern on fringe benefits but most employers provide medical insurance and life insurance as well as paid sick leave and vacations for full-time employees.

What undoubtedly attracts most people to the broadcasting industry is the glamour, excitement, and power of the profession. All of these are present in broadcasting, albeit to a lesser degree than most people think, and they do make for a richer, fuller, more rewarding life than many other people experience in their day-to-day occupations.

One by-product of this glamour, excitement, and power, however, is extreme insecurity. Except for those in a few highly unionized jobs, no one is shielded from the pink slip. Last year's superstar can be this year's forgotten person—and, worse yet, have no means of support. Many people who "make it" in the business tend to spend like millionaires in order to maintain an image. Then, when the image is only a fad of the past, they have no nest egg to comfort them. The industry encompasses many free-lancers who are constantly in the state of being fired and hired and whose outrageously high salaries for one week's work are balanced by two years of unemployment. It is a hard field to break into and a hard field to stay in, but the rewards are worth it to those who endure.

Summary

There are just over 120,000 people employed in broadcasting, which is generally divided into four areas: *programming, engineering, sales,* and *business.* Many other people are in related jobs.

Programming positions include *program managers, disc jockeys, music librarians, reporters, studio production coordinators, announcers, writers, broadcast standards personnel, producers, directors, unit managers, stage managers, stagehands, film services personnel, makeup artists, graphic designers,* and *set designers.* Engineering jobs include *chief engineers, camera operators, audio engineers, technical directors, projectionists, videotape recorder operators, video shaders,* and *lighting directors.* Sales jobs usually involve selling commercials, but *traffic, public relations, promotion,* and *research* are also often in the sales department. Business functions are similar to those in any company. Some of the allied organizations include program producers, ad agencies, rating companies, brokers, consultants, microwave services, and processing labs. Most actors, actresses, writers, producers, and directors need *agents* in order to obtain broadcast employment. Some of the broadcasting unions are *AFTRA,*

SAG, AFM, IBEW, NABET, IATSE, DGA, WGA, and *PGA.* Students wishing to enter broadcasting are advised to obtain a well-rounded education, to avail themselves of any opportunities to get experience in the industry, and to meet people in the industry. Broadcasting is not a particularly financially rewarding occupation, but it has other compensations.

15 Around the World
Broadcasting in Foreign Countries

The whole world's becoming a stage—a TV-screen stage—for American movies and television series.

Broadcasting *magazine*

Cartoon copyrighted by *Broadcasting* magazine

"It's made in Japan under license from a Dutch firm, shipped here by a British importer and serviced by some local guy."

"Different strokes for different folks" is a truism that applies to broadcasting around the world. Organization, purpose, programming, technology, and impact tend to vary as boundary lines are crossed, and yet there are common elements that glue the world's communication systems into a unified whole.

While some foreign broadcast systems resemble that of the United States, more are different from it than are similar to it. Some of the variations can be seen by comparing major ownership, programming, finance, and technological aspects.

Comparative Characteristics

In the United States, broadcasting facilities are owned by private companies which are usually responsible to stockholders, but this form of ownership is rare throughout the rest of the world. In many countries the government owns and controls all broadcasting. In other countries private corporations have actual ownership but are closely tied to the government because the government issues **charters** outlining provisions which the corporations must follow. Often several types of ownership—government, charter, private company—exist side by side in the same country.

United States programming is created primarily by privately owned groups—stations, networks, production companies. The government has only limited control over the content, and controversial ideas and criticisms of government procedures appear frequently. The majority of programs are oriented toward entertainment with education and culture taking a back seat. Outside the United States such a hands-off attitude by the government is rare. In most totalitarian countries, programming is created within the government, usually by a department of education or department of propaganda, and material is often censored by a government committee. Programming tends to be paternalistic and propagandistic, with a preponderance of educational programs and programs espousing the virtues of the government. In some countries programming is produced by private companies but the content is closely supervised by the government. This programming usually emphasizes culture and education. Although controversial ideas are allowed, they are often scrutinized by the government.

In the United States broadcasting is supported almost entirely by advertising revenue obtained from numerous commercials. In many foreign countries there is no such thing as a commercial. Revenue is generated through general government taxation or through taxes on radio and TV sets collected and dispersed by the government. Broadcasting in some countries is supported by a combination of taxes and advertising, but the commercials are generally low key and shown at only certain times during the day.

Technologically, the United States operates on a system that **scans** 525 lines and employs a **color coding system** approved by the National Television System Committee and referred to as NTSC. The Americans hoped that this color system would be adopted throughout the world, but European engineers quipped that NTSC stood for "Never Twice the Same Color" and developed their own system, called SECAM, which American engineers in turn labeled "Something Essentially Contrary to the American

Method." Another system, PAL, was developed in the hope that it would yield "Peace At Last." But such was not the case, and at present approximately 37 countries use PAL, 25 use NTSC, and 22 use SECAM.[1] Generally the SECAM and PAL countries scan at 625 lines rather than 525. Both the scanning and color coding differences, along with different electrical systems and noninterchangeable connectors, make it almost impossible for an American videotape to be shown in a foreign country unless it is first **dubbed** to that country's technical system, a procedure which is accomplished without enormous difficulty.

There are numerous fine point differences in various broadcasting systems, but the salient features of broadcasting around the world can be seen by sampling a few representative countries in some detail.

Broadcasting in Britain

American viewers are familiar with British broadcasting because a number of English-produced programs are aired in the United States, particularly on public television.

Most of British radio is operated by the British Broadcasting Corporation (BBC), a monopoly created by royal charter on January 1, 1927. It is controlled by a board of governors, twelve members appointed for five-year terms by the monarch. The chief executive officer is called the director-general. In theory and practice, both he and the BBC are free from direct governmental influence.

Figure 15.1
Broadcasting House in London, where most of the BBC radio originates.
Photo from the British Broadcasting Corporation

A station receives its license from the Minister of Posts and Tele-communications, who lays down laws regarding transmitters, antennas, frequencies, power, and other technical specifications. These licenses also prohibit the radio stations from carrying advertisements and stipulate that stations must broadcast day-by-day impartial accounts of the two houses of Parliament. Since there are no commercials, the money to produce and transmit radio programs comes from taxes which people pay on their radio sets, which are both collected and dispersed by the government.

Originally, the programming on BBC was very paternalistic. Designed to upgrade tastes, it was often referred to as "Auntie BBC." The original organization was three program services, each designed to lead the listener to the next for a higher cultural level. At the lowest level was the Light Programme, which consisted of quiz shows, audience participation programs, light music, children's adventure, and serials. Level two was the Home Service, which included good music and drama, school broadcasts, information about government, and news. The highest level, called the Third Programme, was classical music, literature, talk, drama, and poetry.

The programming was an easy target for outside competition. When Radio Luxembourg began broadcasting popular music, many of the British people began tuning in, and British companies even began buying ads on Luxembourg stations.

Then in 1963 **"pirate ships"** anchored off the coast of England began broadcasting rock music on frequencies that could be picked up with ordinary radios. This programming became so popular that when the government planned to suppress it, there was such public outcry that the BBC had to change its programming before these pirate ships could be eliminated.

Figure 15.2
A performance for "Saturday Night Theatre" aired on BBC Radio 4. Sylvia Syms (left), Peter Jeffrey (center), and Philip Bond head the cast for "The Calendar," Edgar Wallace's play about horse-racing chicanery.
Photo from the British Broadcasting Corporation

The result was a new, renamed four-level radio setup. Radio 1 programs popular rock music. It even hired some of the disc jockeys formerly on the pirate ships, thus eliminating the need for these ships to continue. Radio 2 resembles the old Light Programme, with quiz shows and children's programs in addition to music. Radio 3 is cultural so is similar to the old Third Programme. Radio 4 emphasizes news and other programming similar to the old Home Service. Since 1972 there has been some independent radio separate from the BBC.

British television is organized under two different services, the BBC and the Independent Broadcasting Authority (IBA). BBC television began in 1936 and in 1937 televised the coronation of George VI. The operation was stopped in 1939 because of the war and then resumed in 1946 utilizing a 405-line scanning system. After color was introduced in 1967, the BBC began converting to a 625-line system. BBC television has been organized like BBC radio in that it is operated from taxes on sets and is controlled by a board of governors. Two services were originally established, BBC I and BBC II, with the intent of giving viewers a choice of programming fare. Unlike radio, the overall program content of both TV services was similar, but the individual programming hours were different. For example, at 8:00 BBC I might have sports and BBC II a drama; then at 9:00 BBC I might have a drama and BBC II a documentary. The original intent of this programming was to upgrade appreciation and provide programs for minority interests. During the day most programming was designed for in-school viewing. The late afternoon and evening program fare on both BBC I and BBC II ran to drama, documentaries, current affairs, features, children's programs, education, religion, and occasional light comedy, some of which was imported from the United States.

This paternalistic programming, like its radio counterpart, came under fire—with the result that the Independent Broadcasting Authority was established and BBC I programming was lightened. Most of the BBC programs which reach America ("Civilisation," "The Ascent of Man," "Elizabeth R," "Monty Python") are shown on BBC II, which usually attracts only 8 percent of the audience. The rest of the audience is watching the lighter programming of BBC I and the Independent Broadcasting Authority.

The IBA was originally formed in 1954 as the Independent Television Authority (ITA) after a heated debate in Parliament regarding the quality and role of television. In 1972 its responsibilities were extended to include the setting up of close to 100 radio stations, and its name was changed to Independent Broadcasting Authority.

The British government has much closer control over the IBA than the American government has over broadcasting in the United States. The IBA operates under ten-year charters from the government, has a director-general as chief officer, and is overseen by an eleven-member board of directors appointed by the minister of Posts and Telecommunications.

Unlike the BBC, the IBA is financed primarily through advertising. However, advertisers or agencies cannot produce programs or be identified

Figure 15.3
An aerial view of BBC Television Centre.
Photo from the British Broadcasting Corporation

Figure 15.4
The late Dr. Jacob Bronowski, narrator of "The Ascent of Man," a thirteen-part series on mankind's scientific and cultural history. This BBC series is one of several which have aired very successfully in the United States.
Photo courtesy of WGBH Educational Foundation

Figure 15.5
High-power antenna combining units at the IBA's UHF transmitters in London. This was the first one-megawatt unattended UHF station in Europe.
Photo courtesy of the Independent Broadcasting Authority

as sponsoring them and cannot control program content. They can buy **spots** during certain time periods but cannot choose the precise time. Only six minutes of ads can be aired in one hour, and these must be at the beginning or end of a program or at a natural break. The minister of Posts and Telecommunications can forbid any ads for goods considered undesir-

Figure 15.6
Cast and crew of "The
Muppet Show" watching
a playback to improve
on technique and
angles. This show is
produced by the in-
dependent production
company ATV Network,
aired over IBA, and syn-
dicated to other coun-
tries.
Photo courtesy of the
Independent Broadcasting
Authority

able or methods deemed in bad taste. No commercials are allowed for religious or political groups or for labor disputes. An advisory committee on advertising has a binding code for advertising practices which prevents misleading statements.

The IBA does not produce any programs itself but rather makes agreements with program contractors, then oversees the programs and transmits them. The contractors are in different areas of the country and provide different types of programs—e.g., one contractor might supply children's programs, another news, and another comedies.

Program contractors receive money from selling spots on their programs. They then pay IBA for rental of transmitters and pay additional money based on the amount earned from ads. The IBA runs its operation from this money and pays high taxes to the government.

Some of the most popular programming on IBA includes two soap operas, "Coronation Street" and "Crossroads," which have been on the air for almost twenty years; "Oh No, It's Selwyn Froggitt," a comedy about a handyman who regularly breaks things; "Opportunity Knocks," an amateur talent show; and reruns of the American "This Is Your Life."

Political broadcasting is handled differently in Britain than in the United States. When an election is due, both the BBC and IBA offer a specified amount of time for political messages which the politicians divide up according to each party's strength in the last election. Broadcasters are not held responsible for applying **equal time** rules because the candidates themselves do so. In England it is understood that broadcasters are permit-ting their facilities to be used by politicians, so time is not sold for political ads, and prime ministers cannot **preempt** all channels for special speeches.[2]

Figure 15.7
Ottawa journalist Bruce Philips (*left*) interviewing Prime Minister Pierre Trudeau for a Canadian radio program.
Photo courtesy of Bushnell Communications, Ltd., Ottawa, Canada

Broadcasting in Canada

Canadian broadcasting is a mixed system mainly because of the geography of the country. Originally broadcasting consisted entirely of privately owned stations supported by advertising. But these stations tended to be only in the large cities because stations in sparsely populated areas could not attract enough advertising to make money. As a result, the Canadian Broadcasting Corporation (CBC) was formed by the government to program to these sparsely populated areas as well as to the cities. The CBC obtains most of its money from the government, but it also has limited advertisements.

Two radio and two television networks are operated by the CBC, one in English and one in French. The privately owned stations have their own network, Canadian TV or CTV. Both the CBC and CTV systems are regulated by the Canadian Radio-Television Committee, which licenses stations and also requires that 60 percent of programs be Canadian-produced in order to keep American influence to a minimum.

From time to time disputes arise between the United States and Canada, particularly regarding advertising practices of stations or cable TV facilities near the border and taxing policies initiated by one country or the other.[3]

Broadcasting in Mexico

Mexico too has a mixed system of both private and governmental broadcasting. The four private TV channels are all owned by a company called Televisa, which was formed in 1973 after a series of mergers involving the Mexican channels 2, 4, 5, and 8. All four channels originate from Mexico City, but channels 2 and 5 are beamed throughout all of Mexico and channels 4 and 8 are regional. Commercials abound on all channels and are

Figure 15.8
A Canadian TV program called "Sports Flashback." This program features host Brian Smith (*left*) with Bill Galloway, of the National Film Archives, Yvon Durelle, a prize fighter, and Torchy Peden, a five-day bicycle rider.
Photo courtesy of Bushnell Communications, Ltd., Ottawa, Canada

Figure 15.9
A program produced by Televisa-México with Sara García (*left*) and María Victoria. Sara is considered "the Grandmother of Mexico."
Photo courtesy of Televisa-México and KMEX-TV, Los Angeles

Figure 15.10
A popular Televisa-México comedy show, "Chespirito," starring Roberto Gómez Bolaños (*right*).
Photo courtesy of Televisa-México and KMEX-TV Los Angeles

responsible for the total income for Televisa. Programming includes series from the United States dubbed into Spanish as well as Mexican-produced soap operas, cultural programs, news, and variety shows. Since Mexico is a large country, a network system takes channels 2 and 5 throughout the country to local stations, all of which have call letters beginning with "X." Some of these local stations only **retransmit** the network programs while others produce local programs of their own. There are also a few local stations which are not network-**affiliated.** A number of the programs produced for Televisa are also aired on Spanish-language stations in the United States.

The government operates two TV channels, 11 and 13. Channel 11 is strictly educational and political and contains no ads. Channel 13 has cultural and entertainment programs and limited ads.

There is one national radio network, but most radio service is local. Although the stations are privately owned and broadcast commercials, the government oversees them through the office of the director general of Telecommunications. This office requires thirty minutes of information about the government each day and also oversees the broadcast of a one-hour program from 4:00 to 5:00 p.m. each Sunday called "National Hour." This program, which is carried by virtually every radio station in the country, consists of editorials, readings from the Mexican constitution, propaganda, and some music and drama.[4]

Broadcasting in the Soviet Union

Broadcasting in the Soviet Union is in strong contrast to that in the United States. Ownership, programming, and financing are all under the control of the Communist Party, and the responsibility for overall broadcasting lies with the State Committee for Radio and TV. This committee, which oversees all programming ideas and content, is made up of members appointed by the Council of Ministers of the Communist Party.

The main headquarters for broadcasting is in a massive production facility in Moscow consisting of twelve studios with modern equipment topped by a 1,500-foot transmission tower. The tower beams four channels of programming from 9:00 a.m. until midnight, with two satellites and a series of relay stations acting as a distribution net. Since the Soviet Union encompasses eleven time zones and some sixty different languages and dialects, translation and distribution of programs represents a monumental effort. There are also local stations in the various states which program local or regional material.

Financing is by government allocation. There are no commercials in the American sense, but several times a week there are blocks of commercial-type information featuring news about what is being sold in the shops.

Program content includes music, formal education, political addresses, documentaries, science programs, children's shows, and sports, with occasional variety or game shows. Programming is essentially devoid of sex and violence. American-produced programs are not shown, but occasionally programs about facets of the United States such as its parks or animals do appear. The principal newscast is scheduled at 9:00 p.m. and does not differ greatly in format from American network news. A talk show interviews tourists in Russia to learn their reaction to the country, mini-series dramas feature Soviet heroes, and a children's program consists of bedtime fairy-tale reading.[5]

Broadcasting in Japan

The Japanese have a well developed system of broadcasting which brings radio and TV to most of the people in the country. Four commercial channels cover most of this small country. The channels resemble American networks, both in terms of program concepts and commercial insertions within programs. In fact, many of the programs broadcast are American with Japanese soundtracks.

There is also educational TV, NHK (Nippon Hoso Kyokai), which is somewhat similar to the BBC in that its revenue is collected from taxes on sets. However, unlike the BBC, NHK is completely free from government control and collects its fees directly from its viewers without the government acting as the financial middleman. NHK operates two television networks and three radio networks. One of each is exclusively for education; the others provide general cultural programming. Most of NHK's programming is produced in Japan.

Japan is on the forefront of technological advances. It has been credited with many breakthroughs in television equipment, particularly miniaturizing equipment and its components.[6]

Broadcasting in Other Countries

No two countries have identical broadcasting setups, but most are similar to one of the forms discussed above. The iron curtain countries follow the authoritarian lines of the Soviet system, although some of the countries have lighter, more entertaining programming than is seen in the U.S.S.R.[7]

In most of Europe broadcasting is operated by companies chartered by the government in a manner similar to the BBC. These companies, like the BBC, are financed by taxes collected on radio and TV sets. Before the advent of TV, this revenue was sufficient to support radio, but many of the European countries have found that in order to meet the high costs of TV, they have had to allow limited TV advertising while maintaining radio as totally noncommercial. Since most European countries are small, any programs broadcast from a central location can be received throughout most of the nation.[8]

Some South American nations have commercial television roughly patterned after Mexico and the United States. However, in countries where dictatorships are strong, the broadcasting setup more closely parallels that of the Soviet Union.[9]

Many of the emerging nations of Africa and Asia have no television at all but do have radio stations. Those that have television have gone through similar steps. Usually there is a heated debate about whether or not television will unduly alter the social patterns. The debate ends with a decision to begin television on a limited basis as a government service. Broadcasting is then begun in black and white. Locally produced program-

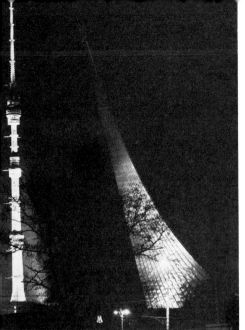

Figure 15.11

Figure 15.12

Figure 15.11
A Moscow TV tower situated next to a monument to conquerors of space.
Photo courtesy of the Embassy of the USSR

Figure 15.12
The popular Japanese children's cartoon "Arasatan."
Photo courtesy of Hippon Hoso Kyokai

Figure 15.13
A documentary about fishing for a mud fish called dojo.
Photo courtesy of Hippon Hoso Kyokai

Figure 15.14
A musical program dealing with songs of a woman's heart.
Photo courtesy of Hippon Hoso Kyokai

Figure 15.15
South Africa's huge broadcasting center constructed in Johannesburg in the 1970s. Part of the TV complex is seen at the left; the tower contains mainly offices; radio facilities are in the foreground.
Photo courtesy of the South African Broadcasting Corporation

ming is generally poor in both technical and content quality—e.g., in a program about carpet-making the camera stays on one piece of carpet for fifteen minutes while a voice in the back drones on. Only the rich can afford their own TV sets, but sets are usually placed in public squares, where people congregate to watch. Programming is imported from other countries, primarily the United States, resulting in increased popularity of the medium. Eventually the system is converted to color and the price of sets is reduced so that more people can own them.

Even the most sophisticated African country, South Africa, did not begin TV broadcasting until the mid-1970s. Discussions of TV began in the 1950s but always bogged down because of fears of cultural disturbance in that multiracial country controlled by a white minority.[10]

There are many individual peculiarities of systems throughout the world. In Switzerland programs must be produced in German, Italian, and French in order to meet the multilingual needs of the country. Belgium, similarly, has three distinct services for French, Dutch, and German. Much of the programming in the Netherlands is produced by religious and political groups. And in Greece the army operates a system which it supports by obtaining ads.[11]

Each individual state of West Germany has its own chartered corporation to produce programs for that state, and a "ratings war" of sorts exists between East and West Germany since radio waves do not stop at the Berlin wall.[12]

Israel has one noncommercial government-owned TV station. It airs American programs, locally produced cultural and news programs dealing with Israel, and several hours a day in Arabic. Two of its four government-owned radio stations have commercials.[13]

In Venezuela, although most people have color TV sets, transmission is in black and white because of dissension that arose when a committee tried

Figure 15.16
A South African television drama.
Photo courtesy of the
South African Broadcasting
Corporation

to decide between the NTSC and PAL color systems. The "compromise" was black and white.[14]

India is using satellite transmission to beam black and white educational TV programs to children and adults in rural areas. Its radio network has recently been increased to cover over 90 percent of the population.[15]

Australia has a series of small networks covering sections of the sprawling continent. These networks are organized by channel numbers; for example, there is a channel 9 network and a channel 7 network.[16]

Most of China's limited programming is highly political, with news that is generally twenty-four hours behind time and presented in a dull way. The feature films that are shown are primarily model revolutionaries and ballets which have been produced by a former Chinese actress who is now in her sixties.[17]

Many countries sell or exchange their programs throughout the world. Mexico provides much of the programming for South America, and the Soviet Union does likewise for the iron curtain countries. Britain, Canada, France, and Germany sell to various countries. But the granddaddy of all in supplying programs to foreign countries is the United States, which sells more internationally than all other countries combined.

In some ways this United States programming hinders local program development. Since it is impossible for most nations to produce shows of similar quality for the price at which they can buy the American shows, they tend to produce little and rely mainly on imports. United States program producers have become dependent upon the world market and frequently do not turn a profit on productions until they are sold overseas. These foreign sales are often filled with financial vicissitudes, for what one nation

International Exchange

is willing to purchase for $40,000, another may only be willing to purchase for $40.

Politically, American programming is often unwelcome in foreign nations because many of the cultural modes displayed are different from those of the nation where the program is aired. News and information programming supplied by American radio and TV is often accused of having a western bias. Many governments are selective about the content of American programs they buy, and some even limit the number of such imports. However, large doses of American cultural ideas affect the people of foreign lands for good or for ill.[18]

The United States has exported more than programs. It has also exported the concept of advertising to support broadcasting. Most world broadcasting systems were noncommercial during the days of radio only, but with the advent of TV, nations found that the American way was very helpful in supplementing the tax money that was falling short of financing the high costs of television production. Most commercials are limited and clustered, however—an intriguing idea to those used to viewing television in the United States. Government-owned, tax-supported broadcasting systems do not need the large advertising base required by private systems in order to acquire production funds. On the other hand, government-owned systems are much more likely to encounter the hand of censorship—an unpopular idea within the American culture.

Summary

Broadcasting systems vary greatly from country to country in *ownership, programming, financing,* and *technology.*

The most common ownership patterns are *private, government,* and *charter.* Programming ranges from propagandistic to entertainment. Financing comes from *advertising, taxes on sets,* and *general taxes.* Different *scanning* and *color systems* exist throughout the world. In Britain, broadcasting is supplied by the *BBC,* a government-chartered organization, and the *IBA,* a private organization. BBC radio has four services and BBC-TV has two. The IBA airs ads and receives its programming from production companies. Canada has both private and government systems because of its geography. The four Mexican TV channels, two regional and two national, are all owned by *Televisa.* Soviet broadcasting is totally government-owned, and originates mainly from a huge complex in Moscow. Japan has four privately owned commercial channels and two educational channels operated by *NHK.* Most iron curtain countries have authoritarian systems; Europe is largely charter; South America is commercial or dictatorship; and emerging nations usually begin with black and white transmission and community viewing areas. Many countries rely heavily on American programs, usually *dubbed* into their own language.

16 Into the Crystal Ball
The Future of Broadcasting

The messages wirelessed ten years ago have not yet reached some of the nearest stars.

Guglielmo Marconi, inventor

Cartoon copyrighted by *Broadcasting* magazine

"We know we've reached the satellite. It's busy."

Certainly any attempt to forecast the future of broadcasting is fraught with hazards beyond number. The imponderables are many; the certainties are few. There are, however, some elements which can logically be considered signposts pointing toward our broadcasting tomorrows. Among them are the newer forms of video viewing that may serve as an alternative to the traditional broadcasting structure; technical advances already developed or on the horizon; and forces working for program and structural concept changes.

The most debated topic concerning the future of television is the concept of "**alternative TV.**" This is a relatively new term which is generally used to designate all forms of television which might allow the viewer an alternative to the fare presently aired by the three major networks and the local stations. The major concepts presently falling under the umbrella of alternative TV are **pay cable, discs,** and **cassettes.** Within this framework are considered many combinations involving hardware not developed—some in the experimental stage, and some still in the dream stage.

Alternative Television—Pay Cable

The future role of cable TV or pay cable is hotly contested. There are those who predict that cable can and should entirely replace the present network-station structure. They envision programs being produced by various production houses and beamed from one location to satellites which will retransmit the programs to cable reception points throughout the country. The cable systems will, in turn, transmit the material entirely by wire to customers who pay for the service.

The proponents of this point of view argue that local TV stations would therefore no longer need the huge band of **spectrum** space they occupy. At present each TV station uses up as much space as all the AM radio stations combined. Disseminating TV on wire instead of through the airwaves would be an act greatly appreciated by many groups (airplane pilots, boating enthusiasts, policemen, taxi drivers, "**ham**" radio operators) who are constantly banging at the Federal Communication Commission's door begging for more spectrum space in order to carry out their duties more effectively and safely.

The proponents point out that such a system could be free of annoying interruptions from insulting commercials because the reception would be paid for by the viewers. They claim that as a corollary, programming would improve because it would no longer need to aim for the lowest common denominator demanded by advertisers.

People who favor elimination of conventional TV also point out that local programming, especially news and public service, could become more local than it is at present. Signals from present-day local TV stations cover a broad area and generally the stations do not program material of interest only to particular subareas within their range. Each cable TV system covers a narrower area than does a station; hence, through **local origination,** it could program material related directly to the needs of the community it serves.

The other obvious advantage which cable proponents espouse is the increase in viewer choice of programming. With the many more channels available through cable than under the present system, there would be room for highly specialized programming in both the entertainment and information fields.

Not surprisingly, a large number of people do not agree with the reasoning of the pro-cable camp. The most vocal opposition is from people entrenched in the present network-station system. They argue that the public will not, and should not need to, pay for television. If a pay cable system replaces the present system, the public at large will be deprived of television, for only the urban elite will be able to afford the service. Like it or not, television has become the primary means by which the nation becomes informed about news, politics, and public affairs. It is also the nation's number one entertainment escape. Depriving people who cannot pay for this service when they are the ones who may need it most would be against our democratic principles.

Spokespeople within the established systems have also tried to point out to both the cable TV community and to the FCC that pay cable is neither economically nor practically viable. It costs a great deal of money to produce quality television, as the networks are well aware. If cable systems intend to offer viewers a choice of 20, 30, 40 channels, where will they obtain the resources necessary to produce the programs? This quantity of programming would so escalate the costs to the viewers that fewer subscribers would be able to afford it, escalating the costs even more to the subscribers left.

Even if money could be found to produce the multitude of specialized programs that cable systems would expect to offer, from a practical point of view it would be difficult to accomplish—if for no other reason, the amount of creative talent in the country has a limit. At present, there are not enough quality movies available to fill pay cable's voracious appetite. Networks occasionally have had to cancel series simply because they have run out of ideas for stories. The opponents of cable systems wonder what secret formula cable people will use as a catalyst for creativity.

Members of the established broadcasting community point out that polls have repeatedly shown that the public thinks that advertising is an acceptable price to pay for the privilege of having television, that many people actually enjoy ads and welcome the break in programming they provide, and that the present network programming fare pleases most of the people.[1]

The strongest opponents of the pay cable system feel that it should be curtailed immediately into nothing more than a retransmission service for station and network programs. They feel that if it is force-fed by the government and begins to operate as its own programming service, it may initially build enough audience to outbid free TV for programs and thus cause irreparable damage to the network structure and deprive the public at large of television. If pay cable is allowed this toehold, the die will be cast.

Although it will not be able to maintain quality programming, it will be able to demolish the networks economically, and everyone will lose.

Of course, many people think that **fee TV** and **free TV** can exist side by side. Some look at pay TV as having a very limited market—perhaps existing only for hotels, motels, and large apartment complexes—while the rest of the nation will still embrace free TV as the primary medium for viewers and advertisers.

Others see cable TV as serving ancillary or two-way functions not now covered by conventional broadcasting. This two-way communication would revolutionize a system that has always been one-way—toward the audience. For example, grocery shopping might be accomplished by cable TV if the various products were displayed on the screen and someone could push buttons for those products desired. Instead of going to a library, it might be possible to request that desired information be displayed on the TV set. Other information, such as public records, could be kept in a computer bank and accessed and displayed by a two-way cable TV system. Similarly, newspapers could be broadcast instead of delivered. Cable TV could open garage doors, trigger burglar alarms, and read gas and electric meters. But the basic news and entertainment functions would be left to conventional stations and networks and merely retransmitted by the cable systems. Under this plan, some people think that cable may sell advertisements to defray costs just as broadcasting does, but the advertisement money would be taken from newspapers, not TV, since the ads would be very local.

Another point of view is that all entertainment programming would be carried commercial-free by cable TV on a pay basis. The networks would program news, documentaries, and sports events only—free to the viewers and with advertisements. Some people think that it would be healthy to have cable and free TV compete with each other for entertainment attractions. The thought is that pay TV will offer quality programming that will **siphon** off enough middle class viewers that the TV networks will have to upgrade their programming to lure them back. It is impossible to predict how the free versus fee concept will end, but many of the battle lines have been drawn.[2]

Pay cable is not the only method being discussed to allow the viewer an alternative to network TV. Also of prime significance are video discs and video cassettes. These devices enable viewers to watch television at their convenience rather than at the time when the material is fed to them by broadcasters. The proposed systems have many similarities to audio equipment already in abundance in the consumer market. Discs are similar to phonograph records, and cassettes are similar to audio tape cassettes.

In the forefront of disc development are Radio Corporation of America (RCA) and a team composed of Philips, an electronic equipment manufacturer based in Holland, and MCA-Universal, the California entertainment program producer. Both RCA and Philips-MCA have developed machines which can be attached to the antenna lead of a conventional TV

Alternative Television— Discs and Cassettes

receiver and then play the material on the disc through the receiver. Unfortunately, the two systems are not compatible. In other words, discs developed for the RCA system cannot be played on the Philips-MCA system and vice versa. This may lead to a winner-take-all situation; it may cause both systems to fail; or it may foster a healthy competition which spurs improvements and economy and allows both to prosper.

The RCA system called SelectaVision employs a stylus which slides over the top of a plastic disc much as a stereo needle slides over a phonograph record. The disc, however, is rotating at a much higher speed—450 **RPM** as opposed to a phonograph record of 33 **RPM**. Most of RCA's discs contain thirty minutes per side. The discs are specially coated to increase their durability, but they will begin to show wear after approximately 500 plays. The stylus will last 300 to 500 hours and can be replaced inexpensively. The SelectaVision stylus can be placed anywhere on the disc, much as a phonograph stylus can, so the viewer can cue a particular portion of the program. RCA's product is easy to operate and repair and is estimated to retail for about $400, with discs costing in the neighborhood of $10 each.

The Philips-MCA system, called Disco-Vision, employs a **laser** beam bounced off the bottom of the disc by means of mirrors. This beam reads the information from the disc and sends another beam to the TV receiver. For Disco-Vision, the disc rotates at 1,800 RPM and contains thirty minutes of programming. Because nothing actually touches the disc while it is revolving, it will last indefinitely. The laser will last several thousand hours and replacement cost is low. Each frame has an index number which appears on the TV screen, so the viewer can tune in any frame desired. The price of the player is claimed to be $500 with discs ranging from $2 to $10 depending on program content.

Both companies have invested millions in the development of video discs and admit that several million players must be sold before they can turn a profit. It is generally conceded that the video quality of both machines is excellent and that the discs are easy to stamp from the master so can be turned out economically.

Of course, the success of either or both of these machines will depend on the software—the programming made available on discs. One of the reasons Philips and MCA joined forces was the possibility of making discs from some of MCA's library of 2,000 feature films. RCA is lining up feature films from other companies. In addition to films, the companies are considering educational lectures, self-help programs, cooking shows, how-to programs, formal education, and maybe even disc-of-the-month clubs. Of course, none of the programming will contain commercials.[3]

Another home video system on the consumer market is the video cassette. The first to hit the market was Sony's Betamax, which is basically a videotape recorder system employing 1/2 " cassette tape. It is not radically different from video cassette tape recorders already being used in industry and education except that it is designed for the consumer market and can tape one show while another is being watched and incorporates a clock

device that can tape material while the owner is away. Prerecorded cassettes containing feature films, lectures, and other programming fare similar to that planned for discs will be made available for Betamax and other cassette systems. Cassette machines have a much higher price tag than the disc machines—about $1,000 for the player/recorder itself and $2,000 for a console that also includes TV receivers. Cost of the tapes runs about $16 per hour. Cassettes have two advantages over disc machines. Not only can they tape material off the air, they are capable of receiving input from a TV camera, enabling the owner to make "home movies" on videotape which can be played back through the TV set just as the other material is.

There is no guarantee that any of these consumer viewing devices will be accepted to the point where they become profitable. Many similar ideas have fallen by the wayside. One of the first, called EVR, was developed by CBS during the 1960s. It employed electronic images placed on photographic film. The film did not record images as when run through a motion picture camera; it contained electronic impulses. The advantage of putting the electronic impulses on film rather than tape was that prints could be made of the film quickly and inexpensively, in contrast to duplications of videotape, which were slow and expensive. The film was placed in the EVR machine and the output was displayed on a TV monitor. CBS predicted that EVR would replace films, but a combination of technical and marketing problems made this outcome impossible.

Other companies have made initial investments in the development of consumer video products but dropped out because of technical or financial problems.

At present the companies working on alternative TV products believe in their machines and feel the market is there. They admit that in order to sell players, there must be programming, and in order to finance programming, they must sell players, but they point optimistically to the fact that over $2 billion a year is spent by Americans on phonograph records.

Some people are opposed to discs and cassettes on the grounds that TV programming should be free. They argue that discs and cassettes will

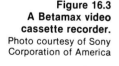
**Figure 16.3
A Betamax video
cassette recorder.**
Photo courtesy of Sony
Corporation of America

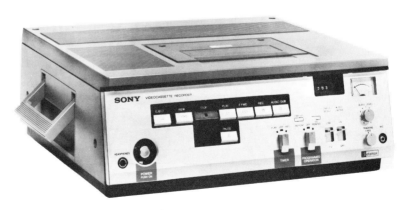

undermine the network system and force TV to become an entirely different type of instrument with people able to see programs at their convenience. No longer will last night's TV offerings offer a common bond for conversation. Other people counter this argument by pointing out that radio is still alive and well despite booming record and audio cassette businesses.[4]

It has been said that television eats its young. While the playback-only disc machines, barely born, are struggling to capture a market, companies are working to develop disc machines that allow viewers to record their own material, as they can with cassette machines. While infant pay cable is crawling to gain a foothold with satellite transmission, feasibility studies are being conducted into the possibility of transmitting directly from satellites to homes, eliminating the need for the cable. No sooner is 2″ videotape developed than it is superseded by 1″ tape, to be superseded by 1/2″ tape, to be superseded by 3/4″, to be superseded by 1/4″. . . . A camera that weighs forty pounds is replaced by one that weighs thirty pounds, just as one weighing twenty pounds hits the market, one weighing ten pounds is developed, and one the size of a wristwatch is envisioned.

Large-scale use of **projected TV** may be on the horizon. Several methods have been tried to project the TV image to a large screen so it can be seen by a large group of people, but usually the projected image is difficult to distinguish because it is not bright enough. However, the state of the art is improving, and recent developments show promise.

One such product presently on the market consists of a small plastic projector and a curved 84″ aluminum screen, at a cost of several thousand dollars. The projector and the screen must be at least eight feet apart, making this particular product rather unwieldy for home use but appropri-

**Figure 16.4
A TeleBeam II large-screen TV projector.**
Photo courtesy of Kalart Victor Corporation

ate for meetings and conventions. Another product consists of one unit that contains a color television set, whose image is projected by a finely ground lens onto a 50″ screen. It is priced under $1,000 and intended for home use. [5]

Flat-screen TV is also in the developmental stage. It is entirely possible that in the not-too-distant future television sets may hang on the wall like pictures and be carried to the beach like radios. This will be due to the fact that the sets will employ **microcircuitry** and will no longer contain tubes which operate on the beam scan principle. Instead, they will probably be operated on a gas discharge principle, like a fluorescent lamp. Two glass panels will hold **electrodes** which will form the picture elements with a gas mixture filling the gap between electrodes. When current pulses are applied to the electrodes, one line at a time, the gas will emit **ultraviolet** light, making the **phosphor** above it glow. Color will be created by triads of red, green, and blue bars which, when illuminated, will be blended by the eye into proper colors. [6]

TV sets, whether conventional or flat-screen, may become inexpensive enough to compete with radios. They might then be treated as a carry along item, and people riding buses or walking along the street could watch their favorite program.

Three-dimensional TV may be a reality someday, but at present it is in a highly experimental stage, with little interest in rushing to bring it to production.

Television cameras continue to shrink. They too may be able to eliminate the last remaining tube—the vidicon or plumbicon pickup tube. If they can do this by utilizing devices that act as **solid state sensors,** then their

**Figure 16.5
A developmental model
flat-screen TV.**
Photo courtesy of Sharp
Electronics Corporation

size can become even smaller than the present hand-held cameras used frequently for news and sports reporting.

Not only are cameras becoming smaller, they are also becoming more sensitive. The original cameras needed intense, and therefore hot, lighting to produce an acceptable picture. Today's cameras can pick up an image with no more available light than that produced by a match.[7]

Videotape recorders continue to shrink too, especially the helical machines using 1″, 1/2″, and 3/4″ tape. Improvements in the electronics of machines combined with improvements in videotape are allowing more and more information to be packed onto less and less tape. A system is being developed to compress into a single cassette the equivalent of all the TV programming of thirty one-hour videotapes. These thirty programs could be shown simultaneously on thirty different TV sets.[8]

The overall concept of smallness will be a great asset to electronic journalism. It is predicted that in the future one TV news reporter will be able to cover a story alone. He or she may carry a small videotape recorder about the size of a present audio cassette recorder and use a TV camera the size of a super 8 film camera. In addition, the reporter may wear a small hearing-aid-type device that is actually a microminiaturized satellite receiver to maintain constant contact with the office, and may carry a briefcase that will really be a satellite terminal allowing transmission from anywhere at any time, making each reporter a James Bond of the airwaves.

Figure 16.6
Possible camera newsperson of the future.

Satellites are bound to figure ever more heavily in TV's future. Networks can use satellites rather than microwave to transmit their programs across the country. Satellites may play a larger role in international TV. Commercials may be sent to local stations by satellite rather than by reels of tape or film mailed or messengered to local stations.

Other technological improvements may be in the offing. **Resolution** of the TV picture may be improved by changing the present 525-line system to the greater density of 635 or 840 lines as used in other countries. Improved standards have not been implemented in the United States mainly because everyone would have to purchase a new TV set. The 525-line system and a new system could not be compatible on the same set. If this problem is solved, improved resolution may become a reality.

Sound quality on TV may improve by stereo TV becoming economical and widespread. Methods of rapid duplication of material from one videotape to another will no doubt be perfected. The present system of **dubbing** requires one hour to make a copy of a one-hour videotape.

Research is underway to improve the technical quality of UHF so it will be equal to VHF in clarity and signal strength. If it is successful, the economic condition of UHF stations may improve.

At the same time, somewhat contradictory plans are afoot to increase the number of VHF stations in some markets. Proponents of this scheme feel that low-powered VHFs with **directional antennas** and offset frequency controls could be dropped into the spectrum space without causing interference to existing stations. They could be used as community stations to present educational and minority group programming.

The laser beam may unlock myriad developments which are as yet unthought of. It can pick up signals in total darkness, and it may enable signals to be transmitted by **light waves** rather than **radio waves.**[9]

Radio too may undergo some technological improvements. Recent years have seen an impressive growth in the broadcasting of music in **stereo** by FM stations. Now it's time for **quadraphonic** FM and stereo AM. Radio receivers can be manufactured even smaller than ones now on the market, but somewhere along the way this reaches a point of diminishing returns because they become so tiny they can be easily lost. There may be changes in equipment capability that will enable daytime-only stations to broadcast for longer periods of the day. Tape may become obsolete as a means of recording and playing sound and instead a minicomputer's digital memory may store continuous hours of programming on punchcards or discs or tiny chips.[10]

Programming Predictions

Critics of broadcasting may fear that there will be no major changes in radio and television programming of the future. They imagine that in the future **prime-time** entertainment shows will still cycle cops, doctors, B-grade movies, and corny comedians with only an occasional worthwhile special that may approach what the medium is capable of exhibiting; news will still be biased and superficial, and documentaries will be relegated to undesirable time slots; daytime TV will still reek with low budget cartoons, weepy soap operas, and hysterical game shows; radio stations will continue to assault the ears with top 40 music; and commercials will still be overabundant, insulting, and repetitious.

Needless to say, many people, especially within the industry, do not share that negative view of present-day broadcasting. They feel the present program fare is serving the needs and desires of the public and should continue as is. Others feel that programming should be more responsive to community needs and represent high cultural values. Citizen groups throughout the country are at work to try to improve programming, and many people employed within broadcasting entities wish to provide programming which they feel is on a higher plane than most present-day offerings.

If any of the forms of alternative TV take hold, there may be significant changes in programming; barring this eventuality, the changes are likely to represent small steps. Both the **fairness** doctrine and the **equal time** provisions may be reexamined. Perhaps the fairness doctrine will be eliminated entirely, allowing stations more editorial latitude in the presentation of points of view. Perhaps it will be modified in such a way that stations do not need to seek actively to uncover opposite points of view. On the other hand this doctrine may be strengthened even further so that all points of view can be heard more fully. The area of equal time may see more exceptions in the future. Perhaps less splinter party candidates will have the right to the equal time given to Republicans and Democrats. The shades of gray surrounding the President as the chief executive of the land and the President as a candidate for reelection may be refined. Then it will be easier for broadcasters to know when they need to give equal time to candidates challenging incumbents.

The future may see some changes in commercials. They may be removed entirely from children's programs or changed greatly in content and method of presentation. Perhaps they will be grouped to make fewer program interruptions.

A fourth network, perhaps interconnected by satellite, may be established to service UHF and **independent** stations. More of the programming fare may be supplied by **syndicators** than by networks. On the other hand, the reverse may happen: networks may begin producing even more of their own programs. The amount of time the network is allowed to program for stations may be changed, either upward or downward.

News and documentaries may consume a larger portion of the broadcast day than they presently do. The amount and type of sex and violence on TV and the hours at which broadcasting of such nature may occur will undoubtedly continue to be researched and debated. There may be no such thing as a prime-time "**season.**" All programs may simply start at convenient times and run for as long as the ratings hold and then be replaced.

Entirely new forms of what may be termed "semi-private" video communication may increase in popularity. One of these is the use of video to express personal feelings and involvements and to aid interpersonal relationships. Generally, this involves a close-knit group of people using port- o-pak equipment to create images and ideas expressing their inter-relationships. Another new form of video, usually referred to as **video art,** is the creation of unusual and/or abstract video imagery, often with the aid of computers or **video synthesizers,** in order to comment on society or create "art for art's sake."

Perhaps more foreign programming will reach American TV. If and when satellites can transmit directly to homes, it may be possible for American audiences to view the BBC directly. In the same way, American programs may be beamed to other countries.

Structural Changes

One of the big question marks of the future is the continuing role of government in broadcasting. No doubt the FCC will continue its technical regulation and make sure that stations broadcast in ways that will not interfere with each other. But the future function of the FCC in programming is less clear. The FCC now has no direct control over network programming, but the threat that it will, or hope (depending on one's point of view), is always present. The NAB Code may become mandatory in order to keep the government from enforcing similar provisions.

The role of the FCC in station licensing may be changed. In the future, stations may receive **licenses** for five years instead of three as at present. Citizen groups may gain a louder voice or may be restrained by law from challenging station licenses.

In the future there may be no joint ownership of newspapers and broadcast stations; or perhaps this trend will be reversed and the two will be more closely aligned than in the past. The vague terms "interest, convenience, and necessity" may receive new interpretations as yet unthought of by either the government or broadcasters.

Public broadcasting's future is closely tied to the dollar, since the quality of its programming is so largely dependent on the appropriations it obtains from Congress. It may receive this funding on a longer term basis, such as five years, or on a shorter term basis, perhaps one year at a time. Public broadcasters hope for the former so they may make long-term plans. Public radio may begin to receive either more or less of the overall educational broadcasting financial pie.

Cable TV guidelines change almost daily, but it is possible that in the near future the FCC may issue an entirely new set of principles. Probably more women and minorities will be hired into the broadcasting industry as pressure for affirmative action continues.

Broadcasters themselves predict that station value will continue to soar and the amount advertisers are willing to pay will continue to grow. Perhaps ratings will take somewhat of a back seat to community service where the worth of a station's programming is judged. Future rating systems may give more emphasis to quality of viewers rather than quantity.[11]

Most ideas for the future of broadcasting must be presented in tentative terms, for it is impossible to tell what direction the industry will take. Broadcasting is such a young industry that there are very few areas where one can take comfort in the fact that history repeats itself.

Within the past fifty years broadcasting has entered and filled the American home, for good or for ill. Tomorrow's place for this entity depends primarily on all of us. In the final analysis, a radio receiver or a TV set is an inanimate object—voiceless or pictureless until we command. Though our influence on local stations, on sponsors, on government agencies, and on program producers is often indirect, we do have a degree of control. The extent to which we as citizens, listeners, and viewers exercise that control will determine in large measure what the influence of future broadcasting will be. In the final analysis, the air is still ours.

Summary It is difficult to predict the future of broadcasting, but *alternative programming, technological advances, programming changes,* and *structural changes* will probably fit into the picture.

The role of *pay cable* is hotly contested. Some people think it should totally replace the present network-station structure. Others think it should be a retransmission service only. Still others think the two can coexist, perhaps with pay cable specializing in two-way communication and conventional broadcasting emphasizing news and public affairs. *Video discs* and *video cassettes* allow viewers to watch programs at their convenience. Discs employ a *stylus* or *laser,* and cassettes use tape. Other technological possibilities include *projected TV, flat-screen TV, three-dimensional TV, smaller equipment, higher density storage* and *faster duplication, satellite advances, improved resolution,* and advances in *microcircuitry* and *lasers.* The programming area may see changes in equal time and fairness, commercials, news, and foreign programming. Structurally, the roles of the FCC, joint ownership, public broadcasting, and cable TV may change.

Glossary

Most of the terms in this glossary appear in boldface type the first time they are used in any chapter in the text. In addition, the full names represented by abbreviations and acronyms commonly used in the broadcasting industry are included. The definitions given here relate to terms as they are used in the text. Some of the definitions for electronic terms go into more technical detail than the context requires, however. These definitions are for technically minded students.

a

AAAA
American Association of Advertising Agencies

ABC
American Broadcasting Company

above-the-line
creative costs of a particular program or series for such items as talent and producer

AC
alternating current

ACT
Action for Children's Television

ADI
Area of Dominant Influence

advertising agency
an organization which plans, organizes, and executes a promotion plan for companies which have products or services to sell

affiliate
a station which receives programming from one of the major networks

AFM
American Federation of Musicians

AFRTS
Armed Forces Radio and Television Service

AFTRA
American Federation of Television and Radio Artists

allocation table
a list compiled by the FCC which indicates where FM or TV stations can be located

alternative TV
any method of receiving television programs other than the conventional network-station setup; the most common forms are pay-cable, video discs, and video cassettes

alternator
a device for converting mechanical energy into electrical energy in the form of alternating current (AC)

AM
amplitude modulation: changing the height of a transmitting radio wave according to the sound being broadcast

amplifier
a circuit, tube, transistor, or other apparatus that draws power from a source other than the input signal and then produces as an output an enlarged reproduction of the essential features of the input

amplitude
the variation of a fluctuating phenomenon, such as alternating current, from its zero value

antenna
a wire or set of wires or rods used both to send and to receive radio waves

antitrust act
act of Congress designed to oppose business deals made to control or centralize industries

AP
Associated Press

ASCAP
American Society of Composers, Authors, and Publishers

ascertainment
a process stations must undertake to keep their licenses; it involves interviewing community leaders to learn what they believe are the major problems in the community

AT&T
American Telephone and Telegraph Company

audimeter
an electronic device attached to TV sets by the A. C. Nielsen Company in order to determine, for audience measurement purposes, when a set is turned on and to what station it is tuned

audio frequency
energy corresponding to the portion of the electromagnetic spectrum perceived as sound by the human ear: approximately 20 to 20,000 Hz, or cycles per second

audion
a three-electrode vacuum tube invented by Lee De Forest which was instrumental in amplifying voice so it could be sent over wireless

average measures
audience measurement counts of the average number of households listening to or watching a station over a preselected period of time

AWRT
American Women in Radio and Television

b

balance sheet
a statement of the assets, liabilities, and net worth of a company at a particular time, usually the close of a fiscal year

bandwidth
the number of continuous frequencies within given limits that are allowable for transmission of a given signal; for example, an AM radio station has a much smaller bandwidth than a TV station

barter
to give goods or services in return for other goods or services

BBC
British Broadcasting Corporation

beat
an area in which a news reporter is expected to gather news

below-the-line
costs which are constant regardless of the particular program or series, such as camera operators, transmitter engineers, and videotape

bicycle network
a method by which the same program is shown on different stations but at different times because the program is not sent over wires or microwave but rather is mailed, flown, or driven from one station to another

bidirectional
picking up on two sides; used to refer to microphones with two live sides

blacklisting
a phenomenon of the 1950s, when many people in the entertainment business were accused of leaning toward communism and as a result could not find work

BMI
Broadcast Music, Inc.

booster
a carrier frequency amplifier which strengthens a signal at one fixed point so it can be retransmitted to another fixed point

BRC
Broadcast Rating Council

broadcast standards
the department at a network or station that decides the general standards of acceptability of program content

broker
a person or company that acts like a real estate agency for people wishing to buy and sell radio and TV stations

c

call letters
a series of government-assigned letters which identify a transmitting station

canned
preproduced; programs, commercials, or program elements that arrive at the station already on tape or film

capacitor
a device consisting of two conducting surfaces separated by insulating material which stores electrical energy and permits the flow of various degrees of alternating current, depending on the frequency

carbon mike
a microphone which operates on the variations of resistance of carbon contacts, a nonmetallic conductive material

cardioid
a heart-shaped pickup pattern for a microphone

carrier wave
a high-frequency wave which can be sent through the air and which is modulated by a lower-frequency wave containing information

cartridge
a self-contained case of magnetic tape wound in a continuous loop; also, the portion of a turntable pickup arm that receives vibrations

cassette
a two-reeled self-contained case for magnetic tape

cathode ray tube
a tube in which an electronic beam can be focused to a small cross section on a luminescent screen and can then be varied in position and density to produce what appears to be a moving picture

CATV
Community Antenna Television; cable TV

CBC
Canadian Broadcasting Corporation

CBS
Columbia Broadcasting System

cease and desist
a formal order which states that a person or company must stop a certain practice immediately

charter
a written grant from the government to a company permitting it to engage in broadcasting under stipulations laid out by the government

circulation
the number of homes that tune in to a particular station over a set period of time, usually one week

citizens' band
a radio communication service intended for short-distance personal and business communication

closed-circuit
television signals that are transmitted via a self-contained wire system rather than broadcast through the air

coaxial cable
a transmission line in which one conductor completely surrounds the other, making for a cable that is not susceptible to external fields from other sources

coil
a number of turns of wire around an iron core

coincidental telephone technique
an audience measurement method whereby people are called on the telephone and asked what they are watching on TV or listening to on radio at that moment

color coding system
the system by which red, blue, and green information is encoded on a TV signal

commission
a percentage of money given to a salesperson based on the amount of the sale

composite week
seven randomly selected days from a three-year period which the FCC reviews in order to determine appropriateness of license renewal

condensor
another term for capacitor

construction permit
(CP) a document issued by the FCC which allows the recipient to begin building a radio or television station

CONTAM
Committee on Nationwide Television Audience Measurement

control track
the portion of videotape that contains sync information such as horizontal and vertical picture alignment

co-op advertising
joint participation in the content and cost of a commercial by two entities, usually a national company which manufactures the product and a local company which sells it

cosmic rays
rays in the vicinity of 10^{18} megahertz that have high penetrating power produced by transmutations of atoms in outer space

counter-programming
scheduling programs to reduce the audience size of a competitor's programs

coverage
the number of homes a particular radio or TV station has the potential to reach if all conditions are perfect

CP
construction permit

CPB
Corporation for Public Broadcasting

CPM
cost per thousand; the price which an advertiser is paying for each thousand households which the commercial reaches

crane
a mechanism on which a camera can be mounted that allows the camera to move from close to the floor to a fairly high distance above the floor

crystal
a thin slab or plate of quartz ground to a thickness that causes it to vibrate at a specific frequency when energy is applied

CTW
Children's Television Workshop

cue
to set up something such as a record or tape ahead of time so it will begin at the right place

cue tone
a sub-audio signal on a tape that enables a specially equipped tape recorder to start or stop the tape at an appropriate point

cume
the total number of households that tune in to a particular station at different times

cycles per second
the number of times a second that an alternating wave goes from zero to a negative peak to zero to a positive peak and back to zero

d

DC
direct current

defamation of character
utterings either written or oral that attack the reputation of a person

demodulate
to operate on a previously modulated wave in such a way that it will have the same characteristics as the original wave

demographics
information pertaining to vital statistics of a population such as age, sex, marital status, and geographic location

depth of field
the range of distance from the camera within which all objects will appear in focus

detector
a part of a radio receiver that demodulates the wave or separates the carrier wave from the information it carries

DGA
Directors Guild of America

diaphragm
a flexible membrane used in dynamic microphones to produce electric impulses from audio-frequency vibrations

diary
a booklet used for audience measurement in which people write down the programs they watch or hear

directional antenna
an antenna which sends out radio waves more effectively in some directions than others

director
the person who calls for the various shots and generally oversees produc-

tion once it is in the TV studio or
remote location

disc
a phonograph record; also a device
resembling a phonograph record used
to play video information

dissolve
going gradually from one picture to
another in such a way that the two
pictures overlap briefly

d.j.
disc jockey

double-system
a method of filming whereby the picture is recorded on film while the
sound is recorded on audiotape some
distance from the camera

down converter
a device for changing high frequency
signals to lower frequency signals

dub
to make another copy; refers especially
to making a copy of a film or tape
through electronic processes

duopoly
a rule which states that a network
organization cannot operate two or
more networks covering the same ter-
ritory at the same time

dynamic mike
a microphone in which a diaphragm is
attached to a coil positioned in a
magnetic field

e

electrode
a conducting element that emits or collects electrons or ions or controls their
movement by an electric field

electromagnetic spectrum
a continuous range of electromagnetic
energy, including radio waves and light
waves

electromagnetism
the magnetic field created around a
wire or other conductor when current
passes through it

electron gun
a structure which produces and controls an electron beam in a TV camera

electronic scanning
a method which analyzes the density
of areas to be copied and translates
this into a moving arrangement of
electrons which can later reproduce the
densities in the form of a picture

endowment
a gift of money often designated for a
specific purpose

ENG
electronic news gathering; specifically,
portable video equipment first used in
obtaining on-the-spot news stories

equalizer
an attachment for a turntable that can
eliminate high frequencies and therefore scratchy noises

equal time
a rule stemming from Section 315 of
the Communications Act, which states
that TV and radio stations should give
the same treatment and opportunity to
all political candidates for a specific
office

extra
a person who has a small, nonspeaking
part in a movie or TV show

f

fairness
a policy which has evolved from FCC
decisions and court cases which states
that radio and TV stations must
present all sides of controversial
issues which they discuss

family hour
a policy included temporarily in the
NAB Code which stated that all
programs aired between 7:30 and
9:00 p.m. should be suitable for
children as well as adults

FCC
Federal Communications Commission

fee TV
another name for pay TV; a counterpart to conventional network-station
free TV

field
one-half a complete scanning cycle, or
a scanning of all the odd or all the
even lines

film chain
equipment used for placing slides or
motion picture film on a TV monitor,
usually consisting of at least one slide
projector, at least one film projector,
a multiplexer, and a TV camera

filter
a device to eliminate certain colors and
let others pass

fixed lens
a lens that cannot have its focal length
changed, so always frames a picture of
the same angle width

flat-screen TV
a form of TV reception being
developed that does not use a picture
tube; it can hang on the wall like a
picture

floor manager
the person who is in charge of studio
operations during production, cuing
the talent and communicating with the
director

FM
frequency modulation: placing a sound
wave upon a carrier wave in such a
way that the number of recurrences is
varied

format
type of programming of a radio station, usually described in terms of the
music it plays

frame
one complete scanning cycle of a TV
camera or receiver; one individual picture of motion picture film

franchise
a special right granted by a government or corporation to operate a
facility such as cable TV

FRC
Federal Radio Commission

free lance
a person who is not under contract for
regular work but sells his or her
services, such as acting or writing,
independently to organizations on a
per-project basis

free TV
TV as it is broadcast by networks and
stations; a counterpart to pay TV

freeze
immobilization or cessation of an activity, such as a stop in the assigning of radio stations

frequency
the number of recurrences of a periodic phenomenon, such as a carrier wave, during a set time period, such as a second

frequency deviation
the degree to which the actual frequency of a station varies from the FCC-assigned frequency

f-stop
a calibration on a lens indicating the aperture, or how wide open the iris is

FTC
Federal Trade Commission

g

gamma rays
electromagnetic radiations with wavelengths in the vicinity of 10^{16} megahertz

GE
General Electric Company

gear shift
the part of a turntable used to select the speed

grid
a pipe structure for hanging lights, usually attached to a TV studio ceiling

ground station
a receiving station for information transmitted by a satellite

guild
an organization similar to a union, usually organized for above-the-line personnel

h

ham
a person who operates a radio station as a hobby rather than a business

head
a small electromagnet used to read, record, or erase information on magnetic tape

helical
a method of videotape recording whereby video information is placed on the tape at a slant

hertz
a frequency unit of one cycle per second; abbreviated Hz

HUT
home using television; the percentage of homes which have a TV set tuned to any station

hypoing
the practice of airing special programs or holding special contests in order to increase audience size during a rating period

Hz
hertz

i

IATSE
International Alliance of Theatrical and Stage Employees and Moving Picture Machine Operators of the United States and Canada

IBEW
International Brotherhood of Electrical Workers

iconoscope
the earliest form of TV camera tube in which a beam of electrons scanned a photoemissive mosaic

IEEE
Institute of Electrical and Electronic Engineers

image orthicon
a TV camera tube used for over twenty years in which a photoemitting surface focused an image on a glass target that was scanned by an electron beam

independent
a station which is not aligned with one of the major networks

information retrieval
a system by which material stored in one place can quickly be displayed in another upon request

infrared rays
waves just beyond the red end of visible light with wavelengths longer than light but shorter than radio waves

initiation fee
a one-time payment of a set amount of money to join an organization such as a union or guild

input
the current, voltage, or power coming into a component of an electronic system, usually by means of a connector

INS
International News Service

instantaneous measure
the number of households tuned to a station at a particular moment

instant replay
the playing back of videotaped material immediately after it is recorded, usually by using a video disc machine

intercom
a two-way communication system without a central switchboard that allows all to hear and often allows all to talk

in the can
finished; material which is on tape or film in a manner ready for airing

IPS
inches per second

iris
the adjustable opening in a camera lens that admits light

ITFS
Instructional Television Fixed Service

j

jack panel
a board with many sockets to which the wires of a circuit are connected at one end, and a male plug can be inserted in the other end

k

key
a switching device for turning a circuit off or on which usually consists of concealed spring contacts and an exposed handle or button

kilohertz
1,000 Hertz; abbreviated kHz

l

laser
acronym for Light Amplification by Simulated Emission of Radiation; a device for transforming light of various frequencies into a very narrow, intense beam

legitimate theater
performance of plays before a live audience

lens
the part of a camera which projects an image on the television pickup tube

libel
to say or print something unfavorable and false about a person

license
a document which the FCC issues to stations authorizing them to operate

light waves
the portion of the electromagnetic spectrum that is visible to the human eye

line-of-sight
a straight line between a broadcast antenna and a receiver

lip sync
a post-production method of adding audio to a motion picture film by recording speaking or singing in synchrony with the picture

local origination
programs produced about the local community, particularly as it refers to cable TV programming

log
a sheet which lists a second-by-second breakdown of a station's program schedule

lottery
the involvement of chance, prize, and consideration (money) for a game or contest

m

magazine concept
placing ads of various companies within a program rather than having the entire program sponsored by one company

magnetic field
an area where magnetic forces can be detected around a magnet

market
an area, often consisting of one city, that a particular station serves

master antenna
the main antenna of a system which sometimes collects signals for a cable TV so that they can be sent on by wire

matching funds
money provided when an equal amount of money has been raised by other means

mechanical scanning
an early form of scanning by which a rotating device such as a disc broke up a scene into a rapid succession of narrow lines for conversion into electrical impulses

megahertz
1,000,000 hertz; abbreviated MHz

microcircuit
a small circuit with high density composed of interconnected elements that perform an electronic circuit function

microwave
radio waves 1,000 megahertz and up, which can travel fairly long distances

minicam
a small, lightweight television camera generally used in remote locations to cover news events

MNA
Multi-Network Area Report published by A. C. Nielsen Co.

modulate
to vary the amplitude or frequency of one wave by placing another on it

monitor
to listen to something without interrupting it; also a device for seeing a TV picture directly from the video output

MSA
Metropolitan Survey Area

multiple system owner
a company which owns several cable TV operations

multiplex
to transmit two or more messages at the same time on a single channel

multiplexer
a set of mirrors within a film chain which direct the selected image to the film chain's TV camera

music licensing
paying for the use of music by giving a set fee to a company which then distributes the revenue according to the popularity of the music

n

NAB
National Association of Broadcasters

NABET
National Association of Broadcast Employees and Technicians

NAD
National Advertising Division (of the Council of Better Business Bureaus)

NAEB
National Association of Educational Broadcasters

NARB
National Advertising Review Board

NATPE
National Association of Television Program Executives

NBC
National Broadcasting Company

network feed
a program or other information coming over wires from a network to a station, sometimes at a time other than when the station plans to air it

NPR
National Public Radio

NTI
Nielsen Television Index

NTSC
National Television System Committee

o

omnidirectional
not favoring any one direction; used to refer to a microphone that picks up on all sides

oscilloscope
a mechanism which makes visible instantaneous values of scanned in-

formation and may or may not produce a permanent record

output
the current, voltage, or power coming out of a component of an electronic system, usually by means of a connector

overnights
ratings which are known the day after they are taken

owned
a station whose financial control and programming are both supplied by a network

p

PACT
Public Access Cable TV

pay cable
a joining of cable TV and subscription TV whereby subscribers pay for special programs which they then can see commercial-free over a cable TV channel

payola
the practice of paying disc jockeys "under the table" to plug certain records in the hope that sales would be increased

pay TV
a method by which people pay in order to receive television programming free of commercials

PBS
Public Broadcasting Service

pedestal
a mechanism on which a camera can be placed permitting the camera to be raised or lowered, usually by hydraulic or pneumatic means

PGA
Producers Guild of America

phosphor
a layer of material on the inner face of a TV tube which fluoresces when bombarded by electrons

photosensitive surface
an area capable of emitting electrons when it is hit by light

pilot
film or tape of a single program of a proposed series which is prepared in

order to obtain acceptance and commercial support

pirate ships
ships anchored off the coast of England which broadcast rock and roll music to the British people because the BBC was not broadcasting it

plate current
the electron flow inside an electron tube from the cathode to the plate

plate voltage
the voltage which exists in a tube between the cathode and the plate

play list
a radio station's listing of the musical selections it has aired over a set period of time

plumbicon
an improved vidicon tube with a lead-oxide target that cuts down on image retention or lag

potentiometer or **"pot"**
an electromechanical device which varies resistance in a circuit and therefore increases and decreases loudness

power deviation
the degree to which the actual power of a transmitter differs from the FCC-assigned power

preamplifier
an amplifier which raises a low-level source so that its signal may be further processed

preemption
removing a program from the air temporarily in order to broadcast a special event or another program

pressure groups
organizations that try to change television organization or programming, sometimes by challenging license renewals

prime time
the time of day when most people are tuned to broadcasting, generally driving time for radio and evening hours for TV

prime-time access
an FCC ruling which declared that stations should program their own material rather than network fare one hour during prime time

prism
a transparent glass with shape and properties that allow it to refract white light into its "rainbow" of colors

producer
the person in charge of a particular program or series who oversees such things as the budget, personnel, and facilities

profit and loss statement
a bookkeeping form which shows the amount of income and expenses of a company and whether the company has made or lost money

projected TV
a TV picture seen on a large screen

q

quadraphonic
sound reproduction using four channels through four separate speakers to blend separate sounds

r

RADAR
Radio All-Dimension Audience Research

radio frequency
the portion of the electromagnetic spectrum from about 30 kilohertz to 300,000 megahertz

radio waves
the waves of the radio frequency band of the electromagnetic spectrum

random sampling
a method of selection whereby each unit has the same chance of being selected as any other unit

rate card
a listing of the prices a station charges for advertisements at different times of the day and under different circumstances

rating
the percentage of people who are watching or listening to a particular station

RCA
Radio Corporation of America

recall
an audience measurement method by which people are asked what they have watched or heard in the past

receiver
the part of a communication system that converts electric waves into visible or audible form

reflection
the phenomenon of a wave striking an object of some type and being bounced back

residuals
payments made to those involved in a production when the program is rerun

resolution
the degree to which fineness of detail can be distinguished

retransmit
to feed the output of a transmitter on to another receiver or transmitter

ribbon mike
a microphone in which the conductor of electricity is a metallic ribbon driven by the speed of the sound waves

roster-recall
an audience measurement method in which people are asked what they have watched or heard in the past; if they cannot remember, they are shown call letters and slogans to assist recall

RPM
revolutions per minute; generally refers to the number of times a record turns in a minute

run-of-the-schedule
a method of selling time whereby the advertiser pays the station's lowest rate and the station schedules the ad at the best available time

S

SAG
Screen Actors Guild

sample
a part that is representative of a whole

scan
to examine the density of an area point by point and convert that information into an electronic code which can later recreate the density

season
the period of time from the start of one block of programs to the start of another block of new and rescheduled programs

Section 315
the portion of the Communications Act that states that political candidates for the same office must be given equal treatment

SESAC
Society of European Stage Artists and Composers

shader
a person who adjusts remote controls for cameras in order to keep color and other electronic elements consistent

share
the percentage of households watching a particular program in relation to all programs available at that time

single-system
a method of filming whereby both picture and sound are recorded on the film at the same time

siphon
a process whereby pay TV systems might drain programming from networks by paying a higher price for it initially

slander
false statements harmful to a person's character or reputation

slant track
another name for helical recording

solid state sensors
devices that convert mechanical energy into an electrical signal without the use of moving parts

special effects generator
a piece of TV equipment often incorporated within the switcher which enables pictures to form wipes, stars, squares, cutouts, and other patterns and effects

spectacular
an early term for what is now known as a special

spectrum
see "electromagnetic spectrum"

spot
a commercial inserted in or between programs

stage manager
another name for a floor manager

static
noise caused by weather and electrical charges in the atmosphere

station representative
a company which sells time for a number of stations

stereo or **stereophonic**
sound reproduction using two channels through two separate speakers to give more feeling of reality

story board
a chart that contains step-by-step pictorialization of a commercial or program

story line
a basic idea of a plot in summary form

strike
to tear down and clean up a set

stringer
a person who gathers news information and is paid only for the material used

strip
the airing of programs on a daily basis at the same time each day

stylus
a device which picks up a signal from a phonograph record

sub-audio
sounds that have a lower frequency than can be heard by the human ear

subscription TV
another name for pay TV

sustaining
a regularly aired program without commercials

sweeps
audience measurement reports which encompass the entire country

switcher
a piece of equipment which changes the TV picture going out over the air or going to a videotape recorder

sync
the precise matching of electron beams

sync generator
the piece of equipment which assures that all TV cameras will be scanning at the same place at the same time

synchronous satellite
a satellite that travels in orbit at such a rate that it appears to hang stationary above the earth

syndicate
to sell a radio or TV program outside the network structure to a number of different stations

take
changing the on-air television picture quickly

target
the portion of a TV camera tube which is scanned by the electron beam

technical director
the person who operates the switcher during production and oversees the technical crew

teletype
a form of telegraph where the striking of keys on a keyboard produces electrical impulses that cause corresponding keys on an instrument at a distant point to type

testimonial
a type of commercial in which a person states the value a certain product has had for him or her

time
the broadcast space which a commercial occupies

time bank
an advertising practice whereby an advertiser supplies a program in exchange for specified advertising time

time period measurement
an audience measurement calculation indicating the percentage of households which tune in a station during a certain period, such as a half-hour

"toll" station
a name for the type of programming WEAF initiated in 1922, which allowed anyone to broadcast a public message by paying a fee, in the same way that one pays a toll to communicate a private message by telephone

toll TV
another name for pay TV

top 40
a radio station format that involves playing the most popular forty songs repeatedly

traffic
the department of a TV or radio station which handles the log and schedules commercials

transmitter
a piece of equipment which generates and amplifies a carrier wave and modulates it with information which can be radiated into space

transverse quadraplex
a type of videotape recorder which uses 2″ tape and places the signal on the tape vertically

tripod
a three-legged structure on which a camera can be placed

TSA
Total Survey Area

tuner
the portion of a receiver that can select frequencies

turret
a round plate in front of a camera holding several lenses, each of which can be rotated into a "taking" position

UHF
ultra high frequency; the area in the spectrum between 300 and 3,000 megahertz

ultraviolet rays
electromagnetic radiations with wavelengths beyond the visible violet end of the spectrum, in the vicinity of 10^{11} megahertz

underwrite
to finance an undertaking such as a TV show

unidirectional
picking up on one side; used to refer to microphones with only one live side

union
an organization that represents the welfare and interests of workers to management

unit manager
a person responsible for facilities for a particular show or shows

universe
a total number from which a sample is selected

UPI
United Press International

vacuum tube
an electron tube evacuated of air to the extent that its electrical characteristics are unaffected by the remaining air

vaudeville
a stage show which presented a variety of performers whose acts had no necessary connection with each other

VHF
very high frequency; the area in the spectrum between 30 and 300 megahertz

video art
the product of utilizing video equipment like a paintbrush to create an aesthetic or personal experience

video synthesizer
a device usually used for video art which creates effects such as adding color

vidicon
a camera tube in which an electron beam scans the surface of a photoconductor

viewfinder
a monitor on a TV camera that allows the camera operator to see the picture which the camera is shooting

VOA
Voice of America

VTR
videotape recorder

VU meter
volume unit meter, a device which measures the power level of an audio wave and therefore indicates the volume of the sound

wavelength
the distance between points of corresponding phase in electromagnetic waves

WGA
Writers Guild of America

wireless
any apparatus which transmits messages by means of radio frequencies rather than devices connected to each other by wires

wire recording
an early form of magnetic recording that used wire rather than tape

wire service
an organization that supplies news to stations by use of teletype

X

X rays
penetrating radiation similar to light with wavelengths in the vicinity of 10^{13} megahertz

Z

zoom lens
a lens with a variable focal length, which allows a TV camera to frame more or less of a scene without the camera being moved

Notes

1 In the Beginning: A History of Radio

1. For a more detailed account of Maxwell, see Orrin E. Dunlap, Jr., *Radio's 100 Men of Science* (New York: Harper and Brothers Publishers, 1944), pp. 65-68.

2. For a more detailed account of Hertz, see ibid., pp. 113-117.

3. For a more detailed account of Marconi, see Degna Marconi, *My Father Marconi* (New York: McGraw-Hill, 1962).

4. For a more detailed account of Fleming, see Dunlap, *Radio's 100 Men,* pp. 90-94.

5. For a more detailed account of Fessenden, see Helen M. Fessenden, *Fessenden: Builder of Tomorrows* (New York: Coward-McCann, 1940).

6. For a more detailed account of De Forest, see Lee De Forest, *Father of Radio: the Auto-biography of Lee De Forest* (Chicago: Wilcox and Follett, 1950).

7. Erik Barnouw, *A Tower in Babel: A History of Broadcasting in the United States to 1933* (New York: Oxford University Press, 1966), pp. 57-61.

8. For a more detailed account of Sarnoff, see Eugene Lyon, *David Sarnoff: A Biography* (New York: Harper, 1966).

9. David Sarnoff, *Looking Ahead: the Papers of David Sarnoff* (New York: McGraw-Hill Book Company, 1968), pp. 31-33.

10. Barnouw, *Tower in Babel,* pp. 39-41.

11. Ibid., pp. 61-64.

12. For a more detailed account of Conrad, see Dunlap, *Radio's 100 Men,* pp. 180-183.

13. Robert E. Summers and Harrison B. Summers, *Broadcasting and the Public* (Belmont, California: Wadsworth Publishing Company, 1966), p. 34.

14. Barnouw, *Tower in Babel,* p. 85.

15. Ibid., p. 86.

16. Ibid., p. 100.

17. Ibid., p. 102.

18. For a more detailed account of WEAF, see William Peck Banning, *Commercial Broadcasting Pioneer: The WEAF Experiment* (Cambridge, Massachusetts: Harvard University Press, 1946).

19. "The First 50 Years of NBC," *Broadcasting,* June 21, 1976, pp. 29-42.

20. For a critique of CBS, see Robert Metz, *CBS: Reflections in a Bloodshot Eye* (Chicago: Playboy Press, 1975) and "The Winning Ways of William S. Paley," *Broadcasting,* May 31, 1976, pp. 25-45.

21. It is difficult to find definitive summaries of ABC and Mutual. They are dealt with in various places in the Barnouw volumes, and the overall situation is delineated in the FCC *Report on Chain Broadcasting* (Washington, D.C.: Government Printing Office, 1941).

22. Summers and Summers, *Broadcasting and the Public,* p. 69.

23. Joan Huff Wilson, *Herbert Hoover: Forgotten Progressive* (Boston: Little, Brown, and Company, 1975), pp. 112-113.

24. Summers and Summers, *Broadcasting and the Public,* p. 26.

25. Ibid., pp. 45-50.

26. For a first-hand account of Amos 'n' Andy, see Charles J. Correll and Freeman F. Gosden, *All About Amos 'n' Andy* (New York: Rand McNally, 1929).

27. An excellent accounting of the history of radio programming was the TV program "The Good Old Days of Radio," aired by PBS March 19, 1976 and rerun several times thereafter. Also of excellent

value is an educational audiotape on early programming developed by KNX radio, Los Angeles. For books dealing with the subject, see Irving Settel, *A Pictorial History of Radio* (New York: Grossett and Dunlap, 1967), and Frank Buxton and Bill Owen, *The Big Broadcast 1920-1950* (New York: Viking, 1972).

28. Erik Barnouw, *The Golden Web: A History of Broadcasting in the United States 1933-1953* (New York: Oxford University Press, 1968), pp. 8-18.

29. Giraud Chester, Garnet R. Garrison, and Edgar E. Willis, *Television and Radio* (New York: Appleton-Century-Crofts, 1971), p. 35.

30. "Genesis of Radio News: the Press-Radio War," *Broadcasting,* January 5, 1976, p. 95.

31. For a more detailed account of radio during World War II, see Paul White, *News on the Air* (New York: Harcourt, Brace, 1947).

32. Barnouw, *Golden Web,* p. 46.

33. Summers and Summers, *Broadcasting and the Public,* p. 46.

34. For more insight into the rise of d.j.s, see Arnold Passman, *The DJ's* (New York: Macmillan, 1971).

35. Summers and Summers, *Broadcasting and the Public,* p. 70.

36. Ward L. Quaal and James A. Brown, *Broadcast Management* (New York: Hastings House, 1976), p. 292.

37. For a more detailed account of Armstrong, see Lawrence Lessing, *Man of High Fidelity: Edwin Howard Armstrong* (New York: Lippincott, 1956).

38. "FM Gets Closer to Going It Alone," *Broadcasting,* May 10, 1976, p. 40.

2 A Sound Look: Technical Aspects of Radio

1. General information regarding overall audio theory and equipment can be found in Lynne S. Gross, *Self-Instruction in Radio Production* (Los Alamitos, California: Hwong Publishing Company, 1976), pp. 38-116; Sydney W. Head, *Broadcasting in America* (Boston: Houghton Mifflin Company, 1976), pp. 21-44; and Robert L. Hilliard, *Radio Broadcasting* (New York: Hastings House Publishers, 1967), pp. 45-73. More technically oriented information can be gained from electronics books, such as Edward M. Noll, *First-Class Radiotelephone License Handbook* (Indianapolis, Indiana: Howard W. Sams and Company, 1974); John Pierce, *Electrons and Waves* (New York: Doubleday, 1964); and Monroe Upton, *Electronics for Everyone* (New York: Signet, 1962). Also of great value are equipment brochures produced by major audio manufacturers, such as Collins, Electrovoice, Fairchild, Gates, Harris, McMartin, QRK, RCA, Schafer, Scully, Shure, Sony, Spotmaster, Teac, and Vega.

2. For more information, see Alex Nisbett, *The Use of Microphones* (New York: Hastings House Publishers, 1975).

3. For more information, see Gross, *Self-Instruction,* pp. 63-72.

4. For more information, see *Recording Basics* (St. Paul, Minnesota: 3M Company, [n.d.]).

5. For more information, see Gross, *Self-Instruction,* pp. 94-104.

6. For more information, see G. A. Chapel, *Radio Stations: Installation, Design, and Practice* (Elmsford, New York: Pergamon Press, 1959).

7. For more information, see "Radio Automation Equipment—1974," *BM/E,* August, 1974, pp. 44-45.

8. For more information, see Milton Kiver, *FM Simplified* (Princeton, New Jersey: Van Nostrand, 1960).

9. For more information, see *The Radio Frequency Spectrum: United States Use and Management* (Washington, D.C.: Office of Telecommunication Policy, 1973).

10. For more information, see K. R. Sturley, *Radio Receiver Design* (New York: Barnes and Noble, 1965).

3 Telvolution: The Evolution of Television

1. The best overall chronicle of the history of television can be found in the three-volume history of broadcasting by Erik Barnouw published in New York by Oxford University Press. The titles and dates are: *A Tower in Babel: A History of Broadcasting in the United States to 1933* (1966); *The Golden Web: A History of Broadcasting in the United States 1933-1953* (1968); and *The Image Empire: A History of Broadcasting in the United States from 1953* (1970). This work will be cited as the major source of information because it gives the most back-up detail and because it is so scholarly and thoroughly researched through innumerable interviews, unpublished papers, and oral history collections as well as the more traditional books, articles, and documents. Barnouw has condensed and updated much of the television material into a one-volume book, *Tube of Plenty: The Development of American Television* (1975). Other, briefer histories of television can be found in many books, including Girard Chester, Garnet R. Garrison,

and Edgar E. Willis, "Chapter 3, The Rise of Television," *Television and Radio* (New York: Appleton-Century-Crofts, 1971); Sydney W. Head, "Chapter 10, History of Television," *Broadcasting in America* (Boston: Houghton Mifflin Company, 1976); Elizabeth J. Heighton and Don R. Cunningham, "Chapter 2, Broadcast Advertising Since 1946," *Advertising in the Broadcasting Media* (Belmont, California: Wadsworth Publishing Company, 1976); Don R. Pember, "Chapter 4, Media History, Part II," *Mass Media in America* (Chicago: Science Research Associates, 1974); and Bob Shanks, "Chapter 3, Networks: History and Structure," *The Cool Fire* (New York: W. W. Norton and Company, 1976).

2. Barnouw, *Tower in Babel*, pp. 210, 231. These early mechanical systems are best described in A. A. Dinsdale, *First Principles of Television* (New York: John Wiley, 1932).

3. Barnouw, *Golden Web*, pp. 42, 127, 145. See also "Portrait," *Business Week*, June 7, 1952, p. 106; and "Portrait," *Fortune*, February, 1954, p. 47.

4. Barnouw, *Tower in Babel*, p. 210, and *Golden Web*, pp. 39-40, 42, 283. See also George Everson, *The Story of Television: The Life of Philo T. Farnsworth* (New York: Norton, 1949).

5. Barnouw, *Tower in Babel*, pp. 66, 154, 210. For Zworykin's own view of the electronics of television, see Vladimir Zworykin, *Television: The Electronics of Image Transmission in Color and Monochrome* (New York: John Wiley, 1954).

6. Barnouw, *Golden Web*, p. 126.

7. Ibid., pp. 126-130.

8. Ibid., pp. 242-244; Girard Chester, Garnet R. Garrison, and Edgar E. Willis, *Television and Radio* (New York: Appleton-Century-Crofts, 1971), pp. 43-44; and Sydney W. Head, *Broadcasting in America* (Boston: Houghton Mifflin Company, 1976), pp. 161-162.

9. See footnotes 19, 20, and 21 of chapter 1, "A History of Radio."

10. Barnouw, *Golden Web*, pp. 285-290; Head, *Broadcasting in America*, pp. 162-165; Heighton and Cunningham, *Advertising*, pp. 26-28; and Summers and Summers, *Broadcasting and the Public*, pp. 75, 88.

11. A large number of excellent, highly pictorial works have been published which deal with TV programming through the years. These include: Linda Beech, *TV Favorites* (New York: Scholastic Book Services, 1971); *Emmy's Twentieth Anniversary Album* (New York: The National Academy of Television Arts and Sciences, 1968); Arthur Schulman and Roger Youman, *How Sweet It Was: Television: A Pictorial Commentary* (New York: Bonanza Books, 1966); Arthur Schulman and Roger Youman, *The Television Years* (New York: Popular Library, 1973); and "A Special Issue on Television, Past, Present, and Future," *Saturday Evening Post*, November 30, 1968, pp. 12-84. Each year's "Fall Preview" issue of *TV Guide* is also valuable for information on programming. Also of great value was NBC's TV special "The First 50 Years," which aired 7:00 to 11:30 p.m., November 21, 1976.

12. Barnouw, *Golden Web*, p. 295; Head, *Broadcasting in America*, pp. 165-167; and Heighton and Cunningham, *Advertising*, pp. 28-29.

13. Most of this information was gained from a 1976 interview with True Boardman, one of the writers blacklisted during the '50s. Two sources interesting to peruse from a historical point of view are John Cogley, *Report on Blacklisting* (Washington, D.C.: The Fund for the Republic, 1956), and Red Channels: The Report of Communists in Radio and Television (New York: Counterattack, 1950).

14. Barnouw, *Image Empire*, pp. 22-23.

15. See note 11.

16. Barnouw, *Image Empire*, pp. 58-61.

17. See note 11.

18. Issues of *Broadcasting* and *Variety* of this era attest to the great confusion surrounding this issue.

19. See note 11.

20. Barnouw, *Image Empire*, pp. 122-129. Some of the more interesting articles written at the time are: "Dress Rehearsals Complete With Answers?" *U.S. News*, October 19, 1959, pp. 60-62; "Is It Just TV or Most of Us?" *New York Times Magazine*, November 15, 1959, p. 15+; "Out of the Backwash of the TV Scandals," *Newsweek*, November 16, 1959, pp. 66-68; "Quiz Probe May Change TV," *Business Week*, November 7, 1959, pp. 28-30; "Tarnished Image," *Time*, November 16, 1959, pp. 72-74+; and "Van Doren on Van Doren," *Newsweek*, November 9, 1959, pp. 69-70.

21. See note 11.

22. Barnouw, *Image Empire*, pp. 160-170; P. M. Stern, "Debates in Retrospect," *New Republic*, November 21, 1960, pp. 18-19; and "TV Debate Backstage: Did the Cameras Lie?" *Newsweek*, October 10, 1960, p. 25.

23. Ward, L. Quaal and James A. Brown, *Broadcast Management* (New York: Hastings House, 1976), pp. 400-403.

24. "Covering the Tragedy: President Kennedy's Assassination," *Time*, November 29,

1963, p. 84; "Did Press Pressure Kill Oswald?" *U.S. News,* April 6, 1964, pp. 78-79; "President's Rites Viewed Throughout the World," *Science Newsletter,* December 7, 1963, p. 355; and J. H. Winchester, "TV's Four Days of History," *Readers Digest,* April, 1964, pp. 204I-204J +.

25. For Friendly's analysis of this whole situation, see Fred Friendly, *Due to Circumstances Beyond Our Control . . .* (New York: Random House, 1967).

26. For more information on TV's relationship to Vietnam, see Michael J. Arlen, *Living Room War* (New York: The Viking Press, 1969).

27. Barnouw, *Image Empire,* p. 197.

28. See note 11.

29. Barnouw, *Image Empire,* pp. 251-252.

30. Heighton and Cunningham, *Advertising,* pp. 268-271.

31. Head, *Broadcasting in America,* pp. 215-218.

32. "'Family Hour' OK But Not by Coercion," *Variety,* November 5, 1976, p. 1 +.

33. See note 11.

4 How Pictures Fly Through the Air: Technical Aspects of TV

1. General information regarding overall television theory and equipment can be found in Alan Bermingham, *The Small TV Studio: Equipment and Facilities* (New York: Hastings House, 1975); Larry G. Goodwin and Thomas Koehring, *Closed-Circuit Television Production Techniques* (Indianapolis, Indiana: Howard W. Sams, 1970); John Quick and Herbert Wolff, *Small Studio Video Tape Production* (Reading, Massachusetts: Addison-Wesley Publishing Company, 1976); and Herbert Zettl, *Television Production Handbook* (Belmont, California: Wadsworth Publishing Company, 1976). More technically oriented information can be gained from electronics books such as Len Buckwalter, *Television: How It Works* (New Augusta, Indiana: Editors and Engineers, 1967); Donald G. Fink and David M. Lutyens, *The Physics of Television* (Garden City, New York: Anchor Books, 1960); Milton Sol Kiver and Milton Kaufman, *Television Simplified* (New York: Van Nostrand Reinhold, 1973); and George Shiers, *The Technical Development of Television* (New York: Arno Press, 1976).

2. For additional information, see equipment brochures produced by lens manufacturers, such as Angenieux and Canon.

3. For additional information, see equipment brochures produced by camera manufacturers, such as Akai, Ampex, Concord, Hitachi-Shibaden, International Video Corporation, Panasonic, Philips-Norelco, RCA, Sony, and Telemation.

4. For additional information, see equipment brochures produced by mounting gear manufacturers, such as Davis and Sanford and Quik-Set.

5. For additional information, see equipment brochures produced by film camera, projector, and editor manufacturers, such as Bell and Howell, Bolex, Eastman Kodak, and Moviola.

6. For additional information, see equipment brochures produced by film chain manufacturers, such as International Video Corporation, Philips-Norelco, and RCA.

7. For additional information, see equipment brochures produced by sync generator and test equipment manufacturers, such as Cohu, Grass Valley, Tektronix, and Telemation.

8. For additional information, see equipment brochures produced by monitor manufacturers, such as Conrac, Magnavox, Panasonic, Setchell-Carlson, Sharp, and Sony.

9. For additional information, see equipment brochures produced by switcher manufacturers, such as Alma, Ball Brothers, Cohu, Dynair, and Grass Valley.

10. For additional information, see chapter 8, "The Television Studio and Control Center" of Zettl, *Television Production Handbook,* pp. 187-210.

11. For additional information, see equipment brochures produced by videotape recorder and videotape manufacturers, such as Ampex, Concord, International Video Corporation, JVC, Memorex, Panasonic, RCA, Shibaden, Sony, and 3M.

12. For additional information, see equipment brochures produced by portable equipment manufacturers, such as Ampex, Ikegami, JVC, Philips-Norelco, Sony, and Thomson-CSF.

13. For additional information, see equipment brochures produced by companies manufacturing transmission equipment, such as Boston Insulated Wire and Cable Company, Collins, Gates, Harris, and Microwave Associates.

14. For additional information, see equipment brochures produced by TV receiver manufacturers, such as General Electric, Magnavox, Motorola, Panasonic, RCA, and Sony.

5 The Escape Machine: Entertainment Programming

1. "Average TV B'cast Day As Seen by the FCC," *Variety,* July 5, 1977, p. 1.

2. Many books and articles which deal in general with television programming were used heavily

in compiling this and the following chapters. Some programming areas have large bibliographies covering specific material. When this is the case, particular sources will be cited. Otherwise, additional information on any type of programming can usually be found in Linda Beech, *TV Favorites* (New York: Scholastic Book Services, 1971); Frank Buxton and Bill Owen, *The Big Broadcast, 1920-1950* (New York: Viking Press, 1972); Barry G. Cole, *Television* (New York: The Free Press, 1970); "Fall Preview," *TV Guide,* September 8, 1973, pp. 7-72; "Fall Preview," *TV Guide,* September 7, 1974, pp. 4-74; "Fall Preview," *TV Guide,* September 6, 1975, pp. 7-74; Peggy Hudson, *TV Today* (New York: Scholastic Book Services, 1969); Horace Newcomb, *TV the Most Popular Art* (New York: Anchor Books, 1974); Eugene Paul, *The Hungry Eye* (New York: Ballantine Books, 1962); Tony Schwartz, *The Responsive Chord* (Garden City, New York: Anchor Books, 1974); Arthur Schulman and Roger Youman, *How Sweet It Was: Television: A Pictorial Commentary* (New York: Bonanza Books, 1966); Arthur Schulman and Roger Youman, *The Television Years* (New York: Popular Library, 1973); "A Special Issue on Television Past, Present, and Future," *Saturday Evening Post,* November 30, 1968, pp. 12-84; and "TV's Fall Season," *Newsweek,* September 8, 1975, pp. 44-48.

3. Schwartz, *Responsive Chord,* p. 52.

4. Interview with Sterrett Neale, Broadcast Music Inc., 1975.

5. Specific references on drama include "After Haley's Comet," *Newsweek,* February 14, 1977, p. 97; Dave Kaufman, "10 Best Programs in Television's History," *Variety,* 43rd Anniversary Issue, pp. 148, 185; Saul N. Scher,

"Anthology Drama: TV's Inconsistent Art Form," *Television Quarterly,* Winter, 1976-77, pp. 29-34; and Louis Solomon, *The TV Doctors* (New York: Scholastic Book Services, 1974).

6. Eli A. Rubinstein, "The TV Violence Report: What Next?" *Journal of Communication,* Winter, 1974, pp. 34-40.

7. George Gerbner and Larry Gross, "Scary World of TV's Heavy Viewer," *Psychology Today,* April, 1976, pp. 41-45 +; "More Violence Than Ever Says Gerbner's Latest," *Broadcasting,* February 28, 1977, p. 20; and "Schneider Attacks Gerbner's Report on TV Violence," *Broadcasting,* May 2, 1977, p. 57.

8. Max Gunther, "All That TV Violence: Why Do We Love/Hate It?" *TV Guide,* November 6, 1976, pp. 6-10.

9. Statistical studies on violence include: Seymour Feshbach and Robert D. Singer, *Television and Aggression: An Experimental Field Study* (San Francisco: Jossey-Bass, 1970); Melvin S. Heller and Samuel Polsky, *Studies in Violence and Television* (New York: American Broadcasting Company, 1976); "Good and Bad in TV Violence," *Variety,* February 23, 1977, p. 1; and Murray Feingold and G. Timothy Johnson, "Television Violence—Reactions from Physicians, Advertisers, and the Network," *The New England Journal of Medicine,* February 24, 1977, special article.

10. Other material dealing with violence includes: "A Blizzard of Paper on Violence," *Broadcasting,* May 16, 1977, pp. 22-24; "PTA Ends Hearings on TV Violence But Issue Lingers," *Broadcasting,* February 28, 1977, p. 21; Harriet Steinberg, "Must Night Fall So Hard?" *Television Quarterly,* Winter, 1976-77,

pp. 49-51; Lee Strobing, "And Now, 'The Family That Screams Together . . ,'" *Television Quarterly,* Winter, 1976-77, pp. 61-64; and "Top Prime-Time Advertisers Reject AMA's TViolence Rx; Baretta Takes Gloves Off," *Variety,* March 4, 1977, pp. 1, 6.

11. For additional information on situation comedies, see Kaufman, "10 Best Programs," pp. 148, 185; and Larry Wilde, "The Genesis of Comedy," *Television Quarterly,* Winter, 1976-77, p. 70.

12. For additional information on variety shows, see Shulman and Youman, *How Sweet It Was,* passim.

13. For additional information on specials, see "Stay Tuned for Ten Great TV Events," *Saturday Evening Post,* September, 1976, p. 39; and "Silverman Has a Surprise for the Competition," *Broadcasting,* December 5, 1977, pp. 24-25.

14. For additional information on movies for TV, see Tom Allen, "TV: Father of the Film," *America,* October 30, 1976, pp. 286-288; and Saul Kaufman, "Films: TV Versions of Moving Pictures," *New Republic,* August 30, 1975, pp. 20 +.

15. For additional information on talk shows, see Dwight Whitney, "Is the Talk Show an Endangered Species?" *TV Guide,* July 30, 1977, pp. 2-6; and Michael J. Arlen, "Host and Guests: Hospitality on Talk Shows," *New Yorker,* January 3, 1977, pp. 62-65.

16. For additional information on game shows, see Arleen Francis, "I Was There from First to Last: What's My Line," *Saturday Evening Post,* September, 1976, p. 43, and "Dress Rehearsals Complete with Answers?" *U.S. News,* October 19, 1959, pp. 60-62.

17. For additional information on soap operas, see Lenore Silvian,

"Spinoffs from Soapland," *Television Quarterly,* Winter, 1976-77, pp. 37-21; "Love of Lunch," *TV Guide,* May 22, 1976, pp. 10-11; and "Sex and Suffering in the Afternoon," *Time,* January 12, 1976, pp. 46-53.

18. Some of the major studies concerning children and TV are John D. Abel and Maureen E. Beninson, "Perception of TV Program Violence by Children and Mothers," *Journal of Broadcasting,* Spring, 1976, pp. 335-364; George Comstock, *Effects of Television on Children: What's the Evidence?* (Santa Monica, California: Rand Corporation, 1975); Gerald S. Lesser, *Children and Television: Lessons from Sesame Street* (New York: Random House, 1974); *Learning While They Laugh: Studies of Five Children's Programs on the CBS Television Network* (New York: Columbia Broadcasting System, 1977); Mark M. Miller and Byron Reeves, "Dramatic Content and Children's Sex-Role Stereotypes," *Journal of Broadcasting,* Winter, 1976, pp. 35-50; and "What TV Does to Kids," *Newsweek,* February 21, 1977, pp. 63-70.

19. Other material dealing with children's television includes Douglas Cater and Stephen Strickland, *TV Violence and the Child: The Evolution and Fate of the Surgeon General's Report* (Palo Alto, California: Aspen Series on Communication and Society, 1975); James D. Culley, William Lazer, and Charles K. Atkin, "The Experts Look at Children's Television," *Journal of Broadcasting,* Winter, 1976, pp. 3-22; "The Ferment in Television for Children," *Broadcasting,* June 30, 1975, pp. 41-50; Hilde Himmelweit, *Television and the Child* (New York: Television Information Office, 1961); Robert M. Liebert, *The Early Window* (New York: Pergamon Press, 1973); William Melody, *Children's Television: The*

Economics of Exploitation (New Haven, Connecticut: Yale University Press, 1975); Fred Rogers, *Mister Rogers Talks About . . .* (Bronx, New York: Platt and Munk, 1974); and Marie Winn, *The Plug-In Drug* (New York: Viking, 1975).

6 A Mirror of the World? Informational Programming

1. *Changing Public Attitudes Toward Television and Other Mass Media, 1956-1976* (New York: Television Information Office, 1977), passim.

2. See note 2, chapter 5.

3. For more information on news sources, see Irving E. Fang, *Television News* (New York: Hastings House, 1972), and "Television Today: The State of the Art," *TV Guide,* February 19, 1977, pp. 6-11.

4. For more information, see Eric Levin, "Anatomy of a Newscast," *TV Guide,* February 28, 1976, pp. 4-8; Eric Levin, "How the Networks Decide What Is News," *TV Guide,* July 2, 1977, pp. 6-11; and Maury Green, *Television News: Anatomy and Process* (Belmont, California: Wadsworth Publishing Company, 1968).

5. "News Turns Into Net Money-Maker; Kidvid Profits Off," *Variety,* April 27, 1977, pp. 1 and 8.

6. For more on this controversy, see "Opposite Views on TV Objectivity," *Broadcasting,* March 29, 1976, p. 61; "The First Amendment and the Fifth Estate," *Broadcasting,* January 5, 1976, pp. 45-101; Edward Jay Epstein, "The Values of Newsmen," *Television Quarterly,* Winter, 1973, pp. 9-20; Edith Efron, *The News Twisters* (Los Angeles: Nash, 1971); and Joseph Keeley, *The Left Leaning Antenna: Political Bias in*

Television (New Rochelle, New York: Arlington House, 1971).

7. For additional information, see Fred W. Friendly, *Due to Circumstances Beyond Our Control* (New York: Random House, 1967).

8. Other materials about news include Harry J. Skornia, *Television and the News* (Palo Alto, California: Pacifica Books, 1968); and David J. LeRoy and Christopher H. Sterling, *Mass News: Practices, Controversies, and Alternatives* (Englewood Cliffs, New Jersey: Prentice-Hall, 1973).

9. For more information about documentary programs, see A. William Bluem, *Documentary in American Television* (New York: Hastings House, 1965), and Ted C. Smythe and George A. Mastroianni, *Issues in Broadcasting* (Palo Alto, California: Mayfield Publishing Company, 1975).

10. For more information on editorials, see L. S. Feuer, "Why Not a Commentary on Sevareid?" *New Republic,* August 15, 1975, pp. 874-876; Karl E. Meyer, "Uncommon Commentary of ABC's Howard K. Smith," *Saturday Review,* December 11, 1976, p. 82; and *Legal Guide to FCC Broadcast Rules, Regulations, and Policies* (Washington, D.C.: National Association of Broadcasters, 1977).

11. "Olympic Group Rejects CBS and NBC Claims, Says Network Bidding for Games Was Fair," *Broadcasting,* May 24, 1976, p. 54; "Football Rights Rise Slightly to $82.5 Million But Get Set to Soar in '78," *Broadcasting,* August 1, 1977, pp. 47-50; Don Kowet, "The Great TV Sports Hype," *TV Guide,* October 22, 1977, pp. 28-32; and Don Kowet, "Playing for Blood," *TV Guide,* October 15, 1977, pp. 4-8.

12. Kowet, "Great TV Sports Hype," passim.

13. William Leggett, "They've Boxed Themselves In," *Sports Illustrated*, September 19, 1977, p. 68.

14. Stanley Frank, "What TV Has Done to Sports," *TV Guide*, February 4, 1967, pp. 4-8.

15. Melissa Ludtke, "Big Scorers in the Ad Game," *Sports Illustrated*, November 7, 1977, p. 50.

16. "Struck by Sabres, WKBW-TV Blames It on Pay Cable Rule," *Broadcasting*, March 24, 1976, p. 55.

17. For additional information on educational programming, see "How Television Tries to Close the Health Information Gap," *Today's Health*, January, 1976, pp. 30-33 +; and "TV and Political Knowledge for Elementary School Pupils," *Intellect*, January, 1976, pp. 284-285.

18. For more information on religious programming, see William A. Bleum, *Religious Television Programs* (New York: Hastings House, 1968); and "Getting Time on the Tube," *Christianity Today*, May 7, 1976, pp. 27-28.

19. For more information, see Frank Wolf, *Television Programming for News and Public Affairs: A Quantitative Analysis of Networks and Stations* (New York: Praeger, 1972), and William A. Bilson, *The Impact of Television* (Hamden, Connecticut: Archon Books, 1967).

20. Neil Hickey, "Equal Time," *TV Guide*, May 22, 1976, pp. 12-16, and "Section 315: Be Prepared," *Broadcasting*, March 29, 1976, p. 44. For further discussion, see chapter 8, The Tenuous Relationship: Broadcasting and Government.

21. Lee M. Mitchell, *Presidential Television* (New York: Basic Books, 1973), and Joe McGinnis, *The Selling of a President, 1968* (New York: Trident Press, 1969).

22. Howard McMillen, "Portrait of a Candidate—in the Age of Television," *TV Guide*, January 18, 1975, pp. 2-6.

23. "NBC Forum Was the Mill: Politics and the Media Were the Grist," *Broadcasting*, March 14, 1977, pp. 40-50.

24. Elmer Lower, "Primer for an Election Year," *Television Quarterly*, Special Election Issue, 1976, pp. 5-13.

7 Time on Our Hands: Programming Decisions

1. These are major formats listed in *Broadcasting Yearbook 1975* (Washington, D.C.: Broadcasting Publications, 1975), pp. D-63-D-81.

2. These are major categories of special radio programming listed in *Broadcasting Yearbook 1975*, pp. D-81-D-88.

3. Ibid., p. A-2.

4. Much of the information for this section resulted from interviews with Joe Keane, former program director for Channel 9, KHJ-TV, Los Angeles, California, 1976.

5. *Broadcasting Yearbook 1975*, p. A-2.

6. More detail can be gleaned from studying one of the network-affiliate contracts.

7. Much of the information for this section resulted from interviews with Howard Sturm, manager of public affairs for Channel 4, KNBC, Los Angeles, California, 1976, and Kaslon Zollar, production manager for Channel 7, KABC, Los Angeles, California, 1976.

8. For more information, see Richard Warren Lewis, "The Man on the 34th Floor," in Barry G. Cole, *Television* (New York: Free Press, 1970), pp. 127-134.

9. The following is based on the budget worksheets of ABC, Los Angeles, California, 1976, and of Channel 9, KHJ-TV, Los Angeles, California, 1975.

10. Richard K. Doan, "Why Shows are Cancelled," in Cole, *Television*, pp. 122-126.

11. Bill Davidson, "Those Reruns: The Facts Behind the Complaints," *TV Guide*, June 9, 1973, pp. 10-14.

8 The Tenuous Relationship: Broadcasting and Government

1. Two sources from the FCC which give general information about its organization are *What You Should Know About the FCC* (Washington, D.C.: FCC Information Bulletin, 1975); and *Letter to a Schoolboy* (Washington, D.C.: FCC Information Bulletin, 1975).

2. "Worsening Jam in CB Radio Swamps FCC," *Broadcasting*, January 19, 1976, p. 30.

3. The FCC booklet to use for passing the third-class license test is entitled *Broadcast Operator Handbook: Radiotelephone 3rd Class Operators' Permit, Broadcast Endorsement* and can be purchased from the U.S. Government Printing Office, Washington, D.C. 20402. One of the many sources for material covering the first-class license test is: Edward M. Noll, *First-Class Radiotelephone License Handbook*, 4th ed. (Indianapolis, Indiana: Howard W. Sams, 1975).

4. *Station Identification and Call Signs* (Washington, D.C.: FCC Information Bulletin, 1972), passim.

5. More information can be found in *How To Apply for a Broad-*

cast Station (Washington, D.C.: FCC Information Bulletin, 1974).

6. "The Divestiture Debate," *Newsweek,* March 14, 1977, p. 43.

7. *Public Law No. 416, June 19, 1934, 73rd Congress* (Washington, D.C.: Government Printing Office, 1934), Section 326.

8. Ibid., Section 307(a).

9. Giraud Chester, Garnet R. Garrison, and Edgar E. Willis, *Television and Radio* (New York: Appleton-Century-Crofts, 1971), pp. 133-136.

10. *How To Apply for a Broadcast Station,* passim.

11. Don R. Pember, *Mass Media in America* (Chicago: Science Research Associates, 1974), p. 283.

12. "The Next Best Thing to Renewal Legislation," *Broadcasting,* January 10, 1977, p. 20.

13. Sydney W. Head, *Broadcasting in America* (Boston: Houghton-Mifflin, 1976), p. 366.

14. Interview with Tracy Weston, Executive Director of the Communications Law Program at the University of California at Los Angeles, 1977.

15. *Your Federal Trade Commission: What It Is and What It Does* (Washington, D.C.: The Federal Trade Commission, 1971), p. 5.

16. The entire booklet listed in footnote 15 is excellent for an overview of the FTC.

17. "From Fighting Bob to the Fairness Doctrine," *Broadcasting,* January 5, 1976, p. 46.

18. More information regarding editorializing cases can be found in "From Fighting Bob to the Fairness Doctrine," and William L. Rivers, Theodore Peterson, and Jay W. Jensen, *The Mass Media and Modern Society* (San Francisco:

Rinehart Press, 1971), pp. 228-229.

19. *Public Law No. 416,* Section 315.

20. Some of the more interesting material on Section 315 includes "From Fighting Bob to the Fairness Doctrine" and also "Section 315: Be Prepared," *Broadcasting,* March 29, 1976, p. 44.

21. "From Fighting Bob to the Fairness Doctrine," p. 48.

22. More regarding the fairness doctrine can be found in David Schoenbrun, "Is Perfect Fairness Possible?" *Television Quarterly,* Special Election Issue, 1976, pp. 77-79; "From Fighting Bob to the Fairness Doctrine"; and Pember, *Mass Media in America,* pp. 283-286.

23. Interview with True Boardman, one of the original members of AFRS, 1977.

24. *Broadcasting Yearbook, 1975* (Washington, D.C.: Broadcasting Publications, Inc., 1975), p. F-33.

25. "Percy Amendment to Spin Off VOA 'Watered Down' in Mark-Up Session," *Broadcasting,* May 16, 1977, p. 38.

26. Insightful books and articles dealing with the pros and cons of government regulation are: John C. Busterna, "Division of Ownership as a Criterion in FCC Licensing Since 1965," *Journal of Broadcasting,* Winter 1976, pp. 101-110; Walter P. Emery, *Broadcasting and Government: Responsibilities and Regulations* (East Lansing: Michigan State University Press, 1971); Edwin G. Krasnow and Lawrence D. Longley, *The Politics of Broadcast Regulation* (New York: St. Martin's Press, 1972); and William L. Rivers and Michael J. Nyhan, *Aspen Notebook on Government and the Media* (Palo Alto, California: Aspen Series on Communication and Society, 1973).

27. One such book is *NAB Legal Guide to FCC Broadcast Rules,*

Regulations, and Policies (Washington, D.C.: National Association of Broadcasters, 1977).

9 Unto Thyself Be True: Self-Regulation

1. Elizabeth J. Heighton and Don R. Cunningham, *Advertising in the Broadcast Media* (Belmont, California: Wadsworth Publishing Company, 1976), p. 284.

2. Erik Barnouw, *Tower in Babel: A History of Broadcasting in the United States to 1933* (New York: Oxford University Press, 1966), p. 120.

3. "Subscriber Status," *Code News* (February, 1977), p. 4.

4. Heighton and Cunningham, *Advertising,* p. 285.

5. These provisions are explained at the back of the code books—*The Radio Code* (Washington, D.C.: National Association of Broadcasters, 1975), pp. 19-27, and *The Television Code* (Washington, D.C.: National Association of Broadcasters, 1975), pp. 23-33.

6. *The Television Code,* p. 23.

7. Ibid., pp. 1-20.

8. *The Radio Code,* pp. 16-17.

9. Ibid., pp. 8-9.

10. Ibid., p. 11.

11. Ibid., p. 11.

12. Heighton and Cunningham, *Advertising,* pp. 291-297.

13. This information was gathered from interviews with station and network personnel—primarily James Harden, general manager for radio station KNAC, Long Beach, California, 1976; Hank Rieger, vice president of public information for NBC-TV, Los Angeles, California, 1977; Dave Sweeney, general manager for radio station KFOX, Long

Beach, California, 1976; and Kaslon Zollar, production manager for Channel 7, KABC, Los Angeles, California, 1976.

14. A more complete list of broadcasting associations, their officers and addresses, can be found in *Broadcasting Yearbook, 1975* (Washington, D.C.: Broadcasting Publications, Inc., 1975), pp. F-17-F-31.

15. A more complete list of broadcasting awards can be found in *Broadcasting Yearbook,* pp. D-55-D-57.

16. For a description of other journals, see Kenneth Harwood, "A World Bibliography of Selected Periodicals on Broadcasting (Revised)," *Journal of Broadcasting,* Spring, 1972, pp. 131-146.

10 The Bottom Line: Advertising and Business Practices

1. Excellent information about advertising and business practices can be found in Les Brown, *Television: The Business Behind the Box* (New York: Harcourt, Brace, and Jovanovich, 1971); Howard W. Coleman, *Case Studies in Broadcast Management* (New York: Hastings House, 1970); Elizabeth J. Heighton and Don R. Cunningham, *Advertising in the Broadcast Media* (Belmont, California: Wadsworth Publishing Company, 1976); Ward L. Quaal and James A. Brown, *Broadcast Management* (New York: Hastings House, 1975); and Bob Shanks, *The Cool Fire* (New York: W. W. Norton and Company, 1976).

2. These are actual rate cards, but the stations did not want to be identified because their rates change so often.

3. Heighton and Cunningham, *Advertising,* p. 47.

4. Ibid., p. 43.

5. Shanks, *Cool Fire,* p. 106.

6. For more information on commercial production, see Norman D. Cary, *The Television Commercial: Creativity and Craftsmanship* (New York: Decker, 1971), and Lincoln Diamant, *The Anatomy of a Television Commercial* (New York: Hastings House, 1971).

7. Lincoln Diamant, *Television's Classic Commercials* (New York: Hastings House, 1970), and Arthur Shulman and Roger Youman, *The Television Years* (New York: Popular Library, 1973).

8. See chapter 7, on "programming decisions."

9. "Radio Financial Data, 1975," *Broadcasting,* November 8, 1976, pp. 57-66; and "Television Financial Data, 1976," *Broadcasting,* August 29, 1977, pp. 23-28.

10. "FCC: 985 TV and 8322 Radio Stations on Air," *Variety,* June 23, 1977, p. 1.

11. *Statistical Abstract of the United States, 1975.* Washington, D.C.: Bureau of the Census, U.S. Dept. of Commerce, 1975, pp. 406, 513, 515, 720, 723.

12. *Broadcasting Yearbook, 1975* (Washington, D.C.: Broadcasting Publications, Inc., 1975), p. A-2.

13. Joseph S. Johnson and Kenneth K. Jones, *Modern Radio Practices* (Belmont, California: Wadsworth Publishing Company, 1977), p. 4.

14. "Peak TV Viewing This Season, Per Nielsen," *Variety,* March 11, 1977, p. 1.

15. "Roper Study Finds a Little Lost Ground Doesn't Keep TV from Dominating," *Broadcasting,* April 4, 1977, p. 42.

16. Gerald F. Kline and Philip J. Tichenor, *Current Perspectives in Mass Communications Research* (Beverly Hills, California: Sage, 1972), p. 35.

17. Tony Schwartz, *The Responsive Chord* (Garden City, New York: Anchor Books, 1974), p. 52.

18. Johnson and Jones, *Modern Radio Practices,* p. 4.

19. *Trends in Public Attitudes Toward Television and Other Mass Media, 1959-1974* (New York: The Roper Organization, 1975), passim, and *Changing Public Attitudes Toward Television and Other Mass Media, 1959-1976* (New York: Television Information Office, 1977), passim.

20. Schwartz, *Responsive Chord,* p. 52.

21. *Broadcasting Yearbook, 1975,* p. A-2.

22. "Radio Financial Data, 1975," passim, and "Television Financial Data, 1976," passim.

23. "Sellers Market Reigns in Radio Properties," *Broadcasting,* July 25, 1977, pp. 70-74.

24. For more on advertising and children, see William Melody, *Children's Television: The Economics of Exploitation* (New Haven, Connecticut: Yale University Press, 1973), and the section Children's Programs in chapter 5, The Escape Machine: Entertainment Programming.

11 The Rating Game: Audience Measurement

1. Accounts of early ratings can be found in several early books— Frederick Lumley, *Measurement in Radio* (Columbus, Ohio: Ohio State University Press, 1934), and Paul F. Lazarfield and Frank N. Stanton, *Radio Research* (New York: Duell, Sloan, and Pearce, 1942).

2. Nielsen publishes materials regarding its ratings, such as *Demonstration Report and User's Manual* (Northbrook, Illinois: A. C. Nielsen, 1974). Other material regarding Nielsen can be found in

Elizabeth J. Heighton and Don R. Cunningham, *Advertising in the Broadcast Media* (Belmont, California: Wadsworth Publishing Company, 1976), pp. 185-194, and Bob Shanks, *The Cool Fire* (New York: W. W. Norton and Company, 1976), pp. 244-253.

3. Arbitron publishes materials regarding its ratings, such as *Arbitron Super Sweeps* (New York: American Research Bureau, 1975), and *Major Improvements in the Arbitron Radio Report* (New York: American Research Bureau, 1975). Material can also be found in Heighton and Cunningham, *Advertising,* pp. 178-185.

4. *Broadcasting Yearbook, 1975* (Washington, D.C.: Broadcasting Publications, Inc., 1975), pp.F-13–F-15.

5. Shanks, *The Cool Fire,* pp. 253-256.

6. Ward L. Quaal and James A. Brown, *Broadcast Management* (New York: Hastings House, 1976), p. 139.

7. Sydney W. Head, *Broadcasting in America* (Boston: Houghton Mifflin, 1976), p. 250.

8. Quaal and Brown, *Broadcast Management,* p. 139.

9. Ibid., p. 139.

10. Heighton and Cunningham, *Advertising,* pp. 153-157.

11. Head, *Broadcasting in America,* p. 251.

12. Heighton and Cunningham, *Broadcasting,* pp. 159-162.

13. Pros and cons of ratings (mostly cons) can be found in many cleverly written articles or sections of books, including Dick Adler, "The Nielsen Ratings—and How I Penetrated Their Secret Network," *New York Times,* October 1, 1974, p. 74B; Shanks, *The Cool Fire,* pp. 244-258; Michael Wheeler, "Life and Death in the Little Black Box," *Television Quarterly,* May-July, 1976, pp. 5-14; and three articles in Barry G. Cole, *Television* (New York: The Free Press, 1970), pp. 385-408.

14. Details can be found in Committee on Interstate and Foreign Commerce, House of Representatives, *Broadcast Ratings: The Methodology, Accuracy, and Use of Ratings in Broadcasting* (Washington, D.C.: Government Printing Office, 1963-1965).

15. Heighton and Cunningham, *Advertising,* p. 249.

16. Details can be found in CONTAM, *Television Ratings Revisited: A Further Look at Television Audiences* (New York: Television Information Office, 1971).

17. Head, *Broadcasting in America,* p. 249.

18. Details can be found in Committee on Interstate and Foreign Commerce, House of Representatives, *Broadcast Ratings: A Progress Report on Industry and Programs Involving Broadcast Ratings* (Washington, D.C.: Government Printing Office, 1966).

19. Details can be found in *ARMS—What It Shows, How It Has Changed Radio Measurement* (Washington, D.C.: National Association of Broadcasters, 1966).

20. Details can be found in *CRAM—Cumulative Radio Audience Method* (New York: National Broadcasting Company, 1966).

12 What! No Commercials? Noncommercial Radio and Television

1. Erik Barnouw, *A Tower in Babel: A History of Broadcasting in the United States to 1933* (New York: Oxford University Press, 1966), p. 61.

2. Ibid., pp. 97-98.

3. Ibid., p. 218.

4. Erik Barnouw, *The Golden Web: A History of Broadcasting in the United States, 1933-1953* (New York: Oxford University Press, 1968), p. 37.

5. Donald N. Wood and Donald G. Wylie, *Educational Telecommunications* (Belmont, California: Wadsworth Publishing Company, 1977), p. 32.

6. *Broadcasting Yearbook, 1975* (Washington, D.C.: Broadcasting Publications, Inc., 1975), p. A-7.

7. Ibid., p. A-6.

8. Wood and Wylie, *Educational Telecommunications,* p. 24.

9. An excellent history of the NAEB can be found in Harold E. Hill, *The National Association of Educational Broadcasters: A History* (Urbana, Illinois: National Association of Educational Broadcasters, 1954).

10. *Broadcasting Yearbook, 1975,* pp. C-1-C-216.

11. "Public Radio Ponders Switch to One National Organization," *Broadcasting,* March 22, 1976, p. 81.

12. *Broadcasting Yearbook, 1975,* pp. C-1-C-216.

13. For more information on educational radio, see James Robertson and Gerald G. Yokom, "Educational Radio: The Fifty-Year Old Adolescent," *Educational Broadcasting Review,* April, 1973, pp. 107-115; *Facts About Educational Radio* (Washington, D.C.: National Association of Educational Broadcasters, 1967); and Wood and Wylie, *Educational Telecommunications,* pp. 107-109.

14. Lynne S. Gross, "A Study of College Credit Literature Courses Offered on Open Circuit Television," *NAEB Journal,* November-December, 1962, pp. 87-88.

15. Interview with Dr. James Loper, General Manager of KCET, Los Angeles, California, 1977.

16. *Broadcasting Yearbook, 1975,* p. A-7.

17. Interview with Dr. James Loper.

18. Clifford G. Erickson and Hyman M. Chausow, *Chicago's TV College: Final Report of a Three-Year Experiment* (Chicago: Chicago City Junior College, August, 1960).

19. Mary Howard Smith, "Midwest Program on Airborne Television Instruction," *Using Television in the Classroom* (New York: McGraw-Hill, 1961).

20. *Broadcasting Yearbook, 1975,* p. A-7.

21. Carnegie Commission on Public Television, *Public Television: A Program for Action* (New York: Harper and Row, 1967).

22. *The Public Broadcasting Act of 1967, Public Law 90-129, 90th Congress,* November 7, 1967.

23. "CPB, PBS Strike Truce in Atlanta," *Broadcasting,* February 14, 1977, p. 31.

24. "Public TV Comes of Age," *Newsweek,* March 8, 1976, pp. 72-73.

25. William D. Houser, "Satellite Interconnection," *Television Quarterly,* Fall, 1976, pp. 78-80.

26. *Broadcasting Yearbook, 1975,* Section B.

27. Figures come from *Status Report on Public Broadcasting, 1973* (Washington, D.C.: Corporation for Public Broadcasting, 1974).

28. More information is available from *Factsheet on the PBS Station Cooperative* (Washington, D.C.: Public Broadcasting Services, June-July, 1974).

29. Additional material about programming can be found in Robert J. Blakely, *The People's Instrument: A Philosophy of Programming for Public Television* (Washington, D.C.: Public Affairs Press, 1971); Patrick Buchanan, "Of Public TV, Public Affairs and Politics," *TV Guide,* May 15, 1976, pp. A-3-A-4; "Public TV Goes Pro," *Broadcasting,* August 30, 1976, pp. 38-40; and Michael G. Reeves and Tom W. Hoffer, "The Safe, Cheap, and Known: A Content Analysis of the First (1974) PBS Program Cooperative," *Journal of Broadcasting,* Fall, 1976, pp. 549-566.

30. Sources for more detail on these controversies include Blakely, *People's Instrument;* Buchanan, *Public TV;* John W. Macy, *To Irrigate a Wasteland: The Struggle to Shape a Public Television System in the United States* (Berkeley, University of California Press, 1974); Don R. Pember, *Mass Media in America* (Chicago: Science Research Associates, 1974), pp. 217-222; "Public TV Comes of Age," *Newsweek,* March 8, 1976, pp. 72-73; "Public TV Goes Pro," *Broadcasting,* August 30, 1976, pp. 38-40; *Public Television: Toward Higher Ground* (Palo Alto, California: Aspen Series on Communications and Society, 1975); and Wilbur Schramm and Lyle Nelson, "Financing Public TV," *Columbia Journalism Review,* January-February, 1973, pp. 209-217.

31. More on instructional television can be found in Anaheim School District, *Preliminary Report of ITV Project for School Year 1959-60* (Anaheim, California: Board of Education, 1960); John Barwich and Stewart Kranz, *Profiles in Video* (White Plains, New York: Knowledge Industry Publications, 1975); Charles Callaci, *Learning Through Television* (Chino, California: Ramo II Publishers, 1975); C. R. Carpenter and L. P. Greenhill, *An Investigation of Closed-Circuit Television for Teaching University Courses* (University Park: Penn State University, 1955); Larry G. Goodwin and Thomas Koehring, *Closed-Circuit Television Production Techniques* (Indianapolis, Indiana: Howard W. Sams and Company, 1970); David Green and Michael O'Sullivan, "In-Service ETV for Hospitals," *Educational Broadcasting,* September/October, 1976, pp. 25-30; Lynne S. Gross, "Producing and Using Single-Concept Tapes," *Educational Television,* December, 1971, pp. 19-21; Lynne S. Gross, "Utilizing ITV for Performance Classes," *Audio-Visual Instruction,* November, 1969, pp. 54-59; Hagerstown Board of Education, *Closed-Circuit Television Teaching in Washington County, 1958-59* (Hagerstown, Maryland: The Board, 1959); Herb Hammer, "Medicine Replays Video Discs—And the Beat Goes On," *Video Systems,* January/February, 1976, pp. 10-14; and William G. Millington and Lynne S. Gross, "Video for Teaching the Non-Verbal Language," *Educational and Industrial Television,* August, 1976, pp. 20-22.

13 A Wired Nation? Cable Television

1. Chronicles of cable's history appear in David L. Jaffe, "CATV: History and Law," *Educational Broadcasting,* July/August, 1974, pp. 15-17 and 34-36; Mary Alice Mayer Philips, *CATV: A History of Community Antenna Television* (Evanston, Illinois: Northwestern University Press, 1972); and Albert Warren, "What's 26 Years Old and Still Has Growing Pains?" *TV Guide,* November 27, 1976, pp. 4–8.

2. The relationship between cable and government can be found in *Cable Television and the FCC: A Crisis in Media Control*

(Philadelphia: Temple University Press, 1973); Steven R. Rivkin, *Cable Television: A Guide to Federal Regulations* (Santa Monica, California: Rand Corporation, 1973); and Martin H. Seiden, *Cable Television USA: An Analysis of Government Policy* (New York Praeger, 1972).

3. A great deal about franchising can be learned from Leland L. Johnson and Michael Botein, *Cable Television: The Process of Franchising* (Santa Monica, California: Rand Corporation, 1973).

4. Jaffe, in *Educational Broadcasting,* July/August, 1974, p. 17.

5. Two sources that deal with local origination are Ron Merrell, "Origination Compounds Interest with Quality Control," *Video Systems,* November/December, 1975, pp. 15-18, and Sloan Commission on Cable Communications, *On the Cable: The Television of Abundance* (New York: McGraw-Hill, 1972).

6. "Cable Survey Shows Growth," *Video Systems,* January/February, 1976, p. 6.

7. Two sources dealing with public access are Richard C. Kletter, *Cable Television: Making Public Access Effective* (Santa Monica, California: Rand Corporation, 1973), and Charles Tate, *Cable Television in the Cities: Community Control, Public Access, and Minority Ownership* (Washington, D.C.: The Urban Institute, 1972).

8. Rivkin, *Cable Television,* passim.

9. "A Short Course in Cable, 1975," *Broadcasting,* April 14, 1975, p. 56.

10. "Righting Copyright," *Time,* November 1, 1976, p. 92.

11. Several articles dealing with pay TV and/or pay cable are: David Lachenbruck, "Pay-TV Makes a Comeback," *TV Guide,* February 24, 1973, pp. 5-8; Daryl Lembke, "Fourth Video Network Debuts," *Los Angeles Times,* March 10, 1976, Pt. IV, p. 18; and Vincent T. Wasilewski, "Pay Cable . . .," *Variety,* January 8, 1975, pp. 97-106.

14 Behind the Scenes: Broadcasting Personnel

1. Federal Communications Commission, *39th Annual Report: Fiscal Year 1973* (Washington, D.C.: U.S. Government Printing Office, 1974), pp. 238, 249, and 253, and Caroline Isber and Muriel Cantor, *Report of the Task Force of Women in Public Broadcasting* (Washington, D.C.: Corporation for Public Broadcasting, October 8, 1975), p. 37.

2. According to the May, 1977 *Fortune* list of the 500 largest industrial corporations, Eastman Kodak employs 127,000 people.

3. For a slightly different approach to station personnel, see Herbert Zettl, "Chapter 14: Station Personnel," *Television Production Handbook,* 2nd ed. (Belmont, California: Wadsworth Publishing Company, 1968).

4. Many sample organization charts are available in two booklets: *Television Station Organization Charts* (Washington, D.C.: National Association of Broadcasters, 1968) and *Radio Station Organization Charts* (Washington, D.C.: National Association of Broadcasters, 1969).

5. Most of these numbers were determined by counting the listings in *Broadcasting Yearbook, 1975* (Washington, D.C.: Broadcast Publications, Inc., 1975). Cable TV figures are from "Cable Survey Shows Growth," *Video Systems,* January/February, 1976, p. 6. College and university figures are from Harold Niven, *Broadcast Programs in American Colleges and Universities* (Washington, D.C.: National Association of Broadcasters, 1975).

6. For more on agents, see Bob Shanks, "Chapter 6: Talent Agencies and Personal Managers," *The Cool Fire* (New York: W. W. Norton, 1976).

7. Ward L. Quaal and James A. Brown, *Broadcast Management* (New York: Hastings House, 1976), p. 104.

8. Shanks, *Cool Fire,* p. 125.

9. For a more complete listing of broadcast unions, see *Broadcasting Yearbook, 1975,* pp. F-33 and F-34.

10. "Parker Assails Hiring Practices at TV Stations," *Broadcasting,* November 27, 1972, p. 26.

11. "FCC Notes Rise in Hiring Women and Minorities," *Broadcasting,* January 31, 1977, p. 46.

12. For information regarding public broadcasting, see Isber and Cantor, *Task Force of Women.*

13. Niven, *Broadcast Programs,* passim.

14. Quaal and Brown, *Broadcast Management,* pp. 97-98.

15 Around the World: Broadcasting in Foreign Countries

1. Joe Roezin, "The Status of International Television," *Video Systems,* October, 1977, p. 26.

2. Alan Coren, "The Awful Truth About British TV," *TV Guide,*

July 9, 1977, pp. 4-6; Alex Twogood, "British Politics on TV: The Civilized Way," *Television Quarterly,* Special Election Issue, 1976, pp. 29-32; and Burton Paulu, *British Broadcasting* (Minneapolis: University of Minnesota Press, 1961).

3. Don R. LeDuc, "Cable TV Control in Canada: A Comparative Policy Study," *Journal of Broadcasting,* Fall, 1976, pp. 435-450, and Vernone Sparkes, "Community Cablecasting in the U.S. and Canada: Different Approaches to a Common Objective," *Journal of Broadcasting,* Fall, 1976, pp. 451-460.

4. "Mexican TV Sales Robust—Still Expanding," *Broadcasting,* October 13, 1975, p. 36; "H'wood Chapter of TV Acad Holds Bash for Televisa, S.A.," *Variety,* March 16, 1976, p. 5, and J. M. Frost, *World Radio TV Handbook* (London: Cardfont Publishers, 1977).

5. Laddie, Marshack, "A Tall Story: Russian TV," *TV Guide,* April 10, 1976, p. 13, and interview with Svetlana Starodomskaya, TV talk show hostess for Soviet TV show, 1977.

6. "Signals Across the Sea: Only the Technology is Essentially Common to All," *Broadcasting,* October 3, 1977, pp. 40-46, and *The History of Broadcasting in Japan* (Tokyo: Nippon Hoso Kyokai, 1967).

7. Burton Paulu, *Radio and Television Broadcasting in Eastern Europe* (Minneapolis: University of Minnesota Press, 1974), and interview with Dragana Dimitrijevic, news producer for channel 6 in Belgrade, Yugoslavia, 1977.

8. Burton Paulu, *Radio and Television Broadcasting on the European Continent* (Minneapolis: University of Minnesota Press, 1967), and interview with John Gregory, Professor of Telecommunications, Pasadena City College,

concerning his sabbatical to study European broadcasting, 1977.

9. Frost, *World Radio TV Handbook,* and interview with Ruben Ferrer, Brazilian broadcasting student.

10. Sydney W. Head, *Broadcasting in Africa: A Continental Survey of Radio and Television* (Philadelphia: Temple University Press, 1974); Alan Bender, "After a 25-Year Wait . . . South Africans Have Television," *TV Guide,* August 14, 1976, pp. 24-26; and interview with Ngebeti Mnisis, Producer/Announcer for Educational Programming of the Swaziland Broadcasting Services.

11. Interview with John Gregory.

12. Edwin J. Kiester, "The Great International Ratings War," *TV Guide,* January 29, 1977, pp. 34-41.

13. Interview with Mark Feldman, Israeli broadcasting student, 1977.

14. Interview with Ruben Ferrer.

15. N. V. Eswar, "All India Radio Net Covers Nearly 90% of Population," *Variety,* January 25, 1977, p. 20; and "From Ahmadabad to Makapura," *TV Guide,* June 19, 1976, pp. 10-12.

16. *Broadcasting and Television Yearbook* (Sydney, Australia: Greater Publications, 1977).

17. David Bonavia, "It's a Long Bike Ride to the TV Set," *Television Quarterly,* Fall, 1976, pp. 55-57.

18. "MIP-TV Cannes: Starting Point for a Worldwide Grand Prix in Television," *Broadcasting,* May 9, 1977, pp. 88-94; "Who Will Pay What for U.S. Programs Abroad," *Broadcasting,* August 15, 1977, p. 34, and Don Kowet, "Maybe They Lose Something in Translation," *TV Guide,* December 10, 1977, pp. 12-14.

16 Into the Crystal Ball: The Future of Broadcasting

1. *Changing Public Attitudes Toward Television and Other Mass Media, 1959-1976* (New York: Television Information Office, 1977), passim.

2. Some of the ideas expressed here can be found in "TV Chiefs Think Medium is Going to be Around for Quite a While," *Broadcasting,* December 15, 1975, p. 40, and "At NAB: A Rerun of Arguments Over Pay Cable," *Broadcasting,* March 29, 1976, p. 32.

3. For additional information on video discs, see John Free, "Video-Disc Players," *Popular Science,* February, 1977, pp. 85-87, and Frank S. Swertlow, "Giving Television a Spin," *TV Guide,* August 16, 1975, pp. 6-10.

4. For additional information on video cassettes, see "Video's New Frontiers," *Newsweek,* December 8, 1975, pp. 52-57; and Joe Roizen, "Future of Television," *Video Systems,* June, 1977, pp. 10-15.

5. "Large Screen TV Sets are Luring Buyers Despite Picture Quality and Price Problems," *The Wall Street Journal,* April 2, 1976, p. 26.

6. John R. Free, "Here Comes Hang-on-the-Wall Flat-Screen TV," *Popular Science,* March, 1975, pp. 94, 96.

7. "No Slackening of Interest in ENG, Still Rising Star of TV News," *Broadcasting,* March 29, 1976, p. 60.

8. "Compact Storage, Swift Transmission Offered in New TV Recording System," *Broadcasting,* February 16, 1976, p. 84.

9. More information can be found in "The States of the Art in Broadcast Equipment," *Broadcasting,* December 13, 1976, pp. 26-41.

10. "Overview: How Tomorrow's Radio Looks From Today's" *Broadcasting,* July 25, 1977, p. 32.

11. Both programming and structural predictions usually come from speeches delivered by broadcasting executives. Several articles in this vein are "NAB Offers Food for Thought About Future of Television," *Broadcasting,* October 13, 1975, pp. 30-31; "The Future of Television: More of Everything," *Broadcasting,* March 1, 1976, p. 38; and "Word to the Wise in Radio: A Complicated Future is Just Around the Corner," *Broadcasting,* March 29, 1976, pp. 34-36.

Selected Bibliography

Below are 100 significant sources of information regarding broadcasting, all of which are fairly accessible in libraries and/or bookstores. For a more complete bibliography see the notes for each chapter and the bibliography in the instructor's manual.

a

Arlen, Michael J. *Living Room War.* New York: The Viking Press, 1969.

b

Baer, Walter S. *Cable Television: A Handbook for Decision Making.* Santa Monica, California: Rand Corporation, 1973.

Barnouw, Erik. *The Golden Web: A History of Broadcasting in the United States, 1933-1953.* New York: Oxford University Press, 1968.

———. *The Image Empire: A History of Broadcasting in the United States from 1953.* New York: Oxford University Press, 1970.

———. *A Tower in Babel: A History of Broadcasting in the United States to 1933.* New York: Oxford University Press, 1966.

———. *Tube of Plenty: The Development of American Television.* New York: Oxford University Press, 1975.

Barrett, Marvin. *The Politics of Broadcasting.* New York: Crowell, 1973.

Beech, Linda. *TV Favorites.* New York: Scholastic Book Services, 1971.

Bermingham, Alan. *The Small TV Studio Equipment and Facilities.* New York: Hastings House, 1975.

Bilson, William A. *The Impact of Television.* Hamden, Connecticut: Archon Books, 1967.

Bleum, A. William. *Documentary in American Television.* New York: Hastings House, 1965.

———. *Religious Television Programs.* New York: Hastings House, 1968.

Broadcasting Yearbook 1975. Washington, D.C.: Broadcasting Publications, 1975.

Brown, Les. *Television: The Business Behind the Box.* New York: Harcourt Brace Jovanovich, 1971.

Buckwalter, Len. *Television: How It Works.* New Augusta, Indiana: Editors and Engineering, 1967.

Buxton, Frank, and Bill Owen. *The Big Broadcast, 1920-1950.* New York: Viking, 1972.

c

Cary, Norman D. *The Television Commercial: Creativity and Craftsmanship.* New York: Decker, 1971.

Changing Public Attitudes Toward Television and Other Mass Media, 1956-1976. New York; Television Information Office, 1977.

Chapel, G. A. *Radio Stations: Installation, Design, and Practice.* Elmsford, New York: Pergamon Press, 1959.

Chester, Giraud, Garnet R. Garrison, and Edgar E. Willis. *Television and Radio.* New York: Appleton-Century-Crofts, 1971.

Cirino, Robert. *Power to Persuade.* New York: Bantam Books, 1974.

Cole, Barry G. *Television.* New York: The Free Press, 1970.

Coleman, Howard W. *Case Studies in Broadcast Management.* New York: Hastings House, 1970.

d

De Forest, Lee. *Father of Radio: Autobiography of Lee De Forest.* Chicago: Wilcox and Follett, 1950.

Diamant, Lincoln. *The Anatomy of a Television Commercial.* New York: Hastings House, 1970.

———. *Television's Classic Commercials.* New York: Hastings House, 1971.

Dunlap, Orrin E., Jr. *Radio's 100 Men of Science.* New York: Harper and Brothers, 1944.

e

Eargle, John. *Sound Recording.* New York: Van Nostrand and Reinhold, 1976.

Everson, George. *The Story of Television: The Life of Philo T. Farnsworth.* New York: Norton, 1949.

f

Fang, Irving E. *Television News.* New York: Hastings House, 1972.

Feshbach, Seymour, and Robert D. Singer. *Television and Aggression: An Experimental Field Study.* San Francisco: Jossey-Bass, 1970.

Fessenden, Helen M. *Fessenden: Builder of Tomorrows.* New York: Coward-McCann, 1940.

Fink, Donald F., and David M. Lutyens. *The Physics of Television.* Garden City, New York: Anchor Books, 1960.

"The First Amendment and the Fifth Estate," *Broadcasting,* (January 5, 1976), pp. 45-101.

"The First 50 Years of NBC," *Broadcasting,* (January 5, 1976), pp. 29-42.

Friendly, Fred. *Due to Circumstances Beyond Our Control.* New York: Random House, 1967.

Frost, Jim. *World Radio TV Handbook.* London: Cardfont Publishers, 1977.

g

Gerbner, George, and Larry Gross. "Scary World of TV's Heavy Viewer," *Psychology Today,* (April, 1976), pp. 41-45 +.

Goodwin, Larry G., and Thomas Koehring. *Closed-Circuit Television Production Techniques.* Indianapolis, Indiana: Howard W. Sams, 1970.

Gross, Lynne S. *Self-Instruction in Radio Production.* Los Alamitos, California: Hwong Publishing Company, 1976.

h

Harmon, Jim. *The Great Radio Comedians.* Garden City, New Jersey: Doubleday, 1970.

Head, Sydney W. *Broadcasting in Africa: A Continental Survey of Radio and Television.* Philadelphia: Temple University Press, 1974.

———. *Broadcasting in America.* Boston: Houghton Mifflin, 1976.

Heighton, Elizabeth J., and Don R. Cunningham. *Advertising in the Broadcast Media.* Belmont, California: Wadsworth Publishing Company, 1976.

Heller, Melvin S., and Samuel Polsky. *Studies in Violence and Television.* New York: American Broadcasting Company, 1976.

Hilliard, Robert L. *Radio Broadcasting.* New York: Hastings House, 1967.

Himmelweit, Hilde. *Television and the Child.* New York: Television Information Office, 1961.

Hudson, Peggy. *TV Today.* New York: Scholastic Book Services, 1969.

j

Johnson, Joseph S., and Kenneth K. Jones. *Modern Radio Station Practices.* Belmont, California: Wadsworth Publishing Company, 1977.

Johnson, Nicholas. *How to Talk Back to Your Television Set.* Boston: Atlantic, Little, Brown, 1970.

Jolly, W. P. *Marconi.* New York: Stein and Day, 1972.

k

Kiver, Milton S. *FM Simplified.* Princeton, New Jersey: Van Nostrand, 1960.

Kiver, Milton S., and Milton Kaufman. *Television Simplified.* New York: Van Nostrand Reinhold, 1973.

Krasnow, Erwin G., and Lawrence D. Longley. *The Politics of Broadcast Regulation.* New York: St. Martin's Press, 1972.

l

Learning While They Laugh: Studies of Five Children's Programs on the CBS Television Network. New York: CBS, 1977.

Lesser, Gerald S. *Children and Television: Lessons from Sesame Street.* New York: Random House, 1974.

Lessing, Edwin Lawrence. *Man of High Fidelity: Edwin Howard Armstrong.* New York: Lippincott, 1956.

Liebert, Robert M. *The Early Window.* New York: Pergamon Press, 1973.

Lyons, Eugene. *David Sarnoff: A Biography.* New York: Harper and Row, 1966.

m

Macy, John W. *To Irrigate a Wasteland: The Struggle to Shape a Public Television System in the United States.* Berkeley, California: University of California Press, 1974.

Marconi, Degna. *My Father Marconi.* New York: McGraw-Hill, 1962.

McGinnis, Joe. *The Selling of the President, 1968.* New York: Trident Press, 1969.

McLuhan, Marshall. *Understanding Media*. New York: McGraw-Hill, 1964.

Melody, William. *Children's Television: The Economics of Exploitation*. New Haven, Connecticut: Yale University Press, 1975.

Metz, Robert. *CBS: Reflections in a Bloodshot Eye*. Chicago: Playboy Press, 1975.

Millerson, Gerald. *TV Camera Operation*. New York: Hastings House, 1973.

Minow, Newton, John Bartlow Martin, and Lee M. Mitchell. *Presidential Television*. New York: Basic Books, 1973.

Mitchell, Curtis. *Cavalcade of Broadcasting*. Chicago: Follet, 1971.

n

Newcomb, Horace. *TV, the Most Popular Art*. New York: Anchor Books, 1974.

Nisbett, Alec. *The Use of Microphones*. New York: Hastings House, 1975.

o

Oringel, Robert S. *Audio Control Handbook*. New York: Hastings House, 1972.

p

Passman, Arnold. *The DJ's*. New York: Macmillan, 1971.

Paul, Eugene. *The Hungry Eye*. New York: Ballantine Books, 1962.

Paulu, Burton. *Radio and Television Broadcasting in Eastern Europe*. Minneapolis: University of Minnesota Press, 1974.

Pember, Don R. *Mass Media in America*. Chicago: Science Research Associates, 1974.

Philips, Mary Alice Mayer. *CATV: A History of Community Antenna Television*. Evanston, Illinois: Northwestern University Press, 1972.

q

Quaal, Ward L., and James A. Brown. *Broadcast Management*. New York: Hastings House, 1976.

Quick, John, and Herbert Wolff. *Small Studio Video Tape Production*. Reading, Massachusetts: Addison-Wesley, 1976.

r

The Radio Code. Washington, D.C.: National Association of Broadcasters, 1974.

Rivers, William L., Theodore Peterson, and Jay W. Jensen. *The Mass Media and Modern Society*. San Francisco: Rinehart Press, 1971.

Rogers, Fred. *Mister Rogers Talks About. . . .* Bronx, New York: Platt and Munk, 1974.

s

Sarnoff, David. *Looking Ahead: The Papers of David Sarnoff*. New York: McGraw-Hill, 1968.

Schwartz, Tony. *The Responsive Chord*. Garden City, New York: Anchor Books, 1974.

Seiden, Martin H. *Cable Television U.S.A.: An Analysis of Government Policy*. New York: Praeger, 1972.

Settel, Irving. *A Pictorial History of Radio*. New York: Grossett and Dunlap, 1967.

Shanks, Bob. *The Cool Fire*. New York: W. W. Norton, 1976.

Shiers, George. *The Technical Development of Television*. New York: Arno Press, 1976.

Shulman, Arthur, and Roger Youman. *How Sweet It Was: Television, A Pictorial Commentary*. New York: Bonanza Books, 1966.

———. *The Television Years*. New York: Popular Library, 1973.

Small, William J. *To Kill a Messenger*. New York: Hastings House, 1970.

Smith, Ralph Lee. *The Wired Nation: The Electronic Communications Highway*. New York: Colophon Books, 1972.

Smythe, Ted, and George A. Mastroianni. *Issues in Broadcasting*. Palo Alto, California: Mayfield Publishing Company, 1975.

Solomon, Louis. *The TV Doctors*. New York: Scholastic Book Services, 1974.

Summers, Robert E., and Harrison B. Summers. *Broadcasting and the Public*. Belmont, California: Wadsworth Publishing Company, 1966.

t

The Television Code. Washington, D.C.: National Association of Broadcasters, 1974.

Trends in Public Attitudes Toward Television and Other Mass Media, 1959-1974. New York: The Roper Organization, 1975.

u

Upton, Monroe. *Electronics for Everyone*. New York: Signet, 1962.

w

Winn, Marie. *The Plug-In Drug*. New York: Viking, 1977.

Wood, Donald N., and Donald G. Wylie. *Educational Telecommunications*. Belmont, California: Wadsworth Publishing Company, 1977.

z

Zettl, Herbert. *Television Production Handbook*. Belmont, California: Wadsworth Publishing Company, 1976.

Index

b

"Backstage Wife," 20
Baird, John, 55
Ball, Lucille, 60–61, 115
Bandwidth, 49
Banzhaf, John F. III, 183
"Batman," 75
Beatles, 76, 116
"Beat the Clock," 121
Belgium broadcasting, 316
Below-the-line, 161
"Ben Casey," 75
Benet, Stephen Vincent, 24
Benny, Jack, 18, 20, 118
Berg, Gertrude, 115
Bergen, Edgar, 20–21
Berle, Milton, 59, 60, 144
Bernstein, Leonard, 67–68, 111
Betamax, 324–326
"Beverly Hillbillies, The," 75, 115
"Bewitched," 75
"Big Blue Marble, The," 126
Billboard, 203
"Biography of a Bookie Joint," 71
"Bionic Woman, The," 78–79
Bishop, Joey, 116
"Black History: Lost, Strayed, or
    Stolen," 72
"Black Journal," 259
Blacklisting, 63
Blue Book, 174
Blue Network, 14, 15, 18, 20
Boardman, True, 24, 185
"Bonanza," 67
Boston Herald Traveler, 175
Bowes, Major Edward, 20, 24
"Break the Bank," 60, 121
"Breakfast Club, The," 36
"Brian's Song," 119
Brinkley, David, 68, 70–71
Brinkley, J.R., 180
British broadcasting, 306–310. See also
    British Broadcasting Corporation;
    Independent Broadcasting
    Authority
British Broadcasting Corporation, 55,
    255, 259, 261, 306–309
Broadcasting, 203, 304
Broadcasting Yearbook, 203, 301
Broadcast Measurement Bureau
    (BMB), 231
Broadcast Music, Inc. (BMI), 109
Broadcast Rating Council (BRC), 245
Broadcast standards, 199–200, 285
Brokers, 297
Bronowski, Jacob, 259, 309
Buffalo Bob, 60–61, 124
Bulova, 58
Burke Marketing Research, Inc., 239
Burnett, Carol, 76, 111, 117
Burns, George, 19–20
Business manager, 151, 292
Byrd, Admiral Richard, 25

c

Cable television (CATV), 77, 105,
    270–281, 321–323, 332
Caesar, Sid, 60–61, 117
Call letters, 171
Camera operators, 81, 95, 140,
    289–290
Cameras, 81–87, 328–329
Campbell's, 225
Canadian broadcasting, 311–312
Canadian Broadcasting Corporation
    (CBC), 255, 311
Canadian Radio-Television Commit-
    tee, 311
Canadian TV (CTV), 311
Canon 35, 135
Cantor, Eddie, 54
"Captain Kangaroo," 68, 124
Carnegie Commission on Educational
    Television, 250
Carnegie Foundation, 256
Carpentier, Georges, 10, 139
Carroll, Diahann, 72
Carson, Johnny, 76, 120
Cartridges, 40–41
Caruso, Enrico, 6
"Case Against Milo Radulovich
    A0569839, The," 64
Cassettes, 40–41, 99, 266, 323–327
Castro, Fidel, 68, 71
Cathode ray, 55, 105
CATV. See Cable television
Cavett, Dick, 76
CB. See Citizen band radio
CBS Program Analysis Unit, 238
"CBS Reports," 70
Censorship
    by advertisers, 223; Communication
    Act provisions, 174; controversy
    over, 189; of drama, 113; and
    license renewal, 180–181; of movies,
    79, 120; of Smothers Brothers, 117
Chamberlaine, Neville, 29
Channel 1, 32, 58
Chayefsky, Paddy, 65
Cher, 117
"Cheyenne," 67
Chicago Democratic Convention, 74
Chicago TV College, 255–256
Child, Julia, 259–260
Children's programs, 20, 60, 74,
    124–127, 225
Children's Television Workshop, 125,
    259
"Children Were Watching, The," 70
Chinese broadcasting, 317
Cigarette commercials, 76, 183, 224
Citizen band radio (CB), 41, 170
Citizens groups, 193, 330. See also
    Pressure groups
"Civilisation," 308
Clarabell, 61, 124

Clark, Dick, 67–68, 111
Clayton Act, 177
Clio, 202
Closed-circuit TV, 266
"Close-Up," 70
Coaxial cable, 105, 272
Coca, Imogene, 60–61, 117
"Colgate Comedy Hour, The," 66,
    211
"Collier's Hour," 24
Collingwood, Charles, 30
Color television, 57–59, 66–67,
    305–306, 308
"Colt 45," 67
Columbia Broadcasting System
    color TV stand, 57–59, 66–67; early
    TV development, 59; EVR develop-
    ment, 326; and Fred Friendly's
    resignation, 74; news development,
    28, 62; during the 1930s, 18;
    operating VOA, 184; origin, 14;
    tape recording policies, 30; violence
    index, 114
Columbia Phonograph Company, 14
Columbia Pictures Television, 297
Comedians, 20, 116
Comedy shows, 20, 75, 115–116
"Command Performance," 184
Commercials. See also Advertising
    on AFRTS, 184; audio recording of,
    41; on automated equipment, 45;
    Blue Book requirements for, 174; on
    children's programs, 124–126; for
    cigarettes, 76; during the depression,
    25; first TV, 58; in foreign coun-
    tries, 305; future of, 331; on game
    shows, 122; on postwar radio, 32;
    production of, 215–219; rise of,
    12–13; of sports stars, 141; TV and
    radio Code provisions for, 198
Committee on Local Television and
    Radio Audience Measurement,
    246
Committee on Nationwide Television
    Audience Measurement, 245–246
Communications Act of 1934
    censorship provisions, 174, 189;
    Congressional involvement, 184;
    educational reservation, 252; in-
    terest, convenience, and necessity
    provisions, 136; new interpretations,
    188; original passage, 16, 269; Sec-
    tion 315, 145, 182; UHF and VHF
    reception provisions, 63
Communications Satellite Corporation
    (COMSAT), 73
Community Antenna Television
    (CATV). See Cable television
Composers, 109–110
Composite week, 161, 177
"Concentration," 122
Congress. See also House of Repre-
    sentatives; Senate

Turn of the century

James C. Maxwell predicts existence of radio waves—1873

Heinrich Hertz provides the theory of radio transmission and generated radio energy—1888

Guglielmo Marconi transmits the letter "s" across the Atlantic—1901

The early 1900s

David Sarnoff hears the *Titanic's* distress signals—1912

Frank Conrad broadcasts at KDKA, Pittsburgh—1919

Vladimir Zworykin with an early iconoscope TV tube

The twenties

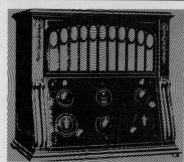

Radio receivers improve and include speakers—1924

Early TV equipment is developed—1927

Amos and Andy sweep the country—1929

The thirties

Jack Benny's radio program provides endless humor

President Franklin Delano Roosevelt delivers "fireside chats"

David Sarnoff has "coming out" party for TV at 1939 New York World's Fair